ORIGINS OF THE COLD WAR

For forty-five years the Cold War was the central factor in world politics. It dominated the foreign policies of the United States and the Soviet Union and affected the diplomacy and domestic politics of most other nations. Understanding the origins of the Cold War is central to understanding the international history of the last half of the twentieth century.

Focusing on the international system and on events in all parts of the globe, this pathbreaking volume provides a fresh and comprehensive analysis of the origins of the Cold War. Moving beyond earlier controversies over responsibility for the Cold War and avoiding myopic preoccupation with Soviet-American relations, the editors have brought together articles that deal with geopolitics and threat perception, technology and strategy, ideology and social reconstruction, national economic reform and patterns of international trade, decolonization and national liberation. The essays demonstrate how tensions between the United States and the Soviet Union spawned an arms race, polarized domestic and international politics, and split the world into military as well as political blocs.

This volume explains how and why the Cold War spread from the industrialized core of Europe and Japan to the Third World periphery, eventually engulfing the whole world. It also shows how groups, classes and elites used the Cold War to further their own interests. Finally, by highlighting the systemic factors that contributed to the onset of the Cold War, this volume provides new insights into the Cold War's unexpected and precipitous end.

Melvyn P. Leffler is Professor and Chair of History at the University of Virginia and **David S. Painter** is Associate Professor of History in the School of Foreign Service at Georgetown University.

Rewriting Histories focuses on historical themes where formerly standard conclusions are facing a major challenge. Each book presents 10–15 papers (edited and annotated where necessary) at the forefront of current research and interpretation, offering students an accessible way to engage with contemporary debates.

Series editor **Jack R. Censer** is Professor of History at George Mason University.

REWRITING HISTORIES
Series editor: Jack R. Censer

Already published

ATLANTIC AMERICAN SOCIETIES
From Columbus through Abolition 1492–1888
Edited by Alan L. Karras and J. R. McNeill

DIVERSITY AND UNITY IN EARLY NORTH AMERICA
Edited by Philip D. Morgan

GENDER AND AMERICAN HISTORY SINCE 1890
Edited by Barbara Melosh

THE INDUSTRIAL REVOLUTION AND WORK IN
NINETEENTH-CENTURY EUROPE
Edited by Lenard R. Berlanstein

SOCIETY AND CULTURE IN THE SLAVE SOUTH
Edited by J. William Harris

Forthcoming

NAZISM AND GERMAN SOCIETY 1933–45
Edited by David Crew

ORIGINS OF THE COLD WAR

An International History

Edited by
Melvyn P. Leffler and
David S. Painter

London and New York

First published 1994
by Routledge
11 New Fetter Lane, London EC4P 4EE

Simultaneously published in the USA and Canada
by Routledge
29 West 35th Street, New York, NY 10001

Typeset in Palatino by Florencetype Ltd, Kewstoke, Avon
Printed and bound in Great Britain by
T.J. Press (Padstow) Ltd, Padstow, Cornwall
Printed on acid free paper

British Library Cataloguing in Publication Data
A catalogue record for this book is available from the British Library

Library of Congress Cataloging in Publication Data
Origins of the cold war: an international history/edited by
Melvyn P. Leffler and David S. Painter.
p. cm.
Includes bibliographical references and index.
1. Cold War. 2. World politics – 1945– .   I. Leffler, Melvyn P.
II. Painter, David S.
D842.086 1994
909.82–dc20 93–23298

ISBN 0–415–09693–6 (hbk)
ISBN 0–415–09694–4 (pbk)

For my brothers, Sheldon and Fred Leffler
and
For my son, Charles, and wife, Flora Painter

CONTENTS

vii

MAPS

EDITOR'S PREFACE

Rewriting history, or revisionism, has always followed closely in the tow of history writing. In their efforts to reevaluate the past, professional as well as amateur scholars have followed many approaches, most commonly as empiricists, uncovering new information to challenge earlier accounts. Historians have also revised previous versions by adopting new perspectives, usually fortified by new research, which overturn received views.

Even though rewriting is constantly taking place, historians' attitudes toward using new interpretations have been anything but settled. For most, the validity of revisionism lies in providing a stronger, more convincing account that better captures the objective truth of the matter. Although such historians might agree that we never finally arrive at the "truth," they believe it exists and over time may be better and better approximated. At the other extreme stand scholars who believe that each generation or even each cultural group or subgroup necessarily regards the past differently, each creating for itself a more usable history. Although these latter scholars do not reject the possibility of demonstrating empirically that some contentions are better than others, they focus upon generating new views based upon different life experience. Different truths exist for different groups. Surely such an understanding, by emphasizing subjectivity, further encourages rewriting history. Between these two groups are those historians who wish to borrow from both sides. This third group, while accepting that every congeries of individuals sees matters differently, still wishes somewhat contradictorily to fashion a broader history that incorporates both of these particular visions. Revisionists who stress empiricism fall into the first of the three camps, while others spread out across the board.

Today the rewriting of history seems to have accelerated to a blinding speed, as a consequence of the evolution of revisionism. A variety of approaches has emerged. A major factor in this process has been the enormous increase in the number of researchers. This explosion has reinforced and enabled the retesting of many assertions. Significant ideological shifts have also played a major part in the growth of revisionism. First, the crisis of Marxism, culminating in the events in Eastern Europe in 1989, has given rise to doubts about explicitly Marxist accounts. Such doubts have spilled over into the entire field of social history, which has been a dominant subfield of the discipline for several decades. Focusing on society and its class divisions implies that these are the most important elements in historical analysis. Because Marxism was built on the same claim, the whole basis of social history has been questioned, despite the very many studies that had little directly to do with Marxism. Disillusionment with social history simultaneously opened the door to cultural and linguistic approaches largely developed in anthropology and literature. Multiculturalism and feminism further generated revisionism. By claiming that scholars had, wittingly or not, operated from a white European/American male point of view, newer researchers argued other approaches had been neglected or misunderstood. Not surprisingly, these last historians are the most likely to envision each subgroup rewriting its own usable history, while other scholars incline toward revisionism as part of the search for some stable truth.

Rewriting Histories will make these new approaches available to the student population. Often new scholarly debates take place in the scattered issues of journals which are sometimes difficult to find. Furthermore, in these first interactions, historians tend to address one another, leaving out the evidence that would make their arguments more accessible to the uninitiated. This series of books will collect in one place a strong group of the major articles in selected fields, adding notes and introductions conducive to improved understanding. Editors will select articles containing substantial historical data, so that students – at the least those who approach the subject as an objective phenomenon – can advance not only their comprehension of debated points, but also their grasp of substantive aspects of the subject.

Some of these wider trends have influenced the study of the origins of the Cold War. The new emphasis on multiculturalism has helped to question the centrality of North America and Western Europe and has allowed the broader view that this volume takes of the subject. Interestingly, the fall of Communist governments has possessed profound implications, though somewhat different from those in other areas of history. The end of the Cold War pulled the subject away from current politics and has rendered its chroniclers more dispassionate. In their refusal to assess blame, the essays here have benefited from the cooling-off of political disagreements. Finally, on a more pragmatic level, the fall of regimes and changes in governmental policies have resulted in the opening of important archival materials and the writing of illuminating memoirs.

Such influences and other factors more specific to this subject have informed this valuable collection on the Cold War. Earlier accounts depended heavily on an ideological and political struggle between the two superpowers. While remaining most significant, the United States and the Soviet Union now share the spotlight with Britain, other European countries, and even smaller nations that could manipulate the Great Powers. The essays presented here highlight the ways that diplomacy, ideology, military strategy, and political economy intersected. This version not only adds richness but entirely refocuses previous interpretations.

Jack R. Censer

INTRODUCTION

The International System and the Origins of the Cold War

David S. Painter and Melvyn P. Leffler

For forty-five years the Cold War was the central factor in world politics. It dominated the foreign policies of the United States and the Soviet Union and affected the diplomacy and domestic politics of most other nations around the globe. Few countries, in fact, escaped its influence. Because the distinctive characteristics of the Cold War era took form in the years immediately following the Second World War, examining its origins is central to understanding international history in the last half of the twentieth century.

Now that the Soviet Union has collapsed and the Cold War is over, an ideal opportunity exists to reassess its beginnings. Scholars and students alike can move beyond earlier controversies over responsibility for the Cold War and try to understand what happened and why without assigning blame. In this volume we focus on the international system and on events in all parts of the globe. We bring together essays that deal with geopolitics and threat perception, technology and strategy, ideology and social reconstruction, national economic reform and patterns of international trade, decolonization and revolutionary nationalism. The essays illuminate how the global distribution of power, the configuration of social forces, and the state of the international economy influenced American and Soviet perceptions of their respective national security interests. They also demonstrate how Soviet-American competition helped shape the political, economic, and social conditions of other nations. And lastly, they reveal how classes, factions, ethnic groups, and revolutionary nationalist movements in other

1

countries used the Cold War to further their own interests and manipulate the Great Powers. The interconnected tapestry of domestic histories and international history is one of the most salient features of the Cold War era.

In the United States two views of the Cold War once competed. The traditional approach blamed the Soviet Union for the outbreak of the Cold War. This orthodox rendition of events portrayed the Soviet Union as relentlessly expansionist and ideologically motivated. According to this view, US officials wanted to get along with the Soviets but slowly came to realize that accommodation was impossible because of the Kremlin's drive for world domination. In contrast, the revisionist review of events interpreted Soviet policy as more circumspect and American policy as more expansionist. Since the early 1970s the contrasting explanations of US behavior have become blurred by a proliferation of studies that have been characterized as post-revisionist, neo-realist, corporatist, and world systems. Although a consensus on the roots of American cold war policies no longer exists, this new generation of scholarship has greatly enriched our knowledge of a wide range of issues by focusing more carefully on geopolitics, social structures, institutional arrangements, and the functioning of the US economy within the world capitalist system.

American archival materials for this period are plentiful, but there still remains a dearth of Soviet documents. It has been difficult to discern with a high degree of confidence the motives and goals of the Soviet Union. Even though Soviet records are now becoming more widely available, we are still very far away from a definitive account of Soviet foreign policy in this period. Nevertheless, historians and political scientists have become more nuanced in their interpretations of developments in the Kremlin. Early views that the Soviet Union had a clear blueprint for world domination have been discredited. In place of the older interpretations attributing the sources of Soviet conduct to Marxist-Leninist desires for world revolution or to the dynamics of a totalitarian society, more recent studies have highlighted such factors as Russian history and geography, traditional Russian expansionism, bureaucratic differences within the Soviet decisionmaking elite, and baseline security requirements arising from the Soviet Union's unique geopolitical position. Soviet archival materials and Russian memoirs underscore the brutality of Communist dictator Joseph Stalin. None the less, they also suggest that he was opportunistic and pragmatic in his foreign policy, seeking to further Soviet power but keenly attuned to constraints and risks. While these accounts (like their predecessors) are based on inadequate primary documents, they represent interesting and provocative new approaches to studying the sources and dynamics of Soviet foreign policy.

Additional archival materials are not necessary to see that the Second World War wrought profound changes in the international state system, bringing about a massive redistribution of power, ending centuries of European dominance, and influencing the evolution of the Cold War. Before the Second World War there were six important powers (or seven if Italy is included): Great Britain, France, Germany, the Soviet Union, Japan, and the United States. By the end of the conflict, the United States stood alone as the strongest nation in the world, its power enhanced, its rivals defeated, and its allies exhausted. The Soviet Union experienced almost incalculable human and material losses and was a distant second. Great Britain, drained by six years of fighting (which cost it a quarter of its wealth) and facing upheaval in its empire, was an even more distant third. Humiliated by its collapse in 1940, deeply divided over the issue of collaboration, severely damaged by the war, and beleaguered by rebellious colonies, France slipped from the ranks of the Great Powers. Germany lay in ruins. Having been thwarted in its second bid for European hegemony, it was occupied by its enemies and was anticipating partition. Japan, too, was devastated and demoralized. Shocked by the atomic attacks on Hiroshima and Nagasaki, shorn of their colonial empire, and occupied by US forces, the Japanese appeared powerless.

The United States entered the postwar era in a uniquely strong position. Practically unscathed by the fighting, the United States almost doubled its gross national product [GNP] during the conflict: By 1945, it accounted for around half of the world's manufacturing capacity, most of its food surpluses, and almost all of its financial reserves. The United States held the lead in a wide range of technologies essential to modern warfare as well as economic prosperity. Possession of extensive domestic oil supplies and control over access to vast repositories of foreign oil provided an additional and essential element in its power position. Although the United States demobilized its armed forces from 12.1 million people in 1945 to 1.7 million by mid-1947, the nation still possessed the world's mightiest military machine. Its navy controlled the seas, its air forces dominated the skies, and it alone possessed atomic weapons and the means to deliver them. Yet the depression and the war left the United States feeling vulnerable and uncertain. Consequently, American officials entered the postwar era thinking more expansively than ever before about their nation's security requirements.

In the first essay in this volume, Melvyn P. Leffler argues that US policymakers believed that their nation's security depended on a favorable balance of power in Eurasia, an open and prosperous world economy, a strategic sphere of influence in Latin America, an elaborate overseas base system, and continuation of the American monopoly of atomic weapons. Leffler demonstrates that the key obstacles to US objectives were socioeconomic dislocation, revolutionary nationalism, and vacuums of power in Europe and Asia, rather than the policies and actions of the Soviet Union. Leffler's work, which is based on extensive research in US military and diplomatic records, demolishes the myth of a naive and reactive United States. It raises interesting questions about the accuracy of US perceptions and the ramifications of US actions, however unintended, on the Kremlin.

The Soviet Union, despite its victory in the war, suffered massive damage. Estimates of Soviet war dead begin at 20 million; damage to the economy left it one-quarter the size of its American counterpart. The Soviets also demobilized rapidly, from approximately 11.3 million people in 1945 to around 2.9 million in early 1948. Notwithstanding the size of Soviet ground forces in central Europe, overall Soviet military capabilities could not match those of the United States. In addition to a greatly inferior industrial base and meager air defenses, the Soviets had no long-range strategic air force, no meaningful surface fleet, and no atomic weapons. But in comparison to those of its neighbors, the relative power position of the Soviet Union had improved, primarily as a result of the defeat of Germany and Japan, countries that historically had checked Russian power in central Europe and northeastern Asia.

In the second essay in this volume Michael MccGwire utilizes an imaginative methodology to examine the impact of the

4

Second World War on Soviet foreign policy. Instead of analyzing Soviet conduct through the few available documents, MccGwire reconstructs how the world must have looked to Soviet officials. More than anything else, he says, they wanted to safeguard their nation against future German aggression. Although they also sought to preserve good relations with the United States, they assigned primacy to securing their borders, reconstructing their industrial base, and refurbishing their military establishment. MccGwire's provocative arguments provide a fresh perspective on Soviet policies. The Kremlin, he suggests, should not be condemned for exceeding its legitimate security needs until those requirements are properly examined from the Soviet perspective.

The Second World War also accelerated dramatic changes in the technology of warfare. Conventional weapons reached new heights of destructiveness. Power projection capabilities, in particular, took a quantum leap forward, with the development of the aircraft carrier and long-range bombers. The atomic bomb magnified the scale of destruction, and fears of an "atomic Pearl Harbor" placed a premium on preparedness and preemption. While the existence of atomic weapons may have helped prevent a war between the superpowers, the arms race that resulted contributed greatly to international tensions as Great Britain, the Soviet Union, and other nations sought to develop their own atomic weapons and the United States tried to maintain its lead.

Over the last two decades historians have examined the strategic arms race between the two superpowers, and one of the most important developments in historical scholarship has been the attempt to unravel the interdependence of strategy and diplomacy in the making of the Cold War. Martin J. Sherwin's essay takes us back to the days of the great coalition between the United States, the Soviet Union, and Great Britain during the Second World War. Sherwin demonstrates how the US decision to drop the atomic bomb on Japan grew out of Anglo-American thinking about its use as a diplomatic tool in peacetime as well as a winning weapon in wartime. Looking at Washington's adversary and making effective use of existing sources, David Holloway examines the origins of Soviet efforts to develop atomic and thermonuclear weapons. Stalin, he argues, grasped the implications of the bomb for postwar diplomacy and expedited its development. Taking the analysis another step further, Marc Trachtenberg examines the relationship between military capabilities, threat perception, and foreign policy goals. He illuminates how American policymakers' calculations about correlations of atomic and strategic power influenced their diplomacy even while they waged limited wars, like the one in Korea.

A growing number of historians in Great Britain and on the continent contest the bipolar interpretation of the origins of the Cold War. The division of Europe, they argue, must be understood in the context of the social, economic, and political history of Europe as well as in terms of Soviet-American rivalry. European nations and elites, they maintain, had more responsibility for developments than is usually assigned to them by American scholars. Indigenous economic, political, and social developments, regional rivalries, and traditional ethnic animosities significantly shaped the relationship between the United States and the Soviet Union. In an essay synthesizing recent scholarship on the European dimension of the Cold War, David Reynolds argues that circumstances within Europe affected the options and tactics available to US and Soviet policymakers. In turn, US and Soviet actions helped determine the outcome of many of Europe's internal struggles.

Many historians have found British records to be an invaluable source for understanding the origins of the Cold War. Arguing that Britain played a key role in postwar developments, these scholars claim that British Foreign Secretary Ernest Bevin and his advisers initially were more alert to the threat posed by the Soviet Union than were officials in Washington. Faced with the rumblings of revolutionary nationalism in their far-flung empire, British policymakers were acutely sensitive to the intersection of their own reconstruction plans with nationalist upheaval in the Third World and the expansion of Soviet power and influence. In a provocative essay John Kent contends that British concerns about the strategic position of the British empire and Bevin's hopes to draw on the resources of the Middle East and Africa prompted Britain to take a defiant stand against the Soviet Union and thus contributed to the outbreak of the Cold War.

Geopolitics and strategy alone did not cause the Cold War. Transnational ideological conflict merged domestic and international developments and affected the relative power positions of different countries. In terms of ideology, the outcome of the Second World War seemed to favor the left and the Soviet Union, at least in the short run. Almost everywhere people yearned for significant socioeconomic reforms, for structural changes in their economies and political institutions, and for improvements in their living conditions. Right-wing groups were totally discredited because of their association with the defeated Axis powers. After fifteen years of depression, war, and genocide, many of the bourgeois middle-of-the-road parties of interwar Europe also were weakened. In contrast, Communist Party membership soared because of the major role Communists played in anti-fascist resistance movements. In many countries the Communists and their allies appeared ready to take power either peacefully or forcefully. US policymakers worried that wherever and however Communist groups attained power they would pursue policies that served the interests of the Soviet Union. The potential international impact of internal political struggles invested the latter with strategic significance and embroiled the United States and the Soviet Union in the internal affairs of other nations. Yet this process was subject to pull as well as push: in many cases the super-powers were drawn into the internal politics of other nations by local allies who sought external assistance in order to prevail in the internal struggle for power.

The postwar transnational ideological conflict between the United States and the Soviet Union must be understood as part of the ongoing structural refashioning of European political economies and internal power relationships. In an illuminating essay on Western Europe, Charles S. Maier shows that American officials had to work within the constraints posed by indigenous European traditions, institutions, and power arrangements. Britain, France, Italy, West Germany, and even the smaller European states like Belgium and the Netherlands retained considerable leverage and helped shape the social and economic order that arose in Western Europe. According to Maier, that order was designed to mitigate class conflict and accelerate productivity, and it shared important continuities with reconstruction efforts after the First World War.

In contrast to US policies in Western Europe, Soviet inter-vention in Eastern Europe was crude, heavyhanded, and brutal. Nevertheless political developments in Eastern Europe, as in

Western Europe, were deeply influenced by historical trends, indigenous conflicts, and the impact of the war on social, political, and economic relationships. In his essay on the tangled web of political intrigue in postwar Hungary, Charles Gati shows that Stalin was in no hurry to impose Communism on East-Central Europe. Drawing on a wealth of new material, Gati argues that the Kremlin initially pursued a differentiated policy within its sphere of influence. Until the fall of 1947, the postwar configuration of power in Hungary and Czechoslovakia – as in other parts of the world – was the result of a complex weaving of indigenous circumstances, Great Power rivalries, and transnational ideological conflict. The political and ideological ambiguities were removed only in late 1947 and early 1948 when Stalin felt beleaguered by dissonance within his own orbit, by the launching of the Marshall Plan, and by Anglo-American attempts to rebuild and unify the western zones in Germany.

International economic developments also shaped the Cold War. Economic hardship threatened to spark conflict between nations as well as to rekindle class strife within nations. In the 1930s the world had, in effect, split into economic blocs: the United States turned inward and, to a lesser extent, toward Latin America; the British closed off their empire behind financial and trade barriers; the Germans built an informal economic empire in central and southeastern Europe; the Soviets tried to construct socialism in one country through collectivization of agriculture and forced industrialization; and the Japanese sought to organize all of East Asia in a "co-prosperity sphere." International trade and national production plummeted as attempts to gain unilateral advantages elicited countermeasures which further restricted production, engendered mass unemployment, accentuated class conflict, and exacerbated national rivalries. Subsequently, wartime mobilization intensified the autarkic, insulated, nationalistic tendencies of the 1930s. Although the allies created new financial institutions (like the International Monetary Fund and the World Bank) at the Bretton Woods Conference in 1944, the end of the war threatened to revive the policies of the 1930s rather than create an open world economy. Faced with massive reconstruction requirements and inadequate financial resources, many governments extended economic controls into the postwar period. These developments portended not reform and reconstruction but a repeat of the experiences of the 1930s – economic stagnation, political extremism, and interstate conflict.

Many scholars have examined the problems of postwar economic disorder. In the excerpt in this book Robert E. Wood shows that the United States provided dollars to Western Europe and the western zones of Germany in order to help those nations purchase the raw materials, fuel, and foodstuffs they desperately needed for reconstruction. US assistance was a temporary expedient, however. The leaders of all the Western nations believed that an important way to overcome Western Europe's shortage of dollars was to expand trade and investment in the Third World. Dollars would flow to the Third World primarily through US procurement of raw materials. Western Europe, in turn, could earn these dollars through the repatriation of profits from investments in rubber, petroleum, and other natural resources, and through its own exports to the Third World. As a result, efforts to promote European reconstruction eventually pitted the West against the rising tide of national liberation in Asia and Africa. The Cold War came to engulf the whole world because US, European, and Japanese leaders believed that the needs of the industrial economies of northwestern and northeastern Eurasia demanded the retention of markets and the preservation of access to raw materials in the underdeveloped periphery. Otherwise, the economies of Western Europe and Japan would remain dependent on US grants and loans (like the Marshall Plan) for the indefinite future.

Decolonization had a profound impact on the postwar international system and accentuated Soviet-American competition. Many independence movements in Asia, the Middle East, and North Africa were radicalized by years of protracted struggle and repression. Revolutionary nationalist leaders sought more than political sovereignty. They wanted to free their economies from foreign control and to eradicate vestiges of colonial society and culture. Because they were fighting against Western control, many independence movements brought to power parties and individuals hostile to capitalism. Marxist-Leninist doctrine seemed to explain their countries' backwardness, and the Soviet pattern of development appeared to provide a statist model for rapid industrialization. Decolonization, therefore, challenged the continuation of Western hegemony over the Third World. In terms of the international distribution of power, it did not affect the United States directly, but it did disrupt the economies of key American allies, distracted their attention, and weakened the overall Western position vis-à-vis the Kremlin.

Developments in the postwar Middle East illustrate these themes. After the war, France was forced to grant independence to Lebanon and Syria and faced challenges in Algeria, Tunisia, and Morocco. Britain was weakened by the loss of the Indian Army, its main power projection force east of Suez. It also encountered strong resistance to its rule in Palestine as well as formidable challenges to its privileged position in Egypt and Iran. These developments jeopardized the entire Western position in the Middle East and gave added impetus to indigenous and regional struggles. And all these events occurred precisely when the Middle East's importance to Western security and prosperity was dramatically increasing. Not only had the Second World War demonstrated the crucial importance of oil to modern warfare, but after hostilities ended the West counted on Middle Eastern oil to fuel European and Japanese economic reconstruction. Iran was central to these efforts because it contained extensive petroleum reserves and the world's largest oil refinery at Abadan. Its rugged terrain, moreover, constituted a barrier between the Soviet Union and the oilfields along the Persian Gulf. Taking note of all these developments and drawing on Iranian and Soviet as well as Western sources, Steven L. McFarland's essay shows that efforts by Iranian elites to enlist the United States as an ally against Great Britain and the Soviet Union and as an asset in their internal maneuvering for power played a key role in the Iranian crisis of 1946, a pivotal event in the origins of the Cold War.

But the Middle East was not the only Third World region where local power struggles intersected with Soviet-American rivalries and Western reconstruction efforts. During the last fifteen years many historians have turned their attention to Japan and its former empire. They have explained Asia's revolutionary movements in terms of indigenous developments and the widespread repulsion against European and Japanese domination. Independence movements were particularly strong where the Japanese empire had spread in the early part of the century and where it had supplanted Western colonial regimes during the Second World War. After the war, the Japanese lost their extensive holdings in Taiwan, Korea, and Manchuria; the

British ceded independence to India, Burma, and Ceylon; and the United States redeemed its wartime pledge to grant freedom to the Philippines. In addition, the British, French, and Dutch faced challenges to their control of Malaya, Indochina, and Indonesia respectively, colonies which were economically important, especially as sources of raw materials and foreign exchange earnings.

Among the many analysts of these events, Bruce Cumings has become one of the most respected. In his article on Northeast Asia he restores Japan to a central role in postwar history by demonstrating how the restoration of Japanese prosperity interacted with other developments in the region. He shows that one must combine an analysis of US involvement with an appreciation of indigenous trends. Similarly, in their analyses of the revolutionary movements in China, Vietnam, and the Philippines, Michael H. Hunt and Steven I. Levine stress the role of local dynamics and the consequences of US and Soviet strategic, political, and economic initiatives. And in another article Shuguang Zhang draws on newly available Chinese sources and argues that the security concerns of Mao Tse-tung and his comrades must be grasped if the international history of postwar Asia and the origins of the Korean War are to be placed properly in the broader context of the Cold War.

These essays on the Middle East and East Asia suggest that agency rested not simply with the Great Powers but also with local elites and popular movements. To portray the Cold War in all its complexity scholars now realize that they must analyze the interconnections between the rivalry of the United States and the Soviet Union and the unfolding of internal developments elsewhere. To do this effectively they have to integrate the geopolitical, strategic, and ideological competition of the Great Powers with local and regional socioeconomic trends and political struggles.

Such considerations also apply to Latin America. Traditional accounts of the origins of the Cold War often neglected Latin America. Yet recent scholarship demonstrates that the dynamics of social and political change in postwar Latin America were deeply intertwined with the Cold War. In a synthetic essay drawing on this new scholarship Leslie Bethell and Ian Roxborough make a strong case that windows of opportunity for democratization in postwar Latin America were rapidly

11

closed as the balance of domestic forces in many nations shifted to the right in conjunction with changes in the international scene and in US foreign policy.

After the Second World War the international system was shaped by five developments: Great Power rivalries, changes in the technology of warfare, transnational ideological conflict, reform and reconstruction of the world capitalist system, and movements of national liberation. Events in each of these areas affected one another, accentuating tension between the United States and the Soviet Union, generating an arms race, polarizing domestic and international politics, and splitting the world into military and political blocs. This new international order became known as the Cold War.

Part I

SOVIET AND AMERICAN STRATEGY AND DIPLOMACY

1

NATIONAL SECURITY AND US FOREIGN POLICY

Melvyn P. Leffler

During the late 1960s and the 1970s historians and political scientists bitterly debated the origins of the Cold War. An eclectic group of scholars, known as revisionists, challenged traditional views of how the Cold War got started. Revisionists insisted that the United States was not an innocent bystander. Focusing on the expansionist tradition and the entrepreneurial capitalism that had characterized US history from its inception and influenced by their hostility to the war in Vietnam, some of them argued that deeply embedded economic and ideological imperatives inspired American officials to assume global responsibilities. Other revisionists focused more directly on the legacy of the great depression which, they said, reinforced an elite consensus in favor of overseas market expansion in order to avert domestic business stagnation and unacceptable levels of unemployment. Still others turned a harsh lens on the diplomacy of Harry S. Truman who, they believed, reversed his predecessor's desire to maintain the wartime coalition with the Soviet Union.

These revisionist arguments angered many retired government officials and a good number of traditional scholars. Traditionalists reiterated their views that the Kremlin started the Cold War. They pointed to the paranoid personality of Joseph Stalin and the revolutionary implications of Marxist-Leninist doctrine. Traditional scholars believed that given the experiences of totalitarian aggression in the 1930s and the dramatic failure of appeasement practices, US officials had no alternative but to respond as they did to the possibility of postwar Soviet/Communist expansion.

By the mid-1980s this controversy was losing its intensity. In a famous article John Lewis Gaddis declared that a post-revisionist consensus was emerging. According to this consensus, the United States had become an imperial nation after the Second World War, but

American officials were not inspired by capitalist greed or fears of another depression. The postwar American empire was a response to the entreaties of governments and peoples who felt threatened by the opportunistic expansion of the Soviet Union. Stalin had no blueprint for world domination, but his barbaric regime threatened his neighbors throughout Eurasia. The United States was obligated to respond to their pleas for help and to become embroiled in a host of disputes that many American policymakers would have preferred to avoid.*

Just as Gaddis was declaring a new consensus, Melvyn P. Leffler presented a version of postwar US national security policy that appeared irreconcilable with the emerging post-revisionist paradigm. Using a vast array of newly declassified documents from the armed services and the intelligence agencies, Leffler argued that US officials had a clear definition of national security, that it was the product of the lessons of the Second World War, and that it was inherently in conflict with the strategic imperatives of the Soviet Union. Studying American assessments of Soviet intentions and capabilities, Leffler demonstrated that it was not so much the actions of the Kremlin as it was fears about socioeconomic dislocation, revolutionary nationalism, British weakness, and Eurasian vacuums of power that triggered US initiatives to mold an international system to comport with its concept of security. The Cold War, he suggested, was the unfolding of the security dilemma whereby nations taking steps to enhance their own security infringe upon the security concerns of their adversaries, thus triggering a spiral of distrust.

Leffler's essay evoked strong rebuttals from post-revisionists.** Yet revisionists also were not altogether comfortable with its implications. Readers should try to clarify Leffler's argument and explicate the factors that shaped the American conception of national security. Does Leffler understate the role of Soviet behavior and Stalin's actions? Does he overlook the extent to which the United States demobilized its armed forces at the end of the war and wanted to turn inwards? In what ways does Leffler's interpretation support or contradict key elements of orthodoxy, revisionism, and post-revisionism?

*   *   *

* John L. Gaddis, "The Emerging Post-Revisionist Thesis on the Origins of the Cold War," *Diplomatic History*, 7 (Summer 1983): 171–90.

** See the comments by John L. Gaddis and Bruce Kuniholm in *The American Historical Review*, 89 (April 1984): 382–90.

In an interview with Henry Kissinger in 1978 on "The Lessons of the Past," Walter Laqueur observed that during the Second World War "few if any people thought . . . of the structure of peace that would follow the war except perhaps in the most general terms of friendship, mutual trust, and the other noble sentiments mentioned in wartime programmatic speeches about the United Nations and related topics." Kissinger concurred, noting that no statesman, except perhaps Winston Churchill, "gave any attention to what would happen after the war." Americans, Kissinger stressed, "were determined that we were going to base the postwar period on good faith and getting along with everybody."[1]

That two such astute and knowledgeable observers of international politics were so uninformed about American planning at the end of the Second World War is testimony to the enduring mythology of American idealism and innocence in the world of *realpolitik*. It also reflects the state of scholarship on the interrelated areas of strategy, economy, and diplomacy. Despite the publication of several excellent overviews of the origins of the Cold War,[2] despite the outpouring of incisive monographs on American foreign policy in many areas of the world,[3] and despite some first-rate studies on the evolution of strategic thinking and the defense establishment,[4] no comprehensive account yet exists of how American defense officials defined national security interests in the aftermath of the Second World War. Until recently, the absence of such a study was understandable, for scholars had limited access to records pertaining to national security, strategic thinking, and war planning. But in recent years documents relating to the early years of the Cold War have been declassified in massive numbers.[5]

This documentation now makes it possible to analyze in greater depth the perceptions, apprehensions, and objectives of those defense officials most concerned with defining and defending the nation's security and strategic interests.[6] The goal here is to elucidate the fundamental strategic and economic considerations that shaped the definition of American national security interests in the postwar world. Several of these considerations – especially as they related to overseas bases, air transit rights, and a strategic sphere of influence in Latin America – initially were the logical result of technological developments and geostrategic experiences rather than directly

17

related to postwar Soviet behavior.[7] But American defense officials also considered the preservation of a favorable balance of power in Eurasia as fundamental to US national security. This objective impelled defense analysts and intelligence officers to appraise and reappraise the intentions and capabilities of the Soviet Union. Rather modest estimates of the Soviets' ability to wage war against the United States generated the widespread assumption that the Soviets would refrain from military aggression and seek to avoid war. Nevertheless, American defense officials remained greatly preoccupied with the geopolitical balance of power in Europe and Asia, because that balance seemed endangered by Communist exploitation of postwar economic dislocation and social and political unrest. Indeed, American assessments of the Soviet threat were less a consequence of expanding Soviet military capabilities and of Soviet diplomatic demands than a result of growing apprehension about the vulnerability of American strategic and economic interests in a world of unprecedented turmoil and upheaval. Viewed from this perspective, the Cold War assumed many of its most enduring characteristics during 1947–8, when American officials sought to cope with an array of challenges by implementing their own concepts of national security.

American officials first began to think seriously about the nation's postwar security during 1943–4. Military planners devised elaborate plans for an overseas base system. These bases were defined as the nation's strategic frontier. Beyond this frontier the United States would be able to use force to counter any threats or frustrate any overt acts of aggression. Within the strategic frontier, American military predominance had to remain inviolate. These plans received President Franklin D. Roosevelt's endorsement in early 1944.[8]

Two strategic considerations influenced the development of an overseas base system. The first was the need for defense in depth. Since attacks against the United States could emanate only from Europe and Asia, the Joint Chiefs of Staff concluded as early as November 1943 that the United States must encircle the western hemisphere with a defensive ring of outlying bases. In the Pacific this ring had to include the Aleutians, the Philippines, Okinawa, and the former Japanese mandates.[9] In the Atlantic, strategic planners maintained that their minimum requirements included a West African zone, with primary bases in the Azores or Canary Islands. The object of these defensive bases was to enable the United States to possess complete control of the Atlantic and Pacific oceans and keep hostile powers far from American territory.[10]

Defense in depth was especially important in light of the Pearl Harbor experience, the advance of technology, and the development of the atomic bomb. According to the Joint Chiefs of Staff, "Experience in the recent war demonstrated conclusively that the . . . farther away from our own vital areas we can hold our enemy through the possession of advanced bases . . . the greater are our chances of surviving successfully an attack by atomic weapons and of destroying the enemy which employs them against us." Believing that atomic weapons would increase the incentive to aggression by enhancing the advantage of surprise, military planners never ceased to extol the utility of forward bases from which American aircraft could seek to intercept attacks against the United States.[11]

The second strategic consideration that influenced the plan for a comprehensive overseas base system was the need to project American power quickly and effectively against any potential adversary. In conducting an overall examination of requirements for base rights in September 1945, the Joint War Plans Committee stressed that the Second World War demonstrated that the United States had to be able to take "timely" offensive action against the adversary's capacity and will to wage war. The basic strategic concept underlying all American war plans called for an air offensive against a prospective enemy from overseas bases. Delays in the development of the B-36, the first intercontinental bomber, only accentuated the need for these bases.[12]

In October 1945 the civilian leaders of the War and Navy Departments carefully reviewed the emerging strategic concepts and base requirements of the military planners. Secretary of the Navy James Forrestal and Secretary of War Robert P. Patterson fully endorsed the concept of a far-flung system of bases in the Atlantic and Pacific oceans that would enhance the offensive capabilities of the United States.[13] From these bases on America's "strategic frontier," the United States could preserve its access to vital raw materials, deny these resources to a prospective enemy, help preserve peace and stability in troubled areas, safeguard critical sea lanes, and, if necessary, conduct an air offensive against the industrial infrastructure of any power, including the Soviet Union.

Control of the Atlantic and Pacific oceans through overseas bases was considered indispensable to the nation's security regardless of what might happen to the wartime coalition. So was control over polar air routes. The first postwar base system approved by both the Joint Chiefs of Staff and the civilian secretaries in October 1945 included Iceland as a primary base area. The Joint War Plans Committee explained that American bases must control the air in the Arctic, prevent the establishment of enemy military facilities there, and support America's own striking forces. Once Soviet-American relations began to deteriorate, Greenland also was designated as a primary base for American heavy bombers and fighters because of its close proximity to the industrial heartland of the potential enemy.[14]

In the immediate postwar years American ambitions for an elaborate base system encountered many problems. Budgetary constraints compelled military planners to drop plans for many secondary and subsidiary bases, particularly in the South Pacific and Caribbean. By early 1948, the joint chiefs were willing to forgo base rights in such places as Surinam and Nouméa if "joint" or "participating" rights could be acquired or preserved in Karachi, Tripoli, Algiers, Casablanca, Dhahran, and Monrovia. Budgetary constraints, then, limited the depth of the base system but not the breadth of American ambitions.[15]

Less well known than the American effort to establish a base system, but integral to the policymakers' conception of national security, was the attempt to secure military air transit and landing rights. Military planners wanted such rights at critical locations not only in the western hemisphere but also in North Africa, the Middle East, India, and Southeast Asia. They delineated a route from Casablanca through Algiers, Tripoli, Cairo, Dhahran, Karachi, Delhi, Calcutta, Rangoon, Bangkok, and Saigon to Manila.[16] According to the Joint Chiefs of Staff, military air transit rights would permit the rapid augmentation of American bases in wartime as well as the rapid movement of American air units from the eastern to the western flank of the US base system.[17]

In Latin America, American requirements for effective national security went far beyond air transit rights. In a report

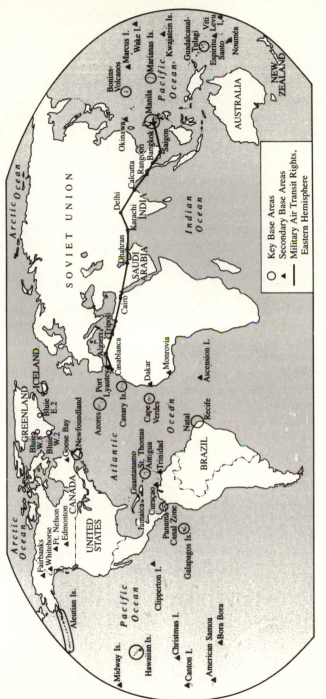

Map 1 US military base requirements following the Second World War

written in January 1945 the War Department urged American collaboration with Latin American armed forces to ensure the defense of the Panama Canal and the western hemisphere. Six areas within Latin America were considered of special significance either for strategic reasons or for their raw materials: the Panama Canal and approaches within 1,000 miles; the Straits of Magellan; northeastern Brazil; Mexico; the River Plate estuary and approaches within 500 miles; and Mollendo, Peru-Antofagusta, and Chile. These areas were so "important," Secretary of War Patterson explained to Secretary of State Marshall in early 1947, "that the threat of attack on any of them would force the United States to come to their defense, even though it were not certain that attack on the United States itself would follow." The resources of these areas were essential to the United States, because "it is imperative that our war potential be enhanced . . . during any national emergency."[18]

The need to predominate throughout the western hemisphere was not a result of deteriorating Soviet-American relations but a natural evolution of the Monroe Doctrine, accentuated by Axis aggression and new technological imperatives.[19] Patterson, Forrestal, and Army Chief of Staff Dwight D. Eisenhower initially were impelled less by reports of Soviet espionage, propaganda, and infiltration in Latin America than by accounts of British efforts to sell cruisers and aircraft to Chile and Ecuador; Swedish sales of anti-aircraft artillery to Argentina; and French offers to build cruisers and destroyers for both Argentina and Brazil.[20] To foreclose all foreign influence and to ensure US strategic hegemony, military officers and the civilian Secretaries of the War and Navy Departments argued for an extensive system of US bases, expansion of commercial airline facilities throughout Latin America, negotiation of a regional defense pact, curtailment of all foreign military aid and foreign military sales, training of Latin American military officers in the United States, outfitting of Latin American armies with US military equipment, and implementation of a comprehensive military assistance program.[21]

Although Truman favored these initiatives to Latin America, not all of them could be implemented. In June 1948, for example, the Inter-American Military Cooperation Act died in the Senate.[22] But this signified no diminution in American

22

national security imperatives; indeed, it underscored that US priorities now lay in Eurasia.

From the closing days of the Second World War, American defense officials believed that they could not allow any prospective adversary to control the Eurasian land mass. This was the lesson taught by two world wars. Strategic thinkers and military analysts insisted that any power or powers attempting to dominate Eurasia must be regarded as potentially hostile to the United States.[23] Their acute awareness of the importance of Eurasia made Marshall, Thomas Handy, George A. Lincoln, and other officers wary of the expansion of Soviet influence there. While acknowledging that the increase in Soviet power stemmed primarily from the defeat of Germany and Japan, postwar assessments of the Joint Chiefs of Staff emphasized the importance of deterring further Soviet aggrandizement in Eurasia.[24] Concern over the consequences of Russian domination of Eurasia helps explain why in July 1945 the joint chiefs decided to oppose a Soviet request for bases in the Dardanelles; why during March and April 1946 they supported a firm stand against Russia in Iran, Turkey, and Tripolitania; and why in the summer of 1946 Clark Clifford and George Elsey, two White House aides, argued that Soviet incorporation of any parts of Western Europe, the Middle East, China, or Japan into a Communist orbit was incompatible with American national security.[25]

Yet defense officials were not eager to sever the wartime coalition. In early 1944 Admiral William Leahy, the President's Chief of Staff, noted the "phenomenal development" of Soviet power but still hoped for Soviet-American cooperation. Eisenhower, Lincoln, and other officers advised against creating a central economic authority for Western Europe that might appear to be anti-Soviet.[26] The American objective, after all, was to avoid Soviet hegemony over Eurasia. By aggravating Soviet fears, the United States might foster what it wished to avoid. American self-restraint, however, might be reciprocated by the Soviets, providing time for Western Europe to recover and for the British to reassert some influence on the Continent.[27] Therefore, many defense officials in 1945 hoped to avoid an open rift with the Soviet Union. But at the same time they were determined to prevent the Eurasian land mass from falling under Soviet and Communist influence.

Studies by the Joint Chiefs of Staff stressed that, if Eurasia came under Soviet domination, either through military conquest or political and economic "assimilation," America's only potential adversary would fall heir to enormous natural resources, industrial potential, and manpower. By the autumn of 1945, military planners already were worrying that Soviet control over much of Eastern Europe and its raw materials would abet Russia's economic recovery, enhance its warmaking capacity, and deny important foodstuffs, oil, and minerals to Western Europe. By the early months of 1946, Secretary Patterson and his subordinates in the War Department believed that Soviet control of the Ruhr-Rhineland industrial complex would constitute an extreme threat. Even more dangerous was the prospect of Soviet predominance over the rest of Western Europe, especially France.[28] Strategically, this would undermine the impact of any prospective American naval blockade and would allow Soviet military planners to achieve defense in depth. The latter possibility had enormous military significance, because American war plans relied so heavily on air power and strategic bombing, the efficacy of which might be reduced substantially if the Soviets acquired outlying bases in Western Europe and the Middle East or if they "neutralized" bases in Great Britain.[29]

Economic considerations also made defense officials determined to retain American access to Eurasia as well as to deny Soviet predominance over it. Stimson, Patterson, McCloy, and Assistant Secretary Howard C. Peterson agreed with Forrestal that long-term American prosperity required open markets, unhindered access to raw materials, and the rehabilitation of much – if not all – of Eurasia along liberal capitalist lines. In late 1944 and 1945, Stimson protested the prospective industrial emasculation of Germany, lest it undermine American economic well-being, set back recovery throughout Europe, and unleash forces of anarchy and revolution. Stimson and his subordinates in the Operations Division of the army also worried that the spread of Soviet power in Northeast Asia would constrain the functioning of the free enterprise system and jeopardize American economic interests. A report prepared by the staff of the Moscow embassy and revised in mid-1946 by Ambassador (and former General) Walter Bedell Smith emphasized that

"Soviet power is by nature so jealous that it has already operated to segregate from world economy almost all of the areas in which it has been established." Therefore, Forrestal and the navy sought to contain Soviet influence in the Near East and to retain American access to Middle East oil; Patterson and the War Department focused on preventing famine in occupied areas and resuscitating trade.[30] But American economic interests in Eurasia were not limited to Western Europe, Germany, and the Middle East. Military planners and intelligence officers in both the army and navy expressed considerable interest in the raw materials of Southeast Asia, wanted to maintain access to those resources, and sought to deny them to a prospective enemy.[31]

While civilian officials and military strategists feared the loss of Eurasia, they did not expect the Soviet Union to attempt its military conquest. In the early cold war years, there was nearly universal agreement that the Soviets, while eager to expand their influence, desired to avoid a military engagement. In October 1945, the Joint Intelligence Staff predicted that the Soviet Union would seek to avoid war for five to ten years. In April 1946, while Soviet troops still remained in Iran, General Lincoln, the army's principal war planner, concurred with Secretary of State Byrnes's view that the Soviets did not want war. In May, when there was deep concern about a possible Communist uprising in France, military intelligence doubted the Kremlin would instigate a coup, lest it ignite a full-scale war. At a high-level meeting at the White House in June, Eisenhower stated that he did not think the Soviets wanted war; only Forrestal dissented. In August, when the Soviet note to Turkey on the Dardanelles provoked consternation in American policy-making circles, General Hoyt Vandenberg, director of central intelligence, informed President Truman that there were no signs of unusual Soviet troop movements or supply build-ups. In March 1947, while the Truman Doctrine was being discussed in Congress, the director of army intelligence maintained that the factors operating to discourage Soviet aggression continued to be decisive. In September 1947, the CIA concluded that the Soviets would not seek to conquer Western Europe for several reasons: they would recognize their inability to control hostile populations; they would fear triggering a war with the United States that could not be won; and they would prefer to gain hegemony by political and economic means.[32]

25

Even the ominous developments during the first half of 1948 did not alter these assessments. Despite his alarmist cable of March 5, designed to galvanize congressional support for increased defense expenditures, General Lucius Clay, the American military governor in Germany, did not believe war imminent. A few days later, the CIA concluded that the Communist takeover in Czechoslovakia would not increase Soviet capabilities significantly and reflected no alteration in Soviet tactics. After talking to Foreign Minister V. M. Molotov in June, Ambassador Smith concluded that Soviet leaders would not resort to active hostilities. During the Berlin blockade, army intelligence reported few signs of Soviet preparations for war. In October 1948, the Military Intelligence Division of the army endorsed a British appraisal that "all the evidence available indicates that the Soviet Union is not preparing to go to war in the near future." In December, Acting Secretary of State Robert Lovett summed up the longstanding American perspective when he emphasized that he saw "no evidence that Soviet intentions run toward launching a sudden military attack on the western nations at this time. It would not be in character with the tradition or mentality of the Soviet leaders to resort to such a measure unless they felt themselves either politically extremely weak, or militarily extremely strong."[33]

Although American defense officials recognized that the Soviets had substantial military assets,[34] they remained confident that the Soviet Union did not feel extremely strong. The Soviets had no long-range strategic air force, no atomic bomb, and meager air defenses. Moreover, the Soviet navy was considered ineffective except for its submarine forces.[35] The Joint Logistic Plans Committee and the Military Intelligence Division of the War Department estimated that the Soviet Union would require approximately fifteen years to overcome wartime losses in manpower and industry, ten years to redress the shortage of technicians, five to ten years to develop a strategic air force, fifteen to twenty-five years to construct a modern navy, ten years to refurbish military transport, ten years (or less) to quell resistance in occupied areas, fifteen to twenty years to establish a military infrastructure in the Far East, three to ten years to acquire the atomic bomb, and an unspecified number of years to remove the vulnerability of the Soviet rail-net and petroleum industry to long-range bombing.[36] For several years at least, the

Soviet capability for sustained attack against North America would be very limited. In January 1946 the Joint Intelligence Staff concluded that "the offensive capabilities of the United States are manifestly superior to those of the U.S.S.R. and any war between the U.S. and the U.S.S.R. would be far more costly to the Soviet Union than to the United States."[37]

Key American officials like Lovett, Clifford, Eisenhower, Bedell Smith, and Budget Director James Webb were cognizant of prevailing Soviet weaknesses and potential American strength. Despite Soviet superiority in manpower, General Eisenhower and Admiral Forrest E. Sherman doubted that Russia could mount a surprise attack, and General Lincoln, Admiral Cato Glover, and Secretaries Patterson and Forrestal believed that Soviet forces would encounter acute logistical problems in trying to overrun Eurasia – especially in the Near East, Spain, and Italy. Even Forrestal doubted reports of accelerating Soviet air capabilities. American experts believed that most Soviet planes were obsolescent, that the Soviets had insufficient airfields and aviation gas to use their new planes, and that these planes had serious problems in their instrumentation and construction.[38]

In general, improvements in specific areas of the Soviet military establishment did not mean that overall Soviet capabilities were improving at an alarming rate. In July 1947, the Military Intelligence Division concluded, "While there has been a slight overall improvement in the Soviet war potential, Soviet strength for total war is not sufficiently great to make a military attack against the United States anything but a most hazardous gamble." This view prevailed in 1946 and 1947, even though the American nuclear arsenal was extremely small and the American strategic bombing force of limited size. In the spring of 1948 the Joint Intelligence Committee at the American embassy in Moscow explained why the United States ultimately would emerge victorious should a war erupt in the immediate future. The Soviets could not win because of their "inability to carry the war to U.S. territory. After the occupation of Europe, the U.S.S.R. would be forced to assume the defensive and await attacks by U.S. forces which should succeed primarily because of the ability of the U.S. to outproduce the U.S.S.R. in materials of war."[39]

Awareness of Soviet economic shortcomings played a key role

in the American interpretation of Soviet capabilities. Intelligence reports predicted that Soviet leaders would invest a disproportionate share of Russian resources in capital goods industries. But, even if such Herculean efforts enjoyed some success, the Soviets still would not reach the pre-Second World War levels of the United States within fifteen to twenty years. Technologically, the Soviets were behind in the critical areas of aircraft manufacturing, electronics, and oil refining. And, despite Russia's concerted attempts to catch up and to surpass the United States, American intelligence experts soon started reporting that Soviet reconstruction was lagging behind Soviet ambitions, especially in the electronics, transportation, aircraft, construction machinery, nonferrous metals, and shipping industries. Accordingly, throughout the years 1945–8 American military analysts and intelligence experts believed that Soviet transportation bottlenecks, industrial shortcomings, technological backwardness, and agricultural problems would discourage military adventurism.[40]

If American defense officials did not expect a Soviet military attack, why, then, were they so fearful of losing control of Eurasia? The answer rests less in American assessments of Soviet military capabilities and short-term military intentions than in appraisals of economic and political conditions throughout Europe and Asia. Army officials in particular, because of their occupation roles in Germany, Japan, Austria, and Korea, were aware of the postwar plight of these areas. Key military men – Generals Eisenhower, Clay, Douglas MacArthur, John Hilldring, and Oliver P. Echols and Colonel Charles H. Bonesteel – became alarmed by the prospects of famine, disease, anarchy, and revolution. They recognized that Communist parties could exploit the distress and that the Russians could capitalize upon it to spread Soviet influence.[41]

Civilian officials in the War, Navy, and State Departments shared these concerns. In the autumn of 1945, McCloy warned Patterson that the stakes in Germany were immense and economic recovery had to be expedited. During the first half of 1946 Secretary Patterson and Assistant Secretary Peterson continually pressed the State Department to tackle the problems beleaguering Germany and Western Europe. Under-Secretary of State Dean Acheson wrote Truman in April 1946, "We have now reached the most critical period of the world food crisis. We must either immediately greatly increase the exports of grain from the United States or expect general disorder and political upheaval to develop in [most of Eurasia]."[42]

American defense officials, military analysts, and intelligence officers were extremely sensitive to the political ferment, social turmoil, and economic upheaval throughout postwar Europe and Asia. In their initial postwar studies, the Joint Chiefs of Staff carefully noted the multiplicity of problems that could breed conflict and provide opportunities for Soviet expansion. In the spring of 1946 army planners were keenly aware that conflict was most likely to arise from local disputes (for example, between Italy and Yugoslavia) or from indigenous unrest (for example, in France), perhaps even against the will of Moscow. A key War Department document in April 1946 skirted the issue of Soviet military capabilities and argued that the Soviet Union's strength emanated from totalitarian control over its satellites, from local Communist parties, and from worldwide chaotic political and economic conditions. "The greatest danger to the security of the United States," the CIA concluded in mid-1947, "is the possibility of economic collapse in Western Europe and the consequent accession to power of Communist elements."[43]

During 1946 and 1947, defense officials witnessed a dramatic unravelling of the geopolitical foundations and socioeconomic structure of international affairs. Britain's economic weakness and withdrawal from the eastern Mediterranean, India's independence movement, civil war in China, nationalist insurgencies in Indo-China and the Dutch East Indies, Zionist claims to Palestine and Arab resentment, German and Japanese economic paralysis, Communist inroads in France and Italy – all were ominous developments. Defense officials recognized that the Soviet Union had not created these circumstances but believed that Soviet leaders would exploit them. Should Communists take power, even without direct Russian intervention, the Soviet Union would gain predominant control of the resources of these areas because of the postulated subservience of Communist parties everywhere to the Kremlin. Should nationalist uprisings persist, Communists seize power in underdeveloped countries, or Arabs revolt against American support of a Jewish state, the petroleum and raw materials of critical areas might be denied the West. The imminent possibility existed that, even without Soviet military aggression, the resources of Eurasia could fall under Russian control. With these resources, the Soviet Union would be able to overcome its chronic economic weaknesses, achieve defense in depth, and challenge American power – perhaps even by military force.[44]

In this frightening postwar environment American assessments of Soviet long-term intentions were transformed. Spurred by the "long telegram," written by George F. Kennan, the US chargé d'affaires in Moscow, it soon became commonplace for policymakers, military officials, and intelligence analysts to state that the ultimate aim of Soviet foreign policy was Russian domination of a Communist world.[45] There was, of course, plentiful evidence for this appraisal of Soviet ambitions – the Soviet consolidation of a sphere of influence in Eastern Europe; Soviet violation of the agreement to withdraw troops from Iran; Soviet relinquishment of Japanese arms to the Chinese Communists; the Soviet mode of extracting reparations from the Russian zone in Germany; Soviet diplomatic overtures for bases in the Dardanelles, Tripolitania, and the Dodecanese; Soviet requests for a role in the occupation of Japan; and the Kremlin's renewed emphasis on Marxist-Leninist doctrine, the vulnerability of capitalist economies, and the inevitability of conflict.

Yet these assessments did not seriously grapple with contradictory evidence. They disregarded numerous signs of Soviet weakness, moderation, and circumspection. During 1946 and 1947 intelligence analysts described the withdrawal of Russian troops from northern Norway, Manchuria, Bornholm, and Iran (from the latter under pressure, of course). Numerous intelligence sources reported the reduction of Russian troops in Eastern Europe and the extensive demobilization going on within the Soviet Union. In October 1947 the Joint Intelligence Committee forecast a Soviet army troop strength during 1948 and 1949 of less than 2 million men. Other reports dealt with the inadequacies of Soviet transportation and bridging equipment and the moderation of Soviet military expenditures. And, as already noted, assessments of the Soviet economy revealed persistent problems likely to restrict Soviet adventurism.[46]

Experience suggested that the Soviet Union was by no means uniformly hostile or unwilling to negotiate with the United States. In April 1946 Ambassador Smith reminded the State

Department that the Soviet press was not unalterably critical of the United States, that the Russians had withdrawn from Bornholm, that Stalin had given a moderate speech on the United Nations, and that Soviet demobilization continued apace. The next month General Lincoln acknowledged that the Soviets had been willing to make numerous concessions regarding Tripolitania, the Dodecanese, and Italian reparations. In the spring of 1946, General Echols, General Clay, and Secretary Patterson again maintained that the French constituted the major impediment to an agreement on united control of Germany. In early 1947 central intelligence delineated more than a half-dozen instances of Soviet moderation or concessions. In April the Military Intelligence Division noted that the Soviets had limited their involvement in the Middle East, diminished their ideological rhetoric, and given only moderate support to Chinese Communists.[47]

In their overall assessments of Soviet long-term intentions, however, military planners dismissed all evidence of Soviet moderation, circumspection, and restraint. In fact, as 1946 progressed, these planners seemed to spend less time analyzing Soviet intentions and more time estimating Soviet capabilities.[48] They no longer explored ways of accommodating a potential adversary's legitimate strategic requirements or pondered how American initiatives might influence the Soviet Union's definition of its objectives.[49] Information not confirming prevailing assumptions either was ignored in overall assessments of Soviet intentions or was used to illustrate that the Soviets were shifting tactics but not altering objectives. A report from the Joint Chiefs of Staff to the President in July 1946, for example, deleted sections from previous studies that had outlined Soviet weaknesses. A memorandum sent by Secretary Patterson to the President at the same time was designed to answer questions about relations with the Soviet Union "without ambiguity." Truman, Clark Clifford observed many years later, liked things in black and white.[50]

The conjunction of Soviet ideological fervor and socioeconomic turmoil throughout Eurasia contributed to the growth of a myopic view of Soviet long-term policy objectives and to enormous apprehension lest the Soviet Union gain control of all the resources of Eurasia, thereby endangering the national security of

31

the United States. American assessments of Soviet short-term military intentions had not altered; Soviet military capabilities had not significantly increased; and Soviet foreign policy positions had not greatly shifted. But defense officials were acutely aware of America's own rapidly diminishing capabilities, of Britain's declining military strength, of the appeal of Communist doctrine to most of the underdeveloped world, and of the opportunities of Communist parties to exploit prevailing socioeconomic conditions. In this turbulent international arena, the survival of liberal ideals and capitalist institutions was anything but assured. "We could point to the economic benefits of Capitalism," commented one important War Department paper in April 1946, "but these benefits are concentrated rather than widespread, and, at present, are genuinely suspect throughout Europe and in many other parts of the world."[51]

In this environment, there was indeed no room for ambiguity or compromise. Action was imperative – action aimed at safeguarding those areas of Eurasia not already within the Soviet sphere. Even before Kennan's "long telegram" arrived in Washington the joint chiefs adopted the position that "collaboration with the Soviet Union should stop short not only of compromise of principle but also of expansion of Russian influence in Europe and in the Far East."[52] During the spring and summer of 1946, General Lincoln and Admiral Richard L. Conolly, commander of American naval forces in the eastern Atlantic and Mediterranean, worked tirelessly to stiffen Byrnes's views and put the squeeze on the Russians.[53] "The United States," army planners explained, "must be able to prevent, by force if necessary, Russian domination of either Europe or Asia to the extent that the resources of either continent could be mobilized against the United States." Which countries in Eurasia were worth fighting over remained unclear during 1946. But army and navy officials as well as the joint chiefs advocated a far-reaching program of foreign economic assistance coupled with the refurbishment of American military forces.[54]

During late 1946 and early 1947, the Truman administration assumed the initiative by creating German Bizonia, providing military assistance to Greece and Turkey, allocating massive economic aid to Western Europe, and reassessing economic policy toward Japan. These initiatives were aimed primarily at tackling the internal sources of unrest upon which Communist parties capitalized and at rehabilitating the industrial heartlands of Eurasia. American defense officials supported these actions and acquiesced in the decision to give priority to economic aid rather than rearmament. "In the necessarily delicate apportioning of our available resources," wrote Assistant Secretary of War Peterson, "the time element permits present emphasis on strengthening the economic and social dikes against Soviet communism rather than upon preparing for a possibly eventual, but not yet inevitable, war."[55]

Yet if war should unexpectedly occur, the United States had to have the capability to inflict incalculable damage upon the Soviet Union. Defense officials sought to perpetuate America's nuclear monopoly as long as possible in order to counterbalance Soviet conventional strength, deter Soviet adventurism, and bolster American negotiating leverage. While Truman insisted on limiting military expenditures, the Joint Chiefs of Staff wanted to enlarge the atomic arsenal and increase the number of aircraft capable of delivering atomic bombs. After much initial postwar disorganization, the General Advisory Committee to the Atomic Energy Commission reported to the President at the end of 1947 that "great progress" had been made in the atomic program. From June 30, 1947, to June 30, 1948, the number of bombs in the stockpile increased from thirteen to fifty. Although at the time of the Berlin crisis the United States was not prepared to launch a strategic air offensive against the Soviet Union, substantial progress had been made in the development of the nation's air-atomic capabilities. By the end of 1948, the United States had at least eighteen nuclear-capable B-50s, four B-36s, and almost three times as many nuclear-capable B-29s as had been available at the end of 1947.[56]

During late 1947 and early 1948, the administration also responded to pleas of the Joint Chiefs of Staff to augment the overseas base system and to acquire bases in closer proximity to the Soviet Union. Negotiations were conducted with the British to gain access to bases in the Middle East and an agreement was concluded for the acquisition of air facilities in Libya. Admiral Conolly made a secret deal with the French to secure air and communication rights and to stockpile oil, aviation gas, and ammunition in North Africa.[57] Plans also were discussed for post-occupation bases in Japan, and considerable progress was made in refurbishing and constructing airfields in Turkey.[58]

The joint chiefs and military planners realized that American initiatives placed the Soviet Union on the defensive, magnified tensions, and made war more likely – though still improbable. In July 1947, intelligence analysts in the War Department maintained that the Truman Doctrine and the Marshall Plan provoked a more aggressive Soviet attitude toward the United States. They also understood that the Soviets would perceive American efforts to build strategic highways, construct airfields, and transfer fighter bombers to Turkey as threats to Soviet security. And defense officials were well aware that the Soviets would react angrily to plans for currency reform in German Trizonia and to preparations for a West German republic. "The whole Berlin crisis," army planners informed Eisenhower in June 1948, "has arisen as a result of . . . actions on the part of the Western Powers."[59]

The real consternation of the Joint Chiefs of Staff and other high-ranking civilian and military officials in the defense agencies stemmed from their growing conviction that the United States was undertaking actions and assuming commitments that now required greater military capabilities. Recognizing that American initiatives, aimed at safeguarding Eurasia from further Communist inroads, might be perceived as endangering Soviet interests, it was all the more important to be ready for any eventuality. Indeed, to the extent that anxieties about the prospects of war escalated in March and April 1948, these fears did not stem from estimates that the Soviets were planning further aggressive action after the Communist seizure of power in Czechoslovakia but from apprehensions that ongoing American initiatives might provoke an attack. On March 14 General S. J. Chamberlin, director of army intelligence, warned the Chief of Staff that "actions taken by this country in opposition to the spread of Communism . . . may decide the question of the outbreak of war and of its timing." The critical question explicitly faced by the intelligence agencies and by the highest policymakers was whether passage of the Selective Service Act, or of universal military training, or of additional appropriations for the air force, or of a military assistance program to Western European countries, or of a resolution endorsing American support for West European Union would trigger a Soviet attack. Chamberlin judged, for example, that the Soviets would not go to war just to make Europe Communist but would resort to war if they felt threatened. The great imponderable, of course, was what, in the Soviet view, would constitute a security threat justifying war.[60]

The priority accorded to Western Europe did not mean that officials ignored the rest of Eurasia. Indeed, the sustained economic rejuvenation of Western Europe made access to Middle Eastern oil more important than ever. Marshall, Lovett, Forrestal, and other defense officials, including the joint chiefs, feared that American support of Israel might jeopardize relations with Arab nations and drive them into the hands of the Soviet Union. Although Truman accepted the partition of Palestine and recognized Israel, the United States maintained an embargo on arms shipments and sought to avoid too close an identification with the Zionist state lest the flow of oil to the West be jeopardized.[61] At the same time, the Truman administration moved swiftly in June 1948 to resuscitate the Japanese economy. Additional funds were requested from Congress to procure imports of raw materials for Japanese industry so that Japanese exports might also be increased. Shortly thereafter, William Draper, Tracy S. Voorhees, and other army officials came to believe that a rehabilitated Japan would need the markets and raw materials of Southeast Asia. They undertook a comprehensive examination of the efficacy and utility of a Marshall Plan for Asia. Integrating Japan and Southeast Asia into a viable regional economy, invulnerable to Communist subversion and firmly ensconced in the Western community, assumed growing significance, especially in view of the prospect of a Communist triumph in China.[62]

The problem with all of these undertakings, however, was that they cost large sums, expanded the nation's formal and informal commitments, and necessitated larger military capabilities. Truman's Council of Economic Advisors warned that accelerating expenditures might compel the President "to set aside free market practices – and substitute a rather comprehensive set of controls." Truman was appalled by this possibility and carefully limited the sums allocated for a buildup of American forces.[63] Key advisers, like Webb, Marshall, Lovett, and Clifford, supported this approach because they perceived too much fat in the military budget, expected the Soviets to rely on political tactics rather than military aggression, postulated latent US military superiority over the Soviet Union, and assumed that the atomic bomb constituted a decisive, if perhaps short-term, trump card.[64]

As Secretary of Defense, however, Forrestal was beleaguered by pressures emanating from the armed services for a build-up of American military forces and by his own apprehensions over prospective Soviet actions. He anguished over the excruciatingly difficult choices that had to be made between the imperatives of foreign economic aid, overseas military assistance, domestic rearmament, and fiscal orthodoxy. In May, June, and July 1948, he and his assistants carefully pondered intelligence reports on Soviet intentions and requested a special study on how to plan American defense expenditures in view of prospective Soviet policies. Forrestal clearly hoped that this reassessment would show that a larger proportion of resources should be allocated to the military establishment.[65]

The Policy Planning Staff of the Department of State prepared the initial study that Forrestal requested. Extensively redrafted it reappeared in November 1948 as NSC 20/4 and was adopted as the definitive statement of American foreign policy. This paper reiterated the longstanding estimate that the Soviet Union was not likely to resort to war to achieve its objectives. But war could erupt as a result of "Soviet miscalculation of the determination of the United States to use all the means at its command to safeguard its security, through Soviet misinterpretation of our intentions, and through U.S. miscalculation of Soviet reactions to measures which we might take."[66] Although NSC 20/4 did not call for a larger military budget, it stressed "that Soviet political warfare might seriously weaken the relative position of the United States, enhance Soviet strength and either lead to our ultimate defeat short of war, or force us into war under dangerously unfavorable conditions." Accordingly, the National Security Council vaguely but stridently propounded the importance of reducing Soviet power and influence on the periphery of the Russian homeland and of strengthening the pro-American orientation of non-Soviet nations.[67]

Language of this sort, which did not define clear priorities and which projected American interests almost everywhere on the globe, exasperated the joint chiefs and other military officers. They, too, believed that the United States should resist Communist aggression everywhere, "an overall commitment which in itself is all-inclusive." But to undertake this goal in a

36

responsible and effective fashion it was necessary "to bring our military strength to a level commensurate with the distinct possibility of global warfare." The Joint Chiefs of Staff still did not think the Soviets wanted war. But, given the long-term intentions attributed to the Soviet Union and given America's own aims, the chances for war, though still small, were growing. The United States, therefore, had to be prepared to wage a war it did not seek, but which could arise as a result of its own pursuit of national security goals.[68]

Having conceived of American national security in terms of Western control and of American access to the resources of Eurasia outside the Soviet sphere, American defense officials now considered it imperative to develop American military capabilities to meet a host of contingencies that might emanate from further Soviet encroachments or from indigenous Communist unrest. Such contingencies were sure to arise because American strategy depended so heavily on the rebuilding of Germany and Japan, Russia's traditional enemies, as well as on air power, atomic weapons, and bases on the Soviet periphery. Such contingencies also were predictable because American strategy depended so heavily on the restoration of stability in Eurasia, a situation increasingly unlikely in an era of nationalist turmoil, social unrest, and rising economic expectations. Although the desire of the national military establishment for large increments in defense expenditures did not prevail in the tight budgetary environment and presidential election year of 1948, the mode of thinking about national security that subsequently accelerated the arms race and precipitated military interventionism in Asia was already widespread among defense officials.

The dynamics of the Cold War after 1948 are easier to comprehend when one grasps the breadth of the American conception of national security that had emerged between 1945 and 1948. This conception included a strategic sphere of influence within the western hemisphere, domination of the Atlantic and Pacific oceans, an extensive system of outlying bases to enlarge the strategic frontier and project American power, an even more extensive system of transit rights to facilitate the conversion of commercial air bases to military use, access to the resources and markets of most of Eurasia, denial of those resources to a prospective enemy, and the maintenance of nuclear superiority. Not every one of these ingredients, it must be emphasized, was considered vital. Hence, American officials could acquiesce, however grudgingly, to a Soviet sphere in Eastern Europe and could avoid direct intervention in China. But cumulative challenges to these concepts of national security were certain to provoke a firm American response. This occurred initially in 1947–8 when decisions were made in favor of the Truman Doctrine, the Marshall Plan, military assistance, the Atlantic alliance, and German and Japanese rehabilitation. Soon thereafter, the "loss" of China, the Soviet detonation of an atomic bomb, and the North Korean attack on South Korea intensified the perception of threat to prevailing concepts of national security. The Truman administration responded with military assistance to Southeast Asia, a decision to build the hydrogen bomb, direct military intervention in Korea, a commitment to station troops permanently in Europe, expansion of the American alliance system, and a massive rearmament program in the United States. Postulating a long-term Soviet intention to gain world domination, the American conception of national security, based on geopolitical and economic imperatives, could not allow for additional losses in Eurasia, could not risk a challenge to its nuclear supremacy, and could not permit any infringement on its ability to defend in depth or to project American force from areas in close proximity to the Soviet homeland.

To say this, is neither to exculpate the Soviet government for its inhumane treatment of its own citizens nor to suggest that Soviet foreign policy was idle or benign. Indeed, Soviet behavior in Eastern Europe was often deplorable; the Soviets sought opportunities in the Dardanelles, northern Iran, and Manchuria; the Soviets hoped to orient Germany and Austria toward the East; and the Soviets sometimes endeavored to use Communist parties to expand Soviet influence in areas beyond the periphery of Russian military power. But, then again, the Soviet Union had lost 20 million dead during the war, had experienced the destruction of 1,700 towns, 31,000 factories, and 100,000 collective farms, and had witnessed the devastation of the rural economy with the Nazi slaughter of 20 million hogs and 17 million head of cattle. What is remarkable is that after 1946 these monumental losses received so little attention when American defense analysts studied the motives and intentions of Soviet policy; indeed, defense officials did little to analyze the threat perceived by the Soviets. Yet these same officials had absolutely no doubt that the wartime experiences and sacrifices of the United States, though much less devastating than those of Soviet Russia, demonstrated the need for and entitled the United States to oversee the resuscitation of the industrial heartlands of Germany and Japan, establish a viable balance of power in Eurasia, and militarily dominate the Eurasian rimlands, thereby safeguarding American access to raw materials and control over all sea and air approaches to North America.[69]

To suggest a double standard is important only in so far as it raises fundamental questions about the conceptualization and implementation of American national security policy. If Soviet policy was aggressive, bellicose, and ideological, perhaps America's reliance on overseas bases, air power, atomic weapons, military alliances, and the rehabilitation of Germany and Japan was the best course to follow, even if the effect may have been to exacerbate Soviet anxieties and suspicions. But even when one attributes the worst intentions to the Soviet Union, one might still ask whether American presuppositions and apprehensions about the benefits that would accrue to the Soviet Union as a result of Communist (and even revolutionary nationalist) gains anywhere in Eurasia tended to simplify international realities, magnify the breadth of American interests, engender commitments beyond American capabilities, and dissipate the nation's strength and credibility. And, perhaps even more importantly, if Soviet foreign policies tended to be opportunist, reactive, nationalistic, and contradictory, as some recent writers have claimed and as some contemporary analysts suggested, then one might also wonder whether America's own conception of national security tended, perhaps unintentionally, to engender anxieties and to provoke countermeasures from a proud, suspicious, insecure, and cruel government that was at the same time legitimately apprehensive about the long-term implications arising from the rehabilitation of traditional enemies and the development of foreign bases on the periphery of the Soviet homeland. To raise such issues anew seems essential if we are to unravel the complex origins of the Cold War.

NOTES

From Melvyn P. Leffler, "The American Conception of National Security and the Beginnings of the Cold War, 1945–48," *The American Historical Review*, 89 (April 1984): 346–81. Reprinted and abridged by permission of the author.

1 Henry Kissinger, *For the Record: Selected Statements, 1977–80* (Boston, MA, 1980), 123–4.
2 For recent overviews of the origins of the Cold War, which seek to go beyond the heated traditionalist-revisionist controversies of the 1960s and early 1970s, see, for example, John L. Gaddis, *The United States and the Origins of the Cold War, 1941–1947* (New York, 1972); Daniel Yergin, *Shattered Peace: The Origins of the Cold War and the National Security State* (Boston, MA, 1978); Thomas G. Paterson, *On Every Front: The Making of the Cold War* (New York, 1979); and Roy Douglas, *From War to Cold War, 1942–48* (New York, 1981).
3 For some of the most important and most recent regional and bilateral studies, see, for example, Bruce Kuniholm, *The Origins of the Cold War in the Near East: Great Power Conflict and Diplomacy in Iran. Turkey, and Greece* (Princeton, NJ 1980); Lawrence S. Wittner, *American Intervention in Greece* (New York, 1982); Aaron Miller, *Search for Security: Saudi Arabian Oil and American Foreign Policy, 1939–1949* (Chapel Hill, NC, 1980); Timothy Ireland, *Creating the Entangling Alliance: The Origins of the North Atlantic Treaty Organization* (Westport, CT, 1981); William W. Stueck, Jr, *The Road to Confrontation: American Policy toward China and Korea* (Chapel Hill, NC, 1981); Dorothy Borg and Waldo Heinrichs (eds), *Uncertain Years: Chinese-American Relations, 1947–1950* (New York, 1980); Robert J. McMahon, *Colonialism and the Cold War: The United States and the Struggle for Indonesian Independence, 1945–49* (Ithaca, NY, 1981); Bruce Cumings, *The Origins of the Korean War: Liberation and the Emergence of Separate Regimes, 1945–47* (Princeton, NJ, 1982); Geir Lundestad, *America, Scandinavia and the Cold War, 1945–49* (New York, 1980); Kenneth Ray Bain, *March to Zion: United States Foreign Policy and the Founding of Israel* (College Station, TX, 1979); Robert M. Hathaway, *Ambiguous Partnership: Britain and America, 1944–47* (New York, 1981); Eduard Mark, "American Policy toward Eastern Europe and the Origins of the Cold War, 1941–46: An Alternative Interpretation," *Journal of American History* [hereafter *JAH*], 68 (1981–2): 313–36; Michael Schaller, "Securing the Great Crescent: Occupied Japan and the Origins of Containment in Southeast Asia." *JAH*, 69 (1982–3): 392–414; and Michael J. Hogan, "The Search for a 'Creative Peace': The United States, European Unity, and the Origins of the Marshall Plan," *Diplomatic History*, 6 (Summer 1982): 267–85.
4 For recent works on strategy, the national military establishment, and the emergence of the national security bureaucracy, see, for example, Richard Haynes, *The Awesome Power: Harry S. Truman as*

Commander in Chief (Baton Rouge, LA, 1973); Alfred D. Sander, "Truman and the National Security Council, 1945–1947," *JAH*, 59 (1972–3): 369–88; Michael S. Sherry, *Preparing for the Next War: American Plans for Postwar Defense, 1941–45* (New Haven, CT, 1977); James F. Schnabel, *The History of the Joint Chiefs of Staff: The Joint Chiefs of Staff and National Policy*, Vol. 1: *1945–1947* (Wilmington, DE, 1979); Kenneth W. Condit, *The History of the Joint Chiefs of Staff: The Joint Chiefs of Staff and National Policy*, Vol. 2: *1947–1949* (Wilmington, DE, 1979); Gregg Herken, *The Winning Weapon: The Atomic Bomb and the Cold War, 1945–1950* (New York, 1980); David Alan Rosenberg, "American Atomic Strategy and the Hydrogen Bomb Decision," *JAH*, 66 (1979–80): 62–87; Harry R. Borowski, *A Hollow Threat: Strategic Air Power and Containment before Korea* (Westport, CT, 1982); Anna K. Nelson, "National Security I: Inventing a Process, 1945–1960," in Hugh Heclo and Lester M. Salamon (eds), *The Illusion of Presidential Government* (Boulder, CO, 1981), 229–45.

5 For the records of the Joint Chiefs of Staff, see Record Group 218, National Archives, Washington [hereafter RG 218]; for the records of the Office of the Secretary of Defense, see Record Group 330, National Archives, Washington [hereafter RG 330]; and, for the records of the National Security Council, see Record Group 273, Judicial, Fiscal, and Social Branch, National Archives, Washington. There are important National Security Council materials in the Harry S. Truman Papers, President's Secretary's File, Harry S. Truman Presidential Library, Independence, MO [hereafter HTL, HSTP, PSF], boxes 191–208. For assessments by the CIA, including those prepared for meetings of the National Security Council (NSC), especially see ibid., boxes 249–60, 203–7. For a helpful guide to War and Army Department records in the National Archives, see Louis Galambos (ed.), *The Papers of Dwight David Eisenhower*, 9 vols (Baltimore, MD, 1970–8), Vol. 9: 2262–70. Of greatest utility in studying the views of civilian and military planners in the War and Army Departments are Record Group 165, Records of the Operations Division [OPD], and Records of American-British Conversations [ABC]; Record Group 319, Records of the Plans and Operations Division [P&O]; Record Group 107, Records of the Office of the Secretary of War, Robert P. Patterson Papers [RPPP], safe file and general decimal file, and Records of the Office of the Assistant Secretary of War, Howard C. Peterson Papers [HCPP], classified decimal file; and Record Group 335, Records of the Under-Secretary of the Army, Draper/Voorhees files, 1947–50. The records of the navy's Strategic Plans Division [SPD] and the Politico-Military Division [PMD] are divided into many sub-series; helpful indexes are available at the Naval Historical Center [NHC]. The center also contains, among many other collections, the records of the Office of the Chief of Naval Operations [CNO], double zero files, as well as the manuscript collections of many influential naval officers, including Chester Nimitz, Forrest Sherman, Louis Denfeld, and Arthur Radford. For air force records, I tried – with only moderate success –

to use the following materials at the National Archives: Record Group 107, Records of the Office of the Assistant Secretary of War for Air, Plans, Policies, and Agreements, 1943–7; Records of the Office of the Assistant Secretary of War for Air, Establishments of Air Fields and Air Bases, 1940–5; and Incoming and Outgoing Cablegrams, 1942–7; and Record Group 18, Records of the Office of the Chief of Air Staff, Headquarters Army Air Forces: Office of the Air Adjutant General, confidential and secret decimal correspondence file, 1945–8. For the records of the State-War-Navy Coordinating Committee [SWNCC] and its successor, the State-Army-Navy-Air Force Coordinating Committee, see Record Group 353, National Archives, Washington, and, for the important records of the Committee of Three (meetings of the Secretaries of State, War, and Navy), see Record Group 107, RPPP, safe file.

6 I use the term "defense officials" broadly in this essay to include civilian appointees and military officers in the departments of the army, navy, and air force, in the office of the Secretary of Defense, in the armed services, in the intelligence agencies, and on the staff of the National Security Council. While I purposefully avoided a systematic analysis of career diplomats in the Department of State, who have received much attention elsewhere, the conclusions I draw here are based on a consideration of the views of high-ranking officials in the State Department, including James F. Byrnes, Dean Acheson, George C. Marshall, and Robert Lovett.

7 Any assessment of postwar national security policy must also take note of the role of the atomic bomb in US strategy and diplomacy. But, since nuclear weapons have received extensive attention elsewhere, I deal with this issue rather briefly. For excellent work on the atomic bomb, see, for example, Martin J. Sherwin, *A World Destroyed: The Atomic Bomb and the Grand Alliance* (New York, 1973); Barton J. Bernstein, "The Quest for Security: American Foreign Policy and International Control of Atomic Energy, 1942–1946," *JAH*, 60 (1973–4): 1003–44; Herken, *The Winning Weapon*; Rosenberg, "American Atomic Strategy and the Hydrogen Bomb Decision"; Richard G. Hewlett and Francis Duncan, *Atomic Shield: A History of the United States Atomic Energy Commission, 1947–52* (University Park, PA, 1969); Gar Alperovitz, *Atomic Diplomacy: Hiroshima and Potsdam* (New York, 1965).

8 Plans for America's overseas base system may be found in RG 218, Combined Chiefs of Staff [CCS] series 360 (12–9–42); Joint Strategic Survey Committee [hereafter JSSC], "Air Routes across the Pacific and Air Facilities for International Police Force," March 15, 1943, JSSC 9/1; Joint Chiefs of Staff [JCS], "United States Military Requirements for Air Bases, Facilities, and Operating Rights in Foreign Territories," November 2, 1943, JCS 570/2; Joint War Plans Committee [hereafter JWPC], "Overall Examination of the United States Requirements for Military Bases," August 25, 1943, JWPC 361/4; and JWPC, "Overall Examination of United States Requirements for Military Bases," September 13, 1945, JWPC 361/5

(revised). For Roosevelt's endorsement, see Roosevelt to the Department of State, January 7, 1944, ibid., JWPC 361/5.

9 JCS, "Strategic Areas and Trusteeships in the Pacific," October 10, 18, 1946, RG 218, ser. CCS 360 (12–9–42), JCS 1619/15, 19; JCS, "United States Military Requirements for Air Bases," November 2, 1943; JCS, "Overall Examination of United States Requirements for Military Bases and Base Rights," October 25, 1945, ibid., JCS 570/40.

10 JCS, "United States Military Requirements for Air Bases," November 2, 1943; JCS, Minutes of the 71st meeting, March 30, 1943, RG 218, ser. CCS 360 (12–9–42); and Joint Planning Staff [hereafter JPS], "Basis for the Formulation of a Post-War Military Policy," August 20, 1945, RG 218, ser. CCS 381 (5–13–45), JPS 633/6.

11 JCS, "Statement of Effect of Atomic Weapons on National Security and Military Organization," March 29, 1946, RG 165, ser. ABC 471.6 Atom (8–17–45), JCS 477/10.

12 For the emphasis on "timely" action, see JWPC, "Overall Examination of Requirements for Military Bases" (revised), September 13, 1945; for the need for advance bases, see JCS, "Strategic Concept and Plan for the Employment of United States Armed Forces," September 19, 1945, RG 218, ser. CCS 381 (5–13–45), JCS 1518. Also see, for the evolution of strategic war plans, many of the materials in RG 218, ser. CCS 381 USSR (3–2–46).

13 For the discussions and conclusions of civilian officials, see William Leahy to Patterson and Forrestal, October 9, 1945, RG 165, OPD 336 (top secret); Patterson to the Secretary of Navy, October 17, 1945, ibid.; and Forrestal to Byrnes, October 4, 1945, RG 218, ser. CCS 360 (12–9–42). For Forrestal's views, also see Forrestal to James K. Vardaman, September 14, 1945, Mudd Library, Princeton University, James Forrestal Papers [hereafter ML, JFP], box 100.

14 For the utility of Iceland and Greenland as bases, see JWPC, "Attributes of United States Overseas Bases," November 2, 1945, RG 218, ser. CCS 360 (12–9–42), JWPC 361/10; NSC, "Report by the NSC on Base Rights in Greenland, Iceland, and the Azores," November 25, 1947, ibid., NSC 2/1. For the dilemma posed by prospective Soviet demands for similar base rights at Spitzbergen, see, for example, JCS, "Foreign Policy of the United States," February 10, 1946, RG 218, ser. CCS 092 US (12–21–45), JCS 1519/2; Department of State, *Foreign Relations of the United States* [hereafter FRUS], 1947, 8 vols (Washington, DC, 1971–3), Vol. 1: 708–12, 766–70, and Vol. 3: 657–87, 1003–18; and Lundestad, *America, Scandinava, and the Cold War*, 63–76.

15 See, for example, Report of the Director, Joint Staff, March 18, 1948, RG 218, ser. CCS 360 (12–9–42), Joint Strategic Plans Group [hereafter JSPG] 503/1. For the special emphasis on North African bases, see, for example, Forrestal to Truman, January 6, 1948, HTL, HSTP, PSF, box 156. And, for further evidence regarding plans for the development of the base system in 1947–8, see notes 57–8, below.

16 JCS, "Over-All Examination of United States Requirements for Military Bases and Rights," September 27, 1945, RG 218, ser. CCS

360 (12–9–42), JCS 570/34; JPS, "Over-All Examination of Requirements for Transit Air Bases in Foreign Countries," January 8, 1946, ibid., JPS 781.

17 JPS, "Over-All Examination of Requirements for Transit Air Bases," January 20, 1946, RG 218, ser. CCS 360 (10–9–42), JPS 781/1; and McCloy, Memorandum to the Department of State, January 31, 1945, RG 165, OPD 336 (top secret).

18 P&O, "The Strategic Importance of Inter-American Military Cooperation" [January 20, 1947], RG 319, 092 (top secret). Also see H. A. Craig, "Summary," January 5, 1945, RG 107, Records of the Assistant Secretary of War for Air, Establishment of Air Fields and Air Bases, box 216 (Latin America); and War Department, "Comprehensive Statement" [January 1945], ibid.

19 This evaluation accords with the views of Chester J. Pach, Jr; see his "The Containment of United States Military Aid to Latin America, 1944–1949," *Diplomatic History*, 6 (1982): 232–4.

20 For fears of foreign influence, see, for example, [no signature] "Military Political Cooperation with the Other American Republics," June 24, 1946, RG 18, 092 (International Affairs), box 567; Patterson to the Secretary of State, July 31, 1946, RG 353, SWNCC, box 76; Eisenhower to Patterson, November 26, 1946, RG 107, HCPP, general decimal file, box 1 (top secret); S. J. Chamberlin to Eisenhower, November 26, 1946, ibid.; Minutes of the meeting of the Secretaries of State, War, and Navy, December 11, 1946, ibid., RPPP, safe file, box 3; and Director of Intelligence to Director of P&O, February 26, 1947, RG 319, P&O, 091 France. For reports on Soviet espionage, see, for example, Military Intelligence Service [hereafter MIS], "Soviet-Communist Penetration in Latin America," March 24, 1945, RG 165, OPD 336 (top secret).

21 See, for example, Craig, "Summary," January 5, 1945; JPS, "Military Arrangements Deriving from the Act of Chapultepec Pertaining to Bases," January 14, 1946, RG 218, ser. CCS 092 (9–10–45), JPS 761/3; Patterson to Byrnes, December 18, 1946; and P&O, "Strategic Importance of Inter-American Military Cooperation" [January 20, 1947].

22 Pach, "Military Aid to Latin America," 235–43.

23 This view was most explicitly presented in an army paper examining the State Department's expostulation of US foreign policy. See S. F. Giffin, "Draft of Proposed Comments for the Assistant Secretary of War on 'Foreign Policy'" [early February 1946], RG 107, HCPP 092 international affairs (classified). The extent to which this concern with Eurasia shaped American military attitudes is illustrated at greater length below. Here I should note that in March 1945 several of the nation's most prominent civilian experts (Frederick S. Dunn, Edward M. Earle, William T. R. Fox, Grayson L. Kirk, David N. Rowe, Harold Sprout, and Arnold Wolfers) prepared a study, "A Security Policy for Postwar America," in which they argued that the United States had to prevent any one power or coalition of powers from gaining control of Eurasia. America could not, they insisted,

withstand attack by any power that had first subdued the whole of Europe or of Eurasia; see Frederick S. Dunn *et al.*, "A Security Policy for Postwar America," NHC, SPD, ser. 14, box 194, A1–2.

The postwar concept of Eurasia developed out of the revival of geopolitical thinking in the United States, stimulated by Axis aggression and strategic decisionmaking. See, for example, the reissued work of Sir Halford F. Mackinder: *Democratic Ideals and Reality* (1919; reprint edn, New York, 1942), and "The Round World and the Winning of Peace," *Foreign Affairs*, 21 (1943): 598–605. Mackinder's ideas were modified and widely disseminated in the United States, especially by intellectuals such as Nicholas John Spykman, Hans W. Weigert, Robert Strausz-Hupé, and Isaiah Bowman.

24 For views of influential generals and army planners, see OPD, Memorandum, June 4, 1945, RG 165, OPD 336 (top secret). Also see the plethora of documents from May and June 1945, US Military Academy, West Point, New York [hereafter USMA], George A. Lincoln Papers [hereafter GLP], War Department files. For the JCS studies, see, for example, JPS, "Strategic Concept and Plan for the Employment of United States Armed Forces," September 14, 1945, RG 218, ser. CCS 381 (5–13–45), JPS 744/3; and JCS, "United States Military Policy," September 17, 1945, ibid., JCS 1496/2.

25 For the decision on the Dardanelles, see the attachments to JCS, "United States Policy concerning the Dardanelles and Kiel Canal" [July 1945], RG 218, ser. CCS 092 (7–10–45), JCS 1418/1; for the joint chiefs' position on Iran, Turkey, and Tripolitania, see JCS, "U.S. Security Interests in the Eastern Mediterranean," March 1946, ibid., ser. CCS 092 USSR (3–27–45). JCS 1641 series; and Lincoln, Memorandum for the Record, April 16, 1946, RG 165, ser. ABC 336 Russia (8–22–43); and, for the Clifford memorandum, see Arthur Krock, *Memoirs: Sixty Years on the Firing Line* (New York, 1968), 477–82.

26 Leahy, excerpt from letter, May 16, 1944, RG 59, lot 54D394 (Records of the Office of European Affairs), box 17. For the views of Eisenhower and Lincoln, see Lincoln, Memorandum for Hull, June 24, 1945, USMA, GLP, War Dept files; and Leahy, Memorandum for the President [late June 1945], ibid.

27 For the emphasis on expediting recovery in Western Europe, see, for example, McCloy, Memorandum for Matthew J. Connelly, April 26, 1945, HTL, HSTP, PSF, box 178; and, for the role of Britain, see, for example, Joint Intelligence Staff [hereafter JIS], "British Capabilities and Intentions," December 5, 1945, RG 218, ser. CCS 000.1 Great Britain (5–10–45), JIS 161/4.

28 Joint Logistic Plans Committee [hereafter JLPC], "Russian Capabilities," November 15, 1945, RG 218, ser. CCS 092 USSR (3–27–45), JLPC 35/9/RD: Military Intelligence Division [hereafter MID], "Intelligence Estimate of the World Situation and Its Military Implications," June 25, 1946, RG 319, P&O 350.05 (top secret); Joint Intelligence Committee [hereafter JIC], "Intelligence Estimate

Assuming that War between the Soviet Union and the Non-Soviet Powers Breaks Out in 1956," November 6, 1946, RG 218. ser. CCS 092 USSR (3–27–45), JIC 374/1; and JIC, "Capabilities and Military Potential of Soviet and Non-Soviet Powers in 1946," January 8, 1947, ibid., JIC 374/2. For concern with the Ruhr-Rhineland industrial complex, especially see Patterson to the Secretary of State, June 10, 1946, RG 107, HCPP, 091 Germany (classified); and, for the concern with Western Europe, especially France, see, for example, JCS, "United States Assistance to Other Countries from the Standpoint of National Security," April 29, 1947, in *FRUS, 1947*, Vol. 1: 734–50, esp. 739–42.

29 See, for example, JIS, "Military Capabilities of Great Britain and France," November 13, 1945, RG 218, ser. CCS 000.1 Great Britain (5–10–45), JIS 211/1; JIS, "Areas Vital to Soviet War Effort," February 12, 1946, ibid., ser. CCS 092 (3–27–45), JIS 226/2.

30 Moscow embassy staff, "Russia's International Position at the Close of the War with Germany," enclosed in Smith to Eisenhower, July 12, 1946, Dwight David Eisenhower Library [hereafter DDEL], Dwight David Eisenhower Papers, file 1652, box 101. Also see, for example, Stimson to Roosevelt, September 15, 1944, ML, JFP, box 100; Stimson to Truman, May 16, 1945, HTL, HSTP, PSF, box 157; numerous memoranda, June 1945, USMA, GLP, War Dept files; numerous documents, 1946 and 1947, RG 107, HCPP, 091 Germany (Classified); and Rearmament Subcommittee, Report to the Special Ad Hoc Committee, July 10, 1947, RG 165, ser. ABC 400.336 (3–20–47). For Forrestal's concern with Middle Eastern oil, see, for example, "Notes in Connection with Navy's 'Line' on Foreign Oil" [late 1944 or early 1945], ML, JFP, box 22; Walter Millis (ed.), *The Forrestal Diaries* (New York, 1951), 272, 356–8.

31 Strategy Section, OPD, "Post-War Base Requirements in the Philippines," April 23, 1945, RG 165, OPD 336 (top secret); MID, "Positive US Action Required to Restore Normal Conditions in Southeast Asia," July 3, 1947, RG 319, P&O, 092 (top secret); and Lauris Norstad to the Director of Intelligence, July 10, 1947, ibid.

32 JIS, "Russian Military Capabilities," October 25, 1945, RG 218, ser. CCS 092 USSR (3–27–45), JIS 80/10; Lincoln to M. B. Gardner and F. F. Everest, April 10, 1946, RG 165, ser. ABC 336 Russia (8–22–43); O. S. P., Memorandum for Hull, May 3, 1946, ibid., ser. ABC 381 (9–1–45); S. W. D., Memorandum for the Record, June 12, 1946, RG 319, P&O, 092 (top secret); Vandenberg, Memorandum for the President, August 24, 1946, HTL, HSTP, PSF, box 249; Chamberlin, "Reevaluation of Soviet Intentions," March 27, 1947, RG 165, Records of the Chief of Staff, 091 Russia (top secret); CIA, "Review of the World Situation as It Relates to the Security of the United States," September 26, 1947, HTL, HSTP, PSF, box 203.

33 MID, "Intelligence Division Daily Briefing," October 18, 1948, RG 319, P&O, 350.05 (top secret); Lovett to John L. Sullivan, December 20, 1948, NHC, double zero files, 1948, box 2. Also see Jean Edward Smith, *The Papers of General Lucius D. Clay: Germany, 1945–1949*,

2 vols (Bloomington, IN, 1974), Vol. 2: 564–5, 568–9, 602; CIA, "Review of the World Situation," March 10, 1948, HTL, HSTP, PSF, box 203; R. H. Hillenkoetter, Memorandum for the President, March 16, 1948, ibid., box 249; Chamberlin, Memorandum to the Chief of Staff, March 14, 1948, RG 319, P&O, 092 (top secret); Smith to Kennan, June 11, 1948, ML, George F. Kennan Papers [hereafter GFKP], box 28; and Carter Clarke to the Chief of Staff, August 6, 1948, RG 330, CD 2–2–2, box 4.

34 The war plans of the Joint Chiefs of Staff outline the extensive ground capabilities of Soviet forces. See especially the documents in RG 218, ser. CCS 381 USSR (3–2–46).

35 See, for example, JIS, "Estimate of Soviet Postwar Military Capabilities and Intentions," November 8, 1945, RG 218, ser. CCS 092 USSR (3–27–45), JIS 80/14; JWPC, "Military Position of the United States in Light of Russian Policy," January 8, 1946, RG 218, ser. CCS 092 USSR (3–27–45), JWPC 416/1; and Inglis, Memorandum of Information, January 21, 1946, ML, JFP, box 24.

36 JLPS, "Russian Capabilities," November 15, 1945; and MID, "Intelligence Estimate of the World Situation for the Next Five Years," August 21, 1946, RG 319, P&O, 350.05 (top secret).

37 JIS, "Soviet Post-War Military Policies and Capabilities," January 15, 1946, RG 218, ser. CCS 092 USSR (3–27–45), JIS 80/24; P&O, "Estimate of the Situation Pertaining to the Northeast Approaches to the United States," August 12, 1946, RG 319, P&O, 381 (top secret).

38 For the views of Eisenhower and Sherman, see S. W. D., Memorandum for the Record, June 12, 1946; Galambos, *Papers of Dwight David Eisenhower*, Vol. 7: 1012–13, 1106–7; Sherman, "Presentation to the President," January 14, 1947, NHC, Forrest E. Sherman Papers, box 2; for the views of Lincoln, Glover, Patterson, Forrestal, and others on Soviet logistical problems, see JPS, Minutes of the 249th meeting, May 22, 1946, RG 218, ser. CCS 381 USSR (3–2–46); Glover to Lincoln and Kissner, June 24, 1947, NHC, SPD, ser. 4, box 86; Louis Denfeld, Memorandum, March 29, 1948, ibid., central files, 1948, A16–3 (5); and Millis, *The Forrestal Diaries*, 272. For assessments of Soviet air power, see, for example, Office of Naval Intelligence [hereafter ONI], "A Study of B-29 Airfields with a Capacity in Excess of 120,000 Pounds" [Spring 1948], NHC, General Board 425 (ser. 315); General Board, "National Security and Navy," Enclosure B, June 25, 1945, ibid., page 16; Forrestal and Clarence Cannon, Excerpt of Conversation, April 9, 1948, ML, JFP, box 48; Inglis to Op-30, December 1, 1948, NHC, SPD, central files, 1948, A8; and Robert Lovett, Diary Entry, December 16, 1947, New York Historical Society, Robert Lovett MS Diaries. For an assessment of Soviet conventional strength, see Matthew A. Evangelista, "Stalin's Postwar Army Reappraised," *International Security*, 7 (1982–3): 110–38.

39 MID, "Estimate of the Possibility of War between the United States and the USSR Today from a Comparison with the Situation as It Existed in September 1946," July 21, 1947, RG 319, P&O, 350.05

(top secret); and JIC, Moscow Embassy, "Soviet Intentions," April 1, 1948.

40 For assessments of the interrelationships between the state of the Soviet economy and Soviet military capabilities, see, for example, JIS, "Postwar Economic Policies and Capabilities of the USSR," November 1, 1945, RG 218, ser. CCS 092 USSR (3–27–45), JIS 80/12; JIS, "Soviet Postwar Economic Capabilities and Policies," January 8, 1946, ibid., JIS 80/22; W. B. Shockley, "Relative Technological Achievements in Weapons Characteristics in USSR and USA," January 30, 1946, RG 107, RPPP, safe file, box 6; MID, "Ability of Potential Enemies to Attack the United States," August 8, 1946, RG 319, P&O, 381 (top secret); US Military Attaché (Moscow) to Chamberlin, March 21, 1947, NHC, Operations Division, ser. 2 (secret and under), box 33, EF 61; JIC, "Soviet Military Objectives and Capabilities," October 27, 1947.

41 For MacArthur's view, see J. W. Dower, *Empire and Aftermath: Yoshida Shigeru and the Japanese Experience, 1878–1954* (Cambridge, MA, 1979), 292–303; for the situation in Germany, see materials in RG 165, ser. ABC 387 Germany (12–18–43), sects 4D, 4E; Smith, *Papers of General Lucius D. Clay*, Vol. 1: 165–6, 184, 187–9, 196–8, 201–2, 207–8, 217; for Eisenhower's concern, see Galambos, *Papers of Dwight David Eisenhower*, Vol. 8: 1516–20.

42 Acheson to Truman, April 30, 1946, RG 107, HCPP, general subject file, box 1. Also see McCloy to Patterson, November 24, 1945, ibid., RPPP, safe file, box 4. For pressure on the State Department, see Patterson to Byrnes, December 10, 1945, RG 165, Civil Affairs Division [hereafter CAD], ser. 014 Germany; Patterson to Byrnes, February 25, 1946.

43 CIA, "Review of the World Situation as It Relates to the Security of the United States," September 26, 1947. Also see, for example, JCS, "Strategic Concept and Plan for the Employment of United States Armed Forces," Appendix A, September 19, 1945; JPS, Minutes of the 249th and 250th meetings; [Giffin (?)] "U.S. Policy with Respect to Russia" [early April 1946], RG 165, ser. ABC 336 (8–22–43); MID, "World Political Developments Affecting the Security of the United States during the Next Ten Years," April 14, 1947, RG 319, P&O, 350.05 (top secret).

44 See, for example, JCS, "Presidential Request for Certain Facts and Information Regarding the Soviet Union," July 25, 1946, RG 218, ser. CCS 092 USSR (3–27–45), JCS 1696; P&O, "Strategic Study of Western and Northern Europe," May 21, 1947, RG 319, P&O, 092 (top secret); and Wooldridge to the General Board, April 30, 1948.

45 For Kennan's "long telegram," see *FRUS, 1946* (Washington, DC, 1970), Vol. 4: 696–709; for ominous interpretations of Soviet intentions and capabilities, also see JCS, "Political Estimate of Soviet Policy for Use in Connection with Military Studies," April 5, 1946, RG 218, ser. CCS 092 USSR (3–27–45), JCS 1641/4; and JCS, "Presidential Request for Certain Facts and Information Regarding the Soviet Union," July 25, 1946.

46 For the withdrawal of Soviet troops, see, for example, MID, "Soviet Intentions and Capabilities in Scandinavia as of 1 July 1946," April 25, 1946, RG 319, P&O, 350.05 (top secret). For reports on reductions of Russian troops in Eastern Europe and demobilization within the Soviet Union, see MID, "Review of Europe, Russia, and the Middle East," December 26, 1945, RG 165, OPD, 350.05 (top secret); Carl Espe, weekly calculations of Soviet troops, May–September 1946, NHC, SPD, ser. 5, box 106, A8; and JIC, "Soviet Military Objectives and Capabilities," October 27, 1947. For references to Soviet military expenditures, see Patterson to Julius Adler, November 2, 1946, RG 107, RPPP, safe file, box 5; and for the Soviet transport system, see R. F. Ennis, Memorandum for the P&O Division, June 24, 1946, RG 165, ser. ABC 336 (8–22–43); Op-32 to the General Board, April 28, 1948, NHC, General Board 425 (ser. 315).

47 Smith to the Secretary of State, April 11, 1946, RG 165, Records of the Chief of Staff, 091 Russia; and, for Soviet negotiating concessions, see Lincoln, Memorandum for the Chief of Staff, May 20, 1946, USMA, GLP, War Dept/files. For the situation in Germany, see OPD and CAD, "Analysis of Certain Political Problems Confronting Military Occupation Authorities in Germany," April 10, 1946, RG 107, HCPP 091 Germany (classified); Patterson to Truman, June 11, 1946, RG 165, Records of the Chief of Staff, 091 Germany. For Clay's references to French obstructionism, see, for example, Smith, *Papers of General Lucius D. Clay*, Vol. 1: 84–5, 88–9, 151–2, 189–90, 212–17, 235–6. For overall intelligence assessments, see Central Intelligence Group [hereafter CIG], "Revised Soviet Tactics in International Affairs," January 6, 1947, HTL, HSTP, PSF, box 254; MID, "World Political Developments Affecting the Security of the United States during the Next Ten Years," April 14, 1947.

48 My assessment is based primarily on my analysis of the materials in RG 218, ser. CCS 092 USSR (3–27–45); ser. CCS 381 USSR (3–2–46); RG 319, P&O, 350.05 (top secret); and NHC, SPD, central files, 1946–8, A8.

49 During 1946 it became a fundamental tenet of American policymakers that Soviet policy objectives were a function of developments within the Soviet Union and not related to American actions. See, for example, Kennan's "long telegram," in *FRUS, 1946*, Vol. 4: 696–709; JCS, "Political Estimate of Soviet Policy," April 5, 1946.

50 Norstad, Memorandum, July 25, 1946, RG 319, P&O, 092 (top secret). For references to shifting tactics and constant objectives, see Vandenberg, Memorandum for the President, September 27, 1946, HTL, HSTP, PSF, box 249; CIG, "Revised Soviet Tactics," January 6, 1947; and, for the JCS report to the President, compare JCS 1696 with JIC 250/12. Both studies may be found in RG 218, ser. CCS 092 USSR (3–27–45). For Clifford's recollection, Clark Clifford, HTL, oral history, 170.

51 [Giffin (?)] "U.S. Policy with Respect to Russia" [early April 1946]. Also see MID, "Intelligence Estimate," June 25, 1946; JPS, "Estimate

of Probable Developments in the World Political Situation," October 31, 1946, RG 218, ser. CCS 092 (10–9–46), JPS 814/1; MID, "World Political Developments," April 14, 1947; and CIA, "Review of the World Situation," September 26, 1947.

52 JCS, "Foreign Policy of the United States," February 10, 1946.

53 Lincoln to Hull [April 1946], RG 59, Office of European Affairs, box 17; Richard L. Conolly, oral history (Columbia, 1960), 293–304.

54 Giffin, "Draft of Proposed Comments" [early February 1946]. Also see, for example, JCS, "Political Estimate of Soviet Policy," April 5, 1946.

55 Peterson, as quoted in Chief of Staff, Memorandum [July 1947], RG 165, ser. ABC 471.6 Atom (8–17–45). Also see, for example, Lovett diaries, December 16, 1947, January 5, 15, 1948; Forrestal to Baruch, February 10, 1948, ML, JFP, box 78.

56 For the views of the General Advisory Committee, see Robert Oppenheimer to Truman, December 31, 1947, HTL, HSTP, PSF, box 200; for the views of the JCS, see, for example, JCS, "Guidance on Military Aspects of United States Policy to Be Adopted in Event of Continuing Impasse in Acceptance of International Control of Atomic Energy," July 14, 1947, RG 165, ser. ABC 471.6 Atom (8–17–45), JCS 1764/1; and, for the size and quality of the stockpile and the number of nuclear-capable aircraft, see especially David Alan Rosenberg, "U.S. Nuclear Stockpile, 1945 to 1950," *Bulletin of Atomic Scientists*, 38 (1982): 25–30. Both Borowski and Rosenberg have stressed the problems beleaguering the Strategic Air Command until the Korean War, but their work also illustrates the significant changes and improvements that began to occur late in 1947 and especially during 1948. See Borowski, *Hollow Threat*; David Alan Rosenberg, "The Origins of Overkill: Nuclear Weapons and American Strategy, 1945–1960," *International Security*, 7 (Spring 1983): 11–27.

57 For negotiations with the British over Middle East strategy and bases, see *FRUS, 1947* (Washington, DC, 1971), Vol. 5: 485–626; for facilities in Libya, see, for example, Leahy to the Secretary of Defense, March 18, 1948, RG 319, P&O, 092 (top secret); and *FRUS, 1948*, (Washington, DC, 1974), Vol. 3: 906–7; for negotiations with the French, see Spaatz to Symington [October 1947], RG 107, Office of the Assistant Secretary of War for Air, 1947, 090, box 187B; Symington to Spaatz, October 30 1947, ibid., and Wooldridge, Memorandum for Op-09, October 25, 1948, NHC, SPD, central files, 1948, A14. For bases in North Africa, see Forrestal to Truman, January 6, 1948, HTL, HSTP, PSF, box 156.

58 For references to Japanese bases, see, for example, "Discussion of Need of Obtaining Long-Term Rights for a U.S. Naval Operating Base in Japan" (approved by Nimitz) [Autumn 1947], NHC, SPD, ser. 4, box 86; Denfeld, Memorandum for Schuyler, February 20, 1948, ibid.; central files, 1948, box 245, EF37; for the uses of military assistance to Turkey, see Leffler, "Strategy, Diplomacy, and the Cold War: The United States, Turkey, and NATO, 1945–1952," *JAH*, 71 (1984–5): 814–19.

59 "National Military Establishment Views on Germany" [appended to memorandum for Maddocks], June 30, 1948, RG 319, P&O, 092 (top secret). For the repercussions of the Truman Doctrine and Marshall Plan, see Chamberlin to Chief of Staff, July 9, 1947, RG 165, Records of the Chief of Staff, 091 Greece; and Hillenkoetter, Memorandum for the President, November 7, 1947, HTL, HSTP, PSF, box 249; and, for a similar view in the State Department, see FRUS, 1947, Vol. 1: 770–5. For prospective Soviet reactions to American assistance to Turkey, also see General Board, "National Security and the Navy," enclosure D, June 25, 1948; and Conolly to CNO, December 4, 1947, NHC, Operations Division, ser. 1, A4/FF7. For assessments of Soviet reactions to Western initiatives in Germany, also see Hillenkoetter, Memoranda for the President, March 16, 1948, and June 9, 1948, HTL, HSTP, PSF, box 249.

60 For Chamberlin's views, see, for example, Chamberlin, Memorandum to the Chief of Staff, March 14, 1948, and Chamberlin, Memorandum for Wedemeyer, April 14, 1948, RG 319, P&O, 092 (top secret). For the view from Moscow, see JIC, "Soviet Intentions," April 1, 1948 (extracts of this report are printed in FRUS, 1948 (Washington, DC, 1976), Vol. 1: 550–7); also see, for example, Hillenkoetter, Memorandum for the President, March 16, 1948; Inglis, Memorandum of Information, March 16, 1948; CIA, "Possibility of Direct Soviet Military Action during 1948," April 2, 1948, HTL, HSTP, PSF, box 255.

61 See, for example, FRUS, 1948, (Washington, DC, 1975), Vol.5: 545–54, 972–6, 1005–7, 1021–2, 1380–1; Leahy, Memorandum for the Secretary of Defense, October 10, 1947, RG 330, box 20, CD 6–1–8; Millis, Forrestal Diaries, 344–9, 356–65, 376–7; Bain, March to Zion, 137–213; and Miller, Search for Security, 175–203.

62 For the rehabilitation of Japan, see Special Ad Hoc Committee [of SWNCC], Country Report on Japan, August 8, 1947, RG 353, box 109; Royall, Memorandum for the Secretary of Defense, May 18, 1948, HTL, HSTP, PSF, box 182; and CIA, "Strategic Importance of Japan," May 24, 1948, ibid., box 255. Also see FRUS, 1948, (Washington, DC, 1974), Vol. 6: 654–6, 694–5, 712–17, 733–4, 750–1, 964–5. For Japan and Southeast Asia, see Ad Hoc Committee, "Study of a United States Aid Program for the Far East," February 16, 1949, RG 319, P&O, 092 Pacific (top secret); and Schaller, "Securing the Great Crescent," 392–414.

63 Edwin G. Nourse, Leon Keyserling, and Clark to Truman, March 24, 1948, HTL, HSTP, PSF, box 143; Truman to Nourse, March 25, 1948, ibid.; Statement by the President to the Secretary of Defense, the Secretaries of the Three Departments, and the Three Chiefs of Staff, May 13, 1948, ibid., box 146; and Truman to Forrestal, July 13, 1948, RG 330, box 18, CD 5–1–20.

64 For the views of Lovett and Webb, see Lovett diaries, December 16, 1947, January 15, 1948, April 21, 1948; for Clifford's view of the importance of the atomic bomb, see Clifford, oral history, 88; and, for Marshall's reliance on the atomic bomb, see McNarney,

Memorandum for the JCS, November 2, 1948, HTL, HSTP, PSF, box 114.

65 For the conflicting pressures on Forrestal and his own uncertainties, see, for example, Excerpt of Phone Conversation between Forrestal and C. E. Wilson, April 2, 1948, ML, JFP, box 48; Forrestal to Ralph Bard, November 20, 1948, ibid., box 78; for Forrestal's intense interest in the assessments of Soviet intentions, see Forrestal to Charles A. Buchanan [July 1948], RG 330, box 4, CD 2–2–2; for Forrestal's request for a comprehensive study of American policy and Truman's responses, see *FRUS, 1948*, Vol. 1: 589–93.

66 NCS 20/1 and 20/4 may be found in Thomas H. Etzold and John Lewis Gaddis, *Containment: Documents on American Policy and Security, 1945–1950* (New York, 1978), 173–211 (the quotations appear on p. 208).

67 Gaddis and Etzold, *Containment*, 209–10.

68 NSC 35, "Existing International Commitments Involving the Possible Use of Armed Forces," November 17, 1948, *FRUS, 1948*, Vol. 1: 656–62. For assessments of Soviet intentions and the prospects of war, see CIA, "Possibility of Direct Soviet Military Action during 1948–49," September 16, 1948, HTL, HSTP, PSF, box 255; CIA, "Threats to the Security of the United States," September 28, 1948, ibid., box 256; and *FRUS, 1948*, Vol. 1: 648–50, and Vol. 5: 942–7.

69 For Soviet losses, see Nicholas V. Riasanovsky, *A History of Russia* (3rd edn, New York, 1977), 584–5. While Russian dead totaled almost 20 million and while approximately 25 percent of the reproducible wealth of the Soviet Union was destroyed, American battlefield casualties were 300,000 dead, the index of industrial production in the United States rose from 100 to 196, and the gross national product increased from $91 billion to $166 billion. See Gordon Wright, *The Ordeal of Total War* (New York, 1968), 264–5.

2

NATIONAL SECURITY AND SOVIET FOREIGN POLICY

Michael MccGwire

Whereas Leffler had vast numbers of documents upon which to base his analysis, students of Soviet foreign relations have not been so fortunate. This situation is now changing as the new Russian government is opening up its archives and former Soviet officials are more willing to talk about and write about past policies. Nevertheless, it will still be several years until we receive well-researched and nuanced appraisals of postwar Stalinist diplomacy.

It will be interesting to see which of the prevailing views of Soviet foreign policy will be substantiated by the opening of archival records. Many postwar accounts of the Kremlin's actions insisted that the Communist regime, inspired by Marxist-Leninist ideology, was intent on world domination. Over the years these accounts evolved as it became unmistakably clear that Stalin did not support all revolutionary movements and that he had his own good reasons to want to perpetuate the wartime coalition. Increasingly, the Soviet dictator was characterized as an opportunist and a prudent expansionist, seeking always to further Soviet power but keenly attuned to power realities.

Some Kremlinologists questioned whether Soviet policy was as clever and coherent as it was often portrayed. Increasingly, scholars saw stark contradictions in the way Soviet policy was conducted, for example, in Germany, and they wondered how these inconsistencies came about. Some analysts dwelled upon the deep divisions among Soviet leaders; some believed that after the war Stalin, at least initially, receded into the background while his lieutenants waged personal and bureaucratic battles with one another. In these struggles doctrine often was used more as a tool than as an inspiration. Indeed over time the role of ideology in Soviet policy became rather blurred.

Michael MccGwire is a well-known British analyst of Soviet strategic doctrine and naval capabilities. In this unpublished essay, written as a guest scholar at the Brookings Institution in Washington, DC, he outlines Soviet national security imperatives as Russian leaders might have conceived of them at the end of the war. He tries to establish historical context and utilizes assessments of threat perception as a vehicle for grasping contradictory elements of Soviet foreign policy. Rather than relying on ideology or bureaucratic explanations, MccGwire explains the variations in Soviet policy by alluding to the diverse and changing threats that Soviet leaders probably perceived and by illuminating the conflicting strategies that Soviet officials might have tried in order to deal with these threats.

Readers should assess whether MccGwire draws reasonable inferences from past history and about the lessons that Soviet leaders might have derived from the Second World War. Does he understate the role of ideology? Does he adequately depict the specter of German revanchism? Does his assessment make sense in light of the way US and other Western leaders might have been estimating their own security needs in the aftermath of the most destructive war ever waged?

* * *

Western perceptions of the Soviet threat have their roots in the 1945–50 period. It was during those years that the public indictment of the Soviet Union was firmly established. That period saw the Soviet subjugation of Eastern Europe, the blockade of Berlin, and the invasion of South Korea. It was toward the end of that period that the claim first emerged that the Soviets' military capability greatly exceeded their requirements for defense.

The Western claim that Soviet military capability is far in excess of its legitimate needs for defense has persisted through to the present and is an important factor in assessing Soviet intentions and the role of military force in Soviet foreign policy. The claim is, however, no more than an assertion, and little consideration has been given to how the Soviets might themselves assess their essential defense requirements. And while there have been numerous studies of the origins of the Cold War, little attention has been paid to how the Soviets' own threat perceptions would have been shaped by the events of 1945–50.

It tends to be forgotten that in 1945 the universal concern of the wartime allies was to prevent a resurgence of German and

54

Japanese aggression, and this remained the focus of Soviet policy. By the spring of 1946, however, the argument had prevailed in America (and, to a lesser extent, in Britain) that the more urgent threat lay in Soviet military domination of Europe. It is now clear that the Western partners grossly overestimated Soviet political and military strength and that even if the Soviets had had the urge to take over Western Europe (which hindsight suggests they did not), they certainly lacked the capability to do so. It was largely because of this inherent weakness that Stalin sought to preserve the remaining shreds of the collaborative wartime relationship, despite the sharp shift in Western policy that became increasingly evident during 1946. It was not until the summer of 1947 that the Soviets turned to reassess the threat, shifting their focus from a resurgent Germany in fifteen to twenty years' time, to a capitalist coalition led by the English-speaking powers that would be ready for war in five to six years. Western Germany and Japan would be part of that coalition, hence the gravity and the immediacy of the threat were sharply heightened.

This analysis makes very little use of Soviet source material, for two reasons. First, it is extremely difficult to distinguish between rhetorical statements and genuine Soviet concerns, and such judgments are always controversial. And second, the Soviets have always been reluctant to acknowledge publicly the weaknesses that must be taken account of in their threat assessments. In such circumstances, Soviet statements concerning their "perceptions" are in general no more to be relied on than contemporary Western statements concerning Soviet "intentions." One must therefore distinguish between the flow of events, with its backdrop of Western commentary and official statements, and the way these data are likely to have been interpreted (and reinterpreted) by the Soviets.

For the historical record of events and contemporary pronouncements, reliance has been placed on generally accepted and well-established Western analyses of the period. This evidence, which is limited to the data that would have been available to the Soviets at the time and does not include information from US documents that have subsequently been declassified, has been evaluated as though through the eyes of a policy-maker in Moscow. Little emphasis has been placed on ideology or Soviet doctrine, because the focus is on a shift in threat perceptions, whereas ideology and doctrine remained constant through the period. Marxist doctrine concerning the inevitability of war between capitalism and socialism would certainly have colored the reevaluation that took place in 1947–8, but it did not prompt it, nor was it a necessary component. The objective factors were sufficient to have forced this reassessment; it was the tardiness of the Soviet reaction to these developments that was surprising.

The story told in this study is deliberately biased to the Soviet viewpoint, reflecting how they are likely to have perceived the consistency of their own policies and the legitimacy of their behavior. It is necessary to understand this viewpoint because the Second World War and its aftermath remained a major reference point for Soviet policymakers, at least through the beginning of the 1980s.

Defense of the homeland is the irreducible core of any national strategy. For Russia, sprawled across 170 degrees of the Eurasian continent, territorial defense looms large and Soviet perceptions of threat were shaped as much by their historical experience as by an objective evaluation of the forces ranged against them.

In the three years following the Bolshevik seizure of power, Russia first suffered invasion and partial dismemberment at the hands of the Germans and their protégés, and was then plunged into three years of civil war. This war included armed intervention by significant British, French, Japanese, and American forces, and a coordinated attack by Polish and Ukrainian armies.

During the first twelve months of the Soviet regime, Germany dominated the external concerns of the Soviet leadership. If the punitive treaty of Brest-Litovsk (March 1918) had been fully implemented, eastern Europe and the westernmost parts of Russia would have been turned into a German preserve through a system of satellite states and economic exploitation. But it was not only the Germans who were eager to dismember Russia. The assault by Poland and its Ukrainian allies in the spring of 1920 revived the threat of an independent and unfriendly Ukraine, and raised the specter of the great Polish-Lithuanian state as it existed prior to 1772. Although the Red Army repelled the assault and moved on to the offensive, its advance was turned back at the gates of Warsaw and, at the time of the armistice in October 1920, about half of Byelorussia and a substantial part of the Ukraine were once again behind Polish lines.

The British, meanwhile, had moved into the Trans-Caucasus, where they already had oil interests, coming overland through Persia and by ship through the Black Sea; in the east, Japan stood ready to annex great tracts of Siberia. The allied intervention, orchestrated and led by Great Britain, confirmed the latter's role as the bulwark of the capitalist world and Communist Russia's main enemy. But the intervention also demonstrated the inability of the capitalist states, war-weary and pursuing their separate and conflicting interests, to combine effectively to overthrow the revolution.

The Soviets recognized that the United States was now the economically dominant capitalist power, but they saw America's capability as offering the means of counterbalancing Japanese aspirations on the Asian mainland, and British imperial ambitions worldwide. Unlike the other major capitalist states, the United States had enjoyed almost uninterrupted good relations with tsarist Russia. It had welcomed the March 1917 revolution without reservation and, after the October coup, was generally in favor of allowing the Russian people to arrange their affairs without interference. The USA was seen as the least imperialist and belligerent of the capitalist bloc, and the Communists (particularly Lenin) were explicit in their admiration of American efficiency and spirit of enterprise; there was a sense that some complementarity existed between the interests of the two states.

The civil war and its attendant troubles were effectively at an end by the spring of 1921, and in 1928 the first Five Year Plan was launched as a forced industrialization program. It is unlikely that the Soviet leadership saw war as being imminent at that time, but the wider perception of threat was captured by Stalin in February 1931 when he rejected the option of slowing the pace of industrialization, because "to slacken the pace would mean to lag behind and those who lag behind are beaten." Old Russia had been beaten by the Tartar Khans, the Turks, the Swedes, the Poles and the Japanese, and the Anglo-French capitalists, and "she was beaten because of her backwardness, because of her military, cultural, political and industrial backwardness."[1]

Meanwhile, more immediate threats began to gather. The early 1930s saw the impotence of the other Great Powers in the face of Japan's occupation of Manchuria, an initiative that posed a serious threat to Russian interests in Asia. By the end of 1933, the Soviet leadership had belatedly grasped the implications of Hitler's rise to power and realized that National Socialism was not only a force to be reckoned with, but one that was highly antagonistic to the Soviet Union. Meanwhile, a full-scale arms race had gotten underway between all the Great Powers; the Berlin–Rome Axis was established in October 1936, followed in November by the explicitly "Anti-Comintern Pact" between Germany and Japan, with Italy joining twelve months later. Whereas Stalin had hoped that the Soviet Union would be able to stand back (but profit) from the conflicts that would inevitably arise between capitalist states, it now looked as if Russia would be the object of a concerted attack on two fronts.

Stalin's immediate concern was to prevent Hitler from achieving a rapprochement with Britain and France, and if possible to persuade the British and French to join the Soviet Union in blocking further aggression by the Axis. However, the Western Powers' feeble performance during the 1938 Czechoslovakian crisis strengthened the Soviet suspicion that some people in London and Paris would not be unhappy to see Hitler's further aggression directed eastward. This suspicion was reinforced in 1939 by the Western Powers' dilatory approach to reaching agreement with Russia on deterring a German assault on Poland. After Munich, the Soviets had therefore pursued the twin objectives of redirecting German aggression back toward the Western Powers, and of developing the means of delaying and then buffering a German invasion, should Hitler still turn east.

Stalin was remarkably successful in achieving these objectives, external developments being exploited with skillful if ruthless diplomacy. Germany had to make significant concessions in order to get the Nazi–Soviet Non-aggression Pact. As soon as the Polish army had been destroyed by Germany as a fighting force, Russia moved to take over the territory lying east of the Curzon Line, the population of the area being predominantly Byelorussian and Ukrainian. These areas were incorporated into the corresponding Soviet republics and their inhabitants purged of the more untrustworthy elements.

Within twelve months, after an unsuccessful attempt to establish a more traditional sphere of influence in the region, a similar process had been applied to the Baltic states (which had been Russian territory prior to 1917), the extra depth making the fragile difference between failure and success to the coming defense of Leningrad. Less satisfactorily, the Isthmus of Karelia (again, Russian territory before the revolution) was wrested from Finland at the cost of some 50,000 dead, although the three-month campaign did serve the unintended purpose of exposing glaring deficiencies in the Soviet military machine.

The time between the German invasions of Poland and of Russia, a period of almost twenty-two months, was characterized by Machiavellian twists and turns as Stalin balanced the requirements to gain time and space against the danger of provoking Hitler to launch an attack. Space was important, both to increase the depth of defense and to incorporate within Soviet borders those ethnic groups which Hitler might otherwise exploit to prise away portions of Russia, as he had done elsewhere. The Ukraine was particularly vulnerable in this respect. Time was desperately needed if Soviet industry was to build up the military capacity to deter a German assault or, if that failed, to absorb the attack. The unexpected collapse of the Western Powers in June 1940 denied Russia a critical breathing space, and it was the vital importance of an extra year's production which probably caused Stalin to miscalculate so badly in June 1941 as he attempted to avoid any possible provocation, such as a defense mobilization.

The results of this miscalculation were disastrous, and the Soviets lost 1 million casualties and 2 million prisoners during the first four months of the war. Nevertheless, sixteen months later the Russians had recovered sufficiently to stem the German advance at Stalingrad, and by the spring of 1943 the fortunes of war were moving steadily in the Soviets' favor.

The impressions created by this experience reinforced the lessons of the 1914–20 period. First, Germany was again the source of a mortal threat, resurgent and seemingly all-powerful within twenty years of a humiliating defeat. But there were also other countries eager to lend a hand in dismembering Russia, including Hungary and Romania.

Second, a secure defense of the homeland called for very large forces. At the outbreak of hostilities in June 1941, there were 188 Soviet divisions on the Western front compared to the Axis 166, and by August the Soviets had fielded 260, yet they still suffered defeat in the field.

Third, there was the importance of the strategic offensive, even if it entailed preemption. One reason was military, enshrined in "the initiative" as a key principle of war. The other reason was political, reflecting the importance of waging war on enemy territory rather than one's own, especially given the political unreliability of various ethnic groups in border regions.

Fourth was the importance of space. Axis forces advanced 600 miles in four months on their whole front, and were held only at the very outskirts of Moscow. They were finally checked in August 1942, when their southern armies had advanced some 1,000 miles. Leningrad would certainly have fallen to the Germans if they had not had to cover 400 miles before launching their assault. Distance was itself a defense.

Fifth was the need to be sufficiently strong on *all* fronts. Although Stalin had managed to negotiate the Soviet-Japanese Neutrality Pact in April 1941, the final direction of Japan's expansionist drive had still remained uncertain. It was only when the Japanese had committed their ground forces to the conquest of Southeast Asia, embroiling the Americans in the process, that Russia could relax its guard in the east. The Soviets could not count on such timely good fortune in a future conflict.

And sixth, the Second World War vindicated the very high priority given by Stalin to building up Russia's military-industrial base. The Russian success depended on a massive flow of arms and equipment from the factories to the front, and while American lend-lease contributed to this flow, it also underlined the need for a vast indigenous production capacity.

Soviet perceptions of the probable threat environment once victory was achieved were strongly influenced by the pattern of inter-allied relationships during the war. In most respects, these confirmed the impressions of the interwar years. There was a great deal of evidence of disagreement and potential hostility between the United States and Britain and while the two nations joined effectively to wage war against Germany, their interests seemed too divergent to allow the capitalist powers to combine and turn on Communism once victory was achieved.

Stalin appears to have felt a personal rapport with Roosevelt. The roots of this rapport may have lain in Roosevelt's success in obtaining diplomatic recognition of the Soviet Union in the first year of his presidency, but it was certainly fostered by Roosevelt's belief in the efficacy of personal diplomacy. Furthermore, Roosevelt seemed to conform to the rather favorable Soviet stereotype of American attitudes and opinion. He shared their deep suspicion of British imperialism. And he appeared sympathetic to Soviet aspirations. By the end of 1943, Roosevelt had cautiously indicated that Stalin could count on a free hand in Eastern Europe. He even acknowledged Soviet interests in Poland and the Baltic states, and although the US government refused to recognize the frontiers established in 1939–40, Roosevelt left the impression that his primary concern there was to avoid any US domestic political repercussions, anyway until after the presidential election in 1944. It was, in fact, generally accepted within the US government that Russia would take such steps as necessary to ensure its territorial security.

Stalin did not establish the same kind of rapport with Churchill, although he had a great respect for the man. Churchill conformed to the Soviet stereotype of British imperial aspirations and his advocacy of military intervention to destroy the Bolshevik revolution at birth was well known. But Stalin accepted British hegemony in Western Europe in return for Soviet hegemony in the Eastern part. It is unlikely that Stalin ever considered that the British, on their own, could pose a serious threat to the Soviet homeland.

The conclusions to be drawn from the allied relationship were therefore generally positive, although there remained grounds for concern. The most serious was the two-year delay in launching the second front. The Western partners' reluctance to make a "blood sacrifice" while the Soviets bore the brunt of the war against Nazi Germany, fostered Soviet suspicions that their capitalist allies would like to arrange matters so that Russia and Germany fought each other to the death, while the Western powers built up their military and economic capacity whereby to dominate the postwar world.

As victory drew near, the dominant concern among most of the allies was the potential resurgence of a powerful Germany in fifteen or twenty years' time. Stalin was obsessed by the thought of a future German revenge and returned to the theme with most of his numerous visitors in the Kremlin. But the immediate prospects were not unfavorable. Roosevelt and Churchill had shown that they were mindful of Soviet security concerns, and it appeared likely that the wartime entente, formalized through permanent membership of the UN Security Council, would endure into the peace. Given the right attitudes, this could provide the means of "preventing new aggression or a new war, if not for ever, then at least for an extended time."[2]

This did not imply that Stalin had changed his mind about the fundamental conflict between capitalism and Communism, or believed that either Britain or the United States was disposed in a friendly fashion toward a Communist Soviet Union. The international system remained inherently hostile but for the time being he perceived a congruence of "vitally important and long-lasting interests" in avoiding war. The United States seemed set on withdrawing all its forces to North America; its continuing aversion to the European style of traditional power politics and its reluctance to become involved in European problems made an Anglo-American coalition unlikely. It even offered the possibility that the USA might be induced to check British machinations, if not to support Soviet interests.

In many ways, therefore, the threat situation in 1944-5 resembled that facing the new Soviet state in the 1920s as it finally emerged from the First World War and the aftermath of revolution and civil war. The United States was seen as sympathetic to Soviet problems, and the complementarity of the two economics had reemerged as the possible basis for economic cooperation. It seemed that the United States did not want to remain politically involved on the Eurasian continent, except in China. There were of course two major differences from the 1920s: the Soviet Union's geostrategic position was significantly improved; and the Americans had the atomic bomb. But all in all, the similarities predominated, not least the devastation wrought on the Soviet political economy by four years of war.

Given these similar circumstances, it is not surprising that Soviet military requirements as perceived in 1944–5 were essentially the same as those formulated in the interwar years, with the additional need to match America's atomic monopoly. The requirement to rebuild the military-industrial base was paramount. Deficiencies in the existing inventory of equipment had to be made up, motorized transport being among the most glaring. But there had also been substantial advances in the technology of warfare, little of which had been applied in the Soviet Union which fought the war using mid-1930s (and older) technology. Russia could not afford to lag behind in this respect, because, as Stalin said in 1931, "those who lag behind are beaten," and much of the Soviet armed forces needed rebuilding from scratch.

The time-horizon was fifteen to twenty years; the most likely enemy, Germany in the west and Japan in the east. Both countries had warred against Russia twice in the last forty years, each had imposed one crushing defeat and Germany had almost succeeded in inflicting two. Besides the modernizing of Soviet military capability, the German threat could be countered in three ways. Stalin rejected the option of collective security, which had failed so disastrously in the 1930s, in favor of the two more concrete approaches. One was to establish a protective barrier of Soviet-oriented buffer states. The other was to impose punitive reparations, which would dismantle Germany's military-industrial base and destroy its warmaking capacity.

Stalin was fully aware that the postwar settlement process would involve very tough bargaining, and while he undoubtedly hoped that the wartime agreements between the "Big Three" would provide the basis for negotiations, he was conscious that the key factors would be troops on the ground and economic power. Stalin would not, therefore, have been unduly perturbed by the denial of any effective Soviet role in the occupation of Italy. The exclusion of Soviet forces from the occupation of Japan was more disturbing, given the latter's role as a traditional enemy of Russia, but it was acceptable since the Soviets had been able to repossess Sakhalin and the Kuriles, and take over the four southernmost islands of the chain, which had never belonged to Russia.

Stalin's geostrategic priorities were reflected in his stance on various European issues. Soviet forces which had advanced some 250 miles in northern Norway were withdrawn promptly, and Stalin forbore to occupy Finland, despite the fact that it had been an autonomous duchy of the Russian empire between 1809 and 1917, and had joined Germany against Russia in 1941. He chose instead to adhere in the main to the relatively moderate territorial provisions of 1940, which were intended to protect Leningrad's maritime flank and to cover the naval base complex on the Kola Peninsula. The Baltic provinces were less fortunate, and were reincorporated into the Soviet state, since they provided maritime access to the central Russian plain and land access to Leningrad.

The continued existence of a Polish state was, however, respected, the long history of Polish rebellions probably arguing against its reincorporation. The state's confines were moved bodily west (so as to exclude Byelorussian and Ukrainian ethnic groups), and Stalin insisted on a Polish government that would be compliant to Soviet wishes, a condition that was accepted (albeit reluctantly) by both Churchill and Roosevelt. They could not ignore the fact that this territory had served as the springboard for three major invasions of Russia in the previous thirty years (plus Napoleon's invasion in 1812), and that in the years to come the role of Poland as a buffer state against a resurgent Germany could be crucial to Soviet security.

To the south of Poland lay three countries which, in the pursuit of their separate interests, had been willing allies of the Germans. Romania had served as the southern springboard for Hitler's invasion and had provided some thirty divisions and incurred nearly half a million casualties against the Russians, as it sought to extend the Romanian frontier to the River Bug. Although Bulgaria had not declared war against the Soviet Union or sent troops to fight there, it had allowed the German navy to use its ports and was strategically placed in relation to the Black Sea exits. Hungary had joined the Axis in November 1940 and its troops fought against Yugoslavia as well as the Soviets, while its transportation system was essential to the supply of both the Balkan and the Russian fronts.

Stalin did not consider that control of these countries was as crucial to Soviet security as control of those to the north. Nevertheless, by March 1945, Communist-controlled "coalition" governments had been installed in Bulgaria and Romania

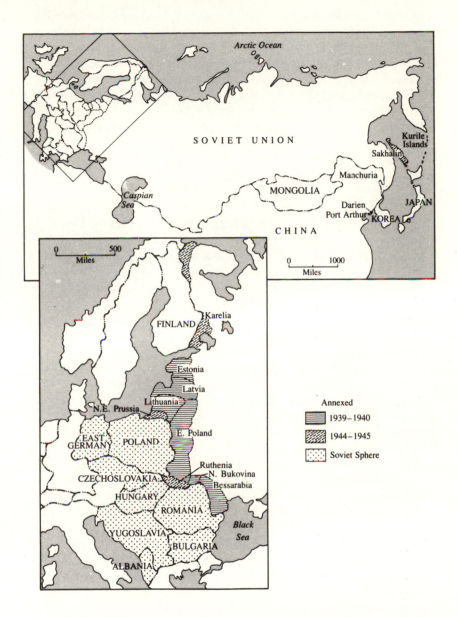

Map 2 The Soviet Union in Eurasia at the end of the Second World War.
Adapted from Woodford McClellan, *Russia: A History of the Soviet Period*
(2nd edn, New York: Prentice Hall, 1990), 199.

(geostrategically, the two more important countries), although genuine coalition government was allowed to persist in Hungary until August 1947, albeit subjected to ever-increasing pressure.

Beyond these three ex-enemies lay four ex-allies, of a kind: Greece, Albania, Yugoslavia, and Czechoslovakia. Stalin had already conceded Greece to the British, despite the fact that left-wing forces could easily have seized power when the Germans withdrew in October 1944. Here again, Stalin's concern to preserve entente overrode other political objectives.

The Communist regimes in Yugoslavia and Albania were apparently pro-Soviet, seeing Moscow as both mentor and liberator. The Czechoslovakians, likewise, saw the Red Army as liberators (there had been no effective indigenous resistance movement), and were sympathetic toward the Soviet Union, choosing it as the only practical protector, Britain and France having demonstrated their impotence in this capacity. By March 1945 a genuine coalition government had been formed in Czechoslovakia, and although the Communist Party could have seized power at this stage, Stalin actively discouraged it. In December 1945, the Red Army evacuated Czechoslovakia in prompt response to a suggestion by President Truman (American forces withdrew at the same time), and in May 1946 free elections gave the Communist Party 38 percent of the poll, more than twice the votes earned by the next most popular party and far more broadly based.

By the end of 1945, then, the geopolitical situation in Eastern Europe was reasonably favorable for the Soviet Union, although there were growing indications that the relatively sympathetic appreciation of Soviet security concerns shown by Roosevelt was not shared by his successor. If anything, the Americans appeared to be at least trying to undermine this security, using the pretext of self-determination, if they were not actually trying to revive the old cordon sanitaire around Russia.

The Western Powers' solicitude for the sanctity of prewar borders rang hollow to someone like Stalin, who had been born among the shifting frontiers of Trans-Caucasia and who, twenty-five years earlier, had watched the same Western Powers attempt to dismember Turkey to their own advantage, at the same time as they were rearranging the Austro-Hungarian empire and prising away bits of Germany. Nor was the West's emphasis on the democratic process particularly persuasive to the Soviet Union, given that Czechoslovakia and Finland were the only newly independent East European states formed in the wake of the First World War that had managed to preserve the semblance of democratic government.

All the others had become more or less fascist. Their leaders had varying degrees of dictatorial powers and most of them were prepared to ride on Hitler's coattails, since these states had substantial territorial claims on their neighbors. Mass fascist parties had existed in Hungary and Romania. Poland, where democracy was effectively at an end by 1930, had been aligned with Germany and supported its policies for the best part of five years. During that time it had been bitterly anti-Russian and anti-Communist; it joined in the dismemberment of Czechoslovakia in 1938 and seized part of Lithuania in early 1939.

Most of these states had substantial ethnic minorities who were severely oppressed, and in the main the lower social strata found themselves worse off than before independence. Political power in the interwar years had lain with traditional groups such as landowners, businessmen, bureaucrats, intellectuals, and the military, with workers and peasants having little or no effective representation. There was no reason to suppose that this pattern would not be repeated after the Second World War, unless positive steps were taken to prevent it. From Stalin's point of view, the issue was not democracy but whose "democrats": those who represented the interests of the traditional ruling classes, or those who represented the interests of the proletariat?

This viewpoint reflected a blend of *realpolitik* and ideology, reinforced by wartime experience. Since Russia needed strong and friendly countries on its borders, this implied Communist-controlled governments, and nowhere more so than in Poland. American interference in Soviet policy toward that country therefore smacked of ulterior motives. So, too, did US complaints about spheres of interest, given Truman's reaffirmation of the Monroe Doctrine covering the American continent and the doctrine's apparent extension to cover the Pacific.

But the Western urge to intrude even in Italy did not affect directly the security interests of the Soviet Union, and was mainly troublesome because it imposed delays on the process of establishing the desired political control over the buffer states to the west. While the increasing tendency for the other powers to gang up on Russia over its policy in Eastern Europe and for Britain and the United States to go back on commitments agreed by the Big Three did not augur well for continuing cooperation, the disagreements were not so fundamental as to require a change in threat assessments. Meanwhile, the Soviet Union's western frontiers were buffered by Communist and/or friendly governments, with the maritime flanks covered by Finland and Bulgaria.

Germany was a problem of a different order. In the simplest terms this could be seen as a race to restore the shattered Soviet economy and rebuild its armed forces, before a resurgent Reich could do likewise. There were two elements to such a competition: one, to rebuild the Soviet military capability; and two, to delay the rebuilding of a German one. American aid could help with the first; German reparations had a role to play with both.

Stalin, a cynic as well as a political realist, would not have counted on capitalist charity to rebuild a Communist Russia and, should it have been forthcoming, would have assumed its purpose was to achieve leverage over Soviet policy. Stalin recognized that the United States was under no obligation to continue lend-lease once fighting was at an end and while he did comment that the manner in which it was stopped was "unfortunate, even brutal," Stalin acknowledged that it was legitimate and would have seen this as a standard power play and nothing to be perturbed about. And while the attractions of substantial reconstruction loans were obvious, these had to be weighed against the probability that such loans (to be spent buying American industrial equipment and other producer goods) would save the United States from an otherwise inevitable postwar slump and another step toward the ultimate downfall of capitalism. By September it had become clear that the US Congress intended to use any such loans as a means of shaping Soviet policy.

As a consequence, German reparations were an essential component of Soviet defense policy, as well as being critical to the Soviet domestic economy. Persistent American and British efforts to whittle down the scale of what the Russians saw as their rightful dues, and to hamper their collection, were therefore a matter for mounting concern.

Soviet requirements for German reparations were consistent and quite specific: (1) Germany would pay reparations in kind to the value of $20 billion, half of which was to go to the Soviet Union; and (2) there would be Four-Power control of the Ruhr industrial complex, the engine-room of the German war machine. Since the Soviets had no means of forcing the Western Powers to deliver up reparations from their occupation zones, they agreed reluctantly at Potsdam that each of the four powers would be allowed to take what it could from its own zone. The decision favored the Western Powers, since their zones comprised about 70 percent of postwar Germany and Austria and contained about 60 percent of Germany's prewar industrial base.

With reparations, there was, indeed, a basic conflict of objectives. The Soviet Union was concerned to severely disable Germany (as was France), contributing to its own reconstruction in the process, while the United States was now primarily concerned with preventing Europe and in particular Germany becoming a charge on the American taxpayer. Nevertheless, Soviet-American relations on the Control Commission were relatively good for the first year. Disagreements at the working level about running the German economy and extracting reparations came within the bounds of tough bargaining between conflicting interests. But in the spring of 1946 it began to appear that American objectives had moved beyond sparing their taxpayers, to integrating a rehabilitated Western Germany into the capitalist economic system.

At the beginning of May 1946, the US military governor suspended all reparation shipments from the American zone, giving as his reason the failure to reach Four-Power agreement on treating Germany as a single economic unit, an explanation the Soviets found hard to take at face value. In July, the American and British occupation authorities began the process of integrating their occupation zones (which would be formally merged at the beginning of 1947), thus consolidating under one authority almost 60 percent of German and Austrian territory and the great bulk of their industrial capacity. At the same period the United States began to develop an export control system for trade with the Soviet Union; it officially quashed the possibility of any reconstruction loan; and to further complicate Russia's economic problems, it withdrew its support from the United Nations Relief and Rehabilitation Administration [UNRRA]. UNRRA's biggest recipients were the countries of Eastern Europe and the Balkans (including Byelorussia and the Ukraine), and its primary contributor had been the United States.

And then in early September, the US Secretary of State made a major policy speech to a large audience of German and

American officials, at the Opera House in Stuttgart. In this he gave strong backing to the concept of German self-government and economic revival, hinted that he did not regard the cession of German territory to Poland as permanent, and, while claiming that he did not want Germany to become a pawn or prize in a struggle between east and west, went on to pledge that "as long as there is an occupation army in Germany, American armed forces will be part of that occupation army."*

These developments were all the more disturbing because the Soviet Union had yet to develop any policy toward Germany beyond the immediate objective of disarming its enemy and using the proceeds to help rebuild Russia. By the summer of 1946, moreover, it was becoming clear that Soviet reparations policy had failed, even in the Soviet zone. The policy had been bedeviled by high-level disagreement about the merits of stripping Germany; the actual plans had been poorly formulated and badly executed, and had then become bogged down in bureaucratic wrangles over the competing claims for current production. This led to more intransigent demands for a Soviet share of reparations from the western zones, which were counterproductive, and harsher measures to extract reparations from the eastern zone, which estranged the German population even further.

Rather than pursuing some Machiavellian scheme to assume political control of Germany, Soviet policy was floundering. While the Soviets had no difficulty in seeing what was to their disadvantage, it was much harder to formulate a coherent policy toward Germany that would serve their long-term interests. Wartime experience would have convinced Stalin that a restored Germany, whatever its political complexion, would inevitably pose a threat to Russia. On the other hand, there were obvious disadvantages to a divided Germany, where the much larger and far more prosperous part adhered to the West. This dilemma bedeviled Soviet policy for the best part of a decade, condemning the Soviets to a mainly reactive German policy, which was as ineffective as it was provocative.

Given this vulnerable situation, the Soviet leaders could not accept at face value American assertions that the policy initiatives in the US zone were defensive responses to illegitimate Russian behavior. To the Soviets, the justice of their claims on

---

* For Secretary of State James F. Byrnes's Stuttgart speech, see *Department of State Bulletin*, 15 (September 15, 1946): 496.

German resources was self-evident, and the need to neutralize this dangerous enemy was not only obvious but had been specifically recognized in the Potsdam accords. It was the Soviets who had been consistent in their demands for reparations, while the Americans had swung from the extreme of Morganthau's pastoralization plan to the opposite policy of rehabilitation. It was the USA that had insisted (to Russia's disadvantage) on breaching the principle of treating Germany as a single economic unit, but was now using the sanctity of that principle as a reason for halting the delivery of reparations from its own zone, and for promising increased German control of a unified British-American zone.

All these shifts in policy worked in the same direction: to Russia's disadvantage and in Germany's interests. In terms of Soviet threat perceptions, an alarming feature of these new developments in Germany was that they were only one aspect of an abrupt shift in US policy toward the Soviet Union which took place in early 1946. The thrust of the new policy of containment was fleshed out by the leak of George Kennan's "long telegram" in February, and publication of a two-part article on the Soviet threat by John Foster Dulles in June.*

Soviet political analysts had been talking for some time of two competing "tendencies" in Britain and the United States. One tendency or faction was prepared to continue with the decision-making system based on tripartite compromise and agreement that developed during the war. The other faction sought world domination for the Anglo-Saxon powers. One would therefore have expected that this sudden change in the thrust and style of US policy toward Russia would have generated a major Soviet reevaluation of the threat. But it seems that Stalin was reluctant to forgo the potential benefits of cooperation and, despite the mounting evidence, he chose not to accept that final victory had gone to the anti-Soviet tendency. He persisted in the hope that vestiges of the wartime collaboration could be made to endure and was conciliatory when vital interests were not at stake. The sharp change in the US style of negotiation appears to have been discounted as diplomatic bargaining tactics, or domestic political rhetoric that was prompted by the mid-term elections. Even the

* For Kennan's "long telegram," see George F. Kennan, *Memoirs, 1925–1950* (New York, Bantam, 1967), 583–98; for Dulles's articles, see *Life*, 20 (June 3, 1946 and June 10, 1946): 113–26 and 118–30.

"all out" speech which launched the Truman Doctrine in March 1947 was treated at the time as anti-Communist propaganda, rather than as a declaration of cold war, possibly because it was timed to coincide with the preliminary stages of the Foreign Ministers' meeting in March–April in Moscow.*

It is unlikely, however, that this sanguineness could have survived the actual meeting, whose main purpose was to consider draft peace treaties for Germany and Austria. The Soviets seemed prepared to adjust their position on the political and economic structure of Germany, in return for the payment to Russia of reparations from current German production in the western zones. But the United States would not agree to such reparations, and before it would even consider studying the factors involved, required the Soviets first to comply with an unrealistic set of demands. Stonewalling on this issue by the British and Americans led to an impasse and it became clear that they were no longer interested in compromise.

Before the continuing of the description of events as they are likely to have been seen from Moscow in 1947, the reader is reminded once more that this study is not concerned to determine the causes of the Cold War, or to apportion blame in the matter. The objective is to identify the genesis of Soviet threat perceptions. The study seeks to explain why Stalin shifted focus from the danger of a resurgent Germany in fifteen to twenty years' time to the more immediate threat of war within five to six years against a capitalist coalition led by the Anglo-Saxon powers.

If there were still doubts in Stalin's mind about the thrust of Western policy after the Foreign Ministers' meeting in Moscow, these would have been finally dispelled by the proposed European Recovery Program. The full implications of this program became clear when the British, French, and Soviet Foreign Ministers met in Paris at the end of June to decide how best to proceed on the American offer. Although the use of US economic strength was not unexpected, it seems that the Soviets assumed initially that Marshall's proposals were primarily

* For Truman's speech that became known as the Truman Doctrine, see *Public Papers of the Presidents of the United States: Harry S. Truman, 1947* (Washington, DC: Government Printing Office, 1964), 176–80.

prompted by the need to find markets for American output. It soon became clear, however, that something more threatening was involved. It appeared that Britain and France, under the guise of coordinating European reconstruction, were acting as US agents in an ambitious scheme to lure as many countries as possible into a binding relationship with the West, by integrating their economies into the capitalist bloc.

Molotov sought to counter this thrust with proposals for a different approach to organizing the administration of aid. When the Western ministers refused to entertain his ideas, Stalin decided that the best way to limit the damage was to refuse to participate in the recovery plan, and to prevent others from doing so where possible. Besides the Soviet Union, seven countries declined outright to attend the first organizing conference, and Czechoslovakia later withdrew its initial acceptance under Soviet pressure.

The lines of battle had finally been drawn and this precipitated a major shift in Soviet foreign policy. Just as there had been "tendencies" in the West concerning how best to handle the Russians, so were there different opinions in Moscow on the costs and benefits of seeking cooperation with the United States, and the extent to which increasingly hostile American statements reflected rhetoric or substance. The Anglo-French stance at the Paris meeting, following as it did on the heels of the Truman declaration, the stonewalling on reparations at the Council of Foreign Ministers, and the eviction of the Communist members of the French and Italian coalition governments, appears to have finally convinced Stalin that the West was indeed on the offensive against Communism. Not only was cooperation no longer a practical option, but even the possibility of "peaceful coexistence" was in doubt. The hard-line pessimists therefore moved into favor in Moscow.

As if on cue, George Kennan's "X" article was published in *Foreign Affairs*[3] and, given his position in the State Department and his role in prompting the policy shift at the beginning of March 1946, it seemed designed to spell out US intentions to the attentive public. It mentioned Soviet weaknesses and suggested that the Communist system already held the seeds of its own decay, and concluded by talking of the need to confront Russian encroachments with "unalterable counter-force." It also argued that American policy was "by no means limited to holding the line" but that US action could "influence . . . internal developments within Russia" and "increase enormously the strains under which Soviet policy must operate." This fitted only too well the pattern of US behavior over the previous eighteen months, particularly since Truman's "all out" speech in March.

Initially, the Soviets perceived the Marshall Plan as designed to consolidate and extend US economic control over Europe, while undermining the Russian sphere of influence. By the early months of 1948 they came to believe that the long-term military implications were more ominous and that the real aim of the Marshall Plan was to arm Western Europe to the point where American client states would be capable of taking on the Soviet ones. Russia would then be faced with the choice of allowing the frontiers of socialism to be pushed back, or of intervening and risking an American nuclear attack.

The difference between this pessimistic assessment in 1948 and the sanguine prognosis in 1944–5 represented a massive failure of Soviet foreign policy, both in terms of shaping the international environment and in forecasting the behavior of other states. The United States had not withdrawn into isolationism. America, Canada, and Australia, the "arsenals of capitalism," had not slumped back into the predicted recession, nor had the need for markets proved to be a constraint on US foreign policy. And, despite conflicting interests, the United States and Britain were working well together as an effective and aggressive team. As for shaping the international environment, the situation was now the opposite to what the Soviets had hoped for, wartime cooperation having been replaced by bellicose confrontation.

The opportunity cost of giving a vanishing entente priority over geopolitical gains had not been insignificant. Northern Iran, rich in agriculture and oil, could easily have been drawn into the Soviet orbit. In Greece, direct Soviet involvement in the fall of 1944 would have given the Greek left control of the government (and the Soviets access to the Mediterranean) and even in 1946, support for the Communist guerrillas could well have ensured their success. Meanwhile, the restraints Stalin placed on Tito, in the latter's negotiations over Trieste and support of Greek Communists, had helped to sour relations with Yugoslavia.

But these were only opportunities lost on the periphery, and the real disaster lay in the total failure of Soviet policy toward Germany. Reparations had contributed much less to the rebuilding of Russia than had been hoped, and had come mainly from the Soviet zone. The objective of crippling Germany's warmaking potential had not been achieved, since the concept of reparations had been replaced by that of rehabilitation in the British and American zones. And even worse, these zones were now being forcefully shaped into an independent German state which, combined with the French zone, would encompass the great bulk of the country's industrial capacity.

In terms of the Soviet Union's security interests, this failure of foreign policy was second only to Stalin's disastrous misjudgment in June 1941, and may explain why he was so tardy in accepting the implications of the steady deterioration in relations with the United States. In retrospect, Moscow could see that the fundamental shift in US policy that occurred in early 1946 signaled the victory of the "imperialistic" tendency within the policymaking elites of Britain and the United States. The Soviets had to identify the reasons for this adverse development and assess its security implications.

The Soviets are unlikely to have placed much weight on the notion that it was their own behavior which evoked this unfavorable Western reaction. In their eyes, it was the Anglo-Saxon partners who had shown bad faith over the wartime agreements, and they considered their own policies to have been generally conciliatory, except where vital interests were at stake.

The Soviets' response was to tighten their grip on the Communist parties of Europe and consolidate their hold on the countries of Eastern Europe, while trying to counter the rise of American influence in Western Europe and to disrupt the progress of the European Recovery Program. The undecided "two tendencies" assessment of Western policy was replaced by the categorical "two camps" formulation and the new line was spelt out at the organizing conference of the so-called Communist Information Bureau (Cominform) in September 1947. The next nine months saw the outbreak of violent Communist-led strikes in France and Italy, and a heightening of Stalinist terror in Eastern Europe as governments were fully Communized and ideological deviations suppressed. At the same time, the states of Eastern Europe were bound tighter to the Soviet Union and to each other through a series of bilateral treaties.

NOTES

From Michael MccGwire, "The Genesis of Soviet Threat Perceptions" (unpublished manuscript), 1–38. Abridged and slightly revised by permission of the author.

1 I. V. Stalin, *Sochineniya* (Moscow, 1955), Vol. 13: 38–9.
2 I. V. Stalin, *Sochineniya* (Stanford, CA: Hoover Institute, 1967), Vol. 2: 164–70.
3 George F. Kennan, "The Sources of Soviet Conduct," *Foreign Affairs*, 25 (July 1947): 566–82.

3

THE ATOMIC BOMB AND THE ORIGINS OF THE COLD WAR

Martin J. Sherwin

The dropping of the atomic bomb on Japan and its relationship to the breakdown of the allied coalition has evoked enormous controversy among historians.* In one of the most important revisionist works of the 1960s Gar Alperovitz argued that the United States used atomic weapons to impress the Soviets more than to defeat the Japanese.

Suggesting that the Japanese were on the verge of surrender, and asserting that US officials knew they would surrender if only they were permitted to retain their emperor, Alperovitz claimed that President Harry S. Truman and his new Secretary of State, James F. Byrnes, could have ended the war without using atomic weapons. But, according to Alperovitz, they dropped the atomic bombs on Hiroshima and Nagasaki because they wanted to end the conflict before the Soviet Union had an opportunity to declare war on Japan, march into Manchuria, and lay claim to the concessions (including Sakhalin and the Kuriles) that Roosevelt had promised Stalin at the Yalta Conference in February 1945. Alperovitz also maintained that Truman and Byrnes hoped that upon seeing the power of atomic weapons, the Soviets would relax their policies in Eastern Europe and accept free elections and open trade. And finally, Alperovitz suggested that the possession of atomic weapons altered US thinking about Germany and encouraged US officials to turn quickly to the problems of reconstructing Germany on the assumption that the power of the atomic bomb afforded the United States the ability to control future German strength.**

* Samuel J. Walker, "The Decision to Use the Bomb: An Historiographical Update," *Diplomatic History*, 14 (Winter 1990): 97–114.

** Gar Alperovitz, *Atomic Diplomacy: Hiroshima and Potsdam* (New York: Vintage, 1965).

Traditional scholars attacked this line of reasoning. They insisted that US officials did not know and could not know (even though Japanese codes had been broken) that the Japanese were about to surrender. The use of atomic weapons, therefore, was essential to save American lives. Other scholars, even some revisionists, argued that the momentum of decisionmaking had its own logic, and that Truman and his advisers took it for granted that they would use the new weapon once it was ready. Still others stressed that officials like Byrnes felt impelled to use the atomic bomb for fear of the political repercussions of not using it, having spent so much money developing it and having insisted that they would accept nothing less than unconditional surrender.

In the selection that follows Martin Sherwin makes a major contribution by taking the issue back from the early months of Truman's tenure in office and placing it in the context of overall wartime diplomacy between Churchill, Stalin, and Roosevelt. Roosevelt died in April 1945 just as the European war was coming to an end. But Sherwin shows that the American President had established patterns for dealing with the Bomb that left a clear legacy to his successor. Sherwin's contribution is not only important for understanding the origins of postwar attitudes toward atomic weapons, but equally significant for inspiring a reassessment of Roosevelt's alleged naivety in dealing with Stalin. Readers should reflect on the conflicting goals that Roosevelt and Truman hoped to accomplish and on the variable strategies that might have been used to achieve those goals. Did Roosevelt try to work out a system of international control of atomic energy? Was he willing to share knowledge of the atomic bomb with Stalin? How did he and Truman expect the bomb to affect postwar diplomacy?

* * *

During the Second World War the atomic bomb was seen and valued as a potential rather than an actual instrument of policy. Responsible officials believed that its impact on diplomacy had to await its development and, perhaps, even a demonstration of its power. As Henry L. Stimson, the Secretary of War, observed in his memoirs: "The bomb as a merely probable weapon had seemed a weak reed on which to rely, but the bomb as a colossal reality was very different."[1] That policymakers considered this difference before Hiroshima has been well documented, but whether they based wartime diplomatic policies upon an anticipated successful demonstration of the bomb's power remains a source of controversy.[2] Two questions delineate the issues in this debate. First, did the development of the atomic bomb affect the way American policymakers conducted diplomacy with the Soviet Union? Second, did diplomatic considerations related to the Soviet Union influence the decision to use the atomic bomb against Japan?

These important questions relating the atomic bomb to American diplomacy, and ultimately to the origins of the Cold War, have been addressed almost exclusively to the formulation of policy during the early months of the Truman administration. As a result, two anterior questions of equal importance, questions with implications for those already posed, have been overlooked. Did diplomatic considerations related to Soviet postwar behavior influence the formulation of Roosevelt's atomic energy policies? What effect did the atomic legacy Truman inherited have on the diplomatic and atomic energy policies of his administration?

Although Roosevelt left no definitive statement assigning a postwar role to the atomic bomb, his expectations for its potential diplomatic value can be recalled from the existing record. An analysis of the policies he chose from among the alternatives he faced suggests that the potential diplomatic value of the bomb began to shape his atomic energy policies as early as 1943. He may have been cautious about counting on the bomb as a reality during the war, but he nevertheless consistently chose policy alternatives that would promote the postwar diplomatic potential of the bomb if the predictions of scientists proved true. These policies were based on the assumption that the bomb could be used effectively to secure postwar diplomatic aims; and this assumption was carried over from the Roosevelt to the Truman administration.

Despite general agreement that the bomb would be an extraordinarily important diplomatic factor after the war, those closely associated with its development did not agree on how to use it most effectively as an instrument of diplomacy. Convinced that wartime atomic energy policies would have postwar diplomatic consequences, several scientists advised Roosevelt to adopt policies aimed at achieving a postwar international control system. Churchill, on the other hand, urged the President to maintain the Anglo-American atomic monopoly as a diplomatic counter against the postwar ambitions of other nations – particularly against the Soviet Union. Roosevelt fashioned his atomic energy policies from the choices he made between these conflicting recommendations. In 1943 he rejected the counsel of his science advisers and began to consider the diplomatic component of atomic energy policy in consultation with Churchill alone. This decisionmaking procedure and Roosevelt's untimely death have left his motives ambiguous. Nevertheless it is clear that he pursued policies consistent with Churchill's monopolistic, anti-Soviet views.

The findings of this study thus raise serious questions concerning generalizations historians have commonly made about Roosevelt's diplomacy: that it was consistent with his public reputation for cooperation and conciliation; that he was naive with respect to postwar Soviet behavior; that, like Wilson, he believed in collective security as an effective guarantor of national safety; and that he made every possible effort to ensure that the Soviet Union and its allies would continue to function as postwar partners.[3] Although this article does not dispute the view that Roosevelt desired amicable postwar relations with the Soviet Union, or even that he worked hard to achieve them, it does suggest that historians have exaggerated his confidence in (and perhaps his commitment to) such an outcome. His most secret and among his most important long-range decisions – those responsible for prescribing a diplomatic role for the atomic bomb – reflected his lack of confidence. Finally, in light of this study's conclusions, the widely held assumption that Truman's attitude toward the atomic bomb was substantially different from Roosevelt's must also be revised.

Like the grand alliance itself, the Anglo-American atomic energy partnership was forged by the war and its exigencies. The threat of a German atomic bomb precipitated a hasty marriage of convenience between British research and American resources. When scientists in Britain proposed a theory that explained how an atomic bomb might quickly be built, policymakers had to assume that German scientists were building one.[4] "If such an explosive were made," Vannevar Bush, the director of the Office of Scientific Research and Development, told Roosevelt in July 1941, "it would be thousands of times more powerful than existing explosives, and its use might be determining." Roosevelt assumed nothing less. Even before the atomic energy project was fully organized he assigned it the highest priority.[5]

The high stakes at issue during the war did not prevent officials in Great Britain or the United States from considering the postwar implications of their atomic energy decisions. As early as 1941, during the debate over whether to join the United States in an atomic energy partnership, members of the British government's atomic energy committee argued that the matter "was so important for the future that work should proceed in Britain."[6] Weighing the obvious difficulties of proceeding alone against the possible advantages of working with the United States, Sir John Anderson, then Lord President of the Council and the minister responsible for atomic energy research, advocated the partnership. As he explained to Churchill, by working closely with the Americans British scientists would be able "to take up the work again [after the war], not where we left off, but where the combined effort had by then brought it."[7]

As early as October 1942 Roosevelt's science advisers exhibited a similar concern with the potential postwar value of atomic energy. After conducting a full-scale review of the atomic energy project, James B. Conant, the president of Harvard University and Bush's deputy, recommended discontinuing the Anglo-American partnership "as far as development and manufacture is concerned."[8] What prompted Conant's recommendations, however, was his suspicion – soon to be shared by other senior atomic energy administrators – that the British were rather more concerned with information for postwar industrial purposes than for wartime use.[9] What right did the British have to the fruits of American labor? "We were doing nine-tenths of the work," Stimson told Roosevelt in October.[10] Early in January 1943 the British were officially informed that the rules governing the Anglo-American atomic energy partnership had been altered on "orders from the top."[11]

By approving the policy of "restricted interchange" Roosevelt undermined a major incentive for British cooperation. It is not surprising, therefore, that Churchill took up the matter directly with the President and with Harry Hopkins, "Roosevelt's own, personal Foreign Office."[12]

Conant and Bush understood the implications of Churchill's intervention and sought to counter its effect. Information on manufacturing an atomic bomb, Conant noted, was a "military secret which is in a totally different class from anything the world has ever seen if the potentialities of this project are realised."[13] Though British and American atomic energy policies might coincide during the war, Conant and Bush expected them to conflict afterward.

The controversy over the policy of "restricted interchange" of atomic energy information shifted attention to postwar diplomatic considerations. The central issue was clearly drawn. The atomic energy policy of the United States was related to the very fabric of Anglo-American postwar relations and, as Churchill would insist, to postwar relations between each of them and the Soviet Union. The specter of Soviet postwar military power played a major role in shaping the Prime Minister's attitude toward atomic energy policies in 1943.

Churchill could cite numerous reasons for his determination to acquire an independent atomic arsenal after the war, but Great Britain's postwar military-diplomatic position with respect to the Soviet Union invariably led the list. When Bush and Stimson visited London in July, Churchill told them quite frankly that he was "vitally interested in the possession of all [atomic energy] information because this will be necessary for Britain's independence in the future as well as for success during the war." Nor was Churchill evasive about his reasoning: "It would never do to have Germany or Russia win the race for something which might be used for international blackmail," he stated bluntly and then pointed out that "Russia might be in a position to accomplish this result unless we worked together."[14] Convinced that the British attitude toward the bomb would undermine any possibility of postwar cooperation with the Soviet Union, Bush and Conant vigorously continued to oppose any revival of the Anglo-American atomic energy partnership.[15]

On July 20, however, Roosevelt chose to accept a recommendation from Hopkins to restore full partnership, and he ordered Bush to "renew, in an inclusive manner, the full exchange of information with the British."[16] At the Quebec Conference, the President and the Prime Minister agreed that the British would share the atomic bomb. The Quebec Agreement revived the principle of an Anglo-American atomic energy partnership, albeit the British were reinstated as junior rather than equal partners.[17]

The debate that preceded the Quebec Agreement is noteworthy for another reason; it led to a new relationship between Roosevelt and his atomic energy advisers. After August 1943 the President did not consult with them about the diplomatic aspects of atomic energy policy. Though he responded politely when they offered their views, he acted decisively only in consultation with Churchill. Bush and Conant appear to have lost a large measure of their influence because they had used it to oppose Churchill's position. What they did not suspect was the extent to which the President had come to share the Prime Minister's view.

Roosevelt was perfectly comfortable with the concept Churchill advocated – that military power was a prerequisite to successful postwar diplomacy. As early as August 1941, during the Atlantic Conference, Roosevelt had rejected the idea that an "effective international organization" could be relied upon to keep the peace: an Anglo-American international police force would be far more effective, he told Churchill.[18] By the spring of 1942 the concept had broadened: the two "policemen" became four, and the idea was added that every other nation would be totally disarmed. "The Four Policemen" would have "to build up a reservoir of force so powerful that no aggressor would dare to challenge it," Roosevelt told Arthur Sweetser, an ardent internationalist. Violators first would be quarantined, and, if they persisted in their disruptive activities, bombed at the rate of a city a day until they agreed to behave. A year later, at the Tehran Conference, Roosevelt again discussed his idea, this time with Stalin. As Robert A. Divine has noted: "Roosevelt's concept of big power domination remained the central idea in his approach to international organization throughout World War II."[19]

Precisely how Roosevelt expected to integrate the atomic bomb into his plans for keeping the peace in the postwar world is not clear. However, against the background of his atomic energy policy decisions of 1943 and his peacekeeping concepts, his actions in 1944 suggest that he intended to take full advantage of the bomb's potential as a postwar instrument of Anglo-American diplomacy. If Roosevelt thought the bomb could be used to create a more peaceful world order, he seems to have considered the threat of its power more effective than any opportunities it offered for international cooperation. If Roosevelt was less worried than Churchill about Soviet postwar ambitions, he was no less determined than the Prime Minister to avoid any commitments to the Soviets for the international control of atomic energy. There could still be four policemen, but only two of them would have the bomb.

The atomic energy policies Roosevelt pursued during the remainder of his life reinforce this interpretation of his ideas for the postwar period. The following three questions offer a useful framework for analyzing his intentions. Did Roosevelt make any additional agreements with Churchill that would further support the view that he intended to maintain an Anglo-American monopoly after the war? Did Roosevelt demonstrate any interest in the international control of atomic energy? Was Roosevelt aware that an effort to maintain an Anglo-American monopoly of the atomic bomb might lead to a postwar atomic arms race with the Soviet Union?

The alternatives placed before Roosevelt posed a difficult dilemma. On the one hand, he could continue to exclude the Soviet government from any official information about the development of the bomb, a policy that would probably strengthen America's postwar military-diplomatic position. But such a policy would also encourage Soviet mistrust of Anglo-American intentions and was bound to make postwar cooperation more difficult. On the other hand, Roosevelt could use the atomic bomb project as an instrument of cooperation by informing Stalin of the American government's intention of cooperating in the development of a plan for the international control of atomic weapons, an objective that might never be achieved.

Either choice involved serious risks. Roosevelt had to balance the diplomatic advantages of being well ahead of the Soviet Union in atomic energy production after the war against the advantages of initiating wartime negotiations for postwar cooperation. The issue here, it must be emphasized, is not whether international control was likely to be successful, but rather whether Roosevelt demonstrated any serious interest in laying the groundwork for such a policy.

Roosevelt knew at this time, moreover, that the Soviets were finding out on their own about the development of the atomic bomb. Security personnel had reported an active Communist cell in the Radiation Laboratory at the University of California. Their reports indicated that at least one scientist at Berkeley was selling information to Russian agents.[20] "They [Soviet agents] are already getting information about vital secrets and sending them to Russia," Stimson told the President on September 9, 1943. If Roosevelt was indeed worried to death about the effect the atomic bomb could have on Soviet-American postwar relations, he took no action to remove the potential danger, nor did he make any effort to explore the possibility of encouraging Soviet postwar cooperation on this problem.

Had Roosevelt avoided all postwar atomic energy commitments, his lack of support for international control could have been interpreted as an attempt to reserve his opinion on the best course to follow. But he had made commitments in 1943 supporting Churchill's monopolistic, anti-Soviet position, and he continued to make others in 1944. On June 13, for example, Roosevelt and Churchill signed an Agreement and Declaration of Trust, specifying that the United States and Great Britain would cooperate in seeking to control available supplies of uranium and thorium ore both during and after the war.[21] This commitment, taken against the background of Roosevelt's peacekeeping ideas and his other commitments, suggests that the President's attitude toward the international control of atomic energy was similar to the Prime Minister's.

Churchill rejected the assumption that international control of atomic energy could be used as a cornerstone for constructing a peaceful world order. An atomic monopoly would be a significant diplomatic advantage in postwar diplomacy, and Churchill did not believe that anything useful could be gained by surrendering this advantage. The argument that a new weapon created a unique opportunity to refashion international affairs ignored every lesson Churchill read into history. "You can be quite sure," he would write in a memorandum less than a year later, "that any power that gets hold of the secret will try to make the article and this touches the existence of human society. This matter is out of all relation to anything else that exists in the world, and I could not think of participating in any disclosure to third or fourth parties at the present time."[22]

When Roosevelt and Churchill met at Hyde Park in September 1944 following the second wartime conference at Quebec, they signed an *aide-mémoire* on atomic energy. The agreement bears the markings of Churchill's attitude toward the atomic bomb. It contained an explicit rejection of any wartime efforts toward international control: "The suggestion that the world should be informed regarding tube alloys [the atomic bomb], with a view to an international agreement regarding its control and use, is not accepted. The matter should continue to be regarded as of the utmost secrecy." The *aide-mémoire* then revealed the full extent of Roosevelt's agreement with Churchill's point of view. "Full collaboration between the United States and the British Government in developing tube alloys for military and commercial purposes," it noted, "should continue after the defeat of Japan unless and until terminated by joint agreement." Finally the *aide-mémoire* offers some insight into Roosevelt's intentions for the military use of the weapon in the war: "When a bomb is finally available, it might perhaps, after mature consideration, be used against the Japanese, who should be warned that this bombardment will be repeated until they surrender."[23]

Within the context of the complex problem of the origins of the Cold War the Hyde Park meeting is far more important than historians of the war generally have recognized.[24] Overshadowed by the Second Quebec Conference on one side and by the drama of Yalta on the other, its significance often has been overlooked. But the agreements reached in September 1944 reflect a set of attitudes, aims, and assumptions that guided the relationship between the atomic bomb and American diplomacy during the Roosevelt administration and, through the transfer of its atomic legacy, during the Truman administration as well. Two alternatives had been recognized long before Roosevelt and Churchill met in 1944 at Hyde Park: the bomb could have been used to initiate a diplomatic effort to work out a system for its international control, or it could remain isolated during the war from any cooperative initiatives and held in reserve should cooperation fail. Roosevelt consistently favored the latter alternative. An insight into his reasoning is found in a memorandum Bush wrote following a conversation with Roosevelt several days after the Hyde Park meeting: "The President evidently thought he could join with Churchill in bringing about a US-UK postwar agreement on this subject [the atomic bomb] by which it would be held closely and presumably to control the peace of the world."[25] By 1944 Roosevelt's earlier musings about the Four Policemen had faded into the background. But the idea behind it, the concept of controlling the peace of the world by amassing overwhelming military power, appears to have remained a prominent feature of his postwar plans.

Harry S. Truman inherited a set of military and diplomatic atomic energy policies that included partially formulated intentions, several commitments to Churchill, and the assumption that the bomb would be a legitimate weapon to be used against Japan. But no policy was definitely settled. According to the Quebec Agreement the President had the option of deciding the future of the commercial aspects of the atomic energy partnership according to his own estimate of what was fair.[26] Although the policy of "utmost secrecy" had been confirmed at Hyde Park the previous September, Roosevelt had not informed his atomic energy advisers about the *aide-mémoire* he and Churchill signed. Although the assumption that the bomb would be used in the war was shared by those privy to its development, assumptions formulated early in the war were not necessarily valid at its conclusion. Yet Truman was bound to the past by his own uncertain position and by the prestige of his predecessor.[27] Since Roosevelt had refused to open negotiations with the Soviet government for the international control of atomic energy, and since he had never expressed any objection to the wartime use of the bomb, it would have required considerable political courage and confidence for Truman to alter those policies. Moreover it would have required the encouragement of his advisers, for under the circumstances the most serious constraint on the new President's choices was his dependence upon advice. So Truman's atomic legacy, while it included several options, did not necessarily entail complete freedom to choose from among all the possible alternatives.

"I think it is very important that I should have a talk with you as soon as possible on a highly secret matter," Stimson wrote to Truman on April 24. It has "such a bearing on our present foreign relations and has such an important effect upon all my thinking in this field that I think you ought to know about it without further delay."[28] Stimson had been preparing to brief Truman on the atomic bomb for almost ten days, but in the preceding twenty-four hours he had been seized by a sense of urgency. Relations with the Soviet Union had declined precipitously. The State Department had been urging Truman to get tough with the Russians.[29] He had. Twenty-four hours earlier the President met with the Soviet Foreign Minister, V. M. Molotov, and "with rather brutal frankness" accused his government of breaking the Yalta Agreement. Molotov was furious. "I have never been talked to like that in my life," he told the President before leaving.[30]

With a memorandum on the "political aspects of the S-1 [atomic bomb's] performance" in hand, Stimson went to the White House on April 25. The document he carried was the distillation of numerous decisions already taken, each one the product of attitudes that developed along with the new weapon. The Secretary of War himself was not entirely aware of how various forces had shaped these decisions: the recommendations of Bush and Conant, the policies Roosevelt had followed, the uncertainties inherent in the wartime alliance, the oppressive concern for secrecy, and his own inclination to consider long-range implications. It was a curious document. Though its language revealed Stimson's sensitivity to the historic significance of the atomic bomb, he did not question the wisdom of using it against Japan. Nor did he suggest any concrete steps for developing a postwar policy. His objective was to inform Truman of the salient problems: the possibility of an atomic arms race, the danger of atomic war, and the necessity for international control if the United Nations Organization was to work. "If the problem of the proper use of this weapon can be solved," he wrote, "we would have the opportunity to bring the world into a pattern in which the peace of the world and our civilizations can be saved." To cope with this difficult challenge Stimson suggested the "establishment of a select committee" to consider the postwar problems inherent in the development of the bomb.[31]

What emerges from a careful reading of Stimson's diary, his memorandum of April 25 to Truman, a summary by Groves of the meeting, and Truman's recollections is an argument for overall caution in American diplomatic relations with the Soviet Union:[32] it was an argument against any showdown. Since the atomic bomb was potentially the most dangerous issue facing the postwar world and since the most desirable resolution of the problem was some form of international control, Soviet cooperation had to be secured. It was imprudent, Stimson suggested, to pursue a policy that would preclude the possibility of international cooperation on atomic energy matters after the war ended. Truman's overall impression of Stimson's argument was that the Secretary of War was "at least as much concerned with the role of the atomic bomb in the shaping of history as in its capacity to shorten the war."[33] These were indeed Stimson's dual concerns on April 25, and he could see no conflict between them.

Despite the profound consequences Stimson attributed to the development of the new weapon, he had not suggested that Truman reconsider its use against Japan. Nor had he thought to mention the possibility that chances of securing Soviet postwar cooperation might be diminished if Stalin did not receive a commitment to international control prior to an attack. Until the bomb's "actual certainty [was] fixed," Stimson considered any prior approach to Stalin as premature.[34] As the uncertainties of impending peace became more apparent and worrisome, Stimson, Truman, and the Secretary of State-designate, James F. Byrnes, began to think of the bomb as something of a diplomatic panacea for their postwar problems. Byrnes had told Truman in April that the bomb "might well put us in a position to dictate our own terms at the end of the war."[35] By June, Truman and Stimson were discussing "further *quid pro quos* which should be established in consideration for our taking them [the Soviet Union] into [atomic energy] partnership." Assuming that the bomb's impact on diplomacy would be immediate and extraordinary, they agreed on no less than "the settlement of the Polish, Rumanian, Yugoslavian, and Manchurian problems." But they also concluded that no revelation would be made "to Russia or anyone else until the first bomb had been successfully laid on Japan."[36]

Was an implicit warning to Moscow, then, the principal reason for deciding to use the atomic bomb against Japan? In light of the ambiguity of the available evidence the question defies an unequivocal answer. What can be said with certainty is that Truman, Stimson, Byrnes, and several others involved in the decision consciously considered two effects of a combat demonstration of the bomb's power: first, the impact of the atomic attack on Japan's leaders, who might be persuaded thereby to end the war; and second, the impact of that attack on the Soviet Union's leaders, who might then prove to be more cooperative. But if the assumption that the bomb might bring the war to a rapid conclusion was the principal motive for using the atomic bomb, the expectation that its use would also inhibit Soviet diplomatic ambitions clearly discouraged any inclination to question that assumption.

Thus by the end of the war the most influential and widely accepted attitude toward the bomb was a logical extension of how the weapon was seen and valued earlier – as a potential instrument of diplomacy. Caught between the remnants of war and the uncertainties of peace, policymakers were trapped by the logic of their own unquestioned assumptions. By the summer of 1945 not only the conclusion of the war but the organization of an acceptable peace seemed to depend upon the success of the atomic attacks against Japan. When news of the successful atomic test of July 16 reached the President at the Potsdam Conference, he was visibly elated.[37] Stimson noted that Truman "was tremendously pepped up by it and spoke to me of it again and again when I saw him. He said it gave him an entirely new feeling of confidence." The day after receiving the complete report of the test Truman altered his negotiating style. According to Churchill the President "got to the meeting after having read this report [and] he was a changed man. He told the Russians just where they got on and off and generally bossed the whole meeting."[38] After the plenary session on July 24 Truman "casually mentioned to Stalin" that the United States had "a new weapon of unusual destructive force."[39] In less than three weeks the new weapon's destructive potential was demonstrated to the world. Upon learning of the raid against Hiroshima Truman exclaimed: "This is the greatest thing in history."[40]

As Stimson had expected, as a colossal reality the bomb was very different. But had American diplomacy been altered by it? Those who conducted diplomacy became more confident, more certain that through the accomplishments of American science, technology, and industry the "new world" could be made into one better than the old. But just how the atomic bomb would be used to help accomplish this ideal remained unclear. Three months and one day after Hiroshima was bombed Bush wrote that the whole matter of international relations on atomic energy "is in a thoroughly chaotic condition."[41] The wartime relationship between atomic energy policy and diplomacy had been based upon the simple assumption that the Soviet government would surrender important geographical, political, and ideological objectives in exchange for the neutralization of the new weapon. As a result of policies based on this assumption American diplomacy and prestige suffered grievously: an opportunity to gauge the Soviet Union's response during the war to the international control of atomic energy was missed, and an atomic energy policy for dealing with the Soviet government after the war was ignored. Instead of promoting American postwar aims, wartime atomic energy policies made them more difficult to achieve. As a group of scientists at the University of Chicago's atomic energy laboratory presciently warned the government in June 1945: "It may be difficult to persuade the world that a nation which was capable of secretly preparing and suddenly releasing a weapon as indiscriminate as the [German] rocket bomb and a million times more destructive, is to be trusted in its proclaimed desire of having such weapons abolished by international agreement."[42] This reasoning, however, flowed from alternative assumptions formulated during the closing months of the war by scientists far removed from the wartime policymaking process. Hiroshima and Nagasaki, the culmination of that process, became the symbols of a new American barbarism, reinforcing charges, with dramatic circumstantial evidence, that the policies of the United States contributed to the origins of the Cold War.[43]

NOTES

From Martin J. Sherwin, "The Atomic Bomb and the Origins of the Cold War: U.S. Atomic Energy Policy and Diplomacy, 1941–45," *American Historical Review*, 78 (October 1973): 945–68. Reprinted and abridged by permission of the author.

1 Henry L. Stimson and McGeorge Bundy, *On Active Service in Peace and War* (New York, 1947), 637.
2 Compare the evidence and interpretations in the following studies: Gar Alperovitz, *Atomic Diplomacy: Hiroshima and Potsdam* (New York, 1965); Herbert Feis, *The Atomic Bomb and the End of World War II* (Princeton, NJ, 1966); Richard G. Hewlett and Oscar E. Anderson, Jr, *The New World 1939/1946: A History of the United States Atomic Energy Commission*, Vol. 1 (University Park, PA, 1962); and Walter Smith Schoenberger, *Decision of Destiny* (Athens, OH, 1969).
3 These views are represented in the following books and articles: Alperovitz, *Atomic Diplomacy*, 12–13; William Bullitt, "How We Won

the War and Lost the Peace," *Life* (August 30, 1948): 82–97; Arthur Schlesinger, Jr, "Origins of the Cold War," *Foreign Affairs*, 46 (1967): 26–9; and Herbert Feis, *Churchill, Roosevelt, Stalin: The War They Waged and the Peace They Sought* (Princeton, NJ, 1957), 596–8.

4 The critical breakthrough was made by Otto R. Frisch and Rudolph E. Peierls in April 1940. For details of the British contribution, see Margaret Gowing, *Britain and Atomic Energy* (London, 1964), pt 1, app. 1.

5 Bush to Roosevelt, July 16, 1941; Roosevelt to Bush, March 11, 1942: President's Secretary's File [hereafter PSF], Bush folder, Franklin D. Roosevelt Library [hereafter FDRL], Hyde Park, NY; Winston S. Churchill, *The Second World War* (New York, 1962), Vol. 4: *The Hinge of Fate*, 330.

6 This option was impractical due to scarce resources and the danger to project sites from German bombing. Quotation from Gowing. *Britain*, 73, 78.

7 "Minute from Sir John Anderson to Prime Minister, 30.7.42," in ibid., app. 3, 437–8.

8 James B. Conant to Vannevar Bush, "Some thoughts concerning the S-1 project," October 26, 1942, Atomic Energy Commission [hereafter AEC] doc. 295.

9 Conant to Bush, March 25, 1943, Harry Hopkins Papers [hereafter HHP], A-Bomb folder, FDRL; Conant to Bush, "U.S. – British Relations on S-1 Project," November 13, 1942, AEC doc. 310: Leslie R. Groves, "Diplomatic History of the Manhattan Project" [hereafter "DHMP"], 7, 9, in Manhattan Engineer District Files [hereafter MED Files], National Archives. The Manhattan Engineer District, most commonly referred to as the Manhattan Project, was the cover name assigned by the United States Army to the atomic energy project.

10 Memorandum by Stimson, October 29, 1942, in Groves, "DHMP," annex 5.

11 "Excerpt from Report to the President by the Military Policy Committee, December 15, 1942, with Particular Reference to Recommendations Relating to Future Relations with the British and Canadians," in ibid., annex 6; Roosevelt to Bush, December 28, 1942, PSF, Bush folder; Conant, "Memorandum on the interchange with the British and Canadians on S-1," January 7, 1943, AEC doc. 152.

12 Robert E. Sherwood, *Roosevelt and Hopkins, An Intimate History* (New York, 1948), 202, 704; Churchill to Roosevelt, April 1, 1943, HHP, A-Bomb folder.

13 Conant to Bush, March 23, 1943, HHP, A-Bomb folder.

14 Harvey Bundy, "Memorandum of Meeting at 10 Downing Street on July 23, 1943," in Groves, "DHMP," annex 11; Bush to Conant, July 23, 1943, AEC doc. 312.

15 Their arguments can be followed in Hewlett and Anderson, *New World*, 270–80; but see also Bush to Hopkins, March 31, 1943, HHP, A-Bomb folder.

16 Hopkins to Roosevelt, July 20, 1943; Roosevelt to Bush, July 20,

1943; Roosevelt to Churchill, July 20, 1943, HHP, A-Bomb folder.

17 Articles of Agreement Governing Collaboration between the Authorities of the U.S.A. and the U.K. in the Matter of Tube Alloys [hereafter Quebec Agreement], in Groves, "DHMP," annex 18; also in Gowing, *Britain*, app. 4. "Tube Alloys" was the British code name for the atomic energy project.

18 *Foreign Relations of the United States* [hereafter *FRUS*], *1941* (Washington, DC, 1958), Vol. 1: 363, 365–6.

19 Roosevelt, quoted in "Mr Sweetser's Notes," May 29, 1942, Arthur Sweetser Papers, box 39, Library of Congress [hereafter LC]. This memorandum was brought to my attention by Mr Günter Brauch. See also *FRUS: The Conferences at Cairo and Teheran, 1943* (Washington, DC, 1961), 530–2, and Robert A. Divine, *Roosevelt and World War II* (Baltimore, MD, 1970), 58.

20 See the testimony of Groves and of John Landsdale, Jr, in United States Atomic Energy Commission, *In the Matter of J. Robert Oppenheimer: Transcript of Hearing before Personnel Security Board* (Washington, DC, 1954), 163–80, especially 171–4, and 258–81; Nuel Pharr Davis, *Lawrence and Oppenheimer* (New York, 1968), 191–2. Though the exact information being passed was not known, there can be no doubt that by the spring of 1944 Roosevelt was aware of Soviet interest in the Manhattan Project. See also Niels Bohr to Roosevelt, July 3, 1944, J. Robert Oppenheimer Papers [hereafter JROP], box 34, Frankfurter-Bohr folder.

21 Agreement and Declaration of Trust, June 13, 1944, in Groves, "DHMP," annex 22a; also in Gowing, *Britain*, app. 7.

22 Churchill, quoted in Gowing, *Britain*, 360.

23 For the *aide-mémoire*, see Gowing, *Britain*, 447.

24 Herbert Feis mentions it in *The Atomic Bomb and the End of World War II*, 33–4. He does not, however, draw out its full implications. See also John Lewis Gaddis, *The United States and the Origins of the Cold War, 1941–1947* (New York, 1972), 87.

25 Bush to Conant, September 25, 1944, AEC doc. 280.

26 See point four of the Quebec Agreement, in Gowing, *Britain*, app. 4: 439.

27 Kenneth Glazier, Jr, "The Decision to Use Atomic Weapons against Hiroshima and Nagasaki," *Public Policy*, 18 (1969): 463–516. Glazier emphasizes the bureaucratic momentum toward this decision.

28 Stimson to Truman, April 24, 1945, in Truman, *Memoirs*, Vol. 1: *1945: Year of Decisions* (Garden City, MO, 1955), 85.

29 Stimson, diary, April 23, 1945, Henry L. Stimson Papers, Yale University Library.

30 Truman, *Year of Decisions*, 82; William D. Leahy, *I Was There* (New York, 1950), 351; Walter Millis (ed.), *The Forrestal Diaries* (New York, 1951), 48–51.

31 Stimson, "Memorandum discussed with the President," in his diary, April 25, 1945.

32 Stimson, diary, April 25, 1945; Groves, "Report of Meeting with the President, April 25, 1945," in Records of the Chief of Engineers,

Commanding General's File 24, tab, D, MED Files; Truman, *Year of Decisions*, 87.

33 Truman, *Year of Decisions*, 87.
34 Stimson, diary, May 31, 1945.
35 Byrnes, quoted in Truman, *Year of Decisions*, 87.
36 Stimson, diary, June 6, 1945.
37 Truman scheduled the Potsdam Conference to coincide with the test of the atomic bomb. See Stimson, diary, June 6, 1945; Joseph E. Davies, diary, May 21, 1945, Joseph E. Davies Papers, box 17, LC; Hewlett and Anderson, *New World*, 352; and Alperovitz, *Atomic Diplomacy*, 62–90.
38 Stimson, diary, July 21, 1945; Churchill is quoted in ibid., July 22, 1945.
39 Truman, *Year of Decisions*, 416. Stalin knew that Truman was referring to the atomic bomb. See Georgii K. Zhukov, *The Memoirs of Marshal Zhukov*, tr. APN (New York, 1971), 674–5. In addition to Truman's own description of his studied attempt to avoid any serious discussion with Stalin about the atomic bomb, see Charles E. Bohlen to Herbert Feis, January 25, 1960, Herbert Feis Papers, box 14, LC.
40 Truman, *Year of Decisions*, 421.
41 Stimson and Bundy, *On Active Service*, 637; Bush to Conant, November 7, 1945, Vannevar Bush Papers, box 27, LC.
42 "The Franck Report," June 11, 1945, in Alice Kimball Smith, *A Peril and a Hope: The Atomic Scientists' Movement, 1945–1947* (Chicago, 1965), app. B.
43 The charge was first made in the West by British physicist P. M. S. Blackett: "So we may conclude that the dropping of the atomic bomb was not so much the last military act of the second World War, as the first major operation of the cold diplomatic war with Russia now in progress." *Fear, War and the Bomb: Military and Political Consequences of Atomic Energy* (London, 1948), 139.

4

THE SOVIET UNION AND THE ORIGINS OF THE ARMS RACE

David Holloway

Western Kremlinologists have debated the impact of Hiroshima and Nagasaki on the Soviet Union. Stalin made numerous statements belittling the importance of the atomic bomb, and some Western analysts have taken the public statements at face value. Others have probed Stalin's actions, paid less attention to his rhetoric, and come forward with different interpretations.

David Holloway is one of the West's best analysts of Soviet atomic and nuclear weapons programs. In this chapter, condensed and excerpted from his book on the Soviet Union and the arms race, he examines the origins of Soviet work on atomic and thermonuclear weapons. Placing these efforts in the context of scientific, technological, and diplomatic developments, he is interested in examining the extent to which initiatives and breakthroughs by one power had a significant impact on the adversary's weapons development. Also of concern is the extent to which weapons development has its own internal dynamic based on scientific knowledge, technological imperatives, and the organizational self-interest of an influential new bureaucracy.

In the course of this chapter Holloway explores the factors that contributed to the success of the Soviet program. He alludes to the contributions of German scientists, US lend-lease, and the information gleaned from British and American spies. But he also shows great respect for the knowledge and capabilities of Russian scientists.

In view of the many factors bearing on Soviet policy, readers should discuss precisely how the use of atomic weapons against Japan (and subsequent US initiatives) influenced developments inside the Soviet Union. In assessing the motives and wisdom of Soviet actions they should recall some of the points made by Sherwin in the preceding article. Did the Kremlin have reason to fear US possession of an atomic monopoly? Is MccGwire (in the second excerpt in this volume) right when he says that the Soviets did not worry about the United States until the middle of 1947? What factors, other than fear of US power, shaped Soviet atomic weapons policy?

* * *

Victory over Germany brought the Soviet Union political gains that must have been inconceivable in the early months of the war. Stalin now had a say in the political arrangements of Eastern Europe, and Soviet security was thereby enhanced. Stalin's policy in Eastern Europe, however, soon brought him into conflict with his allies. Strains were evident at the Postdam Conference in July and August 1945. This was the last meeting of the allied leaders to try to resolve their differences about the postwar settlement. It was also the first occasion on which the atomic bomb cast its shadow over relations between the Soviet Union and the Western powers.

The Americans and the British had pondered for some time what to tell Stalin about the atomic bomb. Neither Roosevelt nor Churchill had been impressed by the advice of the great Danish physicist Niels Bohr that they should inform Stalin before the bomb was tested and try to get agreement on international control.[1] The first atomic bomb test took place on July 16 while the Postdam Conference was in progress. On July 24 President Truman approached Stalin after the formal session had broken up and "casually mentioned" to him that "we had a new weapon of unusual destructive force." Truman wrote later that Stalin replied that "he was glad to hear of it and hoped we would make 'good use of it against the Japanese'." Truman and Churchill (who was watching intently from nearby) were convinced that Stalin had not grasped what the President was referring to.[2] They were mistaken, however, for Stalin knew of the Manhattan Project and had initiated Soviet work on the bomb early in 1943.

When nuclear fission was discovered in Berlin in December 1938, Soviet physicists were as quick as their counterparts in other countries to see that one of its potential applications was the creation of a bomb with unprecedented destructive force. In 1939 Igor Tamm, a leading theoretical physicist, remarked to a group of students, "Do you know what this new discovery means? It means a bomb can be built that will destroy a city out to a radius of maybe ten kilometers."[3]

The discovery of nuclear fission at once stimulated new directions of research in the Soviet Union. Leningrad was the leading center for this work. Here the prime mover was Igor Kurchatov, who headed the nuclear laboratory at the Leningrad Physicotechnical Institute and was later to be scientific director of the atomic project. He coordinated the research not only of his own laboratory, but also of scientists working at the Radium Institute and at the Institute of Physical Chemistry. The Radium Institute was directed by V. G. Khlopin, a radiochemist who later developed the industrial processes for producing plutonium. The director of the Institute of Physical Chemistry was N. N. Semenov, who had done important work on chain reactions for which he later received a Nobel prize.

Nuclear physics in the 1930s was the very model of an international scientific community. The dramatic progress of research was built on discoveries by scientists in several different countries. Although they had no center of nuclear research to compare with Paris, Cambridge, or Copenhagen, Soviet physicists followed international progress avidly and made some significant contributions to it. Their work on nuclear fission parallelled that done elsewhere. In April 1939 two of Kurchatov's junior colleagues established that each fissioned nucleus emitted between two and four neutrons, thus indicating that a chain reaction might be possible. Two physicists at Semenov's institute investigated the conditions under which a chain reaction would take place in uranium, and concluded early in 1940 that an experimental attempt to achieve a chain reaction could now be undertaken. In the same year two other physicists, working under Kurchatov's close direction, discovered the spontaneous fission of uranium (i.e. fission without bombardment by neutrons). Inspired by these results, Kurchatov and his colleagues wrote to the Presidium of the Academy of Sciences, urging an expansion of work on nuclear fission.

Work on nuclear fission continued, though not at the pace or on the scale that Kurchatov desired. He made a further attempt to put his case before the authorities. Semenov wrote on his behalf to the government about the possibility of creating a bomb, the destructive power of which would be incomparably greater than that of any existing explosive. This letter, written at the end of 1940 or early in 1941, elicited no response before the German invasion brought nuclear research in the Soviet Union to a halt.

Early in 1942 the possibility of an atomic bomb became a serious issue for the Soviet leadership, as a result of information obtained about British, American, and German work on the bomb. In April M. G. Pervukhin, Deputy Premier and People's Commissar (i.e. Minister) of the Chemical Industry, was sent for by Molotov, who gave him a thick file containing secret reports about the foreign work. Soviet sources do not say what was in the file, but it may have contained Klaus Fuchs's earliest reports on British work; it appears also that the Soviet Union had by this time received information about German interest in the bomb. Molotov told Pervukhin that he was giving him the papers on Stalin's instruction, and that he was to read them and advise what should be done. Pervukhin recommended that the papers be shown to physicists who would be able to make a precise evaluation of their significance. He himself was given responsibility for the uranium problem.[4]

Information came also from an unexpected source. In May 1942 G. N. Flyorov, one of Kurchatov's former students, wrote to Stalin that "it is essential not to lose any time in building the uranium bomb." Flyorov, now a lieutenant in the air force, was serving at the front in Voronezh, where he had visited the university library to look at the physics journals. He was anxious to see if there had been any response to the discovery, which he had helped to make, of spontaneous fission. A note about this had been published in the American journal *Physical Review*. On looking through the journals, however, he found no reaction to this discovery; moreover, he saw that little of importance was being published about nuclear fission, and that the big names in the field had vanished from the journals. He concluded, rightly, that research was now secret and that the Americans must be working on an atomic bomb. Hence the letter to Stalin.

In the course of 1942 Soviet leaders held consultations with prominent scientists about the development of an atomic bomb. Stalin was worried about the cost of developing a bomb, for he was advised by two of the scientists that it would cost as much

98

as the whole war effort. He decided, nevertheless, to initiate a small-scale project. Kurchatov, who had abandoned nuclear research on the outbreak of war, was chosen as scientific director. He finally began work in February or March 1943.

The decision to build an atomic bomb was taken when the war with Germany still hung in the balance. (The counteroffensive at Stalingrad, planned in September and October 1942, had the code name *Uran*, which, though normally translated as Uranus, is also the Russian for uranium. This may indicate that the atomic bomb was preying on Stalin's mind at the time.)[5] There were many who thought the effort a pointless waste of resources which could be used to meet more pressing needs. Stalin can hardly have thought that a Soviet bomb could be built in time to affect the outcome of the war. Soviet physicists had estimated in 1942 that the development of a uranium bomb would take between ten and twenty years. Perhaps Stalin had it in mind that after the war the Soviet Union would have to face a nuclear-armed Germany, for at this early period he may have had only minimum war aims, which did not necessarily include the destruction of the Nazi state. Perhaps he foresaw that even with the defeat of Germany the Soviet Union would come into conflict with Britain and the United States; after all, they were conducting their atomic projects in great secrecy, without informing the Soviet Union. More probably, the decision should be seen as a hedge against uncertainty. Given that Germany, Britain, and the United States were interested in the atomic bomb, was it not as well to initiate a Soviet project, even though the circumstances in which the new weapon might be used could not be foreseen?

Kurchatov drew up a plan of research with three main goals: to achieve a chain reaction in an experimental reactor using natural uranium; to develop methods of isotope separation; to study the design of both the U-235 and the plutonium bombs. He built up his team slowly, drawing largely on those with whom he had worked before. By the end of 1943 he had fifty people working in his new laboratory; by the end of 1944 he had one hundred scientists. This was a tiny effort compared with the Manhattan Project. As the country was liberated, other institutes were drawn into the project, and in 1945 some German scientists and technicians were brought to the Soviet Union to take part. In the spring of 1945 Kurchatov ordered work to begin on the design of an industrial reactor for producing plutonium.[6] By the time of the Potsdam Conference the Soviet Union had a serious atomic bomb project under way.

In spite of this, however, the American success in building the bomb came as a blow for the Soviet Union. Alexander Werth, who was in Moscow at the time, wrote that the news of Hiroshima had "an acutely depressing effect on everybody." The atomic bomb was seen as a threat to Russia, and "some Russian pessimists . . . dismally remarked that Russia's desperately hard victory over Germany was now 'as good as wasted'."[7] In December 1945 the British ambassador wrote to the Foreign Secretary that "Russia was balked by the west when everything seemed to be within her grasp. The three hundred divisions were shorn of much of their value."[8] Ambassador Harriman reported to Washington in much the same terms.[9]

The small Soviet project laid the basis for the all-out effort that was now launched. Stalin's immediate reaction to Truman's casual remark was to tell Kurchatov to speed up his work. In the middle of August, shortly after his return from Potsdam, Stalin summoned B. L. Vannikov, the People's Commissar of Munitions, and his deputies to the Kremlin. There they were joined by Kurchatov. "A single demand of you, comrades," said Stalin. "Provide us with atomic weapons in the shortest possible time. You know that Hiroshima has shaken the whole world. The balance has been destroyed. Provide the bomb – it will remove a great danger from us."[10] Kurchatov and his colleagues were asked how long it would take to build the atomic bomb if they received all-round support. Five years, they replied. In the event, the first Soviet test took place four years to the month after that August meeting with Stalin.

Compared with his failure to heed the warnings of a German attack in 1941, Stalin's decision about the atomic bomb in 1942 showed considerable foresight. The last thing he can have wanted to hear then was that Germany, Britain, and the United States were working in great secrecy to develop a weapon of unprecedented destructive force. In spite of the critical war situation, he took the precautionary step of setting up a small-scale project. The Soviet leaders were nevertheless shaken by the American success in building a bomb. When Molotov heard what Truman had said at Potsdam, he saw it as an attempt to gain concessions from the Soviet Union. The Soviet leaders regarded the use of the bomb in Japan as part of an effort to put pressure on them, as a demonstration that the United States was willing to use nuclear weapons. Soviet security now seemed to be at risk from a new threat.

If Niels Bohr's advice had been heeded, and Stalin had been told officially about the bomb, his postwar policy might have been just the same. But Western secrecy contributed to Soviet suspicion and spurred the Soviet Union to develop its own bomb. As Margaret Gowing has written, "If Russia had been formally consulted about the bomb during the war . . . it might have made no difference. The fact that she was not, guaranteed that the attempts made just after the war to establish international control, which might have failed anyway, were doomed."[11]

By the summer of 1946 the basic institutional framework had been created in the Soviet Union for developing nuclear weapons, long-range rockets, radar, and jet propulsion. Special bodies were set up in the party, the government, the secret police, and the armed forces to direct these programs. In 1945 scientific-technical councils were created for atomic bomb and rocket development. These consisted of scientists, engineers, and industrial managers, and discussed the major technical and industrial problems connected with the programs. B. L. Vannikov headed the atomic council, with Pervukhin and Kurchatov as his deputies. The rocket council was chaired by D. F. Ustinov, the present [1983] Minister of Defence, who was then the People's Commissar of Armament. A special department of government, also headed by Vannikov, was set up to manage the nuclear program. The secret police had a department for atomic energy; half of all research for nuclear weapons development was done in prison institutes, while most of the construction and mining was done by prison labor. Overall control of the nuclear program lay in the hands of Beria, the chief of the secret police.[12]

The object of these arrangements was to exercise tight central control over the new weapons programs, and to ensure that they had first claim on resources. Soon after the Potsdam Conference Kurchatov became a regular visitor to the Kremlin. Policy was developed in meetings between the party leaders and those directly in charge of the programs. In April 1947, for example, Stalin summoned scientists, industrial managers, and military men to the Kremlin for a series of meetings to decide on an overall plan for rocket development.[13] Stalin's personal interest ensured that these programs had the highest priority; the best scientists, engineers, workers, and managers were assigned to them. Each decision was backed by Stalin's authority, and this helped to overcome obstacles in the way of executing policy.

The war provided the Soviet Union with a major infusion of foreign technology, mainly in the form of captured German scientists, technicians, equipment, and production plant. Foreign technology also came through lend-lease, and by more fortuitous routes. The Tu-4 bomber, for example, was a copy of the American B-29, three of which made a forced landing on Soviet territory in 1944. Foreign technology was important for the postwar programs, but its contribution varied from field to field.[14] In 1945 the Soviet atomic bomb project was better organized than the German, and while the Soviet Union acquired some scientists, technicians, and equipment, most of the leading German nuclear scientists fell into Western hands. The information passed by Klaus Fuchs and other atomic spies was more important for the Soviet effort, perhaps speeding up the development of the atomic bomb by as much as a year or two. But it is certainly wrong to say that this is how the Soviet Union acquired the "secret" of the atomic bomb, for, as Niels Bohr remarked, the only secret of the atomic bomb is that it can be built.

The Soviet Union gained more from German rocket technology. In 1945 a team of Soviet rocket scientists was sent to Germany to study the German effort, and the first Soviet long-range rocket, the R-1, which was test-fired in October 1947, was a modification of the German V-2. The United States too gained from the German rocket program, for as the Red Army approached Peenemunde, the main center of German rocketry, Wernher von Braun took his team and their most important papers to meet the American forces. Unlike the United States, however, the Soviet Union gave high priority to rocket development.[15] In October 1946 thousands of German engineers and technicians were taken to the Soviet Union, where they worked under Soviet supervision. In spite of the purge, there was still a cadre of experienced and gifted rocket scientists who were able to build on the German technology. In 1947 a Council of Chief Designers was set up to coordinate the Soviet program.[16]

The Soviet atomic bomb test of August 1949 helped to speed up American work on thermonuclear weapons, and American policy in turn stimulated Soviet weapons research and development. Soviet work on the thermonuclear bomb began in 1948 when Kurchatov set up a theoretical group (which included Andrei Sakharov) under Igor Tamm, after reports of a super-bomb had been received from the West. Soviet interest in thermonuclear weapons may have been aroused by Klaus Fuchs, who told his Soviet contact about studies of these weapons at Los Alamos. He could have told the Soviet Union that in the spring of 1946 discussion had taken place about two possible types of thermonuclear bombs: one in which a relatively small amount of thermonuclear fuel is ignited by a relatively large fission explosion (later known as a boosted fission weapon) and the other in which a relatively small fission explosion ignites a very large mass of thermonuclear fuel (the superbomb). Fuchs's account of these early discussions of the superbomb would have been misleading rather than helpful to Soviet scientists in a scientific sense, because the early ideas were later shown not to work. But it is possible that Fuchs's reports stimulated Soviet work on these weapons.[17]

By the time of the first atomic bomb test, Tamm's group had concluded that thermonuclear weapons were possible, and two months after the test – that is, about November 1, 1949 – Kurchatov began to work on the development of a thermonuclear bomb as a matter of priority. The first thermonuclear bomb test took place almost four years later, on August 12, 1953. Soviet writers tend to stress the role of American actions in stimulating Soviet nuclear weapons development. It is therefore interesting that they do not mention as providing any impetus to Soviet efforts Truman's announcement on January 31, 1950 of his decision to accelerate development of the superbomb. But one of Kurchatov's biographers does stress that the American test of October 1952 led to an intensification of Soviet work.[18]

This episode in the nuclear arms race is of interest for several reasons. First, it helps to give a clearer picture of the relative stages of development of American and Soviet nuclear weapons. In the mid-1950s the Soviet Union lagged at least three years behind the United States in the development of high-yield weapons. Second, it shows how American and Soviet actions helped to stimulate each other's nuclear weapons development. Yet the actions that were salient on one side were not necessarily so on the other. American accounts of the period highlight the Soviet atomic bomb test of August 1949 and Truman's announcement of January 31, 1950. But Soviet accounts (such as they are) suggest that the Truman announcement was not as important to their own decisions as the early reports of American work on thermonuclear weapons and the American thermonuclear test of October 1952. Third, Soviet decisions show elements both of reaction to American actions and of an internal dynamic. The early thermonuclear studies were initiated in response to reports of American work. The development of a thermonuclear bomb began after the first atomic bomb test and was not, as far as one can tell, directly triggered by American actions. The development of the superbomb was stimulated by the American test of October 1952.

Herbert York is surely right to argue that American national security would not have been harmed if the development of the superbomb had been delayed. The Soviet Union would not have been able to gain a lead in nuclear weapons technology, for the United States would have had time to respond to a continuing Soviet program. Had restraint been practised, the opportunity might conceivably have emerged after Stalin's death for political moves to restrain Soviet-American nuclear arms competition. In the event, the competition in nuclear arms continued unabated.

From August 1945 Stalin faced a dual problem: to build a Soviet bomb as quickly as possible, and to deprive the United States of any military or political advantage from its atomic monopoly. The first part of this problem was solved by launching the new research and development programs. The second was tackled by providing a counterweight to American air power. Soviet forces in Eastern Europe were the main element in this policy. American bombers could threaten Soviet cities and industrial centers, but Soviet forces could not strike the United States. Consequently the Soviet Army was deployed in Eastern Europe not only to safeguard Soviet interests there, but also to strike Western Europe in the event of war. (Soviet forces were certainly not strong enough for Stalin to contemplate an invasion out of the blue.) Conventional weapons were modernized and air defences strengthened.[19]

Stalin took pains to play down the significance of nuclear weapons. In September 1946, for example, he said: "I do not consider the atomic bomb as serious a force as some politicians are inclined to do. Atomic bombs are meant to frighten those with weak nerves, but they cannot decide the fate of wars since atomic bombs are quite insufficient for that."[20] The effort the Soviet Union was making to develop the atomic bomb makes it clear that Stalin did in fact attribute great importance to nuclear weapons. Such statements were designed to weaken any American attempt to use its atomic monopoly to put pressure on the Soviet Union, and also to prevent Soviet troops, who would have to fight without nuclear weapons, from being intimidated by the threat of nuclear war.

Stalin may well have thought that, important though the atomic bomb was, it would not change the character of warfare. He launched major programs to develop the atomic bomb and other modern weapons, but he did not permit any thought to be given to their effect on the conduct of war. Weapons development and military doctrine existed in separate worlds: the former was pushed at a rapid pace, the latter was stifled.[21] By 1952 there were some signs that the implications of nuclear weapons were being reconsidered, but it was not until after Stalin's death in March 1953 that a full reassessment of military thought began.

NOTES

From David Holloway, *The Soviet Union and the Arms Race* (2nd edn, New Haven, CT: Yale University Press, 1984), Chap. 2. Copyright © 1984 by Yale University Press. Reprinted and abridged by permission of the publisher.

1 On Bohr's activities see Margaret Gowing, *Britain and Atomic Energy* (London: Macmillan, 1964), 347–66 and Martin J. Sherwin, *A World Destroyed: The Atomic Bomb and the Grand Alliance* (New York: Vintage Books, 1977), 91–8.
2 Harry S. Truman, *Memoirs*, Vol. 1: *1945: Year of Decisions* (New York: Doubleday, 1965), 458.
3 Quoted by Herbert York, in *The Advisors: Oppenheimer, Teller and the Bomb* (San Francisco: W. H. Freeman, 1976), 29. Unless otherwise noted, the material in this section is taken from David Holloway,

"Entering the Nuclear Arms Race: The Soviet Decision to Build the Atomic Bomb, 1939–45," *Social Studies of Science*, 11 (1981): 159–97.
4 A. I. Ioriysh, I. D. Morokhov and S. K. Ivanov, *A-Bomba* (Moscow: Nauka, 1980), 377.
5 Yu. V. Sivintsev, *I. V. Kurchatov i yadernaya energetika* (Moscow: Atomizdat, 1980), 11.
6 Ioriysh *et al.*, *A-Bomba*, 390.
7 Alexander Werth, *Russia at War 1941–1945* (London: Pan Books, 1965), 925.
8 *Foreign Relations of the United States, 1945* (Washington, DC: Department of State, 1967), Vol. 2: 83.
9 *Foreign Relations of the United States, 1945* (Washington, DC: Department of State, 1967), Vol. 5: 923.
10 Quoted by A. Lavrent'yeva in "Stroiteli novogo mira," *V mire knig*, no. 9 (1970): 4.
11 Margaret Gowing, *Science and Politics*, the Eighth J. D. Bernal Lecture (Birkbeck College, London, 1977), 11.
12 See David Holloway, "Innovation in the Defence Sector: Two Case Studies", in R. Amann and J. Cooper (eds), *Industrial Innovation in the Soviet Union* (New Haven, CT: Yale University Press, 1982), 390–1; the figure for the proportion of research done in prison institutes is taken from Roy A. Medvedev and Zhores A. Medvedev, *Khrushchev. The Years in Power* (New York: Columbia University Press, 1976), 38.
13 A. P. Romanov, *Raketam pokoryaetsya prostranstvo* (Moscow: Politizdat, 1976), 51; G. A. Tokaev, *Comrade X* (London: Harvill Press, 1956), 310–30. Romanov confirms Tokaev's report that meetings were held then, though he does not discuss, as Tokaev does, what was decided.
14 Antony C. Sutton, *Western Technology and Soviet Economic Development 1945 to 1965* (Stanford, CA: Hoover Institution Press, 1973), Chaps 2, 20, 21.
15 See Frederick I. Ordway III and Mitchell R. Sharpe, *The Rocket Team* (New York: Thomas Y. Crowell, 1979), Chaps 13, 14 and 17.
16 N. A. Pilyugin, interview in *Pravda*, May 17, 1978; P. A. Agadzhanov, in *S. P. Korolev. Sbornik statei* (Moscow: Znanje, 1977), 20.
17 David Holloway, "Soviet Thermonuclear Research," *International Security*, 4(3) (Winter 1979/80): 192–7.
18 I. N. Golovin, *I. V. Kurchatov* (3rd edn, Moscow: Atomizdat, 1978), 94.
19 *Sovetskie Vooruzhennye Sily. Istoriya stroitel'stva* (Moscow: Voenizdat, 1978), 384–7, 391–6. Matthew A. Evangelista, "Stalin's Postwar Army Reappraised," unpublished manuscript, Peace Studies Program, Cornell University, 1982.
20 *Pravda*, September 25, 1946.
21 Maj-Gen. S. Kozlov, "The Development of Soviet Military Science after World War Two," *Voennaya Mysl'*, 2 (1964): 33–5.

5

AMERICAN POLICY AND THE SHIFTING NUCLEAR BALANCE

Marc Trachtenberg

Historians have spent a lot of time studying the short-term diplomatic implications of using atomic weapons against Japan. They have spent less time exploring the subsequent relationship between strategy and diplomacy. The declassification of documents pertaining to atomic weaponry has been relatively slow, but since the late 1970s some scholars like David Alan Rosenberg have done a remarkable job outlining the trajectory of American strategic programs and examining the buildup of the atomic arsenal.* But they have not really considered the extent to which strategic and budgetary decisions were related to foreign policy goals or the extent to which perceptions of the military and strategic balance actually affected the conduct of diplomacy.

In this essay Marc Trachtenberg takes a fresh look at American strategic planning and shows the degree to which preemptive thinking lurked in the minds of many US military and some civilian officials. He reevaluates National Security Council Paper no. 68, the most famous statement of American aims and options during the early Cold War. In so doing, he casts the containment policy in new light and suggests an offensive dimension to US diplomacy that not all historians would agree with. But still more importantly, Trachtenberg argues that US policymakers like Dean Acheson and Paul Nitze believed that they needed to possess strategic superiority in order to carry out their diplomatic offensive. This could not be done so long as they entertained a sense of their own military inferiority, catalyzed by the Soviet atomic explosion

---

* David Alan Rosenberg, "American Atomic Strategy and the Hydrogen Bomb Decision," *Journal of American History*, 66 (June 1979): 62–87; Rosenberg, "The Origins of Overkill: Nuclear Weapons and American Strategy, 1945–1960," *International Security*, 7 (Spring 1983): 3–71.

in August 1949, which, combined with Soviet conventional strength, seemed to reconfigure the prevailing balance of power in Moscow's favor. Trachtenberg argues that the immense American strategic build-up undertaken during the Korean War was aimed at regaining the diplomatic offensive. He maintains that once the Americans regained confidence in their own superiority, they were inclined to take the diplomatic offensive on many issues both related to and unrelated to the ongoing Korean conflict.

Trachtenberg's essay opens exciting new avenues of research. Scholars must examine the complex relationships between military capabilities, threat perception, and foreign policy goals. Strategic relationships cast shadows that had powerful influences on how policy-makers defined risks and opportunities and on how they conducted their diplomacy with both friends and foes. Readers should discuss these relationships and analyze how they affected US diplomacy prior to, during, and after the Korean War.

* * *

In January 1946, General Leslie Groves, the wartime commander of the Manhattan Project, prepared a memorandum on the military implications of the atomic bomb. "If we were ruthlessly realistic," he wrote, "we would not permit any foreign power with which we are not firmly allied, and in which we do not have absolute confidence, to make or possess atomic weapons. If such a country started to make atomic weapons we would destroy its capacity to make them before it had progressed far enough to threaten us."[1]

In the late 1940s and well into the early 1950s, the basic idea that the United States should not just sit back and allow a hostile power like the Soviet Union to acquire a massive nuclear arsenal – that a much more "active" and more "positive" policy had to be seriously considered – was surprisingly widespread. The American government, of course, never came close to implementing a preventive war strategy. As far as the public as a whole was concerned, the idea seems to have had only a limited appeal.[2] What ran deep, however, was a tremendous sense of foreboding. If the Soviets were allowed to develop nuclear forces of their own, there was no telling what might happen. If they were so hostile and aggressive even in the period of America's nuclear monopoly, what would they be like once this monopoly had been broken? There was no reason to assume that a nuclear world would be stable; wouldn't the Soviets some day try to destroy the one power that prevented them from achieving their goals by launching a nuclear attack on the United States? The clouds of danger were gathering on the horizon. Was the West, through its passivity, simply drifting toward disaster? Wasn't some sort of more "positive" policy worth considering?

The basic goal here is to study how people dealt with these problems – how they came to terms with the dramatic shifts in the military balance and the extraordinary changes in the overall military environment that were taking place in the first decade of the nuclear age. The nuclear revolution, the loss of the American atomic monopoly, and the coming of thermonuclear weapons in the early 1950s were all of enormous importance to the formation of American policy. It had been clear from the very beginning of the nuclear age that America's nuclear monopoly, even its nuclear superiority, was inevitably a "wasting asset."[3] But what did this imply in terms of foreign and military policy?

Most of the analysis here will focus on the purely historical problem of how this set of concerns worked its way through the political system. But two important points emerge from re-examination of this period. The first has to do with the role of trends in the military balance. Concerns about the way the balance was changing – about the expected opening and closing of "windows of vulnerability" – carried a good deal of political weight; indeed, they turned out to be far more important than I ever would have imagined.[4] The whole concept of "windows," it became clear, was not simply an abstract, academic construct, artificially imposed on historical reality. Although the term itself was not used at the time, one is struck by how real the "window" concept was; its impact on actual policy was both enormous and pervasive. In particular, concerns about anticipated shifts in the military balance played a critical role in shaping not only grand strategy, but also policy on specific issues, especially during the Korean War. The reluctance to escalate during the winter of 1950–1 was due to a sense among "insiders" familiar with the true state of the military balance that a window of vulnerability had opened up, and that the Soviets might be tempted to strike before the United States was able to close it. It followed that this was not the time to run risks. By 1953 the situation had altered dramatically as a result of the extraordinary buildup of American military power then taking place; this shift in the balance led to a greatly increased willingness to escalate in Korea if the war could not be ended on acceptable terms. America's window of vulnerability had been shut; and a window of opportunity opened. A key question during the early Eisenhower period, therefore, was whether this new situation could be exploited before it too disappeared.

The second major point to emerge from the study is that aggressive ideas were taken very seriously in the American government in the early 1950s, even at the highest levels of the administration. This aggressive mood was in part rooted in concerns about the shifting military balance. This is not to say that an aggressive policy was ever implemented. The real question is not whether such a policy was ever adopted, but what sort of political weight this kind of thinking carried.

The sort of argument that General Groves made in 1946 was quite common in the early atomic age. The idea that the United States had to take some sort of action before its nuclear edge was neutralized was by no means limited to the lunatic fringe. William L. Laurence, for example, the science correspondent for the *New York Times* and then America's leading writer on nuclear issues, wanted to force the Soviets in 1948 to accept nuclear disarmament, through an ultimatum if necessary. If they turned down this American demand, their atomic plants should be destroyed before bombs could be produced. If that meant war, he said, it would be one forced on America by Soviet "insistence on an atomic-armament race which must inevitably lead to war anyway. Under the circumstances, it would be to our advantage to have it while we are still the sole possessors of the atomic bomb."[5]

This argument for a more "positive" policy was a favorite theme of a number of scientists and intellectuals. Bertrand Russell had advocated a Laurence-style ultimatum in 1946.[6] By 1948, he was calling for preventive war pure and simple.[7] The famous physicist Leo Szilard had evidently argued for preventive war at the very beginning of the atomic age: it was "from the lips of Leo Szilard," Bernard Brodie wrote, that he had "heard, in October of 1945, the first outright advocacy in [his] experience of preventive war."[8]

Preventive war was a very live issue among the civilian strategists at the RAND Corporation well into the early 1950s, and there is some evidence that the navy was interested in the question in 1948.[9] At the State Department, even moderates like Charles Bohlen and George Kennan were worried about what would happen if matters were allowed to drift and the Soviets began to build large nuclear forces of their own.[10]

The real heart of preventive war thinking at this time, however, lay within the US Air Force. The preventive war policy was, as Brodie pointed out in 1953, "for several years certainly the prevailing philosophy at the Air War College."[11] General Orvil Anderson, the commanding officer at that institution, had in fact "been in the habit of giving students at the college a completely detailed exposition, often lasting three or four hours, on how a preventive war through strategic airpower could be carried out." "Give me the order to do it," he said, "and I can break up Russia's five A-bomb nests in a week. . . . And when I went up to Christ – I think I could explain to Him that I had saved civilization."[12]

The most important government officials at the time, however, were quite hostile to the "preventive war" thesis. But this is not to say that they were not concerned with the problems that would result from the ending of America's nuclear monopoly. The Soviet explosion of an atomic device in late 1949, in fact, led to a major rethinking of American strategy. NSC 68, the basic document here, was written mainly by Paul Nitze, Kennan's successor as head of the State Department's Policy Planning Staff. The report also reflected the views of Secretary of State Dean Acheson, its chief defender in high government circles; it can in fact be seen as a kind of fleshing-out of the Acheson strategy of creating "situations of strength."[13] Contrary to what is commonly believed, the strategy called for in NSC 68 was *not* essentially defensive in nature, and the aggressive thrust of the document was probably linked to concerns about long-term trends in the strategic balance. Indeed, it turns out that window thinking had an important impact on American grand strategy, especially in the period after the outbreak of the Korean War.

The authors of NSC 68 believed that America's atomic

monopoly was the one thing that had balanced Soviet superiority in ground forces; they were concerned, therefore, that with growing Soviet atomic capabilities, America's nuclear edge was being neutralized more rapidly than conventional forces could be created to fill the gap: hence the sense of a danger zone. But they did not believe that, once American ground forces had been built up and an overall balance had been restored, that would be the end of the problem: they did not believe that the threat of retaliation would be an adequate deterrent to nuclear attack. The Soviets, it was predicted, would be able to deliver a hundred atomic bombs on target by 1954. This did not mean that the Soviets could wipe out American industry as such, for this was still the early atomic age, but they could destroy America's "*superiority* in economic potential." The Soviets could thus prevent the United States from "developing a general military superiority in a war of long duration." Even if they had to absorb an American retaliatory attack, it was "hardly conceivable that, if war comes, the Soviet leaders would refrain from the use of atomic weapons unless they felt fully confident of attaining their objectives by other means."[14] In fact, as a Policy Planning Staff paper emphasized in mid-1952, NSC 68 did not hold that "the existence of two large atomic stockpiles" would result in a nuclear stand-off, but instead had predicted that it might well "prove to be an incitement to war."[15]

Because of the advantages of getting in the first blow, there would be a constant danger of surprise attack: the incentive to preempt would be a permanent source of instability. The need, therefore, was not simply to cover a gap; the concern was not limited to the next four or so years. The real problem was more far-reaching, but what could be done about it?

NSC 68 explicitly ruled out a strategy of preventive war, in the sense of an unprovoked surprise attack on the Soviet Union.[16] But a number of the document's key points echoed the standard preventive war arguments: the developing situation was not stable, the country was moving into a period of enormous danger, and this situation could not last indefinitely. Nitze and Acheson took it for granted that America was dealing not with an ordinary adversary, but with a ruthless enemy intent on world domination, and ultimately on the destruction of the United States.[17]

The most important point about NSC 68 is that this was *not* a defensive-minded, status quo-oriented document.[18] For Acheson and Nitze, the fundamental aim of American policy was quite ambitious: to bring about a "retraction" of Soviet power – to force the Soviets to "recede" by creating "situations of strength."[19] The policy of NSC 68 was, in its own terms, a "policy of calculated and gradual coercion"; the aim was "to check and to roll back the Kremlin's drive for world domination." To support such a policy, it was important to go beyond merely balancing Soviet power, and to build up "clearly superior overall power in its most inclusive sense."[20]

This is not to argue that NSC 68 had a hidden agenda and that the real goal of the aggressive strategy was to generate situations that might lead to a war before America's nuclear advantage was lost forever. It is clear, in fact, that neither Nitze nor Acheson actually wanted a war, above all, not in 1950. What they wanted was to create such overwhelming power that the United States could achieve its goals without actually having to fight. But such a military strategy was extremely ambitious. As Nitze put it in mid-1952, it would take "clearly preponderant power" to make progress by peaceful means, "probably more power than to win military victory in the event of war."[21]

At the end of the Truman administration, Nitze would complain that even the extraordinary buildup of military power that had taken place during the Korean War had been inadequate. The defense budget might have tripled, but the "situations of strength" that national policy had called for had never been created. In January 1953, he worried that the United States was becoming "a sort of hedge-hog, unattractive to attack, but basically not very worrisome over a period of time beyond our immediate position"; Nitze was upset that the goals laid out in documents like NSC 68 were not being taken "sufficiently seriously as to warrant doing what is necessary to give us some chance of seeing these objectives attained."[22]

A war itself was never desired, but it does seem clear that Nitze was willing to accept a real risk of a nuclear conflict, but only *after* the trends had been reversed and American power had been rebuilt. For the time being, he wrote in 1950, the United States was weak and needed above all "to build a platform from which we can subsequently go on to a successful outcome of this life-and-death struggle" with the Kremlin. "We must," he stressed, "avoid becoming involved in general hostilities with the USSR in our present position of military weakness if this is at all possible without sacrificing our self-respect and without endangering our survival."[23] But then? The clear implication is that when "our position of weakness" turns into a "position of strength," it would become less necessary to tread cautiously.[24]

In the meantime, however, the country was going to have to cross a danger zone. With the outbreak of the Korean War and the rearmament decisions that were made in its wake, the argument was extended to take note of another danger: the risk that the Soviets might strike preemptively, in order to head off the shift in the balance of military power that American rearmament would bring about. The assumption was that a "window" favoring the Soviets had opened, and that the American attempt to close it might well lead to a war.[25]

The sense that a great window of vulnerability had opened up helps explain why the US government as a whole, and especially those officials who really understood military matters, were so afraid of general war in late 1950 and 1951: for the time being, the military balance favored the Soviets, who might therefore soon choose to precipitate a war with the West. For the same reason, the West had to move with great caution during this period. Indeed, these assumptions had begun to take shape in early 1950, even before the outbreak of the Korean War. It had been predicted that the shift in the balance resulting from the ending of the American nuclear monopoly would embolden the Soviets and lead to an increase in Communist aggressiveness.[26] The events in Korea seemed to confirm this prophecy, and thus to vindicate this whole way of viewing things; a good part of the reason the Korean War had such an extraordinary impact on American policy in this period is that the ground had been prepared in this way. Indeed, what the Korean War seemed to show was that the situation was even more serious than NSC 68 had assumed. The fact that the Soviets had been willing to accept the risk of war with America – first, in approving the North Korean attack, and then in supporting China' intervention in the war – showed how strong they thought their position now was, and thus how far they might now be prepared to go, not just in the Far East, but in Europe as well.[27]

It followed that the central goal of diplomacy, as Bohlen put it in 1951, was to steer the country through the danger zone: "It is axiomatic that when one group of powers seeks to close a dangerous disparity in its armed strength in relation to another group of powers, a period of danger by that factor alone is to be anticipated. The diplomatic arm of the United States should be utilized in this period in such a fashion as to minimize rather than intensify the danger of a general war resulting from a Soviet response to what they might regard as an increasing threat to their existence."[28]

It was, therefore, important to be discreet about America's real long-term aims. There was a great danger, according to a 1952 Policy Planning Staff paper, that if the Soviets thought war was unavoidable, they might initiate a war that would push the United States "back to the Western hemisphere" and allow them to take over the vast resources of Eurasia. To achieve this goal, which would put them in a commanding position for the final phases of the world struggle, they might even be willing to absorb "whatever damage we can inflict" through atomic bombardment. It was thus important at present to avoid giving them the impression that war was inevitable. Talk of rollback was ill-advised at a time when a period of stability was needed to enable the West to develop its power, and in particular to build up its forces in Europe. It followed that public pronouncements for the time being had to be strictly defensive in tone. "It seems dangerous," the paper argued, "to adopt the political posture that we must roll back the Iron Curtain" at a time when the West was not yet able to defend even the present line of demarcation.[29]

So the United States embarked upon an extraordinary buildup of military strength, which acted like an acid, gradually eating away at all those constraints that had kept the United States from escalating at the end of 1950 and in early 1951. The key to the history of the Korean War, in fact, is America's increasing willingness to escalate the conflict. This shift took place in two phases. First, in 1951, it gradually became clear that the government's worst fears about Soviet aggressiveness had been exaggerated: East Germany did not invade the Federal Republic, there was no new Berlin Crisis, Yugoslavia was not attacked, Soviet forces did not move into Iran.[30] As fears of a great risk of war with the Soviets began to fade, the American government felt somewhat freer to act in the Far East.

The second and more dramatic phase began with the

resurgence of American military power in late 1952 and 1953. This led to a much greater willingness to escalate, if that was needed to bring the Korean conflict to a successful conclusion. The decisions of the Eisenhower period, with regard both to the war in Korea and to global strategy as a whole, have to be understood as the climax of a process begun years before in the Truman administration.

The American military buildup was particularly dramatic in the nuclear weapons area. Since 1950, there had been a great expansion in the production of fissionable material, and there had been very important qualitative changes as well, especially with regard to tactical nuclear weapons.[31] By early 1952, the Atomic Energy Commission had developed atomic bombs small and light enough to be used by "such fighter aircraft as the F-84 and some Navy carrier planes." As a result, "between May 1951 and July 1953 the Air Force moved rapidly to build a tactical atomic force."[32] By 1952, "techniques and procedures" for the use of atomic weapons on the battlefield had been worked out.[33] At about the same time, the stockpile of bombs had become so large that, from the point of view of the Joint Chiefs of Staff [JCS], scarcity no longer carried any weight as an argument against the use of nuclear weapons in Korea.[34]

The shift in the military balance between 1950 and 1953 had a major impact on American policy not just in Korea but elsewhere around the globe. There was a striking change in US policy on Berlin in this period. In the policy documents on Berlin from the end of the blockade through early 1951, caution had been the keynote: if the blockade were reimposed, there should be no "probe"; the JCS thought the Western powers were too weak to undertake a ground action of this sort.[35]

By the spring of 1952, however, high officials had already begun to rethink American policy on the use of force in any new Berlin crisis: "We were opposed to it before," General Bradley said on May 14, "but it should be reconsidered now."[36] And in fact, by mid-1952, the US line on Berlin had completely swung around to a much tougher position: in NSC 132/1 of June 12, 1952, a military probe was accepted, and it was now taken for granted that an attack on Berlin would almost certainly lead to general war. The American position on Berlin became even tougher during the early Eisenhower period; and the JCS documents make it clear that it was, at least from their point of view,

116

the improved military situation that had made possible this dramatic shift of policy.[37]

There was a parallel shift in American policy on Indochina during this period. In 1950, the military felt that the United States was too weak to risk escalation of the conflict even if the Chinese intervened in force in the area; by 1952, the American strategy for the defense of Indochina was based on the idea that if the Chinese moved in, the Western powers would have to widen the war and attack China itself.[38]

This examination of the effect of the shifting balance on American foreign and military policy is important because of the light it sheds on the way nuclear forces influence political behavior. It was the overall strategic balance that was crucial, not specific, isolated gestures like particular deployments of nuclear-capable bombers at various points in time. What counted was the actual willingness to escalate, rather than overt threats or ultimata, which the United States government was in fact anxious to avoid.[39]

NOTES

From Marc Trachtenberg, "A 'Wasting Asset': American Strategy and the Shifting Nuclear Balance, 1949–1954," *International Security*, 13 (Winter 1988–9): 5–49. Copyright © 1989. Reprinted and abridged by permission of the author and MIT Press.

1 General Leslie Groves, "Statement on the atomic bomb and its effect on the Army," app. to Joint Chiefs of Staff [JCS] 1477/6, January 21, 1946, in Combined Chiefs of Staff [CCS] 471.6 (8–15–45), sec. 2, Record Group [RG] 218, United States National Archives [USNA], Washington, DC. There is a slightly different version, dated January 2, 1946, in *Foreign Relations of the United States* [hereafter *FRUS*], *1946* (Washington, DC: Department of State, 1972), Vol. 1: 1197–203. Eisenhower, who thought Groves's views were "perhaps extreme in some respects," nevertheless had a high regard for the paper as a whole. See Louis Galambos (ed.), *The Papers of Dwight David Eisenhower*, 9 vols (Baltimore, MD, 1970–8), Vol. 7: 760–1, 641–2, n. 7. See also James F. Schnabel, *The History of the Joint Chiefs of Staff: The Joint Chiefs of Staff and National Policy*, Vol. 1: *1945–1947* (Washington, DC: US Government Printing Office [US GPO], 1979), 281–2.

2 Hazel Gaudet Erskine, "The Polls: Atomic Weapons and Nuclear Energy," *Public Opinion Quarterly*, 27 (1963): 177; George Gallup, *The Gallup Poll: Public Opinion 1935–1971* (New York: Random House, 1972), Vol. 1: 930.

3 The term "wasting asset" was quite common at the time. See, for example, Schnabel, *History of the Joint Chiefs of Staff*, Vol. 1: 258–9.

4 For a discussion of some of the theoretical issues relating to this question, see especially Stephen Van Evera, "Causes of War" (PhD dissertation, University of California at Berkeley, 1984). Chap. 2, and pp. 89–94, 330–9; see also Jack Levy, "Declining Power and the Preventive Motivation for War," *World Politics*, 40(1) (October 1987): 82–107.

5 William L. Laurence, "How Soon Will Russia Have the A-Bomb?", *Saturday Evening Post*, November 6, 1948: 182.

6 See Bertrand Russell's statement in the *Bulletin of the Atomic Scientists*, 2 (7–8) (October 1946): 19–21.

7 See the report of Bertrand Russell's speech of November 20, 1948, at the New Commonwealth School, London, in the *New York Times*, November 21, 1948: 4.

8 Bernard Brodie's recollection is in Brodie to Thomas Schelling, January 8, 1965, enclosure, Brodie Papers, box 2, University of California at Los Angeles [UCLA] Library.

9 The mathematician John Williams, then one of the leading figures at RAND, was the principal champion there of a preventive war strategy. He and Brodie had a very interesting memorandum debate on the issue in 1953 and 1954. See John Williams, "In Response to Paxson's Memo on the Probability of War," February 3, 1953, and "Regarding the Preventive War Doctrine," July 27, 1953, unpublished RAND papers. The memoranda that Brodie, Williams, and others exchanged on the question are in the folder "Strategic Objectives Committee," in James Digby's personal files at RAND; I am grateful to Mr Digby for allowing me to consult them. On navy interest in the idea, see the "Agenda for [Navy] General Board Serial 315. Study of Nature of Warfare within Next Ten Years and Navy Contributions in Support of National Security," March 30, 1948, CD 23–1–10, RG 330, 1947–50 series, USNA, especially question 119. The study itself, evidently written by the future Chief of Naval Operations [CNO] Arleigh Burke, is apparently still classified.

10 Record of the Under-Secretary's Meeting, April 15, 1949, *FRUS, 1949* (Washington, DC: Department of State, 1976), Vol. 1: 284; "Memorandum of National Security Council Consultants' Meeting," June 29, 1950, *FRUS, 1950* (Washington, DC: Department of State, 1977), Vol. 1: 330.

11 Bernard Brodie, "A Commentary on the Preventive-War Doctrine," RAND paper, June 11, 1953, 1. See also his Air War College talk of April 17, 1952, "Changing Capabilities and National Objectives," Brodie Papers, box 12, UCLA, 23 ff.; both in Marc Trachtenberg (ed.), *The Development of American Strategic Thought* (New York: Garland, 1988), Vol. 3.

12 *The New York Times*, September 2, 1950: 8. also the August 1953 air force study "The Coming National Crisis," discussed in David Alan Rosenberg, "The Origins of Overkill: Nuclear Weapons and American Strategy, 1945–1960," *International Security*, 7(4) (Spring

1983): 33. This study, Rosenberg says, argued that "the time was approaching when the U.S. would find itself in a 'militarily unmanageable' position. Before that time arrived, the nation would have to choose whether to trust its future to 'the whims of a small group of proven barbarians' in the USSR, or 'be militarily prepared to support such decisions as might involve general war.'"

13 See, for example, Dean Acheson's "total diplomacy" speech of February 16, 1950, *Department of State Bulletin* (March 20, 1950).

14 National Security Council [NSC] 68, April 7, 1950, *FRUS, 1950*, Vol. 1: 251, 266, 268; emphasis added. See also a Policy Planning Staff paper written in mid-1952, *FRUS, 1952–54* (Washington, DC: Department of State, 1984), Vol. 2: 62, para. 9.

15 Enclosure in Paul Nitze to H. Freeman Matthews, July 14, 1952, *FRUS, 1952–54*, Vol. 2: 62. These were all very controversial issues within the government, especially in 1950. Nitze himself had earlier leaned toward the line that nuclear forces tended to neutralize each other (*FRUS, 1950*, Vol. 1: 14), and it is not clear to what extent NSC 68 marked a genuine shift in opinion on his part, as opposed to an accommodation to those, especially in the military, who took the opposite line. For a fascinating inside account of these disputes, see Harvey to Armstrong, June 23, 1950, Records of the Policy Planning Staff, box 7, folder "Atomic Energy – Armaments 1950," RG 59, USNA. For the views of the military, see Joint Intelligence Committee [JIC] 502, January 20, 1950, CCS 471.6 USSR (11–8–49), "Implications of Soviet Success in Achieving Atomic Capability," sec. 1, in RG 218, USNA; this document was their contribution to the process that culminated in NSC 68. For a Central Intelligence Agency [CIA] contribution, see ORE 91–49, February 10, 1950, file CD 11–1–2, box 61, RG 330 (1947–50 series), USNA.

16 *FRUS, 1950*, Vol. 1: 281–2.

17 *FRUS, 1950*, Vol. 1: 207–8, 145.

18 The large literature on the subject assumes that NSC 68 called for an essentially defensive policy. The early account by Paul Hammond, "NSC-68: Prologue to Rearmament," in Warner Schilling, Paul Hammond, and Glenn Snyder, *Strategy, Politics, and Defense Budgets* (New York: Columbia University Press, 1962), was written before the text of the document became available. The more recent literature is therefore more interesting in this connection. See in particular Samuel F. Wells, Jr, "Sounding the Tocsin: NSC 68 and the Soviet Threat," *International Security*, 4(2) (Fall 1979): 116–58; and Steven Rearden, *The Evolution of American Strategic Doctrine: Paul Nitze and the Soviet Challenge* (Boulder, CO: Westview, 1984), esp. 22–6.

19 For Acheson, see Memorandum of Conversation, March 24, 1950, *FRUS, 1950*, Vol. 1: 208. The term "retraction" appears in many documents from this period. See especially NSC 68, April 7, 1950, *FRUS, 1950*, Vol. 1: 252, 289. Note also a Nitze memorandum of July 14, 1952, in *FRUS, 1952–54*, Vol. 2: 58–9.

20 *FRUS, 1950*, Vol. 1: 253, 255, 284. Note also the reference to the

hydrogen bomb in ibid., 267: "If the U.S. develops a thermonuclear weapon ahead of the U.S.S.R., the U.S. should for the time being be able to bring increased pressure on the U.S.S.R."

21 Paul Nitze to H. F. Matthews, July 14, 1952, *FRUS, 1952–54*, Vol. 2: 59.

22 Nitze to Dean Acheson, January 12, 1953, *FRUS, 1952–54*, Vol. 2: 205.

23 *FRUS, 1950*, Vol. 1: 464.

24 Note also in this context Acheson's complaints in May and June 1953 about the "weakness" of the Eisenhower policy, and the new administration's failure to follow through on Truman's policy of "building strength." Acheson to Truman, May 28, 1953, box 30, folder 391, and Acheson Memorandum of Conversation, June 23, 1953, box 68, folder 172, both in the Dean Acheson Papers, Sterling Library, Yale University, New Haven, CT.

25 See *FRUS, 1951* (Washington, DC: Department of State, 1979), Vol. 1: 40, 111, 126, 131, 153, 198–9, for various documents with similar "window" themes. Note also an interesting variation in an NSC staff document of August 12, 1952, *FRUS, 1952–54*, Vol. 2: 74, para. 3: this was a "bringing matters to a head" argument in reverse.

26 For a typical example of such a prediction prior to the outbreak of the Korean War, see the Policy Planning Staff paper, "The Current Position in the Cold War," April 14, 1950, *FRUS, 1950* (Washington, DC: Department of State, 1977), Vol. 3: esp. 858–9; note also Nitze's comments in *FRUS, 1950*, Vol. 1: 143.

27 See Acheson's remarks in the special NSC meeting held on November 28, 1950, especially the passage summarized on p. 15 of Elsey's notes of this meeting; Elsey Papers, box 72, "Korea. National Security Council Meeting, 3:00 p.m., November 28, 1950," Harry S. Truman Presidential Library [hereafter HSTL], Independence, MO. "Time is shorter than we thought, Mr. Acheson said. We used to think we could take our time up to 1952, but if we were right in that, the Russians wouldn't be taking such terrible risks as they are now." Note also NIE [National Intelligence Estimate]-15, "Probable Soviet Moves to Exploit the Present Situation," December 11, 1950, President's secretary's files [PSF], box 253, HSTL, especially the first paragraph in this document. There were in fact important indications from intelligence sources of a general increase in Soviet aggressiveness and preparations for war. See the memorandum of an intelligence briefing requested by the Secretary of Defense on "Soviet Activity in Europe During the Past Year Which Points Toward Offensive Military Operations," October 26, 1950, CD 350.09, RG 330 (July–December 1950 series), USNA.

28 Bohlen memorandum, September 21, 1951, *FRUS, 1951*, Vol. 1: 172.

29 Policy Planning Staff paper, n.d., *FRUS, 1952–54*, Vol. 2: 67–8.

30 These fears are reflected in many documents from the early Korean War period. See, for example, "Meeting of the NSC in the Cabinet Room of the White House," June 28, 1950, Acheson Papers, box 65, "Memoranda of Conversation, May–June 1950," HSTL; and especially NIE-15, "Probable Soviet Moves to Exploit the Present Situation," December 11, 1950, PSF, box 253, HSTL.

31 See Rosenberg, "The Origins of Overkill," esp. 23–4, and the sources cited there.

32 George F. Lemmer, "The Air Force and Strategic Deterrence, 1951–1960," 14–15. A sanitized, declassified version is available at the Office of Air Force History, Bolling Air Force Base, Washington, DC.

33 Richard Rowe, "American Nuclear Strategy and the Korean War," (MA thesis, University of Pennsylvania, 1984), 61–4. The tactics and operational techniques were developed partly through tests conducted in Korea in October and November 1951 involving "actual atomic bombs, less nuclear components," ibid., 62.

34 ibid., 64. Note also Nitze's comments in a memo to Acheson of January 12, 1952, FRUS, 1952–54. Vol. 2: 204.

35 See especially NSC 24/3, "Possible U.S. Courses of Action in the Event the USSR Reimposes the Berlin Blockade," June 14, 1949, Documents of the National Security Council [hereafter DNSC], University Publications of America, reel 1; Marshall to Lay, October 18, 1950, in NSC 89, FRUS, 1950 (Washington, DC: Department of State, 1980), Vol. 4: 893–4; JCS 1907/62, January 24, 1951, "Records of the Joint Chiefs of Staff," University Publications of America microfilm publication (1979), part II (1946–53), sec. G, reel 5, frame 418FF (henceforth cited as RJCS sec./reel/frame). This last document was the basis for the official JCS memorandum to Secretary of Defense George Marshall, February 7, 1951, FRUS, 1951 (Washington, DC: Department of State, 1981), Vol. 3: 1892 ff.

36 FRUS, 1952–54, (Washington, DC: Department of State, 1986), Vol. 7: 1241.

37 The basic document on Berlin for the late Truman period was NSC 132/1 of June 12, 1952 (FRUS, 1952–54, Vol. 7: 1261 ff.), much of which was evidently carried over into NSC 5404/2, the key Berlin policy document for the early Eisenhower period. This latter document has not been declassified, but one can learn a good deal about it from the Operations Coordinating Board Progress Reports on it of January 7, 1955 and May 17, 1956, DNSC, Supplement 2, reel 1, and Supplement 4, reel 1, respectively. For the military view that the shift in the balance had made all this possible, see the Joint Strategic Survey Committee [JSSC] report on NSC 173, JCS 1907/101 of December 5, 1953, in RJCS/II/G/5/909 ff.

38 See "The History of the Joint Chiefs of Staff. The Joint Chiefs of Staff and the War in Vietnam. History of the Indochina Incident, 1940–1954," JCS Historical Division, 1971, Military Records Branch, USNA, 190, 194–8, 225, 241–58, 294–5, 388, 453–4. A number of the documents summarized here have been published in FRUS and in the Pentagon Papers, but some of the most important ones are still classified.

39 As early as November 1950, Bedell Smith, then CIA director, argued against laying down an ultimatum, and spoke instead of "quiet exploration with implied threats." Memorandum for the President, November 10, 1950, Minutes of the National Security Council,

reel 1. Smith, one of Eisenhower's closest associates from the Second World War, became Under-Secretary of State in 1953. He soon took a hand in a diplomatic initiative aimed at getting the Soviets to help bring about a Korean armistice. Once again, the theme is avoidance of the appearance of "a threat or ultimatum" and just setting forth a "simple statement of facts" as to what was likely to happen if an arrangement was not worked out. *FRUS, 1952–54,* (Washington, DC: Department of State, 1984), Vol. 15: 915; see also 1081, 1096, 1103, 1110–11.

Part II

EUROPE AND THE COLD WAR

6

THE EUROPEAN DIMENSION OF THE COLD WAR

David Reynolds

In their analyses of the Cold War, historians are increasingly showing how indigenous developments, regional rivalries, and traditional ethnic animosities affected the relationships among the Great Powers. These considerations inspired fears in Moscow and Washington and imposed constraints on what Soviet and American policymakers could do. They also established opportunities for transnational linkages.

David Reynolds is one of Britain's best historians of Anglo-American diplomacy and international relations before and after the Second World War. In this article he reviews some of the recent literature on the origins of the Cold War and shows how circumstances within Europe shaped postwar events. The presence of large Communist parties worried officials in Washington; yet, surprisingly, they were not always a source of consolation in Moscow. Communist Party identification did not obliterate the strong ethnic and nationalist sensibilities that existed. Stalin, for example, could not control Yugoslav Communist leader Tito. Nor could his loyal followers easily consolidate their power in countries like Czechoslovakia and Hungary (see the essay by Charles Gati in Chapter 9). For two or three years after the war there was great fluidity within European countries as various parties and factions struggled for domestic power. Their struggles affected the options and tactics available to officials in Moscow and Washington. In turn, Soviet and American actions helped determine the outcome of these internal struggles.

Hovering over much of the internal and external maneuvering was the question of Germany. Uncertainty about Germany's future inspired fears throughout Europe and across the Atlantic. For the time being Germany was occupied, divided, conquered, and devastated. All of Germany's neighbors from Paris to Warsaw to Moscow wanted to use the opportunity to grab part of its territory or its coal or its industrial infrastructure in order to abet the reconstruction processes within their own nations and to weaken permanently their traditional foe. But they all suspected that Germany would rise again and they worried about how it would configure itself internally and how it would align itself externally. Reynolds highlights the importance of the German issue, and readers might compare some of his views to the points raised in the preceding essays by Leffler and MccGwire about threat perception.

But Reynolds does more than outline the European dimensions of the Soviet-American rivalry. He underscores the importance of ideology in shaping the way American and Soviet officials interpreted threats and defined opportunities. Readers need to grapple with the importance of ideology in precipitating the Cold War and they need to analyse precisely how it might have influenced developments. Reynolds seems to be assigning it a degree of importance that is different from MccGwire and Leffler (and from John Kent in the essay that follows). What do you think?

* * *

Conventionally US historiography has focused on the two superpowers. According to Hans Morgenthau in 1954, "the international situation is reduced to the primitive spectacle of two giants eyeing each other with watchful suspicion." In Europe in 1945 there were "two superpowers separated only by a power vacuum," stated John Gaddis in 1978.[1] In recent years, however, various European scholars have stressed that European problems and forces played a decisive part in shaping the US-Soviet confrontation.[2]

One distinctive feature of the European scene after the war was the swing to the left politically. If interwar politics were dominated by fascism and the conservative right, the immediate postwar years saw the triumph of socialism in Britain and Scandinavia. Even more significant was the growth of Communist parties, benefiting from their role in leading the resistance movements in many of the occupied countries. In France CP membership reached over 1 million in 1946; in Italy 1.7 million by the end of 1945. In both these countries the Communists were in coalition governments in 1945–7. Eastern Europe saw even more spectacular increases, from a few hundred CP members to half a million in Hungary in 1945 and from 28,000 to 1.2 million in Czechoslovakia in the year from May

1945. In neither of these two cases can Soviet pressure be considered an all-sufficient explanation: the Hungarians were largely Catholic and historically anti-Slav, while the Red Army pulled out from Czechoslovakia in agreement with the Western allies in November 1945.

This swing to the left posed a real dilemma for the USA and Great Britain, who had little doubt that, whatever the immediate coalitionist tactics of the Communists, their gains would ultimately redound to Stalin's benefit. But the Communist expansion also posed problems for Stalin. After the oppressions of fascist and Nazi rule, the demand for revolution was strong in many of these Communist parties and Moscow's coalitionist line proved unpalatable. Although Stalin was able, in the interests of maintaining the grand alliance, to restrain the Communists in western states like France and Italy, there was enough deviation to imperil his overall policy. China was to be a particular problem later, but in the mid-1940s it was Tito's Yugoslavia (the scene of an indigenous revolution largely unassisted by the Red Army) which did him the most damage. Tito's demands for Trieste, his funneling of support to the Greek Communists and his shooting down of two US transport planes in August 1946 were among the actions that the Western powers readily but erroneously assumed were orchestrated by Stalin.

In 1945–7 neither so-called superpower could therefore control Europe's postwar swing to the left. Nor, secondly, could they order eastern Europe in a mutually acceptable form. In some Slavic areas, such as Bulgaria and the Serbian parts of Yugoslavia, the Russians were not unwelcome, but in much of eastern Europe, such as Romania, Hungary, and Poland, it was a different story. Historic antagonisms, dating back over many centuries, were exacerbated by ethnic rivalries and territorial disputes. In much of eastern Europe an "open sphere" would simply not produce governments and policies sympathetic to Soviet interests.[3] Yet the alternative – exclusive Soviet control – was unacceptable to US political and public opinion. There is no doubt that in 1945–6 Hungary, Czechoslovakia, and even the Soviet zone of Germany were following their own distinctive paths leftward,[4] but, even if superpower relations had not deteriorated as badly as they did in 1947, Stalin (given his attitude to political pluralism at home) would probably have consolidated his hold eventually.

A third semi-autonomous European problem was Germany – in fact the key issue in the emerging Cold War. At stake for the USA and the USSR was control of the country that had started two world wars and might, it was feared, start a third if the victors did not make the right decisions this time. In principle both superpowers inclined to a unified German state, under satisfactory guarantees. It was the French who wanted, as after the First World War, to amputate Germany's economic vital parts, particularly the Ruhr and the Saar, and place them under French or else international control. For the Russians the crucial issue was the settlement of Germany's reparations payments, including substantial amounts from the industrialized western zones controlled by the allies. In reacting to this stalemate, Washington was initially divided in 1945–6. The State Department's European desk, anxious to restore French power, was sympathetic to their arguments, but the War Department and the occupation authorities under General Lucius Clay wanted to get Germany back on its feet economically and end the military regime. Clay's decision to stop reparations payments from the US zone to the USSR (May 1946) was not aimed exclusively at the Soviet Union but was also intended to force the German deadlock to a head in the allied counsels.[5]

Behind American disputes with France and the USSR was mounting domestic pressure to get back to normal. Dean Acheson, Under-Secretary of State, declared in November 1945: "I can state in three sentences what the 'popular' attitude is toward foreign policy today. 1. Bring the boys home. 2. Don't be a Santa Claus. 3. Don't be pushed around."[6]

The implications of American resistance to European commitments bring us naturally to a fourth facet of the European dimension – the place of Britain. Although it is easy to neglect British importance today, Britain in the late 1940s was unquestionably the strongest western European state, economically and militarily, retaining worldwide commitments and interests. Despite the loss of a quarter of its national wealth in the war, Britain's Labour leaders, no less than Churchill and Eden, were determined to maintain its position as a world power. Their view of the United States was ambivalent: the Americans, by language and culture, were seen as natural allies, but they were also rivals for Britain's trade and critics of the British empire. More to the point in 1945, although the British would have liked to have seen firm American commitments to Europe, they recognized that this was unlikely. Consequently it was important to maintain the best possible relationship with the Soviet Union, because together they would have to keep the European peace against a revived Germany.[7]

Despite his reputation as a notorious anti-Communist, Churchill shared these convictions. Like Roosevelt, he acknowledged privately the inevitability of a Soviet sphere of influence in Eastern Europe, but wanted to prevent it becoming a closed Stalinist bloc. Similar views were also held by the new Labour government headed by Clement Attlee, with Ernest Bevin as Foreign Secretary. Bevin, like Churchill, was ready to "talk tough" to Molotov, but in 1945–6 he still had not abandoned the attempt to reach negotiated agreements. As late as December 1947 he could still observe in private that he "doubted whether Russia was as great a danger as a resurgent Germany might become."[8]

Beneath this official policy, however, Whitehall, like Washington, was uncertain about Soviet intentions. The leading hardliners were the Chiefs of Staff, particularly in the form of their post-hostilities planners, who by 1944 were already talking of the USSR as the only likely enemy for Britain in the future. The chiefs and the Foreign Office were particularly disturbed about the eastern Mediterranean – a major area of British interest and historically a center of Anglo-Russian rivalry. In 1945–6 the Soviet Union's pressure on Turkey, its slowness to withdraw from northern Iran and the Communist insurgency in Greece all took on sinister significance for many in Whitehall. Despite the growing doubts, however, the British political leadership in 1945–6 remained anxious for agreement.[9]

The nearest Bevin came to an overt breach with the USSR was the decision in July 1946 to fuse the British and US zones of occupation in Germany. Without economic recovery, Bevin feared disaster. Not only would Communism increase its appeal among discontented and impoverished people, but the burden of running the zone would become unbearable for Britain's weakened economy. With British and US perceptions in line on the issue, the two governments agreed to fuse their zones, to reduce costs. This came into operation in January 1947.[10]

But although the "Bizone" proved a significant development, it did not make inevitable the crisis events of 1947. To understand their full significance, we need to look now at the underlying perceptions of the three allies. For the Cold War developed not so much from the actions of the three powers as from the way these actions were interpreted, or misinterpreted.[11]

One fundamental problem was the "universalist" ideologies publicly espoused by the United States and the Soviet Union. In practice, as we have seen, both countries may well have been adopting a sphere of influence policy, which on Eastern and Western Europe (if not on Germany) involved some acknowledgement of the other's interests and sensitivities. But that is not what they said in public. Privately Roosevelt spoke the language of spheres of influence,[12] but official US foreign policy was couched in terms of one world, open to democratic values, in which, to quote Secretary of State Cordell Hull, "there will no longer be need for spheres of influence, for alliances, for balance of power, or any other of the special arrangements through which, in the unhappy past, the nations strove to safeguard their security or to promote their interests."[13] Roosevelt and Truman believed that the US public would not tolerate the language of the old diplomacy, but by encouraging misleading, even utopian, expectations they paved the way for growing US disenchantment with what the Soviet Union was doing, as well as intensifying Moscow's suspicions. Conversely, the renewed rhetoric of Marxism-Leninism had its effect in the USA. Whether Stalin sincerely supported it or merely utilized this attack on "cosmopolitanism" as part of his domestic battles, it had a deeply unsettling effect in Britain and the USA. Particularly perplexing in Washington was Stalin's election speech of February 9, 1946, which began with a Leninist interpretation of the origins of the Second World War. To many in the west it seemed to confirm that ideology was back in favour in the Kremlin.

Readings of recent history also played their part. In the United States Soviet actions were fitted into an image of totalitarian regimes. Repression at home implied aggression abroad – from the Kaiser, through Hitler, to Stalin. As Truman observed in May 1947: "There isn't any difference in totalitarian states . . . Nazi, Communist or Fascist, or Franco, or anything else – they are all alike."[14] Equally important were the "lessons" of appeasement. Both in Washington and London there was sensitivity about the western failure to react quickly and effectively against Hitler's buildup in the 1930s. Thus, Secretary of the Navy James Forrestal in September 1945 dismissed the idea "that we should endeavor to buy their [Soviet] understanding and sympathy. We tried that once with Hitler. There are no returns on appeasement."[15] Given these views of totalitarianism and of appeasement, there was a tendency for western observers to focus on those aspects of Soviet conduct in 1945–6 that fitted the paradigm – Poland, Romania, Bulgaria, for instance, rather than Finland, Czechoslovakia, or Greece. They saw these as the first steps, 1930s style, to expansion over all of Europe. Though perhaps imperceptive, such an appraisal was understandable if one remembers their view of Stalin as, above all, the architect of the great purges of 1936–9 when perhaps 4 to 5 million were eliminated, half a million of them summarily shot and in which an apparently paranoid dictator disposed of half his own officer corps including his best commanders, thus laying his country open to the disasters of 1941.[16]

If western leaders may have been ill-tuned to possible nuances in Stalin's policy, the Soviet leadership seems fatally to have misread the relationship between the other two members of the Big Three. If the British were too prone to assume underlying Anglo-American harmony, the Soviet Union, guided by Leninism, was too ready to assume inevitable Anglo-American discord. Britain and the United States were in certain respects economic and power-political rivals, but they also shared common liberal values and common interests in the stability of Europe. When those values and interests were threatened in 1940, cooperation overrode competition.[17] When a similar threat seemed to emerge in 1946–7 another rapprochement occurred. Stalin and Molotov had pushed them too far.

It is possible, then, that a spheres of influence arrangement might have worked for eastern and western Europe, if both sides had not been (often willing) prisoners of their ideologies and had they not been heavily influenced by their reading of recent history. On Germany, however, the issues were almost intractable. The Soviet Union had suffered too much in two wars to be able to compromise readily on this matter, and the French, also a continental state easily threatened by Germany, had similar fears. Britain and the United States simply could not comprehend the visceral fears of Germany that gnawed at Soviet leaders – the importance of a secure eastern European buffer and a reliable German settlement to guard against repetition of the traumatic "surprise" attack of 1941. Nor could they fully grasp how their efforts to rehabilitate Germany, made necessary in their view by Soviet intransigence, fed Moscow's anxieties. This was particularly true in 1948 when Stalin blockaded Berlin in a counterproductive effort to head off the creation of a West German state.

But why was the USA so concerned about events in Europe? That, after all, was the big contrast with earlier American foreign policy, when US security was not deemed to be inextricably linked to that of Europe. The 1940s saw a greatly expanded definition of US interests, drawing on two main lines of thought. First, Hitler's victories seemed to show that Americans could not allow a potential foe to control western Europe – the leading economic center outside the USA. If that happened the Americas might be forced into economic isolation and their security eventually eroded by enemy control of Europe's industrial resources. "The greatest danger to the security of the United States," warned the CIA in 1947, "is the possibility of economic collapse in western Europe and the consequent accession to power of communist elements."[18] Linked to this new concern for the European balance was the conviction that air power had revolutionized security. The long-range bomber had "shrunk" the world, the atomic bomb heralded undreamt-of destructive force, and exponents of air power such as Generals "Hap" Arnold and Carl Spaatz argued that the USA now needed an extended defense perimeter with bases across the Atlantic and in Germany and Britain.

These claims had only limited support in 1945–6, even within the Pentagon, and they were partly advanced for bureaucratic reasons, to strengthen the case for a US air force independent of the army. The direct threat to the security of the United States remained extremely remote, particularly before the Soviet atomic bomb (1949) and intercontinental missile (1957). It was ideology as much as interests that underpinned America's new "gospel of national security" – the Wilsonian conviction that the USA could and should use its enhanced power to export liberal, capitalist, democratic, and anti-colonial values for the benefit of a European-dominated world that had torn itself to pieces once again. Harry Hopkins remarked in 1945:

I have often been asked what interests we have in Poland, Greece, Iran, or Korea. Well, I think we have the most important business in the world – and indeed, the only business worthy of our traditions. And that is this – to do everything within our diplomatic power to foster and encourage democratic government throughout the world. We should not be timid about blazoning to the world our desire for the right of all peoples to have a genuine civil liberty. We believe our dynamic democracy is the best in the world.[19]

Bearing in mind what we have just examined – the deteriorating US-Soviet relationship in 1945–6, the European dimension, and the Big Three's underlying perceptions – we are now better able to understand the decisive crisis of 1947. It was a process of action and reaction in which the catalysts came from within Europe. Of particular importance was the abrupt British collapse amid economic crisis in February 1947. Unable to sustain the foreign exchange costs of Britain's overseas commitments, the Treasury, supported by Attlee, forced Bevin and the Chiefs of Staff to abandon the Palestine mandate, pull out of India quickly, and end financial aid to Greece and Turkey. Bevin used the last decision to put the ball firmly in the American court, asking them to assume responsibility for the eastern Mediterranean.[20]

The State Department, guided particularly by Under-Secretary Dean Acheson, was already coming round to this view, but the urgency of the British request posed a major political problem for Truman. The 80th Congress was controlled by the Republicans, whose anti-Communist election rhetoric was balanced by an intense concern to reduce government spending. Sounding out Congressmen, Acheson found them unsympathetic to "pulling British chestnuts out of the fire" but shocked by warnings that Greece was like a "rotten apple in the barrel" from which decay would soon spread through southern Europe. Also effective were presentations of the Greek-Turkish issue in terms of a broader struggle between the democratic and totalitarian ways of life, reminiscent of the Second World War. It was therefore in this universalist language that Truman appealed to Congress on March 12, 1947 for money for Greece and Turkey – "at the present moment in world history nearly every nation must choose between alternative ways of life. The choice is too often not a free one."[21]

The ideological rhetoric of the Truman Doctrine, though exaggerated for political reasons, provided a new statement of policy which then helped shape the US outlook. The strategy of "containment" gradually evolved.[22] At the same time the economic crisis had brought the German problem to a head. Unable to reach agreement at the Moscow Foreign Ministers conference, the US Secretary of State, George C. Marshall, guided by Acheson and Kennan, offered American aid for a joint European recovery programme in his speech on June 5.[23] The central object was the revival of Germany, but the Europe-wide package was intended to make it more palatable to the French and to the Soviet Union, even though the USA and Britain were determined not to let the USSR frustrate further progress. Although Soviet rejection was likely, the attitude of the East European governments was less predictable. Poland, Czechoslovakia, Hungary, and Romania were among those interested in participating, but Stalin, after some indecision, warned them off.[24] Stalin undoubtedly regarded eastern European interest as a further threat to his security zone, but the result of the American offer and the Soviet response was the economic polarization of Europe.

Soviet reaction to the Truman Doctrine had been restrained, but the Szklarska Poreba Conference of Communist parties in September 1947, at which Cominform was created, saw a firm response to American actions and rhetoric. Zhdanov's "two camps" statement and the encouragement of the French and Italian Communist parties to repent their coalitionist past and mount a programme of industrial and political challenge to the bourgeois order represented significant shifts of policy. In Eastern Europe Stalin's overreaction to the Marshall Plan helped precipitate the shift from coalitionist tactics to the tried and tested techniques of Stalinization. From late 1947 the popular front governments in eastern Europe were quickly replaced by Communist rule. Independent-minded Communist leaders who had espoused the earlier doctrine of non-revolutionary roads to socialism, such as Gomulka in Poland, were replaced by Stalinists of unquestioned loyalty, and the collectivization of the economy proceeded apace. It was at this point, *pace* Churchill's Fulton speech of March 1946, that the "Iron Curtain" truly came down.

The breakup of the grand alliance in Europe did not occur immediately in 1945, but developed gradually up to the turning-point of 1947. "Policymakers" were not following confrontational blueprints from an early stage; they gradually lost faith in the strategy of collaboration without having anything clear to put in its place. In the process of breakdown it is perhaps helpful to distinguish *assumptions, perceptions, actions*, and *policies*.[25]

In all three major protagonists the underlying assumptions were skeptical. The Soviet Union assumed fundamental capitalist antipathy; the United States and Britain assumed that Soviet intentions were ultimately revolutionary. At root neither side found it easy to accept that peaceful coexistence was possible or even desirable, with so much of the world apparently at stake in the turbulent aftermath of the Second World War.

In both the USA and Britain perceptions of the Soviet Union were changing in 1945–6, but, although sections of both bureaucracies urged a shift of policy from negotiation to confrontation, the political leaderships were unready to go that far, particularly in public. It was the force of events as much as changing perceptions that drove the British and US governments into action – especially over the problem of Communism in their sphere of influence and over the deadlock in Germany.

At what point Stalin moved from changed perceptions to changed policies is hard to say. Scholars still lack access to the Soviet archives, and Stalin's own public statements, in marked contrast to the prewar period, were few and far between. But as the Marshall Plan took off in the summer and autumn of 1947 he clearly felt obliged to act, for fear that his whole security program was in danger, and it may be that the Cominform statement represented policy catching up with perceptions and actions.

At the end of the war it would seem that the "Big Three" had hoped for some kind of loose spheres of influence arrangement in Europe – but only up to a point. The British still treated much of the Balkans and Middle East as a vital interest, despite dissenting noises from Attlee, and were anxious to contain the expansion of Soviet and Communist influence there. American tolerance for spheres was compromised by a universalist ideology and by their newly extended definition of US security to include the stability of Eurasia. The USSR, in its turn, unsettled the British and Americans by its revival of the universalist language of Marxist-Leninist revolution. An even graver problem was Stalinism itself. Given their recent experiences with "totalitarian" regimes, Britain and the USA feared the worst from a leader for whom security was always closely linked to repression – at home or in eastern Europe.

Even if the wartime allies had been willing to limit their geopolitical and ideological aspirations, however, the problems of Germany made a secure sphere of influence agreement – mutual tolerance of Eastern and Western blocs – an unlikely eventuality. The aftermath of Hitler's war was too profound, too unsettling. For the Western powers the economic dislocation of Germany and the emergence of Communism, whatever Stalin's immediate policy, were unacceptable. For the Soviet Union, any attempt to rehabilitate its mortal enemy, Germany, without security and reparations was equally intolerable. The struggle for mastery of Germany lay at the heart of the grand alliance and also of the Cold War.

NOTES

From David Reynolds, "The 'Big Three' and the Division of Europe, 1945–48: An Overview," *Diplomacy and Statecraft*, 1 (1990): 117–36. Copyright © Frank Cass & Co. Ltd. Reprinted and abridged by permission of Frank Cass & Co. Limited, 11 Gainsborough Road, London E11, England.

1 Hans J. Morgenthau, *Politics among Nations: The Struggle for Power and Peace* (2nd edn, New York, 1954), 339; John Lewis Gaddis, *Russia, the Soviet Union, and the United States: An Interpretive History* (New York, 1978), 180.
2 See Geir Lundestad, "Empire by Invitation: The United States and Western Europe, 1945–1952," *Journal of Peace Research*, 23 (1986): 263–77; also David Reynolds, "The Origins of the Cold War: The European Dimension, 1944–51," *The Historical Journal*, 28 (1985): 497–515. The policies of the leading Western European powers are conveniently summarized in the essays in Josef Becker and Franz Knipping (eds), *Power in Europe?: Great Britain, France, Italy and Germany in a Postwar World, 1945–1950* (Berlin, 1986).
3 The main exception was Czechoslovakia where Benes tried to maintain democracy and independence while conciliating Moscow,

which was a major reason why the Communist takeover there in February 1948 was regarded as so significant by the West.

4 See N. G. Papp, "The Democratic Struggle for Power in Hungary: Party Strategies, 1945–46," *East Central Europe*, 6 (1979): 1–19; Martin R. Myant, *Socialism and Democracy in Czechoslovakia, 1945–1948* (Cambridge, 1981); Gregory W. Sandford, *From Hitler to Ulbricht: The Communist Reconstruction of East Germany, 1945–1946* (Princeton, NJ, 1983).

5 The French dimension of America's German policy is emphasized (and probably exaggerated) in John Gimbel, *The Origins of the Marshall Plan* (Stanford, CA, 1976). On Germany in general there are useful essays in Roland G. Foerster *et al.*, *Anfänge westdeutscher Sicherheitspolitik, 1945–1956*, Vol. 1: *Von der Kapitulation bis zum Pleven-Plan* (Munich, 1982); Josef Foschepoth (ed.), *Kalter Krieg und Deutsche Frage: Deutschland im Widerstreit der Mächte, 1945–1952* (Göttingen, 1985).

6 Walter Isaacson and Evan Thomas, *The Wise Men: Six Friends and the World They Made. Acheson, Bohlen, Harriman, Kennan, Lovett, McCloy* (New York, 1986), 338.

7 For background see Graham Ross (ed.), *The Foreign Office and the Kremlin: British Documents on Anglo-Soviet Relations, 1941–1945* (Cambridge, 1985), which includes a useful introduction; Martin Kitchen, *British Policy towards the Soviet Union during the Second World War* (London, 1986).

8 Alan Bullock, *Ernest Bevin: Foreign Secretary, 1945–1951* (London, 1983), 269. On Churchill see Elisabeth Barker, *Churchill and Eden at War* (London, 1978).

9 Victor Rothwell, *Britain and the Cold War, 1941–1947* (London, 1982) – a digest of Foreign Office opinion; John W. Young, *Britain, France and the Unity of Europe, 1945–1951* (Leicester, 1984); the important article by Raymond Smith and John Zametica, "The Cold Warrior: Clement Attlee Reconsidered, 1945–1947," *International Affairs*, 61(2) (1985): 237–52; and Ray Merrick, "The Russia Committee of the British Foreign Office and the Cold War, 1946–1947," *Journal of Contemporary History*, 20 (1985): 453–68.

10 For a recent argument that Britain forced the pace over Germany, see Anne Deighton, "The 'Frozen Front': The Labour Government, the Division of Germany and the Origins of the Cold War, 1945–1947," *International Affairs*, 63 (1987): 449–65.

11 A useful recent German textbook on the Cold War that embodies this approach is Wilfried Loth, *The Division of the World, 1941–1955* (London, 1988).

12 For instance, he told US Senators in January 1945 "that the Russians had the power in eastern Europe, that it was obviously impossible to have a break with them and that, therefore, the only practicable course was to use what influence we had to ameliorate the situation." Robert Dallek, *Franklin D. Roosevelt and American Foreign Policy, 1932–1945* (New York, 1979), 507–8.

13 Address to Joint Session of Congress, November 18, 1943, in *The*

Memoirs of Cordell Hull, 2 Vols (New York, 1948), Vol. 2: 1314–15.

14 John Lewis Gaddis, *The Long Peace: Inquiries into the History of the Cold War* (New York, 1987), 36.

15 Ernest R. May, *"Lessons" of the Past: The Use and Misuse of History in American Foreign Policy* (New York, 1973), 33.

16 See Roy A. Medvedev, *Let History Judge: The Origins and Consequences of Stalinism* (London, 1972), Chap. 6.

17 See David Reynolds, *The Creation of the Anglo-American Alliance, 1937–1941: A Study in Competitive Co-operation* (London, 1981). For recent scholarship on the war, see David Reynolds, "Roosevelt, Churchill, and the Wartime Anglo-American Alliance, 1939–1945: Towards a New Synthesis," in Wm Roger Louis and Hedley Bull (eds), *The "Special Relationship": Anglo-American Relations since 1945* (Oxford, 1986), 17–41.

18 CIA review of world situation, September 1947, quoted in Melvyn P. Leffler, "The American Conception of National Security and the Beginnings of the Cold War, 1945–48," *American Historical Review*, 84 (1984): 364. See also Daniel Yergin, *Shattered Peace: The Origins of the Cold War and the National Security State* (Boston, MA, 1977), Chap. 8; Richard Best, *"Co-operation with Like-Minded Peoples": British influences on American Security Policy, 1945–1949* (Westport, CT, 1986), Chaps 2–3; Gregg Herken, *The Winning Weapon: The Atomic Bomb and the Cold War, 1945–1950* (New York, 1982), Chap. 10.

19 Thomas G. Paterson, *On Every Front: The Making of the Cold War* (New York, 1979), 72–3.

20 For British influences on US policy see Terry H. Anderson, *The United States, Great Britain, and the Cold War, 1944–1947* (Columbia, MO, 1981); Robin Edmonds, *Setting the Mould: The United States and Britain, 1945–1950* (Oxford, 1986).

21 *Public Papers of the Presidents of the United States: Harry S. Truman, 1947* (Washington, 1963), 176–80.

22 See John Lewis Gaddis, *Strategies of Containment: A Critical Appraisal of Postwar American National Security Policy* (New York, 1982).

23 For useful overviews see Scott Jackson, "Prologue to the Marshall Plan: The Origins of the American Commitment for a European Recovery Program," *Journal of American History*, 65 (1979): 1043–68; Melvyn P. Leffler, "The United States and the Strategic Dimensions of the Marshall Plan," *Diplomatic History*, 12 (1988): 277–306. Two important recent monographs are Alan S. Milward, *The Reconstruction of Western Europe, 1945–1951* (London, 1984), and Michael J. Hogan, *The Marshall Plan: America, Britain and the Reconstruction of Western Europe, 1947–1952* (New York, 1987).

24 Joseph L. Nogee and Robert H. Donaldson, *Soviet Foreign Policy since World War II* (New York, 1981), 65–6. See William Taubman, *Stalin's American Policy: From Entente to Detente to Cold War* (New York, 1982), 172–3.

25 I am developing here the suggestive approach in Deborah Welch Larson, *Origins of Containment: A Psychological Explanation* (Princeton, NJ, 1985), where the last three concepts are articulated and deployed.

7

BRITISH POLICY AND THE ORIGINS OF THE COLD WAR

John Kent

During the past fifteen years historians have found British records to be an invaluable source for understanding the origins of the Cold War. According to some scholars these records demonstrate that the Cold War was not a bipolar affair. They show that British officials shared the fears and concerns of Americans about the potential of a Soviet threat. Indeed some analysts believe that the British alerted and prodded the Americans to assume a bolder posture against Soviet/Communist expansionism. But at the same time the British were also aware that their interests did not always coincide with those of the United States and that it was important to try to maintain a degree of autonomy if they were to preserve their Great Power status.

English historians have done a wonderful job illuminating and debating the degree of continuity between the foreign policies of the Conservative government of Winston Churchill and Anthony Eden and those of the Labour Party headed by Clement Attlee and Ernest Bevin. Although tactics changed after Churchill lost the election in July 1945 and although parts of the empire won their independence, there probably was more continuity than one would have expected. But this is a complex problem because recent research has shown that notwithstanding Churchill's inveterate anti-Communism, he, too, pondered means of accommodating the Kremlin and working out a cooperative relationship. Of course, from his perspective, and from that of his successors, the cooperative relationship had to be on terms that comported with British conceptions of their own vital security interests. At what point this orientation dictated a break with the Kremlin is open to controversy. And so is the degree of Britain's own responsibility for bringing on the Cold War.

Rather than attributing blame or praise for the actions that led to the breakdown of the great wartime allied coalition, some historians are

139

more interested in examining the motivations and goals of the various participants. In this provocative essay John Kent shows that British concerns with their strategic presence in the eastern Mediterranean and Bevin's hopes for maximizing the economic advantages of Britain's African possessions prompted the Foreign Office to take a defiant stand against concessions to the Kremlin.

Readers should compare British thinking about their security require-ments with that of the Americans and the Soviets (as portrayed in the Leffler and MccGwire essays). What factors influenced British think-ing? Were there divisions within the British government? If so, what caused them? To what extent were they related to differences over assessments of Soviet intentions and capabilities? To what extent were they related to different views of British interests, British capabilities, and British economic and military requirements? To what extent were they prompted by hopes of retaining some autonomy vis-à-vis the United States? Why were the British so concerned about holding on to their possessions or maintaining their influence in Africa and the Middle East?

* * *

Standard accounts of postwar foreign and colonial policy assume that Britain's imperial role had to be adapted to the increased international tensions resulting from the breakup of the wartime alliance. The failure of Foreign Secretary Ernest Bevin's attempts to overcome Soviet intransigence and hostility allegedly produced the Brussels Treaty and the securing of an American military commitment to Western Europe. The Cold War therefore encouraged policies geared to the acceptance of a subordinate, if special, position in an American-dominated alliance.

In this essay the links between Britain's imperial policy and the Cold War will be interpreted rather differently. Rather than suggesting that the Cold War simply prompted new Foreign Office initiatives, it will be argued first that attempts to redefine Britain's global role were a prime cause of growing tension in 1945, and therefore an important element in the origins of the Cold War; and second that perceptions of Africa's imperial value influenced overall foreign policy objectives as cold war tensions increased in 1947 and 1948.

It is first necessary to define the central aims, as opposed to the final results, of British foreign policy between 1944 and 1949; these aims are often mentioned in the historiography of the period but seldom given the emphasis they require if perceptions of British policymakers are to be accurately represented.[1] The overriding aim until 1949 was the reestablishment of Britain as a world power equal to and independent of both the United States and the Soviet Union;[2] an aspiration which reflected the Foreign Office view that British weakness was a temporary rather than a permanent phenomenon.[3] In order to achieve this it was believed that the preservation of imperial influence was vital in both economic and power-political terms; use of strategic bases and imperial resources would be supplemented by close political ties with the colonies and Dominions. But the Foreign Office also saw the need to enrol France and the lesser western European powers as "collaborators" with the British empire.[4]

This could obviously not be achieved overnight, and in the intervening period it was deemed necessary to avoid any weakening of Britain's imperial position. It was Bevin and the Foreign Office's determination to prevent this that was to influence attitudes to Anglo-Soviet cooperation in 1945. These attitudes were based not on fears that cooperation with the Soviet Union would be difficult or impossible, but on fears that cooperation would compromise Britain's position in the Middle East and Africa. As a result Anglo-Soviet cooperation was regarded, at least in the short term, as undesirable.

The area initially most affected by the rival claims of British and Soviet imperialism was the Middle East and the eastern Mediterranean. Russian expansion in the Balkans and the Turkish Straits had always threatened what was a predominantly British sphere of influence in the Mediterranean. But in 1944 the Foreign Office was committed to a policy of cooperation with the Soviet Union, although this commitment was to change by the summer of 1945. In the meantime its advocates were faced with two possible options: the negotiation of power-political agreements or the establishment of international arrangements, each of which could prevent Anglo-Soviet rivalries developing into hostile confrontations. But when it was realized that either option would compromise Britain's position in the eastern Mediterranean, and therefore its status as one of the Big Three powers, Anglo-Soviet cooperation was deemed undesirable.

The spheres-of-influence approach was epitomized by the infamous October 1944 percentages deal in which Stalin and Churchill agreed on a 50–50 division in Yugoslavia and a 90–10 arrangement in Britain's favour for Greece;[5] as Churchill explained, the latter was necessary because Britain "must be the leading Mediterranean power." Churchill, however, believed Britain had nothing to fear from the movement of a Russian fleet through the Straits because of Britain's greater naval strength, and told Stalin he was "in favour of Russia's having free access to the Mediterranean for her merchant ships and ships of war."[6] As he noted at the time, "it is like breeding pestilence to try to keep a nation like Russia from free access to the broad waters."[7] In 1945, the key "breeder of pestilence" who was determined to defend Britain's exclusive Mediterranean position was Ernest Bevin. His main opponent was the new Prime Minister, Clement Attlee.

In the summer of 1945, the Foreign Office thought Britain's position in the region was being increasingly challenged by the Soviet Union and this perception was crucial to the formulation of British ideas on future allied cooperation. In June, the Turks approached the Russians about a Turkish-Soviet treaty guaranteeing the joint frontier, and the Turkish ambassador mentioned granting bases in the Straits to the Soviets in certain wartime conditions.[8] Molotov responded by emphasizing the Soviet desire for bases, and explaining that the disputed frontier in the eastern provinces of Turkey could first require revision. In the week before the Potsdam Conference the British ambassador therefore reported that the "most disquieting feature of Soviet policy" was not their activities in eastern Europe, but their attitude to Greece and Turkey which suggested "a threat to our position in the Middle East."[9]

The underlying assumption among strategic planners was that the Soviet Union presented a potential threat to British interests and could not therefore be accepted as a friendly power.[10] This also became the prevalent attitude within the Foreign Office, not because of events in eastern Europe, but because of Soviet desires for greater influence in the eastern Mediterranean. In the summer of 1945, these attitudes produced

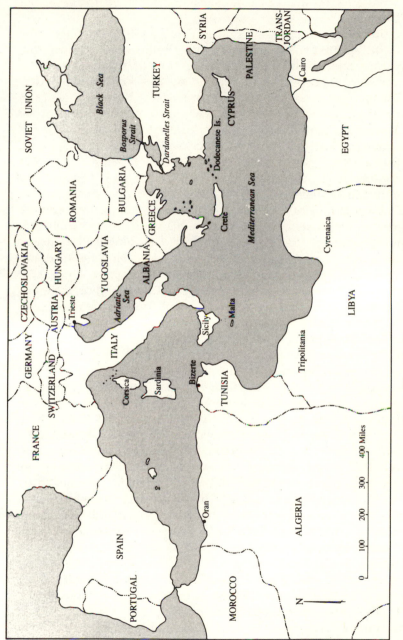

Map 3 The Mediterranean area, 1945–6

a policy of no deals or concessions of any kind to the Soviet Union.

The first indication of a shift in Foreign Office thinking came in the spring of 1945 when Deputy Under-Secretary Sir Orme Sargent changed his views on the best means of dealing with the Soviets. Sargent, later to become Bevin's Permanent Under-Secretary, was not favorably disposed to the Russians.[11] In July, the Deputy Under-Secretary's position changed again when he explicitly called for a diplomatic offensive to challenge the Soviet Union in Finland, Poland, Czechoslovakia, and Bulgaria; but in the two countries in southeastern Europe furthest away from the eastern Mediterranean and the Middle East – Hungary and Romania – Sargent considered Britain might have to acquiesce in Russian domination.[12] "Our strategic position in Greece and the Middle East," stated the Foreign Office, "makes it particularly important to us that Bulgaria should not act simply as an instrument of Soviet foreign policy."[13] The fact that Russian domination in Hungary was acceptable to the Foreign Office if it prevented Soviet control over Bulgarian foreign policy, indicates the lack of importance attached to democratic principles in comparison with Britain's strategic interests.

As has been suggested earlier, the preservation of Britain's Middle Eastern position was deemed essential to the long-term goal of regaining equality with the United States and the Soviet Union. Another threat to this goal was Soviet-American cooperation, based on an assumption that Britain was now very much a junior partner in the alliance, and in July 1945 British representatives in both Moscow and Washington voiced their fears of this. An official of the North American Department reported some feeling in Washington that Britain and the empire were so weakened they could safely be overlooked by the Americans and Russians.[14] In Moscow, Sir Archibald Clark Kerr drew attention to an event which illustrated just such a policy – the bilateral discussions between Truman's emissary, Harry Hopkins, and Stalin on the Polish problem. "This renewed Soviet-American flirtation," he recorded, "of course means more than a mere attempt to break a temporary deadlock. The Americans and the Russians alike are probably hoping to establish a direct relationship with one another." If Britain was not careful, he warned, it would find itself playing a more modest role in allied exchanges.[15]

It was against this background that in July and August 1945 British discussions took place on Anglo-Soviet cooperation and the protection of British interests in the Middle East and the eastern Mediterranean. The new Prime Minister continued to advocate internationalist ideas as the best means of preserving world peace and maintaining Britain's global influence. Attlee believed that key strategic areas, particularly in the Middle East, should be placed under the control of the United Nations and that Britain should confront the Russians with the requirements of a world organization for peace and not with the defense needs of the British empire. Even before the discussions at Potsdam were over, Attlee believed there was a danger of getting into a position where Britain and the Soviet Union would confront each other as rival Great Powers at a number of points of strategic importance.[16]

Bevin was determined to support the Foreign Office view rather than his Prime Minister's. In 1944, as a member of the coalition government, Bevin had expected the Balkans would probably demand British leadership.[17] At the Labour Party Conference of that year he had defended the government's Greek policy on the grounds that it was a necessary part of maintaining Britain's position in the Mediterranean.[18] These imperial instincts were reinforced by a deep dislike of Communism developed during his trade union days and by his private secretary, Pierson Dixon, who worked in the notoriously Russophobe Southern Department from 1941 to 1943. Bevin was keen to resist the extension of Soviet influence in the eastern Mediterranean, and in July 1945 believed that Britain's survival as a Great Power required the reinforcement of its military and economic role in the Middle East, from the Persian Gulf to Cyrenaica.[19]

As a basis for reconciling Anglo-Soviet imperialist ambitions this left some form of power-political agreement on the acceptance of Russian domination in certain areas in return for the assertion of exclusive British rights in others. As noted, these ideas were increasingly geared to keeping the Soviets away from the Turkish Straits and the eastern Mediterranean. One possible option for the British was to agree to Soviet bases in the Straits in return for an acceptance of British bases at Suez and the maintenance of Britain's predominant position in the eastern Mediterranean; another was to satisfy Soviet ambitions

145

in eastern Europe in return for a guarantee of the Middle Eastern status quo. There were two specific difficulties in the way of such policies. In the former case, the British military were convinced of the serious consequences for Britain's strategic interests if such a course was followed. In the latter case the acquiescence of the Americans was unlikely to be secured.

The Foreign Office also considered more general difficulties arising from the need to prevent damage to Britain's imperial credibility. Counsellor Gladwyn Jebb considered the possibility of a deal with the the Russians in the Middle East and the eastern Mediterranean. But he argued that for Britain "to yield to ANY Russian demand would clearly mean that we were not prepared to play the part of a Great Power."[20]

Here was the link between the maintenance of British imperial influence in the Middle East and the preservation of Britain's Great Power status. In both general and specific terms the future of the British empire depended on a policy of no concessions to the Soviet Union. Yet if Britain continued to reject Soviet demands for bases in the Straits its position in Suez was clearly illogical. British withdrawal from the Canal Zone appeared necessary unless the Americans were to side with the British and make it clear they were prepared to oppose Russian claims for bases in the Straits by force.[21] The defense of the British empire in its most vital yet vulnerable area required not only a policy of non-cooperation with the Russians, but an Anglo-American anti-Soviet front until British postwar recovery was assured and the reattainment of a position of equality secured.

This policy was clearly evident within the Foreign Office even before the Potsdam summit was over. It was not conceived in response to oppressive Soviet actions in Europe nor to the difficulties over Poland and Germany. Perceptions of the importance of the empire to Britain's future global role and the preservation of Britain's Mediterranean position as a link between the mother country and the Dominions were much more important. This was to prove a key factor in the breakdown of the first Council of Foreign Ministers in London, which, under the terms of the Potsdam agreement, was to be primarily concerned with the Italian peace treaty. An important Italian issue was the disposal of Italy's colonies; and the future of Libya, divided into its eastern and western parts of Cyrenaica and Tripolitania, had implications for Great Power rivalries in the

Mediterranean. The Chiefs of Staff emphasized that in strategically important areas, notably Cyrenaica, Britain would require the use of military facilities, but there would be no objection to sharing these under the aegis of the United Nations provided they were controlled by Britain or a state on whose friendship the British could rely.[22]

At the London Council Byrnes proposed a ten-year allied trusteeship over the whole of Libya. Bevin's response was to support Byrnes's proposal on condition that certain modifications were made; Britain's priority was to prevent the Soviets getting a foothold in North Africa and then work for arrangements which would meet British needs in Cyrenaica. Molotov argued that Britain was trying to create a monopoly in the Mediterranean because of French and Italian weakness in the region. But if Russia was granted Tripolitania and Britain Cyrenaica, he felt the whole question of the Italian colonies could be settled very quickly. Bevin, true to the policy of no concessions, stood firm, and replied that the Soviet Union had not met him in anything and that Britain did not want an inch of territory.[23] In these circumstances the Conference of Foreign Ministers ended, apparently in deadlock over a procedural point. But, as Pierson Dixon noted in his diary, the real reason was "our refusal to meet Russian ambitions in the Mediterranean."[24]

This was not the policy of the Prime Minister who, unlike Bevin and the Chiefs of Staff, no longer believed in the strategic importance of the Mediterranean because of the advent of air power; and, unlike Bevin and the Foreign Office, Attlee had not ruled out a policy of compromise and cooperation with the Soviet Union.[25] In an attempt to defuse the growing Anglo-Soviet conflict, the Prime Minister suggested disengaging from the eastern Mediterranean and the Middle East where there was a risk of clashing with the Soviet Union. As part of an attempt to reconcile the British empire with a commitment to internationalism, Attlee proposed a British withdrawal from Greece and Egypt in order to form a new line of defence across Africa from Lagos to Kenya.[26] The establishment of a neutral zone in the Middle East, subject to international supervision, where there would be no exclusive spheres of influence or bases could defuse the Anglo-Soviet conflict and provide an unprovocative shield for Britain's African empire. This was the first indication that Africa was being drawn into the Cold War conflict being waged within the government; it was also the first indication of a British interest in the continent, an interest that was soon to grow and to result in colonial Africa assuming much greater importance in Bevin's overall global strategy.

Meanwhile the future of the Italian colonies was to continue to reveal the attitudes of the Foreign Secretary to Britain's imperial role in the eastern Mediterranean and Middle East. On May 10, the Russians made a significant concession and renounced all claims to any trusteeship of Tripolitania; the Soviet position was now that all the Italian colonies should be given in trust to Italy for ten years. Bevin's response was to increase British demands in order to secure an exclusive position in Cyrenaica,[27] a shift, as he acknowledged, made on his own responsibility and without cabinet approval. British communications through the Mediterranean, Bevin explained, were necessary for the defence of the Dominions. Cyrenaica was "vital from the point of view of the British Empire."[28]

This was a vital question in terms of the breakdown of allied cooperation and the origins of the Cold War; it was also relevant to the debate between the imperialists and the internationalists which was under way at the highest levels of the British government. Bevin's views on how best to safeguard the empire were directly opposed to Attlee's, who was convinced the empire could only be defended by its membership of the United Nations. Britain had therefore to try to make international arrangements effective and "not at the same time act on outworn conceptions" based on the need to preserve exclusive maritime control of imperial communications in the Mediterranean.[29]

By the end of 1946, the debate was influenced by perceptions of the increased importance of Africa for Britain's economic recovery. Bevin's interest in colonial development went back to 1929 and his work in the Colonial Development Advisory Committee established by the then Labour government. In 1946, Bevin was particularly interested in a trans-African trunk road which was rejected by an inter-departmental committee on grounds of cost.[30] But with attention being given to the economic and strategic importance of Africa, it could be argued that Britain's position in the Mediterranean and the Middle East was necessary for the defence of the continent. In other words a neutral zone in the Middle East would be infiltrated by the Russians who would then be in a position to threaten Africa. Pierson Dixon accepted that the Middle East was no longer vital for British communications, but believed a strong British presence was necessary to prevent the Russians taking over North and Black Africa; without it, he feared, the Soviets would become established on the Congo and at the Victoria Falls.[31]

At a meeting in January 1947 senior Russophobe officials concluded that any attempt to reach agreement with the Soviet Union was out of the question until Britain's weakness had been overcome; to ignore this "would be to repeat on a larger scale the errors made at Munich" and enable the Russians to threaten South Africa. Then, once the Soviet Union was established on the shores of the Indian Ocean in East Africa, India would gravitate to the Soviet bloc.[32]

This African domino theory was designed to justify Britain's imperial position in the Middle East. But the continent was also important to the reattainment of Great Power status and to the regaining of economic independence from the Americans. The economic crises of 1947 increasingly convinced Bevin and other leading policymakers, notably Sir Stafford Cripps, that colonial development would provide the answer to Britain's dollar difficulties; what Europe was unable to deliver the colonial territories of Africa would eventually provide. Bevin explained his ideas to Attlee in September: "I am sure we must free ourselves of financial dependence on the United States as soon as possible. We shall never be able to pull our weight in foreign affairs until we do so."[33] Moreover, if the development of Africa's resources could be carried out in conjunction with the three other African colonial powers this would provide a means of enrolling Western European nations as collaborators with the British empire. For Bevin maintained "it was essential that Western Europe should attain some measure of economic unity if it was to maintain its independence as against Russia and the United States"[34]

In the wake of the convertibility crisis of July and August 1947, Bevin and Cripps discussed the possibility of developing an area in western Europe and Africa which would allow Britain to become self-supporting, overcome the dollar problem, and thereby regain economic independence. Once Britain had examined the prospects of developing colonial resources, the French and Belgian colonies could be brought in to make a similar contribution to improving the dollar position. This formed an increasingly important element in the original 1945 plan of enrolling the western European nations as collaborators with the British empire; it was more attractive to imperialists like Bevin than a British imperial trading bloc, because of the perceived necessity to build strong economic links with Europe. France and Belgium would be the initial collaborators in Africa, although Bevin soon expected to involve both the Portuguese and the Italians.[35]

The French and British Colonial Offices were already involved in a low-profile scheme of technical cooperation in Africa; but in September 1947, Bevin and Bidault agreed this should be extended to economic and commercial matters and dealt with by ministers.[36] In December, an interdepartmental working party was set up to investigate colonial economic cooperation, and the breakdown of the Council of Foreign Ministers in the same month prompted Bevin to make public his ideas on a third world force led by Britain. Linked economically by what Bevin had earlier termed "vested interests," there would be no formal political ties, but a "spiritual union" in which, as leader of Western Europe and the Commonwealth, Britain could develop its "own power and influence to equal that of the United States." Mobilizing the resources of Africa in support of West European Union would ensure that the British-led grouping equalled the western hemisphere and Soviet blocs in terms of productive capacity and manpower.[37]

In 1948, the Foreign Secretary was not seeking a special position in an American-dominated Atlantic Alliance created to defend Western civilization; his goal was a special role for the British empire, in conjunction with Western Europe, which would enable it to gain economic independence from the United States and achieve equality of status and influence within a tripartite world order. As late as March 1948, the Cabinet was still being told "we should use US aid to gain time, but our ultimate aim should be to attain a position in which the countries of western Europe would be independent both of the US and the Soviet Union." Bevin was hoping "to organize the middle of the planet – W. Europe, the Middle East, the Commonwealth," and if Britain "only pushed on and developed

Africa, we could have US dependent on us and eating out of our hand in four or five years . . . . US is very barren of essential minerals and in Africa we have them all."[38]

Between 1945 and 1947, Bevin and his officials aimed to preserve and strengthen British influence in the eastern Mediterranean and the Middle East; they then sought to develop European and African resources in an attempt to regain Britain's economic independence and reestablish a position of global power and influence equal to that of the Americans and Russians. Historians who interpret Bevin's policy in terms of the contemporary issues of the Soviet threat, Western European defence and the Atlantic Alliance fail to reflect Bevin's Churchillian imperialism and the fact that his policy in terms of its own stated aims was a failure. What was central to Bevin's policy was the role of the empire and its relation to western Europe and the middle of the planet; his aim was to create a third world force independent of the United States and the Soviet Union, not to provide a link between the United States and western Europe. The Atlantic Alliance was not therefore Bevin's overriding aim in 1945 nor indeed in 1948.

In the short term, American backing for British schemes was deemed necessary in order to support the empire during Britain's period of recovery, and also to support Britain's commitment to western Europe when the latter appeared threatened by Communist coups. The fact that American backing for the empire was sought in the summer of 1945 before the Conference at Potsdam, is crucial to an understanding of British policy toward the Russians; it was perceptions of Britain's imperial role, together with a refusal to accept the Soviet Union as a friendly power, which produced a Foreign Office view that any cooperation with the Soviets was undesirable.

Central to this view was the determination to preserve Britain's exclusive position in the eastern Mediterranean and Middle East, and it was the Mediterranean issue which produced the first formal breakdown of allied cooperation. Attlee's internationalism and Molotov's power-political bargaining both proved irreconcilable with Bevin's and the Foreign Office's ideas on the future of the British empire. This is not to affirm that British actions were solely responsible for the breakdown of allied cooperation, or that they were a major influence on

American policy; but a study of Bevin's imperialism does suggest that his policies could only lead to cold war confrontation and were therefore more a cause of allied disagreements than a response to them.

NOTES

From John Kent, "The British Empire and the Origins of the Cold War, 1944–49," in Anne Deighton (ed.), *Britain and the First Cold War* (New York: St Martin's Press, 1990), 165–83. Reprinted and abridged by permission of St Martin's Press and the Macmillan Press Ltd.

1 See especially Alan Bullock, *Ernest Bevin: Foreign Secretary, 1945–1951* (New York, 1983); R. Ovendale, *The English-Speaking Alliance* (London, 1985); David Dilks, *Retreat From Power* (London, 1981).
2 This idea was frequently expounded by both Bevin and his Permanent Under-Secretary from early 1946, Sir Orme Sargent. See, for example, Sargent memo, July 11, 1945, Foreign Office [hereafter FO] 371/50912; Bevin to Attlee, September 16, 1947, FO 800/444; Cabinet papers [hereafter CAB] 129/23 C.P.(48)6, January 4, 1948, CAB 129/23; CAB/128 C.M.(48)2, January 8, 1948, CAB 128; Public Record Office [hereafter PRO], London.
3 A. Adamthwaite, "Britain and the World 1945–49," *International Affairs*, 61(2) (1985): 223–35.
4 Sargent memo, "Stocktaking after VE Day," July 11, 1945, FO 371/50912, PRO.
5 The initial agreement was Russian influence in Romania 90 percent; British influence in Greece 90 percent; Russian influence in Bulgaria 75 percent; British and Russian influence in Hungary and Yugoslavia 50 percent each.
6 Folios 227–35. Record of meeting at the Kremlin, October 9, 1944, FO 800/302, PRO; cited by M. Gilbert, *Road to Victory: Winston S. Churchill 1941–1945* (London, 1986), 993.
7 Churchill Papers 20/153 Prime Minister's Personal Minute M(Tol) 6/4, October 12, 1944; cited by Gilbert, *Road to Victory*, 1003.
8 FO to Washington, July 5, 1945 (copy of telegram to Istanbul), CAB 119/126, PRO.
9 *Documents on British Policy Overseas* [hereafter *DBPO*], Series 1, Vol. I, 1945, Clark Kerr to Eden, July 10, 1945.
10 P.H.P(45)9(0) Final, March 30, 1945, JP(45)170(Final), July 11, 1945, CAB 119/126, PRO.
11 For Sargent's views in the interwar years see J. Haslam, *The Soviet Union and the Struggle for Collective Security in Europe 1933–39* (London, 1984), 99, 228.
12 Sargent memo, "Stocktaking after VE Day," July 11, 1945, FO 371/50912, PRO.
13 *DBPO*, Series I, Vol. II: 699.

14 *DBPO*, Series I, Vol. I: 793–5.
15 ibid., 145–6.
16 *DBPO*, Series I, Vol. I: 364.
17 Bevin Papers 3/1, Bevin to Cranborne, February 1, 1944; cited in V. Rothwell, *Britain and the Cold War, 1941–1947* (London, 1982), 224.
18 43rd Annual Conference Report of December 11–15, 1944; cited in P. Addison, *The Road to 1945* (London, 1975), 254.
19 K. Morgan, *Labour in Power, 1945–1951* (Oxford, 1984), 193.
20 *DBPO*, Series I, Vol. I: 992–4; original emphasis.
21 ibid.
22 Comments by the Chiefs of Staff, January 1, 1945, FO 371/50787, PRO.
23 Note of conversation between Bevin and Molotov, October 1, 1945, FO 371/50920, PRO. Bevin's last point was of course incorrect and was not what he was preparing to tell the Americans, because Britain wanted Cyrenaica.
24 Rothwell, *Britain and the Cold War*, 239, citing Pierson Dixon's diary.
25 For an analysis of Attlee's and Bevin's disagreements: R. Smith and J. Zametica, "The Cold Warrior: Clement Attlee Reconsidered, 1945–1947," *International Affairs*, 61(2) (1985): 237–52.
26 K. Harris, *Attlee* (London, 1982), 299.
27 Ironically this tactic of increasing one's demands when others made concessions was precisely what Bevin ascribed to Communist negotiators. See Dalton Diary, September 10, 1946; cited in Yergin, *Shattered Peace: The Origins of the Cold War and the National Security State* (Boston, MA, 1977), 258.
28 Record of 3rd informal meeting of Foreign Ministers, Paris, May 10, 1946, FO 371/57278, PRO.
29 *DBPO*, Series I, Vol. II, Memo by Attlee, "Future of the Italian Colonies," September 1, 1945.
30 DO(46) Minutes of 10th Meeting of the Defence Committee, April 5, 1946, CAB 131/1, PRO; P. S. Gupta, "Imperialism and the Labour Government," in J. Winter (ed.), *The Working Class in Modern British History* (Cambridge, 1983), 101.
31 Dixon memo, December 9, 1946, FO 800/475, PRO.
32 Foreign Secretary minute for PM, January 9, 1947, FO 800/476, PRO.
33 Bevin to Attlee, September 16, 1947, FO 800/444, PRO.
34 Record of Meeting of Cabinet Economic Policy Committee, November 7, 1947, FO 371/62740, PRO; cited in W. Lipgens, *A History of European Integration: The Formation of the European Unity Movement 1945–47* (Oxford, 1982), 557.
35 Note of a conversation between Bevin and J. Chauvel, October 20, 1947, FO 800/465, PRO; Troutbeck minute, October 20, 1947, FO 371/67673, PRO.
36 ibid. Note of discussions between Bevin, Bidault, Creech Jones, Chauvel, Couve de Murville, Harvey and Dixon, October 19–22, 1947.
37 CP(48), January 4, 1948, CAB 129/23, PRO; CM(48), January 28, 1948, CAB 128/12, PRO.
38 B. Pimlott (ed.), *The Political Diary of Hugh Dalton, 1918–1940* (London, 1986), 443.

8

HEGEMONY AND AUTONOMY WITHIN THE WESTERN ALLIANCE

Charles S. Maier

Beyond the superpowers, nations and groups and classes within nations pursued their own interests and ideals. They set constraints upon what the Great Powers could do or they helped shape the latters' interaction with one another. In turn, the United States and the Soviet Union had to devise policies that accommodated, modified, or crushed these longings for autonomy and self-expression.

The United States had immense power at the end of the Second World War, but it could not and did not simply impose its will on its partners in the Western alliance. According to the Norwegian historian Geir Lundestad the American empire was an "empire by invitation," an empire beckoned by others as well as designed to further US interests. *Historians like John Gaddis and Charles Maier have adopted this model of analysis and have used it to differentiate the "Pax Americana" in Western Europe from the Soviet empire that emerged in Eastern Europe.*

In this essay Maier seeks to assess the structure of coordination in the Atlantic alliance. Shared values among elites were critical to the success of US policy, and Maier shows that American officials worked hard to cultivate an ideological consensus around the theme of productivity, that is, around the notion that economic gains would allay class conflict and minimize redistributive struggles. But US officials had to do more than forge an ideological consensus. They had to grapple with the unique problems within various European nations, and they had to accommodate national aspirations such as France's insistence on con-

---

* Geir Lundestad, "Empire by Invitation? The United States and Western Europe, 1945–1952," *Journal of Peace Research*, 23 (September 1986): 263–77.

trolling German power and Britain's determination to sustain a global presence.

So fearful were US policymakers of Communist gains and Soviet machinations that European statesmen often manipulated American apprehensions to serve their own national advantage. Maier describes here how this was done, how European officials often transformed their weakness into strength. This was a laborious and time-consuming process that often exposed dissension and vulnerability in the Western camp. Yet in the long run the give and take infused the Western alliance with a sense of shared purpose and mutual interdependence that was far more durable than anything the Soviet Union could establish in Eastern Europe. Readers should explore why this type of "consensual hegemony" could be brought about in one part of Europe but not in the other.

* * *

"Pax Americana" is a resonant term that conceals a crucial question: How much power and control did the United States exert in postwar Europe? US policy involved organizing a coalition of nations, encouraging European leaders who shared the political objectives of the United States, and seeking to isolate those who did not. It meant using economic assistance as well as the appeal of a liberal ideology to reinforce centrist political preferences among European voting publics and working-class movements. At the same time Washington policymakers were supposedly committed to encouraging European autonomy. How did alliance and autonomy mesh?

The premise of this essay is that, given the basic inequality of resources after the Second World War, it would have been very difficult for any system of economic linkages or military alliance not to have generated an international structure analogous to empire. Hegemony was in the cards, which is not to say that Americans did not enjoy exercising it (once they resolved to pay for it). To state this, however, is to explain little. The more intriguing issue remains the degree to which the US ascendancy allowed scope for European autonomy. The relationship worked out between Washington and the European centers during the formative Truman years provided cohesive political purpose but simultaneously allowed significant national independence. To explain that dual result is the purpose of this essay.

From Washington's viewpoint as of 1950, US policy might have been described as a process of growing coherence and resolution. From a confused postwar period in which most Americans thought primarily of winding down their wartime commitments, the Truman administration recognized the threat of Soviet Communist expansionism, provided economic and military reassurances that the United States would not simply abandon those who wished to resist Soviet encroachment, launched a major coordinated plan for economic recovery, and then served as architect for a military alliance and tentative political cooperation. Under the aegis of containment and the leadership of Truman, Americans committed themselves to a continuing role in West European affairs. Whether one admires the process of leadership or deplores it as provocative, certainly the policy of the Truman years – carried through by a remarkable phalanx of internationalists such as Robert Lovett, Averell Harriman, George Marshall, and Dean Acheson, all trained to influence and command, and convinced that Washington must in fact exert influence and command – is one of remarkable purposefulness.

To be sure, this policy could not have enjoyed success had there been no West European interlocutors, a team of partners who quickly became convinced that their own countries' interests, and perhaps their own personal political fortunes, were best served by alignment in the new field of US strength. As noted, such a transnational elite forms the backbone of any imperial system. Nevertheless, Europeans had their own problems and their own priorities. These did not always coincide with American preoccupations, even when common interests prescribed the same overall policies. Moreover, Europeans from the different countries understood how to pursue their own independent agendas under the US umbrella. This freedom of action did not weaken Washington's policies. On the contrary, it allowed US actions to seem less dominating and less constraining and thus probably helped make for a more broadly accepted policy. Precisely this possibility for national divergence made American policies more supple and more attractive than they might otherwise have been. John Gaddis has used the term "empire by consent," and I have used "consensual hegemony."

But how was that consent achieved? And how could there be national differentiation within an overarching US-sponsored Atlantic structure?

The major slogan invented to describe US policies was "containment." In some ways containment remained an American concept. It defined policy as seen from the Great Power center. Europeans accepted the notion, but it did not motivate them in the same integrating and substantive way. They remained concerned about economic recovery, economic integration, and national autonomy as much within blocs as between them. Here we will attempt to see the interlocking of the US agenda and the Washington conceptualization of foreign policy with some of the European agendas and their respective notions of foreign policy objectives. There was much shared purpose to be sure, perhaps more than in any earlier or subsequent period. But even with the extraordinary consensus of the late 1940s to the mid-1960s, different national objectives did not cease to exist.

US policy obviously had a political and an economic aspect. I have described the economic aspect in an earlier paper as "the politics of productivity."[1] Unlike "containment," this was not a term applied by policymakers at the time. None the less, the watchword of productivity became important in 1947 as the Marshall Plan (substantial aid to an integrated West European region) emerged out of the ad hoc aid characteristic of immediate postwar efforts.

Aid through early 1947 was keyed to relief. But by the spring of that year, Washington planners, cold war politics aside, believed that that approach would remain insufficient. In effect, foreign assistance would have to recapitulate the earlier progress of the New Deal, going from the Federal Emergency Relief Administration to the Public Works Administration and Work Projects Administration – that is, from relief to job creation and to investment in infrastructure. To be sure, the proximate impulse in the spring of 1947 for Marshall's initiative arose from a balance of payments crisis. Europe simply lacked the dollars to import agricultural goods, coal, and other basic necessities. The severe winter of 1947 had choked off the initial recovery of 1946. European workers were losing patience with counsels of restraint; strikes broke out and political conflict flared. Fuel was catastrophically scarce because coal barges could not move on the frozen northern rivers and German miners were weakened by hunger. Factories had to be cut back to partial work weeks. With massive discontent among labor, all efforts appeared blighted. The need was to rebuild the European economy so it would not be in a state of perpetual dollar hemorrhage. The moment had come for a concept of far more integrated West European assistance, if only to persuade Congress that relief would not be poured perpetually down a rathole.[2]

As the European Recovery Program [ERP] was established over the course of the following year, with its country missions and Washington Economic Cooperation Administration [ECA] headquarters, the rationale of enhancing "productivity" was increasingly developed. Productivity was the allegedly apolitical criterion that motivated recovery assistance. Just as the idea of "totalitarianism" offered an explanatory construct that could account for Soviet behavior, so "productivity" could serve to sum up American economic aspirations. Productivity was an index of efficiency: it implied clearing away bottlenecks to production and getting the highest output from labor and capital, just as the United States had so obviously accomplished. Productivity supposedly dictated no political interference; for what groups could object to such a neutral measure of economic achievement?

Productivity suggested that class conflict was not inevitable and that management and labor did not have to quarrel over the shares of wages and profits. If they only cooperated, the dividend of economic growth might reward them both. Thus, economic growth in a sense promised the adjournment of political and social conflict; it would transform basic struggles into cooperative searches for optimal economic solutions, "the one best way."

Of course, there was an implicit politics in productivity. It effectively declared out of bounds any Marxist or left-wing notion that capitalism itself might be inequitable. Only self-serving parties interested in their own selfish power could object to economic growth. Acceptance of productivity as a goal effectively froze the division of income and managerial power in a society, promising proportional increments of growth to everyone but keeping the basic distributions of authority and wealth the same. Americans were willing to accept this bargain, as agreement on productivity-keyed wages indicated. The

United States was a society whose immigrant base in effect wagered on growth alone for prosperity.

But applied to Europe, such a policy meant by 1947–8 that Communist spokesmen must be viewed as obstructionist, especially after the Soviet Union decided that it could not participate in the Marshall Plan and in the fall of 1947 urged Communist party leaders in the West to enter a new phase of long-term obstruction.[3] Instead, productivity served to rally social democratic labor groups. French and Italian social democrats were dissatisfied with galloping inflation in their countries and wanted the restoration of wage differentials, which Communists opposed. Leaders of the Force Ouvrière in France, the non-Communist trade unionists in Italy, and the anti-Communist Trades Union Congress in Britain looked to US government assistance or sympathetic American Federation of Labor emissaries with well-upholstered checkbooks to help them resist Communist politicization and subversion of their own unions.[4] Productivity thus came to Europe as the ideological watchword of a coalition that would unite progressive management and collaborative labor.

In the United States the idea of productivity was complemented by the theme of sustained economic growth; the first reference to this – outside academic journals – that I am aware of was in the speeches of the New Dealish chairman of the Council of Economic Advisers, Leon Keyserling.[5] Growth and productivity were to remain underlying guidelines for foreign policy. Even as they were being crowded out after Korea by more purely military and security-oriented concepts, Atlantic leaders invoked their efficacy. "The improvement of productivity, in its widest sense, remains the fundamental problem of Western Europe," spokesmen of the Organization for Economic Cooperation and Development [OECD] wrote in 1952. And Thomas Cabot, the director of international security affairs in the State Department, insisted as he turned over the Mutual Security Program to its incoming director, Averell Harriman, "In my view we have been remiss in not giving productivity greater emphasis . . . . If we can sell Europe on the fundamental advantages of a *competitive* and reasonably free system of enterprise, I have no doubt the standard of living there will advance soon to a level where there is no danger whatever of its being subverted."[6]

The politics of productivity, however, formed only one key concept underlying US policy in the years after 1947. The other was the more geopolitical notion of containment and national security. Productivity and containment were the twin themes of postwar US foreign policy: the one upbeat, can-do, confident that with the removal of bottlenecks, abundance could reconcile all political differences; the other somber, minor-key, predicting twilight struggles and the need for untiring resistance until rivulets of reform might eventually thaw the frozen Soviet political system. The simultaneous pursuit of both ideas allowed the bipartisan foreign policy coalition enough unity at home to overcome isolationism, rallying former New Dealers and interventionist strategic thinkers.

The objectives of containment and productivity characterized policy in general, but they also suggested different needs for different European societies. Washington policymakers worked to encourage an integrated Western Europe, but they also understood that each country had particular vulnerability and potential resources. A common urgency underlay the crisis of 1947 – the conviction that Western Europe was an entity that in effect had to be created to be preserved. But there was no undifferentiated bloc; there were specific problems, opportunities, and missions.

The European countries seemed to pose three sorts of challenge for US policy during the Truman period. The most urgent and brutal was that of direct Communist takeover. The image of countries slipping behind the Iron Curtain, of being "lost" to Communism, prompted the articulation of containment. Communist takeover could result from armed subversion, as the Truman administration beheld it in Turkey and Greece. But Communist takeover need not be military. The Italian government in 1947 and early 1948 seemed almost as precarious. Italy's Communist Party appeared to have the power to paralyze economic reform – to be sure, reform carried out along classical deflationary lines that restored management's power to lay off workers, which had been effectively suspended at liberation. Even sober American observers believed that the April 1948 elections might return the Communists to a dominant government role.[7]

Direct Communist takeover was not the only danger, however. More threatening was the danger of political and economic paralysis. Institutional crises would continue to affect Italy even after the peril of outright takeover seemed to pass, and they threatened French governments as well. Although Americans worried briefly in 1947 that Gaullist electoral gains might prompt Communist counteraction, they became more concerned that the government's inability to master inflation might force the centrist parties to readmit the Communist Party to the ruling coalition of Catholics, socialists, and center parties. The outcome that was dreaded was less direct takeover than an inability to generate productivity and recovery – a vicious circle of inflationary wage settlements and continuing state deficits, growing alienation of labor, and eventually a debilitating neutralism.

These dangers overcome, a third order of difficulty still threatened Washington's overall design. By 1949, "integration" had become a major theme of economic and political aspirations.[8] Although some degree of integration had stamped the Marshall Plan from its inception, Paul Hoffman and other administrators pressed the idea vigorously as the European Recovery Program went into its postcrisis phase. Integration had traditionally implied working toward a common market, but in 1948–9, it referred specifically to achieving monetary convertibility. Without multilateral clearances, US subsidies could not generate their most efficient stimulus.

Communist takeover, economic paralysis, and resistance to integration thus emerged as successive perils to US policy for Europe. The countries most worrisome in 1947 were the least-so later. The societies least vulnerable at first were to become more problematic when integration was at stake. But US policymakers also understood that the European countries brought different assets as well as difficulties. The European nations would make diverse contributions to the common effort.

West Germany clearly had an economic vocation. Even as food shortages provoked demonstrations and coal output fell in the spring of 1947, Americans sought to draw on German mining and industrial potential. American businessmen, trade unionists, and political leaders alike believed that German resources could serve Western Europe as a whole. "The best reparations our Western Allies can obtain is the prompt recovery of Germany," Secretary of Commerce Harriman reported to

161

Truman after his investigations of the summer of 1947. "We cannot revive a self-supporting Western European economy without a healthy Germany playing its part as a producing and consuming unit."[9]

Assigning West Germany a role as an eventual economic "locomotive" was possible because politically the country remained under effective control. In light of developments in East Germany, Communism exercised no mass appeal in the West. Socialism was also an excluded alternative. Once the United States took a leading role within the British and American zones, British sympathizers had to defer their plans for the socialization of coal and steel industries in North Rhine-Westphalia, and the Social Democratic Party [SPD] itself retreated into an opposition stance. The possibilities of socialism had been minimal. SPD enthusiasm had been overrated, and the British had never really pressed for it; there was little Labour Party involvement in occupation affairs.[10]

West Germany had an economic mission; France, Britain, and the small countries of Western Europe had political roles to play in the new Western Europe. Administration policymakers believed that these countries were needed to generate stability and Western cooperation. The initial response of both Foreign Secretary Ernest Bevin and French Foreign Minister Georges Bidault to Marshall's speech promised that both countries would take the lead in the new Europe. But France's cooperation was proffered precisely to head off too quick a rehabilitation of Germany. French leaders had to be persuaded to come to terms with the economic role that West Germany must logically play, just as two years later they would have to be pressed into accepting a German military role. "The goal of the European Recovery Program is fundamentally political," said Acting Secretary of State Robert Lovett in December 1948, "and France is the keystone of continental Western Europe."[11]

If France was to be the political keystone, stability had to be ensured inside the country. This meant creating the conditions for a non-Communist coalition to prosper. As early as October 1947, in a striking application of the politics of productivity, Under-Secretary Lovett urged working-class schism: "Politically speaking the break must come to the left of or at the very least in the middle of the French Socialist Party. Translated into labor terms, the healthy elements of organized labor must be kept in the non-Communist camp. Otherwise the tiny production margin of the fragile French economy would vanish and the ensuing civil disturbances would take on the aspects of civil war."[12]

Once the schism did materialize, the task was to brake inflation and restrain wages. Emphasizing that Americans "did not want to take sides in internal French politics," Lovett said that it would be hard to continue aid unless "a strong, unified and cooperative non-Communist government . . . put the French house in order."[13] Such a "nonpolitical" agenda included balancing the budget and ending inflation.

American Treasury officials were pleased with the anti-inflationary policies of René Mayer and Maurice Petsche. Acheson could turn to Paris again to work for European integration: "France and France alone can take the decisive leadership in integrating Western Germany into Western Europe."[14]

Britain also had a political vocation in American eyes. Over the long term, European recovery required meshing resources and production, thus freeing trade and payments from early postwar restrictions. Britain had the least scarred economy and the closest cultural links to the Americans, hence it appeared as a natural leader. But the British devoted their cooperative efforts largely to military matters. With great fanfare Bevin called for a "consolidation of Western Europe" in January 1948, but he proposed building on the Treaty of Dunkirk directed against Germany and helped produce the West European Union, a rather empty institutional vessel designed to encourage Washington to enter a defense commitment.[15] Emphasizing a military role would give Britain more parity with the United States, whereas economic integration would undermine the Commonwealth resources. By 1949 Americans were chafing at London's unwillingness to upgrade the political status of the Organization for European Economic Cooperation [OEEC] and at British resistance to monetary convertibility.[16] British assistance in Korea and the post-1950 emphasis on military cooperation compensated for foot-dragging on economic integration. None the less, London's reluctance to strengthen European institutions remained a disappointment.

Washington policymakers thus dealt with a complex European agenda. They sought to overcome the dangers of Communist paralysis in Italy and France, to mobilize the economic potential of West Germany, to press France as continental "keystone" to allow German integration, and to move Britain toward more far-ranging economic cooperation. They also relied on the small countries to provide a basis for Europe's new supranational agencies, the staffs of NATO, the Coal-Steel Authority, and the OEEC. This very differentiation of tasks, however, provided special political leverage for the European countries. Precisely because US policemakers envisaged a differentiated set of national problems and contributions, scope was provided for each country's political strategies. It is these very strategies that make European history during the Cold War more than just a mere shadow of US power and motivation. European statesmen understood what Washington needed from them and could extract concessions in return. De Gasperi in Italy, the leaders of the French "third force" (from Bidault to Mayer to Monnet and Schuman), Konrad Adenauer in West Germany, and finally the British leadership (a combination of Labour ministers and persuasive Treasury and Foreign Office officials) used the new Atlantic Community for national as well as cold war ends.

For Italy, weakness was itself a strategy. By the spring of 1947, de Gasperi sought to reconstruct his government without the Communists. Throughout 1946 the Christian Democrats had built up their machine in Italy but economic difficulties mounted. When the economic officer of the American embassy, Henry Tasca, returned to Washington in May 1947, he reported a "lack of confidence on the part of the strategic economic groups in the ability of the government to direct and control the country." The Communists were benefiting from the very fear that they might come to power.[17] At the same time Italian Ambassador Alberto Tarchiani sought guarantees from Secretary of State Marshall: if de Gasperi reconstructed his government without the Communists, would he be assured of the economic aid needed to counter the obstruction that was feared? No specific promises could be brought back from Washington, although the crisis lingered even as Marshall made his celebrated Harvard commencement address.

This implicit dependence continued through the 1948 elections. Italy sought aid from the United States by constantly stressing the precariousness of non-Communist democracy. De Gasperi received fewer promises of special assistance than he desired, but he could work within the overall context of the emerging Marshall Plan. When Washington sought to press large amounts of military aid on Italy in early 1948, however, he was shrewd enough to understand that the Americans' fear of a military coup was exaggerated and that such an arsenal could only discredit him if it became public knowledge.

The Italian premier understood how to exploit the politics of dependence. More than elsewhere the fate of the Christian Democrats depended on American intervention; hence it was in de Gasperi's interest to insist on his country's political and economic fragility. He stressed his difficulties in seeking a favorable decision on Trieste and, less successfully, on the Italian colonies. By 1948–9, the Italian authorities' emphasis on deflationary stabilization, even at the cost of rising unemployment, dismayed ECA supervisors, while the State Department similarly resented subordinating Italian defense expenditures to the stability of the lira. But it was hard to exert too much pressure. Even when the Christian Democrats enjoyed a majority after April 1948, the internal party balance was precarious.

Washington sought to encourage the more cooperative and less right-wing and deflation-minded currents. It was also essential in Washington's eyes to keep the Saragat wing of the Social Democrats within the coalition so as to prevent the Italian working class from falling completely under Communist domination.[18] Thus Italy's plea to be included in NATO had to be honored despite the extended defense commitment this entailed and the negligible military assistance the nation might provide. To keep Rome out would have signaled a continuing stigma and undermined the Italian government. Domestic stability was more at stake than military defense. In short, Italy was included in NATO not because of its strength but because of its weakness.[19]

Throughout 1947, French governments were constrained to pursue a tactic similar to that of de Gasperi. Until the winter of 1947–8, Bidault still entertained aspirations that France might retain control of the German Rhineland, the French zone of occupation, and a share in administering the Ruhr. The French minister repeatedly importuned the Americans and the British that unless they heeded French wishes toward Germany the fragile centrist government that had expelled the Communists might collapse. Ambassador Caffery faithfully conveyed a sense of the Ramadier government's standing at the political brink: aid or Armageddon.[20]

Such pleading might win US willingness to provide more coal and financial aid, but it could not do more than slow down Anglo-American insistence that Germany must be made a more paying concern. After long internal debate, in early 1948 the French openly came round, and accepted that their older ideas of a hold on the Rhineland were unrealistic and that they had to endorse West German institutions. French political strategy became less supplicating, more autonomous. By 1948 it was hard to play the menace of the Communists so convincingly. If Caffery could always signal alarms, Tomlinson and other US economic officials wanted action to raise taxes and curb expenditures. Efforts to curb inflation won recognition from Washington.

But firming up policy at home was only part of the French response. The other was to carve out some limited scope for foreign policy autonomy. While British statesmen aspired to be the experienced, senior counselors in an Anglo-American military-political framework, the French in effect sought a secondary, subhegemony within NATO. Abandoning their early effort to retain control over a segment of West Germany, the French sought to satisfy US demands that they take the lead in "integrating" West Germany back into the West. The political genius of the Schuman Plan lay in the fact that it could please Washington, even as it capitalized on the fact that Bonn was momentarily weak but would soon be industrially and perhaps politically resurgent. In effect, Monnet and Schuman offered to serve as Bonn's patrons at a point when Adenauer could not really carry out an independent foreign policy.

Paris also insisted on Italian membership in NATO over British and even American skepticism.[21] The theoretical reason was that France must otherwise defend its long Italian frontier; but the French also wished to become Rome's patron as well as Bonn's. To Rome, France offered military colleagueship; to Bonn, economic partnership. Thus France became the architect of an alignment within Western Europe that seemed advantageous to the United States while it also enhanced France's own role. The French were not able to achieve the tripartite OEEC or NATO directorates they periodically proposed; nevertheless, France, perhaps more than Britain, created a real

European role that could serve national interests.

France retained political assets throughout the period; State Department spokesmen always recognized how crucial France was. But what about West Germany: a divided country, burdened by its recent history, distrusted by its neighbors, and, until 1955, limited in its sovereignty? Even when its cities were in ruins, Germany always retained industrial potential. Typecast as the animator of West European recovery, Germany could continually emphasize its economic vocation. German industrialists and labor leaders joined forces in petitioning for an end to dismantling and to corporate deconcentration. They found sympathetic responses from Lucius Clay's assistant, General William Draper, and later High Commissioner McCloy. German firms pressed their plans for reconstruction and expansion by citing their fervent desire to serve as good Europeans: Thyssen would get its new rolling mills by proposing steel for the Marshall Plan.[22] When France held out the Schuman Plan, Adenauer set aside any opposition on details from his own industrialists. The crucial aspect, he understood, was not whether Germany might or might not extract a few more concessions; it was the political opportunity to achieve partnership with France.

After the outbreak of the Korean War the potential of the German economy became even more prized. Emphasizing economic potential also accorded with the political tasks within West Germany. The constant appeal was for working-class loyalty; labor had to be harnessed for production. In return for codetermination, the union federation effectively accepted wage restraint until the 1960s. Pay claims were subordinated for the evident need to reconstruct the country. Workers remained suspicious of ideology after the experience of the Third Reich and in light of the unwelcome totalitarian development of East Germany. Economics was a surrogate for politics for two decades after 1947, but it was also a way of conducting politics. Reconstruction provided a sense of national purpose at home, and under Adenauer's canny supervision, coal, steel, and skilled labor were bargaining chips for recovering international autonomy. The resources of the Ruhr, reconciliation with France, reparation for Israel, and rearmament for the West became the pillars of German policy.

Within the framework of the new Western Europe, the

smaller countries and Britain chose opposite courses. The Dutch and the Belgians provided the leadership and enthusiasm for the supranational agencies Americans sought to strengthen. In part their ministers may have found this new scope of activity personally rewarding. Dirk Stikker and Paul Henri Spaak were the preeminent Europeanists, although Americans had to balance Spaak's utility to the OEEC with his importance in holding together Belgium's unraveling political coalitions. In addition, Spaak (like Gunnar Myrdal, chairman of the Economic Commission for Europe in 1947–8) was distrusted by London.[23] But beyond Spaak's personal contribution, Belgium was pivotal in US calculations because of its international financial strength. US Treasury advocates of multilateralism approved of Belgium's early postwar policies, and they found Camille Gutt, who went on to chair the International Monetary Fund after presiding over Brussels's successful currency reform in 1944–5, a congenial defender of hard-currency convertibility.

In contrast to Belgium, Britain resisted multilateralism and convertibility. Within the American "hegemony" British leaders chose what a classical historian might call the Polybian strategy – that is, attempting to become the Greeks in America's Roman empire, wagering on the "special relationship" to prolong their influence and status. They brought to this role a certain historical mystique, the experience of managing an empire, the willingness to shoulder heavy defense commitments (which the Pentagon especially appreciated), memories of the wartime alliance, and the considerable resources of a common language and a prestigious culture. State Department officials recognized that the United States was often partial to London and that British leaders "are not on occasion averse to letting their continental colleagues know they are favored above others by us."[24]

Throughout the late 1940s and early 1950s US policymakers struggled against their own partiality as they criticized Britain for its retention of expensive military forces (at least before Korea), its reluctance to accept the Coal-Steel Community, and its resistance to a European Payments Union. But the web of informal associations, probably accentuated by the Anglo-Saxon descent of US foreign service officers, tempered a more ruthless approach. The British sometimes overestimated the deference that their wisdom should command and assumed that they retained the brains even if Washington commanded the money.

None the less, Bevin, Sir Stafford Cripps, and civil servants such as Sir Edwin Plowden understood how to create a sympathetic mood in high-level negotiations. (Congress proved more resistant to US concessions than executive-branch officials did.) And although Britain continued to insist on the special needs of the Commonwealth, Bevin's early anti-Communism and Cripps's continuing "austerity" dissipated American charges of self-indulgence.

None the less, the Marshall Plan presented occasions for disagreement. For Washington, the greater the degree to which Europeans could diminish their balance of payments constraints by multilateral clearance of payments among themselves, the greater could be the effect of scarce dollars for Europe as a whole and the less Europe's overall dollar dependency would cost the American taxpayer. But Britain resisted moves towards free convertibility. To enter a multilateral clearing scheme threatened to require deflationary measures at home that would preclude Labour Party commitments to full employment and generous social welfare. What is more, Britain wanted to pass along Marshall Plan dollars in 1948 to its former Asian dependencies so that they would not liquidate their sterling reserves kept in London. (Much of these reserves, in effect, represented wartime loans from the colonies for the British costs incurred in their defense. They provided London with the same credit facilities that dollar convertibility gave the United States until 1973.)

US ECA and Treasury officials felt that the British were stinting on their own domestic investment for the sake of imperial grandeur, and they argued that Washington could not afford to subsidize the dollar shortages of the Third World. As with other similar issues, compromise solutions were negotiated, which is why the European Recovery Program remained workable, even if it moved less decisively toward the integration that Washington desired.[25]

By and large throughout such negotiations US Treasury spokesmen looked to restoration of currency convertibility, which meant establishing the dollar as a universal medium of exchange. ECA planners in Washington and Paris stressed the recovery of production and consumption. Their activist economists contemplated increasing intervention into European investment plans, and they asked that Marshall Plan aid be evaluated not in monetary aggregates or financial terms but in the "real" categories of national income.[26]

It was not surprising that expansionist concepts of domestic investment and international trade took root in the ECA, for the new agency recruited the young economists being trained in the "Keynesian revolution." But the division between ECA Keynesians and the more orthodox Treasury–IMF spokesmen testified to the ambiguities of the Truman administration, poised between New Deal legacies and a revival of more traditional economic concerns. The two major ECA officials had unconventional business backgrounds: Harriman had joined the New Deal after administering railroads, shipping, and banking; Paul Hoffman had been an organizer of the activist Committee on Economic Development, a business coalition that welcomed demand management and macroeconomic intervention. In contrast, Secretary of the Treasury John Snyder was a midwestern banker.

The ambiguities in America's foreign economic policy reflected the spectrum of approaches within the Truman administration more generally. These conflicting tendencies meant that different European countries might appeal to different sources of American authority. The deflationary leaders of Italy or of Belgium implicitly aligned with the US Treasury to resist ECA prodding; the British relied first on Marshall Plan leaders to compromise, and then on US military and political concerns to buffer Washington's would-be financial disciplinarians.

The result of these and many other bargains in the administration's European policy was to allow significant flexibility for national objectives. Washington policymakers could not smash Britain's residual imperial position, which London relied on in part to finance its welfare state. Nor could Washington push de Gasperi's Italy toward the thoroughgoing political and social modernization the Americans would doubtless have preferred. Rather, the Italian Christian Democrats knew how to use American assistance as part of their own resources for domestic patronage and political networks. The need for industrial revival in Europe provided the West Germans with their opportunity to recover political independence as well, as did the felt need for rearmament after 1950. The overarching Soviet-American bipolarity concealed how much scope there was for customized national polices and strategies to flourish. As Bevin had done in early 1948, Europeans talked boldly of integration and unity. But the policies they pursued looked toward cherished national and particularist objectives as well. US policy offered many footholds precisely because with all its stress on Western Europe as a region, it had to confront individual national needs, weaknesses, and potential resources. The Europeans responded reciprocally. On the one level, integration and unity flagged; the opportunity that the European federalists sought was not fully seized, although this slowing of impetus was more apparent in later years than during the Truman period. But the historical result of the period was truly remarkable. The scope for national political alternatives distinguished Western from Eastern Europe; it followed not from blueprints but from the compromises that policy pluralism required. In an era when Europe seemed initially demoralized as well as devastated, the groundwork was laid not just for an imperial subordination to Washington but for a genuine revival of national traditions and of autonomous historical possibilities for Europeans.

NOTES

From Charles Maier, "Alliance and Autonomy: European Identity and U.S. Foreign Policy Objectives in the Truman Years," in Michael Lacey (ed.), *The Truman Presidency* (New York: Woodrow Wilson International Center and Cambridge University Press, 1989), 273–98. Reprinted and abridged by permission of the author.

1 Charles S. Maier, "The Politics of Productivity: Foundations of American International Economic Policy after World War II," in Peter J. Katzenstein (ed.), *Between Power and Plenty: The Foreign Economic Policies of Advanced Industrial States* (Madison, WI: University of Wisconsin Press, 1978), 23–49.
2 See Michael J. Hogan, "The Search for a 'Creative Peace': The United States, European Unity, and the Origins of the Marshall Plan," *Diplomatic History*, 6(3) (Summer 1982): 267–85.
3 Communist policy has been interpreted differently. See Alfred Rieber, *Stalin and the French Communist Party, 1941–1947* (Cambridge, MA: Harvard University Press, 1962); Wilfried Loth, "Frankreichs Kommunisten und der Beginn des kalten Krieges: Die Entlassung der Kommunistischen Minister im Mai 1947," *Vierteljahrshefte für Zeitgeschichte*, 26 (1978): 9–65; J. P. Hirsch, "'La seule voie possible': Remarques sur les comunistes du Nord et du Pas-de-Calais de la Libération aux grèves de novembre 1947," Actes du Colloque de l'Université de Lille III, 2–3 novembre 1974, in *Revue du Nord*, 57 (1975): 563–78. Up to winter 1947 Communists themselves followed

a politics of productionism, seeking to establish their coalition bona fides in Western Europe by getting their unions to work hard and pursue wage restraint. That policy threatened to fragment their own ranks during the hard winter of 1947, and they were compelled to a more militant stance: precisely the demands that let the French and Belgian socialists argue for their exclusion from "Tripartite" coalitions in early 1947. Only in the fall of 1947 did the "orders" from Moscow seem to arrive, that henceforth they must remain noncooperative. Even then, however, the objective of the mass Communist strikes of 1947–8 seems less to have been to seize power (they knew this was impossible) than to show the centrist parties, including the socialists, that their countries could not be governed without their cooperation. Here, too, they miscalculated. In effect, US capital replaced Communist labor.

4 For the European labor movement, from viewpoints critical of US policy, see Peter Weiler, "The United States, International Labor, and the Cold War: The Breakup of the World Federation of Trade Unions," *Diplomatic History*, 5(1) (Winter 1981): 1–22; Ronald Radosh, *American Labor and U.S. Foreign Policy* (New York: Random House, 1969). For more sympathetic accounts, André Barjonet, *La C.G.T.* (Paris, 1968); Daniel L. Horowitz, *The Italian Labor Movement* (Cambridge, MA: Harvard University Press, 1963); also Irving Brown's detailed if partisan reports in the American Federation of Labor [AFL] papers, Florence Thorne collection, State Historical Society of Wisconsin, Madison.

5 Keyserling, "Prospects for American Economic Growth," address in San Francisco, September 18, 1949, in the Harry S. Truman Presidential Library [hereafter HSTL], Independence, MO, President's Secretary's Files [hereafter PSF], 143: "Agencies: Council of Economic Advisers."

6 Organization for European Economic Cooperation [OEEC], *Europe: The Way Ahead*, 4th Annual Report (Paris, 1952), 195; Cabot to Harriman, October 25, 1951, in *Foreign Relations of the United States 1951* [hereafter *FRUS*] (Washington, DC: Department of State, 1979), Vol. 1: 440.

7 For an example, see the views of George F. Kennan; Kennan to Secretary of State, March 15, 1948, *FRUS, 1948* (Washington, DC: Department of State, 1974), Vol. 3: 848–9.

8 On Washington's hopes for European integration in 1947–8, see Hogan, "Search for a Creative Peace"; also Armin Rappaport, "The United States and European Integration: The First Phase," *Diplomatic History*, 5(2) (Spring 1981): 121–49.

9 W. Averell Harriman to Truman, August 12, 1947, in Harriman papers: Commerce File; Folder: "Germany," Library of Congress, Washington, DC.

10 See, for example, the statements by Franz Neumann in Council on Foreign Relations Archives, Records of Groups, Vol. 19, 1949/50: Study Group on the Problem of Germany, meetings of October 13 and November 9, 1949.

11 Lovett to Harriman, December 3, 1948, *FRUS, 1948*, Vol. 3: 301–3.
12 National Archives [hereafter NA] Washington: RG 59, 851.00/10–2447.
13 *FRUS, 1948*, Vol. 3: 307.
14 Acheson to US embassy, Paris, October 19, 1949, *FRUS, 1949* (Washington, DC: Department of State, 1975), Vol. 4: 469–72.
15 See Rappaport, "The United States and European Integration," 129–31. Bevin followed up his cabinet paper and speech in Parliament with queries to Washington on US readiness to help in the defense of Western Europe. See Alan Bullock, *Ernest Bevin, Foreign Secretary 1945–1951* (New York: W. W. Norton, 1983), 518–22.
16 Meeting of ambassadors at Paris, October 21–2, 1949; *FRUS, 1949*, Vol. 4: 492; and Bruce to State Department, June 4, 1950, *FRUS, 1950* (Washington, DC: Department of State, 1977), Vol. 3: 716.
17 Tasca statement in part in *FRUS, 1947*, (Washington, DC: Department of State, 1972), Vol. 3: 898–901, and in part in NA, Washington: RG 59, 865.51/5–747.
18 For the poormouthing of 1947, see Ambassador Dunn to Secretary of State, May 3, 6, and 28, also memorandum of conversation, May 16, and memoranda of conversation by the director of the Office of European Affairs, May 20 and June 4, 1947; also Marshall to US embassy, Rome, May 20, 1947, in *FRUS, 1947*, Vol. 3: 889–919. For later criticism of Italian policies but unwillingness to press too hard, see the ECA Country Report on Italy (1950) and Acheson to US embassy in London on Italian politics, January 18, 1950, *FRUS, 1950*, Vol. 3: 1984–5, and Acheson to US embassy in Rome, December 2, 1950, ibid., 1501–2.
19 See E. Timothy Smith, "The Fear of Subversion: The United States and the Inclusion of Italy in the North Atlantic Treaty," *Diplomatic History* 7(2) (Spring 1983): 139–55.
20 Caffery cables to State Department, February 19, 1947, and May 12, 1947, in *FRUS, 1947*, Vol. 3: 690–2; also memorandum of conversation, Moscow, April 20, 1947, and Bidault to Secretary of State, July 17, 1947, and Caffery to State Department, July 18, 1947, all in *FRUS, 1947* (Washington, DC: Department of State, 1972), Vol. 2: 367–71, 991–2, 996.
21 For the internal French reassessment of their German policy, see Ministère des Affaires Etrangères, Paris: Série Y: 55, dossier 1: Massigli (ambassador in London) to Bidault, November 22, 1947; and Série Y: 45, dossier 9: Ministère des Aff. Etr. à M. le Commissaire Général du Plan, août 9, 1948 (provisional classifications). For a jaundiced French view of the origins of the Schuman Plan by an adherent of an English orientation, see René Massigli, *Une Comédie des Erreurs 1943–1956* (Paris, 1978), Ch. 5; and on the question of Italian membership in NATO, see minutes of the tenth meeting of the Washington Exploratory Talks, December 22, 1948, in *FRUS, 1948*, Vol. 3: 324–32.
22 See the Thyssen plea for expansion in Duisburg-Hamborn, in

Bundesarchiv, Koblenz: Z 41/23 Verwaltungsamt für Eisen und Stahl.

23 See Kirk to State Department, October 11, 1948, and Lovett to Kirk, October 13, 1948, in *FRUS, 1948*, Vol. 3: 489–92; memorandum by Perkins for Secretary of State, September 9, 1949, *FRUS, 1949*, Vol. 4: 421–2, and related material following.

24 Ambassador Bruce to Secretary of State, April 25, 1950, in *FRUS, 1950*, Vol. 3: 63–5; also the meeting of ambassadors, October 21–2, 1949, *FRUS, 1949*, Vol. 4: 490–4; and the minutes of the seventh meeting of the Policy Planning Staff, January 24, 1950, *FRUS, 1950*, Vol. 3: 617–22.

25 See "Extract of Current Economic Developments," May 24, 1948; Ambassador Lewis Douglas to State Department, June 11, 1948; Richard M. Bissell, Jr, "Memorandum," September 22, 1948, all in *FRUS, 1948*, Vol. 3: 442–3, 450–2, 486–9; and Phillip S. Brown to Bissell, September 23, 1948, in RG 59: 840.50 Recovery/10-148. Background of the earlier issues in Richard Gardner, *Sterling-Dollar Diplomacy* (rev. edn, New York: McGraw-Hill, 1969).

26 On Treasury views, see Acheson's summary of the views of Frank A. Southard, Jr (US executive director of the IMF), April 12, 1949, in *FRUS, 1949*, Vol. 4: 382; also Southard to Secretary of the Treasury John Snyder, September 29, 1949 and January 16, 1950, in HSTL, John W. Snyder Papers, box 34, F. "UK Loan, 1946–48, Alphabetical File," and box 11, F, "ECA and International Trade Organization, 1950." On the activism of the ECA, see Hoffman to Harriman, October 6, 1949, *FRUS, 1949*, Vol. 4: 426–9; and on end-use accounting see Richard M. Bissell, Jr, "Statement on the Long-Term Programme," to the Long-Term Working Group of the OEEC, October 26, 1948, in HSTL, Charles P. Kindleberger papers, box 2, F. "General Correspondence." Admittedly, ECA administrators in the respective countries were often businessmen who held views less Keynesian than those of the young academic economists at headquarters.

9

HEGEMONY AND REPRESSION IN THE EASTERN ALLIANCE

Charles Gati

One of the most exciting areas of inquiry in cold war studies relates to Eastern Europe. Archival materials are becoming more plentiful, and historians have begun to conduct meaningful oral interviews, examine some party archives, and peruse selective yet valuable personal manuscript collections. Charles Gati was one of the first scholars to do this work and his analysis of immediate postwar developments in Eastern Europe in general and in Hungary in particular has been pathbreaking.

Gati stresses the importance of indigenous developments. He illuminates the legacy of the war and the popular clamor for land reform and social justice. He explores the tangled web of political intrigue, the differences among Hungarian Communists, and the relationships between the latter and the men in the Kremlin.

Gati shows that Stalin was in no hurry to communize Hungary. Within Eastern Europe the Kremlin pursued a differentiated policy. In Poland, Romania, and Bulgaria the Soviets clamped down immediately. In Hungary and elsewhere in East-Central Europe (for example, Czechoslovakia) there was a so-called "Democratic interlude," a two- or three-year span when there was considerable fluidity and openness. Readers should reflect on both why Stalin permitted such an interlude in the first place and why he decided to bring it to an end in the autumn of 1947. Readers should also think about how this argument reinforces or conflicts with some of the points put forward in the MccGwire and Reynolds essays. For example, was Stalin motivated by his perception of threat and his fear of US initiatives, or by ideological concerns, or by dissension within his own bloc? And when comparing developments in Eastern and Western Europe, readers should seek to identify the reasons why the Soviet Union could not forge a consensual hegemony similar to the one established by the United States in Western Europe.

* * *

175

Although Hungarian political life during the short-lived democratic interlude – from late 1944 to late 1947 – was quite complex, its basic features can be easily summarized.

For three years, Hungary was governed by a broadly based coalition government composed of representatives from several non-Communist parties, from the interwar regime of Admiral Miklos Horthy, and just a few members of the small Hungarian Communist Party, even as the country – Hitler's last satellite – was being controlled by the Red Army primarily through the Allied Control Commission. As in Czechoslovakia, Austria, and Finland, but nowhere else in Soviet-occupied Europe, Hungary was allowed to hold free elections in November 1945, which confirmed the Communists' minority status. They received only 17 percent of the votes cast by contrast to the 57 percent in favor of the immensely popular Smallholders' Party alone. Until the autumn of 1947, Hungarian political life displayed many of the virtues of political democracy: the composition of the government mirrored the election results, the press was almost free, the National Assembly openly debated controversial issues, the economy was mainly in private hands and based on market forces, the stock market flourished. Indeed, it was only after the Communist Information Bureau (Cominform) was founded in the Polish town of Szklarska Poreba in the summer and autumn of 1947 that Hungary's democratic interlude gave way to Communist hegemony.

This essay, by offering new details about the beginning and the end of Hungary's democratic interlude, raises two questions of interpretation: why was the Communist takeover of Hungary as gradual as it was, and why did it end when it did (sooner than planned)? Put in a broader context, why did Moscow prescribe a relatively long democratic interlude in Hungary (and Czechoslovakia) while engineering far more rapid takeovers elsewhere?

As the Second World War was coming to an end, Stalin's foreign policy objectives developed within a framework of conflicting imperatives and inhibitions. On the one hand, the Soviet Union's new European geopolitical position offered the historic opportunity to realize Moscow's long-suppressed desire to expand "socialism in one country" into "socialism in one region," an opportunity pointing toward the adoption of an assertive foreign policy. On the other hand, Stalin's apprehension over potential Western countermeasures – and, to a lesser extent, his view that some of the European countries were not yet ripe for revolution – was an inhibiting factor.

The consequence of such conflicting circumstances and calculations was a highly differentiated Soviet policy toward Europe.[1]

Given the evidence of his negotiating positions in the autumn of 1944 and his subsequent policies too, Stalin seems to have regarded it as both premature and counterproductive for all the Communist parties to adopt a uniformly militant approach even in what would soon be called the "people's democracies" of Eastern and East-Central Europe. Although his ultimate objective was surely the establishment of the Soviet Union as the predominant European power, Stalin was prepared to pursue that objective gradually. Accordingly, he appears to have envisaged a Europe made up of three political zones or spheres:

1 a non-Communist, relatively stable zone in Western Europe, one that would also include Greece;
2 a Communist zone under Soviet control in Eastern Europe – along the vital routes to Germany and the Balkans – that would range from Poland and the eastern part of Germany to the Black Sea states of Romania and Bulgaria;
3 an intermediate zone in East-Central Europe of coalitional political systems under only gradually increasing Communist influence, extending from Yugoslavia in the south through Austria, Hungary, and Czechoslovakia to Finland in the north.

For the time being, Western Europe – the first zone – was not only beyond Stalin's reach, it was also beyond his ambitions. Seeking a measure of stability in Western Europe to divert attention from the sovietization of Eastern Europe, Stalin was especially eager to provide no reason for the United States to remain active in Europe after the war and involve itself in the political affairs of the continent. For this reason, Stalin instructed the powerful French and Italian Communist parties to avoid all provocative actions and concentrate instead on such innocuous tasks as the reconstruction of their countries' war-torn economies and administrative structures.[2]

Whether any of the Communist parties of Western Europe could have seized power in the autumn of 1944 or early 1945 remains an unanswerable question. It is a fact, however, that after 1941 the Italian and the French Communist parties constituted the largest force within the anti-Nazi resistance during the Second World War, and they emerged from the war well organized and quite popular. By professing to fight for national survival and national independence rather than for revolutionary objectives, they had effectively removed the stigma from the Communist name and thus qualified themselves for participation in a broadly based, democratic coalition government. That they chose to join the postwar governments and postponed all attempts to seize power was not because a Communist-led revolution was definitely destined to fail, but because Stalin settled on a Popular Front or "moderate" strategy for them in order to placate the United States and Great Britain and in order to divert attention from what was happening in Eastern Europe.

In the second zone, for which Stalin had envisaged Soviet dominance at the earliest possible moment, coalition governments of "national unity" came into being in 1944–5 as they did elsewhere in Europe – but they were coalitions in name only. With a few notable exceptions, the bogus coalition governments in Poland, Romania, and Bulgaria – as well as in the Soviet-occupied part of Germany – typically included only such non-Communists as the local Communist parties deemed acceptable: fellow-travellers and political chameleons like the Pole Jozef Cyrankiewicz, nominally a socialist, or the Romanian Petru Groza, nominally of the "Ploughmen's Front."[3] Even though a few courageous Agrarian leaders, such as Stanislaw Mikolajczyk in Poland, Iuliu Maniu in Romania, and Nikola Petkov in Bulgaria, refused to give up or fade away for some time to come, the Communists in fact obtained controlling influence in the wake of the Red Army's arrival almost at once. In contrast to what was happening elsewhere in Europe truly competitive elections were not allowed to be held anywhere in this zone; instead, an all-encompassing, Communist-dominated bloc of parties "won" putative elections whose outcome had been predetermined.

In East-Central Europe – that intermediate zone of states for which Stalin had envisaged coalition governments without

Communist hegemony as yet – the trend of events was more ambiguous than elsewhere in Europe, the results rather mixed. Although their political standing varied from country to country, by 1947 all of the Communist parties in this zone – with the notable exception of the Yugoslav party – had witnessed the erosion of their popular appeal, all had suffered setbacks, all had managed to alienate both Western and domestic opinion.

Following a strategy identical to the Czechoslovak party's, the Hungarian Communists' quest for power entailed extensive cooperation with non-Communist elements and participation in a national effort to rebuild the country. The Hungarian Communists were told that since Moscow's primary aim was the rapid sovietization of Poland (combined with the dismemberment of, and eventual control over, Germany), they had to act in such a way as to placate Western concerns and suspicions.[4] Accordingly, at the first Central Committee meeting held in Soviet-liberated Budapest on January 23, 1945, the party's second-in-command, Erno Gero, explained the Polish tradeoff to a group of puzzled Communist leaders by referring to the complex "international situation" in general and the Churchill–Stalin percentage agreement in particular. "The Soviet Union must win the diplomatic battle in order to obtain decisive influence in Hungary," said Gero, concluding that Hungarian Communists must "not scare the Anglo-Americans" for the time being.[5] The party was not expected to achieve hegemony in less than ten to fifteen years.[6]

Although it could gain only 17 percent of the vote in the free 1945 national elections – in contrast to the Smallholders' Party's 57 percent – the Communist Party was to acquire far more influence than its popular appeal would have warranted. Ranging from persuasion to intimidation and coercion, the technique it most skillfully applied was known as the "salami tactics," which signified the party's ever-increasing demands to remove step by step – or slice by slice – elements it deemed undesirable from the coalition. In 1945, it was the leftovers of the interwar regime of Miklos Horthy; in 1946, it was the so-called right wing of the Smallholders' Party, led by Dezso Sulyok, and of the Social Democrats, led by Karoly Peyer; in 1947, it was Bela Kovacs, the Smallholders' popular Secretary-General, followed by Zoltan Pfeiffer's troublesome faction, followed by the centrist Prime Minister, Ferenc Nagy, and others.

In each case, the Communist Party reiterated its long-term commitment to political cooperation and harmony within the coalition, adding, however, that first these "reactionary" and "anti-democratic" politicians must be dismissed from positions of influence. The "salami tactics" turned out to be effective, not only because the Communists could claim the support of the Soviet occupation forces, but also because some of the non-Communist leaders were not unwilling to acquiesce in the removal of a competing faction within their parties from political life.

The Communist Party's successes in dividing its adversaries through the "salami tactics" and its advance toward hegemony notwithstanding, the highly competitive national elections of August 31, 1947 – in which it received 22 percent of the vote – served as a reminder of its limited appeal. Publicly, the party claimed victory, but it was hard to explain away the 78 percent non-Communist vote. The election demonstrated the inadequacy of the coalition strategy in Hungary – as, indeed, that strategy was found to have been inadequate everywhere else in Stalin's third zone by the autumn of 1947.

Stalin's projected policy for Hungary was first confronted in a series of three secret meetings that took place in Moscow in October 1944. One was between the Soviet leadership and an official delegation sent to the Soviet capital by the regent of old Hungary, Admiral Miklos Horthy. At long last, the regent seemed ready to conclude an armistice agreement with the Soviet Union.

The delegation appointed by Horthy and headed by Lieutenant-General Gabor Faragho left for the Soviet Union on September 28. At first, Moscow would have accepted an armistice along the Finnish pattern: Horthy stays, the Germans leave, and everything else is subject to negotiations. By the time the Faragho delegation arrived in October, the terms became less flexible: Horthy could still stay, but he must turn against Hitler and accept the evacuation of all Romanian, Czechoslovak, and Yugoslav territories regained since 1938. By December, after Horthy had abdicated and after the Red Army had come to control half of Hungary, Stalin made a further adjustment in the Soviet position. His early notion of the "broadest possible anti-German coalition" now gave way to the somewhat narrower "anti-German *and* anti-Horthy coalition," one in which a few leading representatives of the old order could still participate.

Coincidentally, a second series of secret conferences was taking place in October. Accompanied by Foreign Secretary Anthony Eden and others, Churchill arrived in Moscow to discuss with Stalin and Molotov the postwar political orientation of five countries in Eastern and in East-Central Europe – Greece, Bulgaria, Romania, Yugoslavia, and Hungary. The first meeting between Churchill and Stalin was held on October 9; the substance of their famous "percentage agreement" became known with the publication of Churchill's memoirs in 1953.[7] But their encounter was followed by two days of haggling between Eden and Molotov on October 10 and 11, the details of which came to light only in the mid-1970s.[8]

Churchill was not in a strong position to demand Western influence in Eastern or in East-Central Europe. The United States had rejected his recommendation that parts of this region be liberated by Anglo-American forces. Having all but conceded Poland to Stalin in Tehran two years earlier, in 1943, he was now prepared to concede Soviet control over Romania and Bulgaria too in exchange for British control over Greece, assuming that in Yugoslavia and Hungary – and perhaps elsewhere in East-Central Europe – "some kind of Anglo-Soviet influence-sharing" might be possible. Expressing his idea in percentages, Churchill – writing "on a half-sheet of paper" – presented Stalin with a formula for the distribution of Great Power influence after the war.

Molotov's apparent purpose at the follow-up meetings was to increase Soviet influence in Hungary, while Eden – guided by British interests in the Mediterranean – would have preferred to focus on Bulgaria and the Balkans in general. A long, rather petty, and somewhat disjointed haggle followed. Eden was to recall in his memoirs that while Molotov "showed a disposition to haggle over the percentages," he [Eden] "was not interested in figures. All I wanted was to be sure that we had more voice in Bulgaria and Hungary than we had accepted in Romania." Eden believed that "we obtained what we wanted on almost all points. I should say 90 percent overall."[9] Aside from the irony of judging the results of this encounter in percentages, Eden was surely mistaken. Compared to the Churchill–Stalin "deal," he gained nothing. And if Molotov's main purpose was to obtain

British consent to Soviet primacy in Hungary after the war, then that purpose was achieved.[10]

The third set of secret meetings was held in Moscow in the autumn of 1944 just as Soviet forces were moving into Hungary. The cream of Hungarian communist *émigrés* got together on September 13, 20, and 28 and October 7, 1944 to hammer out their program for and define their role in postwar Hungary. At least twenty-four leading cadres participated in the debates. These were the veterans of the Hungarian Communist movement in exile, the "Muscovites" who had survived the short-lived Soviet republic or commune of 1919, Hungary's prisons during the interwar years, and Stalin's purges in the 1930s. They were exhilarated by the prospect of returning to their homeland, not as conspirators and agitators facing certain arrest and imprisonment but as free citizens of a new Hungary. Yet, as their speeches and comments showed, they bore the scars of more than two decades of intense factional disputes and personal antagonisms.[11]

Neither of the two main speakers even intimated that the Communist Party might seek to rule postwar Hungary. One of them, the ideologist Jozsef Revai, a particularly articulate spokesman for the Popular Front approach, argued that his party should seek the slow, long-term transformation of Hungarian society. He put considerable emphasis on the necessity of inspiring a national effort in the months and years ahead, stressing that even "a democratic revolution will not happen at once."[12] The primary task was the distribution of land, Revai stressed, and hence the Communist Party must not allow such popular issues as Hungary's proper borders with its neighbors to distract the country's attention from the implementation of land reform and from the pursuit of other social and economic reforms.

The second main speaker, and a frequent participant at all the other sessions, was Erno Gero. In his lecture of October 7, he noted that although Horthy's ultimate fate was uncertain, the old regime was expected to survive. He also argued that the party had to stand for a democratic transformation and not for the dictatorship of the proletariat. The party's program for a people's democracy must be so flexible, Gero emphasized, that no important stratum of Hungarian society would find it necessary to oppose it. Put another way, the

Table 1 The Soviet-British Bargain of 1944

	Churchill–Stalin agreement (Oct. 9)	Molotov's initial revision proposed (Oct. 10)	Molotov's first "package deal"	Molotov's second "package deal"	Molotov's third "package deal"	Eden's only counter-proposal	Molotov's counter-offer	Molotov's modified counter-offer	Molotov's Oct. 11 final proposal (apparently accepted)
Soviet influence in Hungary	50%	–	75%	50%+	75%	75%	–	–	80%
Soviet influence in Yugoslavia	50%	–	75%	50%	60%	50%	50%	60%	50%
Soviet influence in Bulgaria	75%	90%	75%	90%	75%	80%	90%	75%	80%
Soviet influence in Romania	90%	–	–	–	–	–	–	–	–
Soviet influence in Greece	10%	–	–	–	–	–	–	–	–

Communist Party should be prepared to form an alliance with all classes and not only with the industrial proletariat and the peasantry.[13]

During the rather extensive debate that followed, a number of participants – apparently surprised if not irritated – openly questioned the leadership's conciliatory strategy. Gero, acknowledging the existence of "mistaken views," found it necessary to explain again the reasons for the party's gradualist approach. Still, some kept returning to the issue of how the Communist Party would make headway: how it would proceed to hasten the process toward a people's democracy. Responding to that question, the leaders referred to a system of local national committees that the party would establish concurrently with the formation of a central government. Expecting these national committees to be more responsive to Communist influence and pressure, Gyorgy Lukacs, the noted Marxist philosopher, argued that a national committee in Budapest could play an especially vital role in the country's political life and indeed "push the government forward."[14]

On the basis of these discussions, Revai and Gero composed the party's "action program" during the second half of October. A copy of the draft was forwarded to Stalin and Molotov for approval. The program emphasized the need for national collaboration and unity against Nazi Germany, speedy reconstruction, and the urgency of land reform. Georgi Dimitrov, the Bulgarian prewar leader of the Comintern, laughingly told Gero that the Hungarian Communists were ever so lucky to have the unresolved problem of vast land holdings in Hungary, for this way they could easily champion a popular and quite non-controversial cause.[15] So approved, the Muscovites' program virtually amounted to temporary self-abnegation. The party's best-known leader, Matyas Rakosi, was instructed to stay in Moscow for a while because his return to Hungary might frighten too many of his countrymen. The party was to display both its red flag and the Hungarian national colours of red, white, and green. Although all the participants of the Moscow meetings were not informed about it explicitly, Stalin had told the leadership that in order to distract the attention of the Western allies from the rapid sovietization of Poland, the pluralistic phase in Hungary – the democratic interlude – would have to last at least ten to fifteen years.[16]

The actual implementation of ideas emanating from these three meetings – i.e. obtaining a measure of continuity with the past, deferring if possible to the sensitivities of Great Britain and the United States, and hence carrying out a program of national reconstruction by a broadly based coalition government – was a task initially assigned to Zoltan Vas, the first Muscovite to follow the Red Army to Hungary. Reflecting the party line, Vas deliberately kept the Communist Party in the background; in point of fact, he was instructed to "implement the Party's objectives through other people . . . even through other parties."[17] Vas and his comrades did what they could to make the Communist Party palatable to, and seem representative of, the Hungarian people – and to appear that way to the Western world whose cooperation Stalin needed and whose potential hostility he so deeply feared.

During the course of these first few weeks, the Muscovites' policies ran into resistance from an unexpected source – from many of the local or "home" Communists who found the party line as defined by the Moscow leaders and indeed by the Russians far too conciliatory toward the old regime. Having suffered under Horthy and having fought him under extraordinarily difficult circumstances, these Communists sought revenge and wanted "socialism now." At a party *aktiv* of November 19, 1944 in Szeged, for example, several home Communists heatedly argued for the immediate establishment of the dictatorship of the proletariat. The answer came from Revai who had just arrived from Moscow: "England and America would not recognize a Communist government. Those who want socialism and the dictatorship of the proletariat make the anti-German policy more difficult."[18] On another occasion, Gero exclaimed: "Some Communists think that the order of the day in Hungary is the establishment of socialism. That is not the position of the Hungarian Communist Party. It is not a correct viewpoint to urge the construction of socialism on the rubble of defeat."[19] On still another occasion, Revai was even more emphatic: "I declare that we do not regard the national collaboration [of the several political parties] as a passing, political coalition, as a tactical chess move, but rather as a long-lasting alliance."[20]

For non-Communists, this was as surprising as it seemed appealing. The Communists' proposed "Program for Hungary's

Democratic Reconstruction and Advancement" seemed to represent the general objectives that they had dreamed of, and fought for, for a quarter of a century. They could only welcome the Communist Party's advocacy of a competitive political system, freedom of religion, freedom of the press; of free enterprise and private property, combined with land reform and the nationalization of large banks, mines, and insurance companies; and of a "democratic" foreign policy rooted in good neighborly relations, "close friendship" with the Soviet Union and "sincere cooperation" with Great Britain and the US.[21] Political platitudes, to be sure, but they were identical to those the non-Communists would have put forth.

For the military officers and political figures in Horthy's entourage, the choice between joining the new government or staying on the sidelines was more difficult. Yet, in the end, most of those who were asked to participate decided to do so – at least for now. Political retirement seemed neither useful nor realistic, for the country's place in the emerging European political order was still unclear and its place in the Soviet orbit appeared not to be a foregone conclusion. Despite their reservations and fears about the Communists' ultimate plans, then, the majority of the old guard could join the new era, not because they were opportunists who could not live without the perquisites of power but because they sought to position themselves for a future to whose shape they fervently hoped to contribute.

Meanwhile, discussions in Moscow about the distribution of portfolios in a new provisional government moved along two separate tracks. First, as previously noted, the subject had come up between Horthy's delegation, the so-called Hungarian Committee in Moscow led by General Faragho, and the Soviet government, usually led by Molotov. Second, there had been extensive consultations between the Soviet government and the "Moscow-based" Hungarian Communists, too. Stalin was present on at least one such occasion, on December 1, when the Hungarian Communist side was represented by Rakosi, and by Gero and Imre Nagy.

The three sides finally got together for what turned out to be a decisive session on December 5. They had not met before – these professional revolutionaries and these well-bred officers and politicians of the old order – but they all knew by now what kind of government they were expected to form. As Molotov had told the Hungarian Committee on November 13: "The institution to be created should be democratic, with the participation of every party."[22]

Gero presented the list. He said that the provisional government should be headed by General Bela Miklos and should include the remaining four members of the Hungarian Committee. Thus: Defense – General Janos Voros; Culture/Education – Professor Geza Teleki; Ministry of Food – Lieutenant-General Gabor Faragho; and Liaison with Moscow – Domokos Szent-Ivanyi. Gero further recommended that the other seven portfolios should be distributed among four political parties as follows: two "Moscow-based" Communists in charge of Agriculture (Imre Nagy) and Commerce (Jozsef Gabor); two Social Democrats in charge of Industry (Ferenc Takacs) and Welfare (Erik Molnar); two Smallholders in charge of Foreign Affairs (Janos Gyongyosi) and Finance (Istvan Vasary); and one representative of the National Peasant Party in charge of Internal Affairs (Ferenc Erdei).[23]

Gero's list was accepted without debate. The Hungarian Committee was clearly pleased with the list. With the Horthyites and five non-Communists assuming all but two of the cabinet seats, there was reason to believe that the Soviet Union was indeed committed to continuity, albeit without Horthy, and to the ideal of forging a genuine coalition government.

In reality, Gero seems to have set at least two political traps for the unwary Hungarian Committee.

First, the Communists were about to take control of not two but four, and perhaps five, ministries in the government. For in addition to Nagy and Gabor, the man to head the important Ministry of Internal Affairs, Ferenc Erdei, was a secret member of the Communist Party, even though he remained formally associated with the National Peasant Party at Zoltan Vas's request. Then there was Erik Molnar, listed by Gero as a Social Democrat. In fact, Molnar had been a home Communist, a party member since 1928, whose assignment in the 1930s was to penetrate the Social Democratic Party and influence its policies from within. Lastly, there was the dubious case of Janos Gyongyosi, the designated Foreign Minister and nominally a Smallholder, who was already working for, and on behalf of, the Soviet High Command in western Hungary.[24]

Second, Gero offered a cabinet seat to all members of the Horthyite Hungarian Committee probably because their past could some day be used against them. After all, Bela Miklos, the new Prime Minister, could be justly accused of collaboration with the Third Reich: he had served as the senior general of the army until mid-October 1944 and in that capacity he had directed Hungary's war effort against the Soviet Union. The same could be said about the other officers, Voros and Faragho. As for the civilians, even Professor Teleki and Szent-Ivanyi had been identified with some of the policies of the Horthy regime. In short, Gero's coalition appeared to be far more genuine and inclusive than it actually was.

At the year's end, as Budapest was still to be liberated, the country's postwar political order was already in place. The radical transformation of Hungary's social and economic life was under way. The Soviet-ordained gradualist approach of the Communist Party was not only an eminently workable strategy in Hungary, but it proved to be an effective Soviet signal to the West as well. *The Economist* of London assured its readers on December 30 that the composition of the new Hungarian government had proved the accuracy of "Mr Molotov's promise" that Russia would not attempt to influence the "domestic structure" of countries under its temporary supervision.

Reading this, even Molotov must have allowed himself a rare smile.

Less than three years later, when the founding meeting of the Cominform got under way on September 21, 1947, the Soviet leaders were no longer in a smiling mood. Stalin's differentiated plan for postwar Europe – both the Popular Front strategy of domestic cooperation through coalitions in Western and in East-Central Europe and the Popular Front strategy of international cooperation with the West – ceased to produce new gains for the Soviet Union. The once-prevalent American image of a benign and trustworthy Uncle Joe was replaced by a widely perceived reality called the Soviet totalitarian menace.

With the grand alliance thus shattered – and given the removal of Communists from the governments of Western Europe and the apparent standstill in East-Central Europe – it was time for Stalin to initiate drastic changes in policy. He signaled a dramatic turn in international Communism from right to left, from gradualism to insurrectionism, only in the autumn of 1947. For, by then, his early doubts about the specter of "incipient diversity" in international Communism had crystallized.[25] In Western Europe, the Communist parties had allowed themselves to be removed from their countries' governments. In East-Central Europe, the gradualism he had devised for this area was thwarted by the Yugoslavs who, contrary to his vision, had seized power too soon; it was frustrated by the Finns and the Austrians whose quest for power had failed altogether; and it was even foiled by the Czechoslovaks and the Hungarians who had not moved soon enough to consolidate their power. While Stalin had reason to be satisfied with what was happening in Eastern Europe, even here he could find the Gomulka wing in Poland too pertinacious, too intractable, somewhat independent.

Stalin needed the Yugoslav Communists' help to present the abrupt change in policy without giving the impression that he had been wrong or inconsistent. Then, as always, the Soviet party insisted on being consistently correct, and Stalin of course was infallible. If so, how could the two Soviet representatives at the Cominform meeting, Andrei Zhdanov and Georgi Malenkov, put forth Stalin's militant line without criticizing Stalin's previous gradualist line? And how could they prevent the Yugoslavs, who had advocated such a militant line all along, from asking the embarrassing question as to why Stalin had to wait so long to shelve his "capitulationist" Popular Front ideas? Would not Tito's representatives, Eduard Kardelj and Milovan Djilas, claim to have been "consistently correct"?

To protect Stalin's authority, Zhdanov employed the simple device of shifting blame for the gradualist sins of the recent past by pretending that it was the Communists of Western and East-Central Europe who had failed to implement Stalin's policies correctly and hence it was they, not Stalin, who were at fault.

The more complex device Zhdanov employed aimed at the entrapment of the Yugoslav Communists. The two Yugoslav delegates had been asked to come to the Cominform meeting a day or two before the opening session in order to consult with the Soviet representatives. Hoping to use the occasion to discuss a couple of misunderstandings between the two parties, Kardelj and Djilas were happy to oblige. And what they learned and what they were asked to do were both surprising and satisfying: at long last, Stalin was ready to turn against the gradualist right in international Communism and he asked for the Yugoslavs' support. Would the Yugoslav comrades criticize the "insufficiently militant" Communist parties of Western and East-Central Europe for relying on parliamentary methods to gain power, for trusting Social Democrats, for failing to see through imperialist designs?

Kardelj and Djilas failed to understand in time that Stalin's cordiality toward the Yugoslav Party would be short-lived, and that there was a price to be paid for the harsh attacks they were urged to deliver. For in a deceitful political scheme strikingly similar to the factional struggles in the 1920s,[26] Stalin presently instigated the Yugoslav left to censure the gradualist right, all the while contemplating the next round when he would use the right, by then properly humbled, to bring the self-righteous and stubborn Yugoslavs under control. When, several months later, Kardelj and Djilas finally realized that – in preparation for the 1948 confrontation – Stalin had turned them loose to "create a gulf" between the Yugoslav Party and the others, and that Stalin was thus planting the seeds of bitter hostility toward the Yugoslavs among Communists everywhere,[27] it was too late. Most participants left the founding meeting of the Cominform with a sense of brooding resentment against the humiliation inflicted on them by Kardelj and Djilas, and when the time came to retaliate – in 1948 – they would be as vehement and zealous in their denunciation of the Yugoslavs as Kardelj and Djilas had earlier been of them.

From official accounts published afterwards, the outside world could learn some of what happened at the founding meeting of the Cominform, but not much. Zhdanov's "two camps" speech received the most attention, and his message was clear: the era of "cooperation" between the Soviet Union and the West had come to an end. Although Soviet foreign policy was still to be based on long-term coexistence between socialism and capitalism, Zhdanov no longer expected the West to reciprocate. He identified the Truman Doctrine and the Marshall Plan as extreme expressions of American imperialism, steps which reflected aggressive military and strategic intent as well as a commitment to economic expansion and ideological warfare. Supported by Great Britain and France, American imperialism was said to aim at the enslavement of Europe – making it a "49th state" – and at unleashing a new war against the Soviet Union.[28]

Yet the official record of the conference concealed as much as it revealed. As the unofficial accounts of the conference would subsequently reveal, the delegates may have attended one of the most acrimonious gatherings in the stormy history of the Communist movement. The French and the Italians especially were subjected to bitter accusations, while criticism of the Czechoslovak and the Hungarian Communist parties, and of the Gomulka wing in Poland, was more muted and rather circuitous. Heckling of some of the speakers was the order of the day. Jacques Duclos, the French Communist, was rudely and repeatedly interrupted by the Yugoslavs, the Russians, and the Romanians. Ana Pauker accused him and the Italian Longo of "parliamentary pirouetting." Zhdanov also turned on Duclos: "Do you not believe, Comrade Duclos, that the people would have understood the situation better if you had said that the Communist Party was an opposition party? . . . If the Communist Party observes that it has taken the wrong road, it must openly confess its mistake; this you have not done!" Malenkov joined the rumpus: "We would like Duclos to state his conclusions clearly, to tell us just what errors were committed by the leadership of the French Communist Party."[29]

Humiliated and angry, Duclos at one point left the meeting, sat by himself on a bench in the park, and would not talk to anyone. Back at the conference hall, his voice still trembling, he admitted his party's "opportunism" and apologized to his inquisitors. So did Longo for the Italian Party. With the obligatory and rather pitiful self-criticism behind them, Duclos and Longo left for home to implement the new party line. Puzzled, confused, and probably angry, they must have wondered why they had to accept rebuke for policies which had been initiated, approved, and promoted by Stalin himself.

Although the collusive Soviet-Yugoslav condemnation of the French and the Italian parties, and Zhdanov's "two camps" speech were the two featured events in Szklarska Poreba, the side-show was not without interest either. Three other parties –

the Polish, the Czechoslovak, and the Hungarian – had some difficulty explaining why they had continued to uphold the concept of peaceful transition to socialism for so long, why they still tolerated the existence of other political parties at this late date, why they failed to press for a radical economic program on the Soviet pattern.

Speaking for the Polish party – though he represented only one of its factions – Gomulka turned out to be the only delegate at the conference to express reservations about the proposed militant approach, about the very formation of the Cominform, about adopting a strategy common to all Communist parties. In open session, moreover, he stubbornly repeated the view that political circumstances in Poland still called for Communist cooperation with, rather than the absorption of, the Polish socialists' quite accommodating left wing. Neither the official record nor the unofficial accounts indicate clearly how the other delegates responded to these by now outdated ideas, but Gomulka is known to have left the gathering skeptical about the new line in international Communism.[30] An unreconstructed believer in the "Polish road" to socialism, Gomulka lost and was soon dismissed as his party's Secretary-General and placed under house arrest.

The Hungarian Communist Party's predicament at, and after, Szklarska Poreba was similar to that of the Czechoslovak Communists. Its delegates left Budapest for the conference at short notice, not knowing what to expect. If anything, they had reason to believe that the Hungarian Communists' record of the previous three years would earn them accolades from their foreign comrades. After all, the Hungarian party had applied consummate skill to the implementation of the Popular Front strategy. Operating in a hostile – anti-Soviet and anti-Communist – environment comparable only to Poland's and possibly Romania's, the Hungarian Communists had still managed to obtain 17 percent of the popular vote in the free elections of 1945. In their dealings with the non-Communist parties, the Communist leaders – particularly Secretary-General Rakosi and ideologist Revai – possessed an uncanny knack of knowing when to be accomodating and when to be unyielding, when to rely on parliamentary methods and when to resort to intimidation and even terror, when to make concessions and when to threaten to make public an embarrassing story about a stubborn opponent's past.

So ambiguous was their predicament, so difficult was the balancing act they were expected to perform, and so complex was the task of shaping a political order they concurrently sought to support and subvert, that there were times during the democratic interlude when all the Communists could do was to emulate their coalitionary partners/opponents – and play for time! As Vas sums up his and his comrades' sense of uncertainty (in the as yet unpublished part of his extraordinarily candid memoirs), they were unsure *even in 1946* whether "Stalin might not let Hungary come under the political influence of the [Western] allies in exchange for Soviet demands on Poland and Germany."[31]

To be sure, the Communists had resorted to some harsh measures before the founding meeting of the Cominform in Szklarska Poreba. Early in 1947, they implicated Bela Kovacs, the Smallholders' popular Secretary-General, in a so-called "anti-democratic conspiracy," and the major political crisis they created that summer brought down the Smallholder-led government of Ferenc Nagy. On the eve of the Cominform gathering, on September 16, 1947, the party's Politburo began to prepare guidelines for the "fusion" of the Communist and Social Democratic parties.[32] Still, much of what transpired at Szklarska Poreba took the Hungarian Party by surprise.

Indeed, it was only after Zhdanov classified Hungary as one of the people's democracies at Szklarska Poreba that the Hungarian delegation began to understand that the new militant line, the end of the Popular Front era, required a fundamental change in the party's policies at home. When he returned to Budapest, Revai concluded in a secret memorandum to the Politburo that the Cominform had made "significant changes in the political and tactical direction of the Comintern's 7th Congress."[33] Although he sought to minimize the direct implications of this "significant change" for the Hungarian Party in order to justify the gradualist sins of the recent past, his memorandum was full of self-critical remarks: the party was said to lack a firm ideological basis for its programs and policies, it overestimated the function of "parliamentary combinations," it was given to "practicism." In order to fulfill its new mission, Revai urged the party to adopt six new steps: revision of the party's coalition strategy; reexamination of economic policy with a view toward supplanting the role of the bourgeoisie; changes in state administration and in the army's organizational structure; measures to raise the party's "militant spirit"; improvements in the work of the trade unions to avoid "bureaucratic degeneration"; and a thorough reorientation of ideological work to provide a theoretical basis for the implementation of all the other tasks and to explain anew the evolution of the country's political system since 1944.[34]

At one of many debates in the Politburo later that year – on December 10, 1947 – Imre Nagy, apparently alone, argued against the new militancy. Nagy continued to hold on to the pre-Cominform view that the Hungarian transitional system was a "mixture" of the old and the new, a view which had been the Hungarian party line all along and which had been put forth by Revai as late as the beginning of the Szklarska Poreba gathering. But Nagy's position was by now untimely and therefore inoperative.

The post-Cominform majority view was summed up by Gero, who served as chairman of one of the two commissions which the Politburo appointed to study the lessons of the Cominform meeting:

> As a result of domestic and international developments and contrary to our previous conceptions, a new and serious forward step is possible in the nationalization of industry and, in part, of commerce. As is known, our original plan was to effect nationalization gradually . . . In my view, it would be a mistake to adhere to the original schedule and not to take advantage of the favourable circumstances.[35]

Ideological revisions were accompanied by harsh measures in the political realm. First, the results of the August 1947 elections were *de facto* revoked by the party's decision to encourage non-Communist politicians to leave the country – or cooperate with the new bogus coalition. Dozens if not hundreds of prominent political figures were thus forced to leave for the West in October–November; others signed up to serve the Communist regime. Second, as the centrist leaders of the Social Democratic Party were among those who escaped, the Communists called for the "unification" of the two so-called working-class parties (which took place in 1948).

The third political development in the aftermath of the founding meeting of the Cominform had to do with the intensification of infighting within the Communist Party leadership itself. It seems that Rakosi perceived a potential challenge to his authority less from the gradualist Imre Nagy, who was not given to political infighting and who was reportedly protected by Georgi Malenkov, than from Laszlo Rajk, another Politburo member and then Minister of Internal Affairs. Rajk had been suspected by Rakosi to have favored a more militant approach since 1945; according to one account, Rajk and a few other home Communists had "considered the coalition 'corrupt,' and they craved a cleaner break with the past than Rakosi was offering."[36] Although there is no evidence that he actually did so, Rajk *could* claim to have held the "correct" militant position before Szklarska Poreba and hence he was a potential threat to Rakosi, while Rakosi had pursued the coalition games and hence he felt vulnerable. A consummate master of political intrigues, Rakosi accordingly allowed, perhaps encouraged, Gabor Peter, the head of the political police [AVH] and thus Rajk's subordinate, to accuse Rajk in December 1947 of "anti-party and anti-regime behaviour"; soon thereafter Politburo member Farkas joined in with the equally incredible claim that Rajk was an "enemy."[37] In May 1949 he was arrested as a Titoist, tortured, sentenced, and killed. His only crime was that his more militant sentiments had been perceived or presumed before either Stalin or Rakosi would come to regard them as timely – and he paid for them with his life.

In the winter of 1947–8 Rakosi reduced the Hungarian coalition into a totally bogus coalition, a Communist political order in which a few nominally non-Communist figureheads served in order to cover up the dramatic change that took place in the party's policies after the Cominform meeting. With that change, Stalin drew the curtain – the iron curtain – on the democratic interlude he had composed for Hungary three short years earlier in Moscow. The Communists' solemn declaration – "we do not regard the national collaboration [of the several political parties] as a passing, political coalition, as a tactical chess move, but rather as a long-lasting alliance" – turned out to be a lie.

NOTES

From Charles Gati, "The Democratic Interlude in Postwar Hungary: Eastern Europe before Cominform," *Survey*, 28 (Summer 1984): 99–134. Reprinted and abridged by permission of the author.

1 Cf. Geir Lundestad, *The American Non-Policy Towards Eastern Europe, 1943–1947* (New York: Humanities Press, 1975), especially 435–50.
2 Fernando Claudin, *The Communist Movement: From Comintern to Cominform* (New York: Monthly Review Press, 1975), pt 2, 336.
3 The term "bogus coalition" was first used by Hugh Seton-Watson in *The East European Revolution* (3rd edn, New York: Praeger, 1956), 170.
4 Information by Zoltan Vas, Matyas Rakosi's close associate for over thirty years who spent the war years (1941–4) in Moscow in Rakosi's entourage. Stalin's "Polish tradeoff" was also indicated by Gero (note 5 below).
5 As quoted in Mihaly Korom, *Magyarorszag ideiglenes nemzeti kormanya es a fegyverszunet (1944–1945)* [Hungary's Provisional National Government and the Armistice (1944–1945)] (Budapest: Akademiai Kiado, 1981), 390–1.
6 That the Communist takeover in Hungary should occur in "no less than 10 to 15 years" was a key feature of Communist planning for the postwar years. The phrase itself was repeated in all of my interviews with high-ranking Communist officials, including Vas, Ferenc Donath, Miklos Vasarhelyi, and others. When asked at a May 1945 party *aktiv*, Rakosi also used the phrase. See Gyula Schopflin, "A Magyar Kommunista Part utja, 1945–1950" [The Path of the Hungarian Communist Party, 1945–1950], *Latohatar* (Munich), 7(4–5) (July–October 1955): 239.
7 Winston S. Churchill, *The Second World War*, Vol. 6: *Triumph and Tragedy* (Boston, MA: Houghton Mifflin, 1953), 227–9. A copy of the agreement is in Churchill's file at the Public Records Office in London (PREM 3/66/7, PRO). For an excellent summary and perceptive interpretation, see Vojtech Mastny, *Russia's Road to the Cold War* (New York: Columbia University Press, 1979), 207–12. See also Albert Reis, "The Churchill–Stalin Percentages Agreement," *American Historical Review*, 83(2) (April 1978): 368–87.
8 The British record of these two meetings is at the Public Records Office: "Record of Meeting at the Kremlin, Moscow, on 10th October, 1944 at 7 p.m." (PREM 3/343/2) and "Record of Meeting at the Kremlin, Moscow, on 11th October, 1944, at 3 p.m." (PREM 3/434/2). Brief reference to these meetings is made in Anthony Eden, *The Reckoning* (Boston, MA: Houghton Mifflin, 1965), 559–60.
9 Eden, *The Reckoning*, 560.
10 Mastny, *Russia's Road*, 210–11.
11 The most detailed report on these meetings is in Korom, *Magyarorszag*, 243–60. See also Balint Szabo, *Nepi demokracia es forradalomelmelet* [People's Democracy and Revolutionary Theory] (Budapest: Kossuth, 1974), 75–105. For a fine summary in English based

on Szabo, see Bennett Kovrig, *Communism in Hungary. From Kun to Kadar* (Stanford, CA: Hoover Institution Press, 1979), 154–6.

12 Korom, *Magyarorszag*, 249 and 257. See also Szabo, *Nepi demokracia*, 79.

13 Korom, *Magyarorszag*, 254.

14 Szabo, *Nepi demokracia*, 84–5.

15 Korom, *Magyarorszag*, 268. Entitled "Magyarorszag demokratikus ujjaepitesenek es felemelkedesenek programja" [Program for Hungary's Democratic Reconstruction and Advancement], the program is reprinted in Sandor Rakosi and Balint Szabo (eds), *A Magyar Kommunista Part es a Szocialdemokrata Part hatarozatai, 1944–1948* [Decisions of the Hungarian Communist Party and the Social Democratic Party. 1944–1948] (Budapest: Kossuth, 1967), 37–41.

16 William O. McCagg, Jr was the first to notice overwhelming *public evidence*, by the end of December 1944, that Stalin's gradualism in Hungary was "designed to compensate Western discontent over Poland"; see McCagg, "Communism and Hungary, 1944–1946" (PhD dissertation, Columbia University, 1965), 158. It should be noted, too, that Stalin, who paid close attention to Hungarian affairs during the autumn and winter of 1944–5, repeatedly reminded the Hungarian Muscovites not to hurry and especially not to antagonize anyone. On December 5, for example, he made extensive comments on the Hungarian Communist Party's draft of a new policy declaration, saying (according to Gero's private notes taken that day) that while the draft was "generally good," it would benefit from greater emphasis on the "protection of the average person's private property" and on the possibility of "private initiatives" [*po gushche o chastnov initsiative*]. (Marked by Stalin's initials "I. V." and underlined in Gero's notebook.) Concerning the nature of the coalition government, the Soviet – almost certainly Stalin's – advice was also based on tactical considerations: "Don't be grudging with words, don't scare anyone. But once you gain strength, then move ahead . . . Conclusion of an armistice is the government's [main] task . . . Must utilize as many people as possible, [those] who could be of service to us" [*Mozgatni kell minel tobb embert, akik hasznot hozhatnak*], Korom, *Magyarorszag*, 333–4. On another occasion, Stalin told the Hungarian Communists that although they could count on Soviet fraternal assistance, "Soviet power cannot do everything for you. You must do the fighting, you must do the work." ibid., 330.

17 For the text of the party statutes, see Rakosi and Szabo (eds), *A Magyar Kommunista Part*, 34–6.

18 Korom, *Magyarorszag*, 286. See also Agnes Sagvari, *Nepfront es koalicio Magyarorszagon 1936–1948* [Popular Front and Coalition in Hungary 1936–1948] (Budapest: Kossuth, 1967), 95.

19 As quoted in Kovrig, *Communism in Hungary*, 157.

20 *Delmagyarorszag* (Szeged), December 5, 1944.

21 Rakosi and Szabo (eds), *A Magyar Kommunista Part*, 37–42.

22 Peter Gosztonyi, "Az Ideiglenes Nemzeti Kormany megalakulasanak elotortenetehez" [To the Prehistory of the Founding of the

Provisional National Government], *Uj Latohatar*, 15(3) (August 1972): 228–9.

23 ibid. Cf. Job Paal and Antal Rado (eds), *A debreceni feltamadas* [Resurrection in Debrecen] (Debrecen: Editors' Publication, 1947), 148.

24 Vas claims that both Erdei and Gyongyosi applied to him for membership of the Communist Party and that they became secret members. Other sources could not confirm Gyongyosi's membership.

25 Joseph R. Starobin, "Origins of the Cold War," *Foreign Affairs*, 47 (4) (July 1969): 68–96.

26 At that time, Stalin had first allied himself with Bukharin and others on the right to oust Trotsky, Zinoviev and others on the left, but shortly thereafter he had the remnants of the left help him remove his erstwhile ally and their former antagonist, Bukharin.

27 I am indebted to Robert C. Tucker for suggesting this as a possible interpretation of Stalin's motives. Vladimir Dedijer, *Tito* (New York: Simon & Schuster, 1953), 295.

28 The official report on the conference is *Informatsionnoe soveshchanie predstavitelei nekotorykh v Polshe v kontse sentyabrya 1947 goda* (Moscow: Ogiz, 1948): Zhdanov's speech appears on pp. 13–18. The most complete unofficial account is by one of the Italian delegates, Eugenio Reale, who left the Italian Communist Party after the Soviet intervention in Hungary in 1956: see his *Avec Jacques Duclos au banc des accusés* (Paris: Plon, 1958).

29 Both quotations in Eugenio Reale, "The Founding of the Cominform," in Milorad M. Drachkovitch and Branko Lazitch (eds), *The Comintern: Historical Highlights* (New York: Praeger, 1966), 266.

30 *Nowe Drogi* (September–October 1948): 40 ff. Gomulka's whole career is elegantly traced in Nicholas Bethell, *Gomulka; His Poland, His Communism* (New York: Holt, Rinehart & Winston, 1969).

31 Mr Vas, who died in 1983 at the age of 80, was kind enough to allow me to read the uncensored version of his memoirs.

32 Erzsebet Strassenreiter. "Adalekok a magyarorszagi munkasegyseg tortenetehez es az egyseges munkaspart letrejottehez" [On the History of Workers' Unity and of the Creation of the United Workers' Party], in Karoly Suri (ed.), *A munkasegysegyseg fejlodese Somogy megyeben 1944–1948* [The Development of Workers' Unity in Somogy County 1944–1948] (Kaposvar, 1979), 61.

33 As quoted in Szabo, *Nepi demokracia*, 222. For another summary of Revai's report, see Sagvari, *Nepfront*, 272 ff.

34 Szabo, *Nepi demokracia*, 220.

35 Gero's report to the Politburo is quoted in Ivan T. Berend, *Ujjaepites es a nagytoke elleni harc Magyarorszagon 1945–1948* [Reconstruction and the Struggle Against Big Capital in Hungary 1945–1948] (Budapest, 1962), 373.

36 McCagg, "Communism and Hungary," 268.

37 As quoted in Erzsebet Strassenreiter and Peter Sipos, *Rajk Laszlo* [Laszlo Rajk] (Budapest, 1974), 185.

Part III

LINKING CENTER AND PERIPHERY

10

FROM THE MARSHALL PLAN TO THE THIRD WORLD

Robert E. Wood

The Marshall Plan was one of the decisive turning points in the early Cold War. After deliberating briefly on whether or not the Soviet Union should participate in the plan, Stalin quickly decided against it. He feared that the United States would use it to lure Eastern Europe from the Soviet orbit and to build up a powerful Germany. As indicated in the Gati and MccGwire essays, the Soviet leader then moved decisively to crush all opposition within Eastern Europe and to bring down the iron curtain as it would exist for the next four decades.

US officials were relieved that the Kremlin rebuffed their overture to participate in the European Recovery Program. They feared that the Kremlin might sabotage the program from within, or that Congress might not finance an assistance package that included Communist lands. Using the specter of Soviet domination, Truman administration officials won congressional support. In 1948 the program got under way and it helped to restore hope and provide the marginal assistance that expedited reconstruction in Western Europe.

Economic historians now hotly debate the extent to which the Marshall Plan was responsible for European recovery.* What is incontestable is that industrial growth did not quickly eliminate the dollar gap problem, that is, the shortage of dollars available to European governments which they needed to procure raw materials, foodstuffs, and some machine tools. In other words European countries continued to import more from than they exported to the United States. They had to design ways to overcome this problem. Otherwise when the Marshall Plan ended they would find themselves in a terrible predicament. They

---

* Alan S. Milward, *The Reconstruction of Western Europe, 1945–1951* (Berkeley, CA: University of California Press, 1984).

might have to control trade, subsidize exports, or discriminate against American imports. They might have to look to the Soviet Union or Eastern Europe, now under the Kremlin's control, for markets. They might have to resort to exchange controls, bilateral trade agreements, quotas, and other mechanisms. Or, given the shortage of dollars, they might have to establish domestic controls and set industrial and agricultural priorities. Should any or all of these things occur, the open, multilateral world economic system that the United States wanted might be jeopardized.

In this chapter, Robert Wood shows how the European Recovery Program accentuated US concerns with the Third World. European recipients of Marshall Plan aid sought to use their former colonies to generate the dollars they themselves needed to overcome their dollar shortages. The colonies of Britain, France, the Netherlands, and Portugal sold raw materials to the United States and earned dollars which, in turn, flowed back to London, Paris, and other European commercial and financial centers. Hence retaining the ties, even informal ties, between colony and metropole assumed more importance than ever before.

Wood and some other historians believe that understanding the requirements of the world capitalist system is a key to grasping the developments that led to the Cold War. In their view the Cold War spread to the Third World because US officials and many of their partners in Western Europe and Japan believed they needed to maintain links with the underdeveloped periphery in order to earn dollars, sustain their economic growth, preserve their strength, and maintain open markets and free governments. They feared that revolutionary nationalist movements might sever ties with their former colonial masters and establish links with Moscow or its allies, thereby sapping the strength of Western democracies, undermining their reconstruction efforts, and jeopardizing multilateralism and liberal capitalism. In this respect the reader might turn back to the essay by John Kent and note his portrayal of Bevin's desire to retain Britain's position in Africa in order to help allay Britain's own dollar shortages. Similarly, the reader will want to recall this essay when reading the next excerpt by Bruce Cumings.

Whether or not one agrees with these challenging and thought-provoking arguments, one should take note of the importance of the interrelationships between economic and geopolitical developments in the international system. And one should be aware that the configuration of power in the international system can have a powerful influence on the way officials think they can arrange their own domestic economic and political systems.

* * *

The Marshall Plan has exercised a tenacious grip on the consciousness of US policymakers. It has come to symbolize boldness and success, and virtually whenever new directions in US foreign aid programs have been proposed, the theme of "a new Marshall Plan" has been pressed into service.

Officially known as the European Recovery Program [ERP], the Marshall Plan dispensed over $13 billion between 1948 and 1952 to Western European countries constituted as the Organization for European Economic Cooperation [OEEC]. Over 90 percent of this aid was in the form of grants. The program was administered by a relatively independent agency, the European Cooperation Administration [ECA]. It was formally concluded ahead of schedule at the beginning of 1952, when it was merged into the worldwide Mutual Security Program [MSP].

The European Recovery Program was not simply about either Europe or recovery; it was much more ambitious than that. In reality, the Marshall Plan's uniqueness was that it addressed the breakdown of the prewar economic order with a vision – backed up by a wide range of programs around the world – of a reconstructed set of economic relations binding Europe, North America, and the Third World. The boldness – and real success – of the Marshall Plan lay in its contribution to the construction of a new international order, not in the quantity of capital and raw materials it provided for Western European industries.

The international order constructed during the Marshall Plan period had profound implications for the Third World. The Marshall Plan linked both European reconstruction and the US campaign for multilateralism to a particular model of development in the underdeveloped world.

Five sets of changes in the world economy set the stage for the Marshall Plan. Together these changes created the dollar shortage that was the basis of the worldwide economic crisis in the postwar period. First, there was the breakdown of trade between Eastern and Western Europe. As the "first Third World,"

Eastern European countries had maintained a semicolonial relationship with Western Europe, exchanging food and raw materials for manufactured goods.[1] In 1948, however, Western European exports to Eastern Europe were less than half of the prewar level, and imports from Eastern Europe were only one-third.[2] Instead of recovering, this trade declined over the next five years.[3] This decline meant that European countries had to rely on dollar imports from the United States to fulfill needs formerly met by trade with Eastern Europe.[4]

Second, there was the loss – or threatened loss – of important colonial sources of dollars. France's major colonial dollar earner, Vietnam, was in rebellion. So was the Netherlands' major dollar earner, Indonesia. Guerrilla insurgency was increasing in Britain's most profitable colony, Malaya, although the rebellion never cut off Malaya's dollar exports. In addition to the loss of colonial dollar earnings, the European powers bore the substantial costs of fighting the liberation movements. France had 110,000 troops in Indochina, and the Netherlands had 130,000 in Indonesia.[5]

Third, there was Europe's loss of earnings on foreign investments, particularly in Latin America, brought about by the liquidation of overseas investments to finance the war effort. For both France and Britain, overseas investment earnings and other associated "invisible" payments had long helped offset trade deficits. Net earnings on foreign investment alone had paid for 20 percent of Western Europe's imports in 1938 – $3 billion at postwar prices.[6]

Fourth, many of the European countries and their overseas territories were hit with declining terms of trade. According to one ECA analysis of the sterling area's two most important dollar exports, gold and rubber: "Had the prices of these two commodities gone up as the others did, the same exports to the United States during the five years following the war would have earned an additional $3.5 billion for the sterling area."[7] Total Marshall Plan aid to Great Britain came to $2.7 billion. Without such declining terms of trade, some countries would not have had a dollar deficit at all.

Finally, the European countries found themselves dependent on the US economy in a way they never had been before. This left them susceptible to small fluctuations in the US economy. The UN calculated that a 4 percent fall in employment in the

United States would cost the rest of the world $10 billion in dollar earnings.[8]

These international consequences of the Second World War were only dimly perceived in the United States before the end of the war. Although the strategic brilliance of the Marshall Plan was that it responded to the breakdown of the old economic order in Europe, the original impetus and rationale for it came from the United States, not from Europe. The case for large-scale grant assistance was made long before the particular consequences of the war were known and also long before the beginnings of the Cold War. It was made in terms of a theory of the Second World War's causes and of perceptions of the US economy's structural needs.

From the onset of the war, US policymakers linked the war to a need for a new international order afterwards. Under the leadership of Secretary of State Cordell Hull, the State Department developed a frankly economic interpretation of the causes of the war. This analysis became the basis of US economic policy and was stated as early as 1940 by President Roosevelt. The emergence of a multilateral world economy – based on the unobstructed movement of capital and labor – became a major wartime goal.[9]

Americans believed that their prosperity was due to rearmament and war and feared a postwar depression. A 1941 survey of the American Economic Association found 80 percent of its members predicting a postwar depression.[10] A January 1945 public opinion survey found 68 percent viewing unemployment as the single most important postwar issue.[11] A major effort to deal with these concerns was mounted during the war. "By 1943, the government had become convinced that the greatest obstacle to the success of a postwar multilateral system and increased American exports was the 'dollar shortage.'"[12] During the rest of the war and the immediate postwar period, US government officials reiterated the theme of finding a way to maintain a high level of US exports as the key to avoiding a postwar depression.[13]

Some observers dispute the importance of these concerns by pointing to the problem of the inflation that occurred immediately after the war, caused by pent-up consumer demand.[14] Proponents of the export-dependency argument always recognized, however, that the necessity of overseas markets would not impress itself immediately upon demobilization, but only after backed-up consumer demand had been satisfied. This position was explicitly put forth both by government officials and in corporate-sponsored studies.[15] Whether or not this position was correct, what mattered was that US policymakers believed it.

Domestic economic justifications of aid remained dominant in the business press as late as mid-1948. In February 1948, *U.S. News and World Report* carefully listed the advantages and disadvantages of domestic versus foreign "pump priming," concluding that the latter was superior:

> Some advantages over domestic pump priming are seen in the world program that is about to begin. Effects of spending will not be so visible inside the United States. American taxpayers will not have WPA [Work Projects Administration] leaf-raking projects before their eyes. They won't see courthouses being built, sidewalks laid or murals painted with federal money. The result is that there may be less criticism.
>
> The foreign aid program also may promise an easier way of keeping U.S. business active and of getting rid of surpluses. Most industrial orders will be for heavy goods – machinery, trucks, tractors, electrical equipment – a sector of industry that the New Deal never could revive until the war. Foreign outlets for surplus grains and fruit and cotton may prove more effective than relief stamp programs at home.[16]

Important as US concern over exports was, it does not explain the particular form the Marshall Plan took or its timing. A common assumption is that the Marshall Plan was aimed at the European left. Yet while State Department spokesmen and ECA figures like Paul Hoffman later credited the Marshall Plan with preventing the victory of the left in Europe – an assessment many historians have accepted – there is reason to believe that the European left had already been defeated as a result of its own internal weaknesses, the Great Power conservatism of Soviet foreign policy, and the policies of American and British occupation forces.[17] More recent historical scholarship has clarified that the major target of the Marshall Plan was not socialism but capitalism – or rather the national brand of capitalism that US leaders saw emerging in Europe.[18]

Fred Block has argued that "national capitalism," based on extensive state intervention and planning to ensure full employment, was the dominant trend in Western Europe at the end of the war:

> Although little was actually done before World War II to implement national capitalism, there is good reason to believe that after the war, there might have been substantial experiments with national capitalism among the developed capitalist countries. In fact, in the immediate postwar years, most of the countries of Western Europe resorted to the whole range of control devices associated with national capitalism – exchange controls, capital controls, bilateral and state trading arrangements. The reason these controls were not elaborated into full-scale experiments with national capitalism was that it became a central aim of United States foreign policy to prevent the emergence of national capitalist experiments and to gain widespread cooperation in the restoration of an open world economy.[19]

In the struggle to mobilize the US public in support of massive aid programs, US leaders again and again stressed the danger European economic policies represented. In his speech at Baylor University in March 1947, President Truman publicly sounded the tocsin about the danger of European reconstruction policies, attacking government intervention in trade, even if the actual activities (and profits) were left in private hands. He urged that "the whole world should adopt the American system" and, pointing to the dangers of autarkic capitalism, warned: "Unless we act, and act decisively, it will be the pattern for the next century."[20]

The commitment to fighting autarky and national economic planning took many forms. It guided occupation authorities. It led to the long and often bitter bargaining with the British over the British loan in 1945. It was at the basis of US leaders' vision of the new international institutions they sought: the United Nations, the World Bank, the International Monetary Fund, the International Trade Organization. And it accounts for the unique focus of the Marshall Plan on building and consolidating a new international economic order. Through the Marshall Plan, the United States sought an antidote to national capitalism through new sets of international arrangements. These were to have profound implications for the underdeveloped world.

From the very beginning, the struggle against national capitalism in Europe led US policymakers to look to Africa and Asia to close the dollar gap. US imports from Europe constituted only 0.33 percent of US gross national product. Politically untouchable tariff walls made increasing most European imports impossible. US investors, despite the existence of convertibility guarantees, expressed little interest in investing in Western Europe – an alternative source of dollars that Congress and the ECA had originally counted on.[21] US policymakers looked instead to the overseas territories of European countries to bail out their colonial masters. As John Orchard, a special representative and consultant for the ECA, concluded: "Indeed, the overseas territories hold more promise of contributions to the closing of the dollar gap than the countries of metropolitan Europe."[22]

The overseas territories were expected to contribute to the success of the Marshall Plan in two major ways. First, they would provide the market for European goods that had formerly existed in Eastern Europe and that the United States was not able to provide.[23] Second, the overseas territories were expected to be dollar earners through their raw materials exports to the United States. US demand for these raw materials was expected to draw US private investment in these territories, constituting, in the words of ECA Special Representative Averell Harriman, "one of the most promising ways to assist in reaching a balance of payments."[24]

These two roles of the overseas territories were linked in a triangular trade model, in which dollars would flow into European hands indirectly through their colonies. As one economist put it: "Such a pattern of trade, to be self-sustaining, would mean a surplus of (European) exports to the nondollar world, a surplus of exports by the latter to this country, and a European surplus of imports from us, to be financed in this manner."[25] Although this description does not accurately portray the way the colonial powers actually acquired the dollars their colonies earned, the model was politically attractive because it allowed for the continuation or even the increase of European trade deficits with the United States, as long as the overseas territories ran up trade surpluses with the United States.[26]

The raw material exports of the overseas territories were seen as critical both to the success of the Marshall Plan in Europe and to US prosperity. An important selling point of the plan in the United States was that it would provide access to raw materials and primary products in the underdeveloped world. This goal was to be achieved in three main ways. First, various mechanisms for US stockpiling of raw materials were built into the operating structure of the ERP. For example, the United States could use up to 5 percent of the counterpart funds its aid generated to purchase "strategic" materials. Second, the aid treaties that were negotiated with each metropolitan country guaranteed potential US investors access "to the development of raw materials within participating countries on terms of treatment equivalent to those afforded to the nationals of the participating country concerned."[27] Third, a special fund was established for investments in increased production of strategic materials.

In 1951 congressional hearings on the foreign aid program, Nelson Rockefeller testified that 73 percent of US strategic materials imports came from the underdeveloped areas.[28] In an article titled "Widening Boundaries of National Interest," Rockefeller concluded: "Clearly, the success of the industrial mobilization plans of the North Atlantic Treaty countries is contingent upon the continued and increasing supply from underdeveloped areas of such strategic materials as bauxite, chrome, copper, lead, manganese, tin, uranium, and zinc," and he called for a 50 percent increase in raw materials exports from the underdeveloped areas.[29]

Coincidentally, the three colonies with the greatest raw materials exports – Malaya, Netherlands East Indies, and Indochina – were all areas where significant anti-colonial insurgency had taken place right after the war. The military efforts of Britain, the Netherlands, and France to repress these movements provided an additional link between the overseas territories and the European Recovery Plan. Resolution of colonial wars came to be seen as necessary for fulfilling US political and military aims in Europe. As the US Secretary of Defense testified in the foreign aid hearings in 1951: "The sooner Indochina can be stabilized, the sooner those French divisions, which are the backbone of European land defense, can be brought to full effectiveness by the return of sorely needed professional officers, noncommissioned officers, and technicians."[30]

The role that the ECA envisioned for the underdeveloped areas – particularly the overseas territories – reinforced the type of export-oriented development that had always been the basis of European colonial policy. The difference was that the overseas territories were to be opened more to US investment and their exports directed more to the United States and other "hard currency" areas.

Measuring the significance of the Marshall Plan for the overseas territories is not an easy task. Not all aid directed toward the overseas territories was labeled as such. In the cases of France and the Netherlands (until Indonesia gained its independence), substantial dollar aid to the metropoles was officially earmarked for their colonies. For France and the Netherlands, this came to $388.3 million; unfortunately, the ECA provided no comparable cumulative figures for the other European metropoles. The ECA Special Reserve Fund, later renamed the Overseas Development Fund, made $63.8 million of investments, mostly in Africa. These included $32.1 million in French Africa, $17.3 million in the Belgian Congo, $11.5 million in British Africa, and $663,000 in Portuguese Africa.[31] Another $47 million was invested directly in the production of strategic materials. If we assume that the dollar forms of aid generated counterpart that was spent in the overseas territories, the overall total would surpass $1 billion.

The Marshall Plan's relationship to colonialism in Asia, where the postwar reimposition of colonial authority was resisted by significant popular movements, was more varied and complex than it was in Africa. Within their staunchly anti-Communist and counterrevolutionary framework, US policymakers were flexible in their responses, depending on their assessment of the nature of the popular forces and the options open to the colonial powers. One extreme is represented by British Malaya, where British counterinsurgency efforts seem to have enjoyed full US support. Subsequently, a National Planning Association report concluded: "The United Kingdom effort to suppress guerrilla warfare in Malaya would seem to have been indirectly financed out of aid that ostensibly was going to Europe."[32]

Indochina represents an intermediate case. State Department documents in 1948–9 reflect considerable US frustration with French intransigence toward nationalists of all political stripes. However, recognizing the popularity of Ho Chi Minh and his forces, US policymakers were forced to admit that they could offer no alternative course of action.[33] During this period, they sought to maintain some pressure on the French by refusing to fund projects directly for Indochina, but at the same time, they took account of the dollar cost of France's war in calculating French aid requirements. The Griffin Mission, sent to Indochina and elsewhere in Southeast Asia in early 1950 to expand the US aid presence, noted:

> In the last analysis, of course, the French financial contribution to the area has been made possible by ECA aid to France, and the balance-of-payments deficit of the area has been taken into account in calculating France's need for ECA aid. The United States is therefore already indirectly aiding Indochina.[34]

Indonesia represents the other extreme, where the United States was prepared to use Marshall Plan aid to pressure the Netherlands to relinquish control. After authorizing over $100 million of aid to the Netherlands for use in Indonesia, the State Department desperately sought to convince the Dutch that the way to prevent revolution in Indonesia was to come to terms with anti-Communist nationalists. Acting Secretary of State Robert Lovett urged Dutch acceptance of a US plan to strengthen "Mr Hatta [one of the leaders of the Indonesian Republic] and his government sufficiently to enable him successfully to liquidate Communists within the Republic."[35] After the fledgling republic violently suppressed a military revolt in Madiun that drew Communist backing, the United States secretly informed the Dutch that any military action against the republic would result in the cessation of US aid. When the Dutch proceeded to take such action in December, all US aid earmarked for Indonesia was suspended. In 1950, ECA aid was resumed to the now independent Republic of Indonesia.

Between 1948 and 1952, the ECA gradually became involved in aid programs to other underdeveloped areas besides the overseas territories. The original Marshall Plan legislation included an authorization of $463 million for China, which was to be administered by the ECA. In January 1949, Truman transferred the administration of economic aid in South Korea from the army to the ECA. In the following year, after the Chinese Revolution ended ECA activities on the mainland, Congress authorized the use of the leftover Chinese funds in the neighboring areas of Southeast Asia; this became the basis of programs in Taiwan, Indochina, Thailand, Indonesia, and Burma. A substantial aid program was initiated by the ECA in the Philippines in 1951, and the ECA financed a large shipment of grain to India in the same year. Outside of East Asia, most economic aid was administered by the Technical Cooperation Administration, formed in 1951.

Between 1948 and 1952, the great bulk of aid to the Third World was administered by the ECA and represented an attempt to intervene in civil and revolutionary struggles in Asia. Sixty-four percent of the total went to Taiwan, Korea, and the Philippines, and a $248.7 million loan to India made to avert famine was credited with "preventing the establishment of a new Communist bridgehead in Asia."[36]

NOTES

From Robert E. Wood, *From the Marshall Plan to Debt Crisis: Foreign Aid and Development Choices in the World Economy* (Berkeley, CA: University of California Press, 1986), 29–60. Copyright © 1986 the Regents of the University of California. Reprinted and abridged by permission of the publisher.

1 For analyses of the emergence of Eastern Europe as a peripheral area and as the first "Third World," see Immanuel Wallerstein, *The Modern World System: Capitalist Agriculture and the Origins of the European World-Economy in the Sixteenth Century* (New York: Academic Press, 1974), Chap. 2; and L. S. Stavrianos, *Global Rift: The Third World Comes of Age* (New York: William Morrow, 1981), Chap. 3.
2 United Nations, Economic Commission for Europe, *Economic Bulletin for Europe*, second quarter, 1949, 1(2) (Geneva, October 1949): 27.
3 United Nations, Economic Commission for Europe, *Economic Bulletin for Europe*, second quarter, 1952, 4(3) (Geneva, November 1952): 35.
4 Organization for European Economic Cooperation, *European Recovery Programme: Second Report of the O.E.E.C.* (Paris, 1950), 140.

5 *U.S. News and World Report* (August 13, 1948): 32; ibid. (September 17, 1948): 26.
6 Organization for European Economic Cooperation, *European Recovery Programme*, 140.
7 Economic Cooperation Administration, Special Mission to the United Kingdom, *The Sterling Area: An American Analysis* (London: Economic Cooperation Administration, 1951), 68.
8 Organization for European Economic Cooperation, *European Recovery Programme*, 149.
9 Warren Leroy Hickman, *Genesis of the European Recovery Program: A Study of the Trend of American Economic Policies* (Geneva: Imprimeries Populaires, 1949), 26–7. This book, published in 1949, foreshadows much of the contemporary "revisionist" historiography of this period.
10 Lloyd C. Gardner, *Architects of Illusion: Men and Ideas in American Foreign Policy, 1941–1949* (Chicago: Quadrangle, 1970), 22.
11 ibid., 57.
12 Hickman, *Genesis*, 79.
13 William Appleman Williams, *The Tragedy of American Diplomacy* (New York: Delta, 1962), 236–7. Williams has explored the long-term social roots of the belief in the necessity of export markets in *The Roots of the Modern American Empire: A Study of the Growth and Shaping of Social Consciousness in a Marketplace Society* (New York: Vintage, 1969). For a variety of other statements by US officials linking reliance on exports to avoiding a postwar depression, see J. Fred Rippy, "Historical Perspective," in James Wiggins and Helmut Schoeck (eds), *Foreign Aid Reexamined* (Washington, DC: Public Affairs Press, 1958), 1–24.
14 For example, see Daniel Yergin, *Shattered Peace: Origins of the Cold War and the National Security State* (Boston, MA: Houghton Mifflin, 1977), 309.
15 Hickman, *Genesis*, 138, 208.
16 *U.S. News and World Report* (February 27, 1948): 21.
17 For example, see Joyce Kolko and Gabriel Kolko, *The Limits of Power: The World and United States Foreign Policy, 1945–1954* (New York: Harper & Row, 1972); Gabriel Kolko, *The Politics of War: The World and United States Foreign Policy, 1943–1945* (New York: Vintage, 1968); and Fernando Claudin, *The Communist Movement: From Comintern to Cominform* (New York: Monthly Review Press, 1975), pt 2.
18 Kolko and Kolko, *The Limits of Power*, 367.
19 Fred L. Block, *The Origins of International Economic Disorder: A Study of United States International Monetary Policy from World War II to the Present* (Berkeley and Los Angeles, CA: University of California Press, 1977), 9.
20 James P. Warburg, *Put Yourself in Marshall's Place* (New York: Simon & Schuster, 1948), 46.
21 Hoffman's shift from seeing US private investment as a primary instrument of European recovery to seeing it as an indication that

recovery had been achieved is described in Hadley Arkes, *Bureaucracy, the Marshall Plan and the National Interest* (Princeton, NJ: Princeton University Press, 1972), 250–5.

22 John E. Orchard, "ECA and the Dependent Territories," *Geographical Review* (January 1951): 67.

23 William C. Mallalieu, *British Reconstruction and American Policy* (New York: Scarecrow Press, 1956), 196.

24 *Extension of E.R.P.*, hearings before the Committee on Foreign Affairs, H.R., 81st Congress, 1st Session (February 1949), 25.

25 Williams, *Tragedy of American Diplomacy*, 173.

26 Economic Cooperation Administration, *Twelfth Report to Congress*, quarter ending March 31, 1951: 21.

27 Kolko and Kolko, *The Limits of Power*, 448.

28 Rippy, "Historical Perspective," in Wiggins and Schoeck, *Foreign Aid Reexamined*, 13.

29 Nelson A. Rockefeller, "Widening Boundaries of National Interest," *Foreign Affairs*, 29 (4) (July 1951): 527.

30 *Mutual Security Program Appropriations for 1952*, hearings before a subcommittee of the Committee on Appropriations, H. R., 82nd Congress, 1st Session, 750. This point is reiterated in the *Second Report to Congress on the Mutual Security Program* (June 30, 1952), 24.

31 Harry B. Price, *The Marshall Plan and Its Meaning* (Ithaca, NY: Cornell University Press, 1955), 151.

32 National Planning Association, "The Foreign Aid Programs and the United States Economy," in Special Senate Committee to Study the Foreign Aid Program, *Foreign Aid Program: Compilation of Studies and Surveys* (Washington, DC: Government Printing Office, 1957), 935.

33 See US Department of State, *Foreign Relations of the United States, 1948* (Washington, DC: Government Printing Office, 1974), Vol. 6: 43–9.

34 Samuel P. Hayes (ed.), *The Beginning of American Aid to Southeast Asia: The Griffin Mission of 1950* (Lexington, MA: D. C. Heath, 1971), 98.

35 ibid., 50–1.

36 Price, *The Marshall Plan*, 217.

11

JAPAN AND THE ASIAN PERIPHERY

Bruce Cumings

One of the most striking developments of the Cold War international order was the reconstruction and integration of Japan into an American-led orbit. Another critical feature of postwar Asia was the phenomenally rapid economic growth that began to take place in the 1960s in Japan, South Korea, Taiwan, Hong Kong, and Singapore. More and more historians have been showing that the origins of the American embroglio in Vietnam, itself part of the Cold War, were inspired by the effort of US officials to safeguard the resources and markets of Southeast Asia which were thought to be essential for the Japanese economy. The implementation of containment in Indochina also reflected Washington's desire to buy time so that the burgeoning economies in the region could be integrated in the Japanese semi-periphery and the American-led free world.

Bruce Cumings is a political scientist who has found a home in the History Department of the University of Chicago. In his pathbreaking work on the coming of the Korean War he has combined comprehensive archival research with stimulating theoretical insights. In the following article he shows that developments in postwar Asia must be studied in historical and geographical context. If one is to understand why the Cold War came to Asia and what has happened there during the Cold War, one must take cognizance of the hegemonic position of the United States in the world capitalist system. But that is not enough. The unique evolution of events in Japan, Korea, and Taiwan can be understood only by combining an analysis of US policy with a knowledge of the social structure of these countries and with an appreciation of the strength and autonomy of the state. The dynamic interaction of these factors explains how and why the United States coopted the region into its own orbit and stymied the growth of Soviet/Communist influence. These factors also help to explain the configuration of power relationships within postwar Asia as well as the strategies for successful export-led economic growth.

Readers should discuss several important issues raised here. What, for example, is meant by the functioning of the world capitalist system and its division into core, semiperiphery, and periphery? How does the product cycle affect change within the world capitalist system? What did it mean for the United States to exercise its hegemonic influence over the world capitalist system in general and the Asian periphery in particular? What roles were played by Japan, by Korea and Taiwan, by Southeast Asia? How were these roles conditioned by historical experience, by social structure, by the power of the state, and by US policy? As readers think about these questions they should also ponder how aspects of this article relate to the conclusions put forward in the selections by Wood, Maier, Kent, and Hunt and Levine.

* * *

East Asia today is the center of world economic dynamism. Japan in 1980 became number two in the world in gross national product [GNP]. Its achievement is complemented by the "gang of four," South Korea, Taiwan, Singapore, and Hong Kong. These four East Asian developing countries now account for almost twice the export totals of the entire remainder of the Third World, and their growth rates are usually the highest in the entire world.

A glance back before the Second World War suggests that we may need a longer perspective to capture the true dimensions of this growth. Japan's interwar annual growth rate of 4.5 percent doubled the rates of interwar Europe; colonial manufacturing growth in Korea, 1910–40, averaged 10 percent per annum, and overall GNP growth was also in the 4 percent range, as was Taiwan's. No nation's heavy-industrial growth rate was steeper than Japan's in the period 1931–40; in the textile sector, Japan's automation was ahead of Europe's in 1930. Yet new research now suggests that both Korea and Taiwan experienced higher gross domestic product (GDP) growth rates than Japan between 1911 and 1938 (Japan 3.36 percent, Korea 3.57 percent, Taiwan 3.80 percent).[1]

In the past century Japan, Korea, and Taiwan have also moved fluidly through a classic product-cycle industrialization pattern, Korea and Taiwan following in Japan's wake. Japan's

216

industrialization has gone through three phases, the last of which is just beginning. The first phase began in the 1880s, with textiles the leading sector, and lasted through Japan's rise to world power. In the mid-1930s Japan began the second, heavy phase, based on steel, chemicals, armaments, and ultimately automobiles; its end did not come into sight until the mid-1960s. The third phase emphasizes high-technology "knowledge" industries such as electronics, communications, computers, and silicon-chip microprocessors.

Within Japan each phase, in good product-cycle fashion, has been marked by strong state protection for nascent industries, adoption of foreign technologies, and comparative advantages deriving from cheap labor costs, technological innovation, and "lateness" in world time. Taiwan and Korea have historically been receptacles for declining Japanese industries. Adding agriculture gives a pattern in which in the first quarter of this century Korea and Taiwan substituted for the diminishing Japanese agricultural sector, exporting rice and sugar in great amounts to the mother country (Taiwan was annexed in 1895, Korea in 1910). By the mid-1930s Japan had begun to export iron and steel, chemical, and electric-generation industries, although much more to Korea than to Taiwan. In the 1960s and 1970s, both smaller countries have received declining textile and consumer electronic industries from Japan (as well as from the United States), and in the 1980s some Japanese once again speak of sending steel and autos in the same direction.

Thus if there has been a miracle in East Asia, it has not occurred just since 1960; it would be profoundly ahistorical to think that it did. Furthermore, it is misleading to assess the industrialization pattern in any one of these countries; such an approach misses, through a fallacy of disaggregation, the fundamental unity and integrity of the regional effort in this century.

This article asserts that an understanding of the Northeast Asian political economy can only emerge from an approach that posits the systemic interaction of each country with the others, and of the region with the world at large. Rapid upward mobility in the world economy has occurred, through the product cycle and other means, within the context of two hegemonic systems: the Japanese imperium to 1945, and intense, if diffuse, American hegemony since the late 1940s. Furthermore, only considerations of context can account for the similarities in the

Taiwanese and South Korean political economies. Simultaneously, external hegemonic forces have interacted with different domestic societies in Korea and Taiwan to produce rather different political outcomes.

The concept of the product cycle offers a useful way to understand change and mobility within and among nations. For a world system analyst the product cycle is one among several means of upward and downward mobility; the core assumption is the existence of a capitalist world economy that, at least in our time, is the only world-ranging system. Thus, the core power pursues an imperialism of free trade, and rising powers use strong states, protectionist barriers, or a period of withdrawal and self-reliant development (the Stalinist or socialist option) as means to compete within the world system.[2]

The world system perspective posits a tripartite division of the globe: core, semiperiphery, and periphery. I use the term *hegemony* to refer to core-state behavior. By hegemony I do not mean the Gramscian notion of class ethos, nor a crude Marxist notion of ruling class or imperial domination, nor the diffuse contemporary Chinese usage, referring to big-power domination in all its manifestations. Nor do I use it in Robert Keohane and Joseph Nye's sense "in which one state is able and willing to determine and maintain the essential rules by which relations among states are governed."[3] I mean by hegemony the demarcation of outer limits in economics, politics, and international security relationships, the transgression of which carries grave risks for any nonhegemonic nation.

In the postwar American case, hegemony meant the demarcation of a "grand area."[4] Within that area nations oriented themselves toward Washington rather than Moscow; nations were enmeshed in a hierarchy of economic and political preferences whose ideal goal was free trade, open systems, and liberal democracy but which also encompassed neomercantile states and authoritarian politics; and nations were dealt with by the United States through methods ranging from classic negotiations and tradeoffs (in regard to nations sharing Western traditions or approximating American levels of political and economic development) to wars and interventions (in the periphery or Third World), to assure continuing orientation toward Washington. The hegemonic ideology, shared by most

Americans but by few in the rest of the world, was the ethos of liberalism and internationalism, assuming a born-free country that never knew class conflict. Not a colonial or neocolonial imperialism, it was a new system of empire begun with Wilson and consummated by Roosevelt and Acheson. Its very breadth – its non-territoriality, its universalism, and its open systems (within the grand area) – made for a style of hegemony that was more open than previous imperialisms to competition from below.

These various terms and concepts are applicable to the international system. In Japan, Taiwan, and Korea, much of their success and their variance from one another may be explained by reference to state and society. Strong states can formulate policy goals independently of particular groups, they can change group or class behavior, and they can change the structure of society.[5] Japan rates as very strong on this scale; so, in the later periods, do South Korea and Taiwan. Indeed, these three strong states go far toward explaining their product-cycle virtuosity.

Finally, there is society, by which I mean both the conventional notion of a system structured by groups and classes and Karl Polanyi's sense of society being the human web that reacts to market penetration, capitalist relations, and industrialization in varying but always critical ways around the globe.[6] Attention to society and its reactions can avoid the reductionism of some scholars who place inordinate emphasis on the structuring effect of the world system on national societies, as if they are putty to be shaped and molded. In fact, in the Northeast Asian case the three different societies deeply affect the development of the national and regional political economies.

The place to begin in comprehending the region's economic dynamism is with the advent of Japanese imperialism. Japan's imperial experience differed from the West's in several fundamental respects.[7] It involved the colonization of contiguous territory; it involved the location of industry and an infrastructure of communications and transportation in the colonies, bringing industry to the labor and raw materials rather than vice versa; and it was accomplished by a country that always saw itself as *dis*advantaged and threatened by more advanced countries.

219

Japan entered upon colonization late, in a world with hundreds of years of colonial experience and where, as King Leopold of Belgium said three years before the Meiji Restoration, "the world has been pretty well pillaged already." Most of the good colonial territories were already spoken for; indeed, for several decades Japan faced the possibility of becoming a dependency, perhaps even a colony, of one of the Western powers. With imperial attention mostly focused on China and its putative vast market, however, Japan got what E. H. Norman called a "breathing space" in which to mobilize its resources and resist the West. Its success was manifest in victories over China and Russia within the decade 1895 to 1905, but that should blind us neither to Japan's perception of its position as poised between autonomy and dependency in a highly competitive world system nor to the very real threats posed by the West. While the British and the Americans marveled at Japanese industrial and military prowess at the turn of the century, the Kaiser sent his famous "yellow peril" mural to the Tsar, and the French worried about Japanese skills being tied to a vast pool of Chinese labor, posing a dire threat to the West. In such circumstances the Japanese were hardly prone to worry about the sensitivities of Taiwanese or Koreans but rather to see them as resources to be deployed in a global struggle.[8]

Whereas Taiwan had for the most part only an aboriginal population until the eighteenth century, and a small class of Chinese absentee landlords by the end of the nineteenth century (the *ta-tsu-hu*), Korea had a powerful landed class of centuries' duration, in which property holding and aristocratic privilege were potently mixed.[9] The Japanese found it expedient to root landlords more firmly to the ground, as a means of disciplining peasants and extracting rice for the export market. The landlord class therefore persisted through to 1945, although by then it was tainted by association with imperial rule. In Taiwan, by contrast, land reform at the turn of the century eliminated absentee lords and fostered a class of entrepreneurial landowners, emerging "from below" as they had in Japan. By 1945 most Taiwan landowners held less land than their Korean counterparts and were far more productive. Whereas tenancy increased markedly in Korea, it actually decreased in Taiwan between 1910 and 1941. Samuel Ho has concluded that by 1945 agriculture in Taiwan was quite scientific, and change had occurred "without disrupting the traditional system of peasant cultivation."[10] Korea, on the other hand, had frequent peasant protests and rebellions, guerrilla movements in the border region, and above all a huge population movement off the land that severely disrupted the agrarian political economy.[11]

In the 1930s Japan largely withdrew from the world system and pursued, with its colonies, a self-reliant, go-it-alone path to development that not only generated remarkably high industrial growth rates but changed the face of Northeast Asia. In this decade what we might call the "natural economy" of the region was created; although it was not natural, its rational division of labor and set of possibilities have skewed East Asian development ever since. Furthermore, during this period, Japan elaborated many of the features of the neomercantile state still seen today.

The 1930s' development rested on the "two sturdy legs" of cheap labor and "a great inflow of technology," followed by massive state investments or subsidies to *zaibatsu* investors.* Exports were still mostly "light," mainly textiles; but iron and steel, chemicals, hydroelectric power, aluminium, and infrastructure (transport and communications) grew markedly in the imperium.[12] What is so often forgotten is that this spurt located industry in the colonies as well.

Japan is among the very few imperial powers to have located modern heavy industry in its colonies: steel, chemicals, hydroelectric facilities in Korea and Manchuria, and automobile production for a time in the latter. Even today, China's industry remains skewed toward the Northeast, and North Korea has always had a relatively advanced industrial structure. Samuel Ho remarks that, by the end of the colonial period, Taiwan "had an industrial superstructure to provide a strong foundation for future industrialization"; the main industries were hydroelectric, metallurgy (especially aluminium), chemicals, and an advanced transport system. By 1941, factory employment, including mining, stood at 181,000 in Taiwan. Manufacturing grew at an annual average rate of about 8 percent during the 1930s.[13]

Industrial development was much greater in Korea, perhaps because of the relative failure of agrarian growth compared to

* The *zaibatsu* were privately owned industrial-financial conglomerates.

221

Taiwan but certainly because of Korea's closeness both to Japan and to the Chinese hinterland. By 1940, 213,000 Koreans were working in industry, excluding miners, and not counting the hundreds of thousands of Koreans who migrated to factory or mine work in Japan proper and in Manchuria. Net value of mining and manufacturing grew by 266 percent between 1929 and 1941.[14] By 1945 Korea had an industrial infrastructure that, although sharply skewed toward metropolitan interests, was among the best developed in the Third World. Furthermore, both Korea and Taiwan had begun to take on semiperipheral characteristics. Korea's developing periphery was Manchuria, where it sent workers, merchants, soldiers, and bureaucrats who occupied a middle position between Japanese overlords and Chinese peasants; as Korean rice was shipped to Japan, millet was imported from Manchuria to feed Korean peasants in a classic core – semiperiphery – periphery relationship. As for Taiwan, its geographic proximity to Southeast Asia and South China made it "a natural location for processing certain raw materials brought in from, and for producing some manufactured goods for export to, these areas."[15]

The Japanese managed all this by combining a handful of *zaibatsu*, several big banks, and the colonial state structures. They also foisted upon Koreans and Taiwanese an ideology of incorporation emphasizing a structural family principle and an ethical filiality: the imperium was one (not-so) happy family with Emperor Hirohito as the father.

Although Taiwan seemed to emerge from the last phase of colonialism relatively unscathed, with few disruptions, Korea was profoundly transformed. The period from 1935 to 1945 was when Korea's industrial revolution began, with most of the usual characteristics: uprooting of peasants from the land, the emergence of a working class, widespread population mobility, and urbanization. Because the Japanese industrialized from above, however, social change accompanying this revolution was greatest in the lower reaches of society. The social and regional conflicts that racked Korea in the 1945–53 period have their origins in the immense population shifts, agrarian disruptions, and industrial dynamism of the final phase of the Japanese imperium. This was truly a decade-long pressure cooker; the lifting of the lid in 1945 deeply affected Korea.[16] But

Japan, too, was deeply changed by the experience. Japan was remade in this period.

The modern Japanese state, well described in its contemporary features elsewhere,[17] was initially the great work of the Meiji oligarchs. But it was in the 1930s that it took on many of the neomercantile features that persist today: its virtuosity in moving through the product cycle, from old to new industries; the extraordinary role for the bureaucracy and key agencies like the Ministry of International Trade and Industry [MITI], exercising "administrative guidance" throughout the economy; the peculiar vehicles for credit, which account for much of the mobility in and out of industries; the role of large conglomerates; the systematic exclusion of labor from most important decisionmaking; and the high rates of exploitation of poorly paid female labor.

In September 1945, as US occupation forces filtered into Japan, an American officer walked into a Mitsui office in Tokyo and introduced himself. A man in the office pointed to a map of the Greater East Asian Co-prosperity Sphere and said, "There it is. We tried. See what you can do with it!"[18] It was not until 1948 that the United States would seek to do much with it, however. In the period 1945–7 in Korea, Japan, and Taiwan, society reacted strongly against the effects of imperial militarism and industrial midwifery. American occupation in Japan led by Douglas MacArthur, a nineteenth-century liberal, also reacted strongly in the early years against the political economy of prewar Japan, seeking to destroy the Japanese Imperial Army, break up the *zaibatsu*, eliminate rural landlords, and bequeath to the world a reformed and chastened Japan that would never again mix aggression with economic prowess. Unions and leftist parties were unleashed and, with occupation "New Dealers," mustered a challenge to the prewar system strong enough, at minimum, to establish the countervailing power that enables us to call postwar Japan a democracy. Although the main emphasis was on democratization and an end to militarism, narrower interests also asserted themselves. The first head of the Economic and Scientific Section of the occupation, for example, was Robert C. Kramer, a textile industrialist; he and representatives of American textile, rayon, ceramics, and other industries threatened by Japanese competition opposed reviving Japan's

223

economy, particularly in its potent prewar form.[19] American allies, especially the British, also urged that commitments to reform and reparations be carried through, thereby to weaken Japan's competitiveness in world markets.

From the early 1940s, however, one sector of American official opinion opposed a punitive occupation, for fear that this would play into the hands of the Soviets and make a reintegration of Japan with the world economy impossible. In essence, such people, who included a Japanophile faction in the State Department,[20] wanted a Japan revived to *second-rank* economic status and enrolled in an American-managed free trade regime. Such recommendations remained in the background, however, while Japan's American emperor, General Douglas MacArthur, masterfully imposed a benevolent tutelage upon the Japanese people.

All this began sharply to change in late 1947, leading to what we might call the Kennan Restoration. George Kennan's policy of containment was always limited and parsimonious, based on the idea that four or five industrial structures existed in the world: the Soviets had one and the United States had four, and things should be kept that way. In Asia, only Japan held his interest. The rest were incontinent regimes, and how could one have containment with incontinence? Kennan and his Policy Planning Staff played the key role in pushing through the "reverse course" in Japan.

American policy in the mid-twentieth century resonated with Jacob Viner's description of British policy in the eighteenth: it was governed "by joint and harmonized considerations of power and economics."[21] Security and economic considerations were inextricably mixed. A revived Japan was both a bulwark against the Soviets and a critical element in a reformed and revived world economy. What is surprising, in the multitude of formerly classified American documents now available on early postwar Asian policy, is how powerful were the economic voices. In particular, a cluster of bankers and free traders, now dubbed the "Japan Crowd," were instrumental in the ending of the postwar reforms in Japan and the revival of the regional political economy that persists today.[22] Economics bulked so large because, as Charles Maier points out, the defeated Axis powers (Japan and West Germany) were to become world centers of capital accumulation and growth, not of political or military power.[23] Thus Japan's economy was reinforced, while its political and military power (beyond its borders) was shorn. The result is that in the postwar world economy Japan resembles a sector as much as a nation-state. Until the 1970s it was a distinctly secondary sector when compared to the United States, that is, it was returned to semiperipherality as (it was hoped) a permanent second-rank economic power.

The coalition that brought the reverse course to Japan has been well detailed elsewhere. In brief it included, in addition to Kennan, Dean Acheson, Dean Rusk, Max Bishop and others within the government, several journalists, and a powerful lobby of American firms and individuals who had had large investments in prewar Japan: General Electric, Westinghouse, Goodrich, Owens-Libby, American Can, and others.[24] Percy Johnston, head of the pivotal Johnston Committee whose report in April 1948 was instrumental in the reverse course, was chairman of the Chemical Bank; the "Dodge Line" of fiscal austerity was run by a Detroit banker; many Wall Streeters, including the American maker of the Japan Peace Treaty, John Foster Dulles, supported a revival of Japan's economic prowess. As good free traders from the new hegemonic power, they had nothing to fear from Japan. The old hegemonic power, Great Britain, fought unsuccessfully against the changes.

As thinking about a revived Japan evolved in 1948–50, two problems emerged: first, how could Japan's vital but second-rate status be assured; second, how could a prewar political economy that got raw materials and labor from the Northeast Asian periphery survive in the postwar world without a hinterland? George Kennan raised these problems in a 1949 Policy Planning Staff meeting:

> You have the terrific problem of how the Japanese are going to get along unless they again reopen some sort of empire toward the south . . . .
>
> If we really in the Western world could work out controls . . . fool-proof enough and cleverly enough exercised really to have power over what Japan imports in the way of oil and other things . . . we could have veto power over what she does.[25]

Thus, once the decision to revive Japan was made, two questions predominated: the hegemonic problem and the hinterland problem. The Central Intelligence Agency [CIA] in May 1948 suggested Northeast Asia as the new (old) hinterland:

As in the past, Japan for normal economic functioning on an industrial basis, must have access to the Northeast Asiatic areas – notably North China, Manchuria, and Korea – now under direct, indirect, or potential control of the USSR.[26]

A high official in the Economic Cooperation Administration, a few months later, suggested the same hinterland, and a drastic method of recovering it. Without North China and Manchuria, he argued, Japan would have "no hope of achieving a viable economy"; it (and Korea) would be "doomed to military and industrial impotence except on Russian terms." Therefore, "Our first concern must be the liberation of Manchuria and North China from communist domination."[27] This rollback option, however, was delayed; the victory of Mao's forces throughout China and the possibility in 1949 that Washington might be able to split Moscow and Peking (Acheson's policy) combined to suggest a hinterland for Japan in Southeast Asia.

In July 1949, the CIA asserted that the United States had "an important interest" in "retaining access to Southeast Asia, for its own convenience and because of the great economic importance of that area to Western Europe and Japan." It argued that "the basic problem with respect to Japan is to recreate a viable economy. This in turn requires a stabilization of the situation in Southeast Asia and a *modus vivendi* with Communist China." The latter requirement might be satisfied if China could be drawn away from "vassalage toward the USSR."[28] Southeast Asia was the preferred candidate for Japan's hinterland. It would provide markets for Japan's textile and light industrial exports, in exchange for raw materials Japan badly needed. The problem was that France and Britain sought to hold the countries in the region exclusively, and nationalist movements resisted both the Europeans and a reintroduction of the Japanese. Thus, "Anglo-American consensus over Japan dissolved" as the United States played the hinterland option. Japan was a threat to sterling bloc trade and currency systems, and was "perforce in the dollar bloc"; the United States wanted Japan to earn dollars in the sterling bloc, which would have the dual virtue of supporting Japan's revival while encouraging Britain's retreat from empire.[29]

The occupation also rearranged Japan's monetary and trade policies to support a revival of trade. The yen was fixed in 1949 at the rate of 360 to $1.00, from which it did not depart until 1971; the rate was artificially low to aid Japanese exports. The Dodge Line pursued a strict policy of fiscal restraint. In the same year (1949) the occupation removed price floors on Japanese exports, raising fears of "dumping" in Southeast Asia.

Particularly important is the *triangular* structure of this arrangement: United States (core), Japan (semiperiphery), and Southeast Asia (periphery). This structure was clearly articulated in the deliberations leading up to the adoption of NSC 48/1 in late December 1949, a document so important that it might be called the NSC 68 for Asia. (With this the United States made the decision to send aid to the Bao Dai regime in Vietnam, not after the Korean War began.) The first draft argued the virtues of a "triangular" trade between the United States, Japan, and Southeast Asia, giving "certain advantages in production costs of various commodities" – that is, comparative advantage in the product cycle. It also called for a positive policy toward Communist-held territory in East Asia: the goal was "to commence the rollback of Soviet control and influence in the area." The final document changed this phrase to read, "to contain and where feasible to reduce the power and influence of the USSR in Asia."[30] The roll-back contingency expressed both the fear of continuing Communist encroachment, what with the fall of China in 1949, and the search for a Japanese hinterland.

The Korean War effectively drew the lines of the "grand area" in East Asia. When the war broke out, the Seventh Fleet was interposed between Taiwan and the mainland, suggesting once again an integration of Taiwan with Japan and the world economy. South Korea was almost lost in the summer of 1950. Then, after the Inch'on landing, the course of the fighting opened the realm of feasibility suggested in NSC 48/1; the "contain and reduce" phraseology was used in the State Department to justify the march north and, in passing, to wrench North Korea's industrial base away from the Communists. Roll-back met several hundred thousand Chinese "volunteers," however, and that debacle froze the situation. The geopolitical lines, or hegemonic outer limits, were thus fixed and they have survived.

227

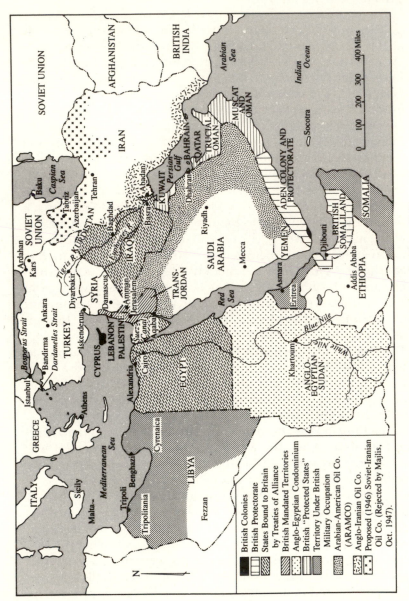

Map 4 East and Southeast Asia, 1948

Taiwan and South Korea were in, North Korea and Manchuria were out. It remained only to reintroduce Japanese economic influence, which the Kennedy administration did in the early 1960s in both Taiwan and South Korea.

Acheson would remark in 1954 that "Korea came along and saved us," and the *us* included Japan. The Korean War not only boosted the Japanese economy but provided MacArthur with justification for reviving police and military and for excluding labor and the left within Japan. The strategic lines of the new Northeast Asian political economy, however, brought the peculiar nature of American hegemony to the fore. There is a paradox at the heart of it: nonterritorial in contrast to Old World imperialism, organizing great spaces and knocking down barriers to trade, it has outer limits sufficient to keep countries *in* the system but not sufficient to protect the home economy against destructive competition, and not sufficient to maintain effective dependency relationships or a frozen hierarchy. The system permits upward mobility. The United States retrieved South Korea and Taiwan from oblivion in 1950, but invoking the threat of oblivion to keep them in line in later years was unthinkable. The United States keeps Japan on a food, oil, and security dependency, maintaining a light hold on the Japanese jugular; yet to squeeze would be disastrous. Outer limits are not enough to bring recalcitrant allies to heel. Furthermore, within those outer limits a dependent but strong state obtains leverage over the American "weak state," weak in the sense of competing centers of power and economic interest that can be played off against one another.[31] Thus, the postwar settlement simultaneously gave Japan, in particular, dependency and autonomous capability.[32]

Japan is ultradependent on the United States, or on American firms, for oil and security, and significantly dependent on the United States for food. During the occupation, the Petroleum Board that set policy was made up of members mostly drawn from American oil majors, and even in the mid-1970s Japan was receiving about 70 percent of its oil deliveries from the majors.[33] In the 1960s and 1970s the United States also supplied 60 to 70 percent of Japan's food imports, and in the 1950s used the PL 480 program to sell grain in Japan, Taiwan, and South Korea. All three have been protected markets dependent upon American grain. And since 1945 Japan has had no military capability remotely commensurate with its economic power.

Within Japan, after the reverse course took hold, was a formidable political economy for competition in world markets. The *zaibatsu* were less smashed than reformed, prospering again by the mid-1950s if in less concentrated form. More important, they were now under *state* influence and control, something that prewar bureaucrats had longed for; the role of the big banks was also enhanced.[34] With the *zaibatsu* weakened, the military smashed, and the landlords dispossessed, but with the bureaucracy untouched (the occupation governed through the existing bureaucracy with few reforms or purges), the Japanese state had more relative autonomy than in the prewar period. Indeed, it was the great victor of the occupation. Autonomy enabled Japan to pursue neomercantile policies of restricting entry to Japanese markets, resisting the intrusion of foreign capital, and providing various incentives and subsidies to restructure the industrial base in the 1950s, and conquer foreign markets in the 1960s and 1970s.

The immediate postwar settlement in Taiwan and Korea fundamentally expressed the differences in the two *societies*. Taiwan "drifted aimlessly" in the late 1940s, having to reorient its trade away from Japan and toward China (until 1949); it sold sugar, cement, aluminum, and food to this now-enlarged periphery.[35] But it remained "an extremely well-ordered society," with "fewer signs of social disintegration" than any place on the Asian mainland.[36] Like Japan, the state emerged stronger after the inflow of the Kuomintang [KMT] and the China mainlanders in 1945–9. The potent colonial bureaucracy was preserved nearly intact; Japanese personnel in many cases stayed on well into 1946, training Taiwanese replacements, and native bureaucrats who had served in the colonial administration continued in office. When the mainlanders took over they added a powerful military component to give the state even more autonomy from society: the Kuomintang had finally found a part of China where its bureaucracy was not hamstrung by provincial warlords and landlords. Thus, for the first time, the Nationalists were able to accomplish a land reform; they could do so because none of them owned any land in Taiwan. The reform, in turn, aided the productivity of agriculture because redistributed land went primarily to entrepreneurial, productive, relatively rich peasants.

Furthermore, a disproportionate number of experts, technicians, and well-educated professionals fled the mainland,
adding to Taiwan's already significant human capital. The
result, once the Seventh Fleet drew the outer limit in 1950, was a
state with significant relative autonomy but now far more
dependent on the United States than in any previous period of
Nationalist rule.

Korea, of course, was divided in 1945. In the North a quick
and efficient social and anti-colonial revolution occurred under
Soviet auspices, the ultimate (but also the predictable) societal
response to nearly half a century of Japanese imperialism. The
South, however, festered for five years through dissent, disorder, major rebellions in 1946 and 1948, and a significant guerrilla movement in 1948 and 1949. Southern landlords succeeded
in recapturing the state in 1945 and 1946, under American
auspices, and used it in traditional fashion to protect social
privilege rather than to foster growth. They prevented major
land reform until the Korean War began, and showed no interest in developing the economy. Instead, they ruled through
draconian police and military organizations. As in Taiwan there
was considerable continuity in the bureaucracy from the colonial
period, but the Japanese officials had mostly fled when the war
ended and those Korean functionaries who remained were
largely unable to function, since they were often hated more
than the Japanese overlords. The southern state entered a general crisis of legitimacy in the late 1940s: marked by the worst
Japanese excesses but unable to carry forward colonial successes, the regime seemed doomed.

When civil war erupted in June 1950 the North had an easy
time of it, sweeping the southern regime away until it met
massive American intervention. But paradoxically, the three-
month northern occupation of the South, which included a
revolutionary land reform in several provinces, cleared the way
to end landlord dominance in the countryside and to reform
landholding on the Taiwan model once the war terminated in
1953. By 1953 South Korea further resembled Taiwan. Its colonial heavy industry had been amputated by Korea's division,
most of it now in the North and beyond reach; like Taiwan,
southern Korea was the home of light industry and the best rice-
producing provinces. During the war many northerners had
fled south, also disproportionately including the educated and

professional classes. By the war's end the South had a standing army of about 600,000, compared with 75,000 in 1950, so it approximated the distended Nationalist Army. Finally, Syngman Rhee, like Chiang Kai-shek, had won an ironclad commitment of American defense from Communism. So, to put it concisely, by 1953 Taiwan and South Korea once more resembled each other, but what was accomplished with ease in Taiwan required a war in Korea.

Industrial development in Japan, Korea, and Taiwan cannot be considered as an individual country phenomenon; instead, it is a regional phenomenon in which a tripartite hierarchy of core, semiperiphery, and periphery was created in the first part of the twentieth century and then slowly re-created after the Second World War. The smooth development of Taiwan has its counterpart in the spasmodic and troubled development of Korea, and neither can be understood apart from Japan. Not only was Taiwan's society less restive and its state less penetrated by societal constraint, but it also had breathing space occasioned by Japan's greater attention to Korea and Manchuria before 1945, and American intervention in and assistance to Korea after 1950. In short, the developmental "successes" of Taiwan and Korea are historically and regionally specific, and therefore provide no readily adaptable models for other developing countries interested in emulation. But the evidence also strongly suggests that a hegemonic system is necessary for the functioning of this regional political economy: unilateral colonialism until 1945, US hegemony since 1945.

NOTES

From Bruce Cumings, "The Origins of the Northeast Asian Political Economy: Industrial Sectors, Product Cycles, and Political Consequences," *International Organization*, 38 (Winter 1984): 1–40. Copyright © 1984. Reprinted and abridged by permission of the author and MIT Press and the World Peace Foundation.

1 G. C. Allen, *Japan's Economic Policy* (London: Macmillan, 1980), 1; see also Kazushi Ohkawa and Henry Rosovsky, *Japanese Economic Growth: Trend Acceleration in the Twentieth Century* (Stanford, CA: Stanford University Press, 1973), 74, 82–3. For the comparisons of growth rates with Korea and Taiwan see Mataji Umemura and

Toshiyoki Mizoguchi (eds), *Quantitative Studies on Economic History of Japan Empire [sic], 1890–1940* (Tokyo: Hitotsubashi University, 1981), 64.

2 For references, see David P. Calleo and Benjamin M. Rowland, *America and the World Political Economy* (Bloomington, IN: Indiana University Press, 1973), and Jacob Viner, "Power versus Plenty as Objectives of Foreign Policy in the Seventeenth and Eighteenth Centuries," *World Politics*, 1 (October 1948): 1–29 on mercantilism and neomercantilism; Raymond Vernon, *Sovereignty at Bay: The Multinational Spread of U.S. Enterprises* (New York: Basic Books, 1971), on the product cycle and free trade; Immanuel Wallerstein, "The Rise and Future Demise of the World Capitalist System: Concepts for Comparative Analysis," in Immanuel Wallerstein (ed.), *The Capitalist World-Economy* (New York: Cambridge University Press, 1979), for the world system approach.

3 See C. Fred Bergsten, Robert O. Keohane, and Joseph S. Nye, Jr, "International Economics and International Politics: A Framework for Analysis," in C. Fred Bergsten and Lawrence B. Krause (eds), *World Politics and International Economics* (Washington, DC: Brookings, 1975), 14; also Robert O. Keohane and Joseph S. Nye, Jr, *Power and Interdependence: World Politics in Transition* (Boston, MA: Little, Brown, 1977), 42–6.

4 The "grand area" was a concept used in Council on Foreign Relations planning in the early 1940s for the postwar period. See Laurence H. Shoup and William Minter, *Imperial Brain Trust: The Council on Foreign Relations and U.S. Foreign Policy* (New York: Monthly Review Press, 1977), 135–40.

5 Steven D. Krasner, "U.S. Commercial and Monetary Policy; Unravelling the Paradox of External Strength and Internal Weakness," in Peter J. Katzenstein (ed.), *Between Power and Plenty: The Foreign Economic Policies of Advanced Industrial States* (Madison, WI: University of Wisconsin Press, 1978). Alexander Gerschenkron, *Economic Backwardness in Historical Perspective* (Cambridge, MA: Harvard University Press, 1962).

6 Karl Polanyi, *The Great Transformation* (New York: Farrar & Rinehart, 1944).

7 See Bruce Cumings, *The Origins of the Korean War: Liberation and the Emergence of Separate Regimes, 1945–47* (Princeton, NJ: Princeton University Press, 1981), Chap. 1. On Taiwan see Samuel Ho, *The Economic Development of Taiwan 1860–1970* (New Haven, CT: Yale University Press, 1978), 26, 32; he puts a similar emphasis on the role of the colonial state in Taiwan.

8 Jean-Pierre Lehmann, *The Image of Japan: From Feudal Isolation to World Power, 1850–1905* (London: Allen & Unwin, 1978), 178.

9 James B. Palais, *Politics and Policy in Traditional Korea* (Cambridge, MA: Harvard University Press, 1975), 1–19.

10 Ho, *Economic Development*, 43, 57.

11 Cumings, *Origins*, Chaps 8–10.

12 Ohkawa and Rosovsky, *Japanese Economic Growth*, 180–3, 197.

13 Ho, *Economic Development*, 70–90; Ching-yuan Lin, *Industrialization in Taiwan, 1949–1972: Trade and Import-Substitute Policies for Developing Countries* (New York: Praeger, 1972), 19–22.

14 Edward S. Mason *et al.*, *The Economic and Social Modernization of the Republic of Korea* (Cambridge, MA: Harvard University Press), 76, 78.

15 Lin, *Industrialization in Taiwan*, 19.

16 Cumings, *Origins*, Chaps 1 and 2.

17 T. J. Pempel, "Japanese Foreign Economic Policy: The Domestic Bases for International Behavior," in Katzenstein (ed.), *Between Power and Plenty*, 139–90.

18 John Emmerson, *The Japanese Thread* (New York: Holt, Rinehart & Winston, 1978), 256. I am indebted to Michael Schaller for providing me with this quotation.

19 Jon Halliday, *A Political History of Japanese Capitalism* (New York: Pantheon, 1975), 183–4.

20 Akira Iriye, "Continuities in U.S.–Japanese Relations, 1941–1949," in Yonosuke Nagai and Akira Iriye (eds), *The Origins of the Cold War in Asia* (Tokyo: University of Tokyo Press, 1977), 378–407.

21 Viner, "Power versus Plenty," 91.

22 John G. Roberts, "The 'Japan Crowd' and the Zaibatsu Restoration," *Japan Interpreter*, 12 (Summer 1979): 384–415.

23 Charles S. Maier, "The Politics of Productivity: Foundations of American International Economic Policy after World War II," in Katzenstein (ed.), *Between Power and Plenty*, 45.

24 Halliday, *Political History*, 183.

25 See Kennan's remarks in "Transcript of Roundtable Discussion," US Department of State, October 6, 7, and 8, 1949, 25, 47, in Carrollton Press, *Declassified Documents Series*, 1977, 316B.

26 US Central Intelligence Agency, ORE 43–48, May 24, 1948, in Harry S. Truman Presidential Library [hereafter HSTL], President's Secretary's Files [hereafter PSF], memos 1945–49, box 255, Independence, Missouri.

27 Economic Cooperation Administration, unsigned memorandum of November 3, 1948, in Dean Acheson Papers, box 27, HSTL.

28 Central Intelligence Agency, ORE 69–49, "Relative US Security Interest in the European-Mediterranean Area and the Far East," July 14, 1949, in HSTL, PSF, memos 1945–49, box 249.

29 Calleo and Rowland, *America and the World Political Economy*, 198–202.

30 Draft paper, NSC 48, October 26, 1949, in National Security Council [NSC] materials, box 207, HSTL. For a fuller elaboration see Bruce Cumings, "Introduction: The Course of American Policy toward Korea, 1945–53," in Bruce Cumings (ed.), *Child of Conflict: The Korean-American Relationship, 1945–1953* (Seattle, WA: University of Washington Press, 1983).

31 Krasner, "US Commercial and Monetary Policy," 63–6; Albert O. Hirschman, *National Power and the Structure of Foreign Trade* (Berkeley, CA: University of California Press, 1946), *passim*.

32 Jon Halliday, "Japan's Changing Position in the Global Political

Economy" (paper presented at the annual meeting of the Association for Asian Studies, 1979, Los Angeles).

33 See ibid.; also Martha Caldwell, "Petroleum Politics in Japan: State and Industry in a Changing Policy Context" (PhD dissertation, University of Wisconsin, 1980), Chap. 2.

34 Chalmers Johnson, "A Japan Model?" (paper presented at the Japan Seminar, University of Washington, School of International Studies, Seattle, May 1981). Also Allen, *Japan's Economic Policy*, 108–9.

35 Ho, *Economic Development*, 103; Lin, *Taiwan's Industrialization*, 27–8.

36 Ho, *Economic Development*, 104.

Part IV

THE COLD WAR AND THE THIRD WORLD

12

THE IRANIAN CRISIS OF 1946 AND THE ONSET OF THE COLD WAR

Stephen L. McFarland

Most histories of the Cold War attribute great significance to the Iranian crisis of 1946. In standard accounts of this crisis, the Soviet Union is portrayed as the predator, intervening in Iran's internal affairs, encouraging separatist movements, demanding oil concessions, and seeking to grab a chunk of Iranian territory. In revisionist accounts, the United States is portrayed as a shrewd and self-interested actor, plotting to gain some leverage over Iranian oil, previously controlled by the British, or, at the very least, scheming to protect the rest of the Middle East's petroleum from the outstretched claws of the Russian bear.

The following excerpt by Stephen McFarland offers an entirely new way to look at this crisis. He does not deny that the United States and the Soviet Union were acting in their respective self-interest. But he shows that the Iranians were important players in the crisis, that they saw themselves threatened by traditional British and Russian rivalries in the region, and that they maneuvered to bring in the Americans as a buffer against their traditional enemies. Moreover, he shows that Iranians were divided, that different regions, ethnic groups, classes, and factions identified their interests with different external powers. Each tried to garner foreign allies in their quest for domestic power and wealth. Out of this complex interplay of domestic and international politics emerged an enduring alliance between the Shah of Iran and the United States, an alliance that would have ominous implications during the 1970s.

Like some of the recent writing on the Cold War, this article shifts the focus of analysis away from Washington and Moscow. Third World nations and peoples were not simply pawns in the great game of power politics, but were often important actors. Indeed their actions may have played a key part in arousing the fears of the Great Powers themselves. During the Second World War what were Iranian leaders concerned about? Why did they look to the United States? Did they purposefully exaggerate the Soviet threat? Who was manipulating whom (and for what reasons) in the Cold War?

* * *

In late 1945 columnist Walter Lippmann tried to come to grips with rapidly changing world events. The wartime alliance was in shambles, and the peace most Americans expected was being pushed beyond reach. Lippmann determined that: "American foreign policy is drifting. The United States is being sucked into conflict with the Soviet Union. Whose fault is it? No honest man can say. The United States is drifting toward catastrophe."[1] Although Lippmann was not referring to the Iranian situation, his analysis described the process by which the United States, during and after the Second World War, was "sucked" into an involvement in Iran that resulted from problems only remotely connected to the Soviet-American dispute over Eastern Europe. The reactions of the United States and the Soviet Union to events in Iran were due to the initiatives of the Iranians as well as to any preconceived policy of Great Power confrontation or global expansion. Domestic crises within Iran attracted Great Power intervention and anticipated the ensuing Cold War struggle.

This intervention, however, did not occur in a vacuum. The United States and the Soviet Union, pursuing their own interests, became conscious of Iran's economic and strategic importance at an early date and their policies evolved accordingly. The Soviets endeavored to preserve their sphere of influence in Iran and invited American intervention by breaking their treaty obligations in Iran. American oil companies, advisers, and officials took up Iranian causes too readily and committed many anti-Soviet acts in Iran. In almost every case, Iranian statesmen, employing the century-old strategy of *movazaneh* (equilibrium), labored to intensify differences between their two traditional enemies, the British and the Soviets, in order to forestall any effort by either to make further inroads into Iranian independence and ultimately to regain complete independence.[2] They endeavored to attract the United States to act as a buffer and

240

counterbalance to the Anglo-Soviet threat. Domestically, the government and various interest groups within Iran used the allies as protectors and promoters in internal power struggles. In this manner, internal and external events were linked so that the Iranian monarchy was able to regain its supremacy and Iran its independence and territorial integrity, both of which had been lost in 1941. Iranians exploited the budding Soviet-American rivalry to their advantage. The main result of this Iranian manipulation was a series of crises that exacerbated Great Power differences and eventually helped to nudge the superpowers to the brink of war.

The crises in Iran began in August 1941. The need for a supply route to the Soviet Union and Iran's pro-German policies necessitated the allied occupation of Iran. The country was divided into three zones: Soviet in the north, British in the south, and nominally Iranian in the center. American forces entered Iran in 1942 to assist in the movement of war supplies to the Soviet Union. The 1942 treaty of alliance (the United States was not a signatory) governed the occupation and was designed to limit allied interference in Iran's internal affairs and guarantee its postwar sovereignty.

Iran collapsed into confusion and disorder following the British and Soviet invasion. The rigidly controlled prewar society came apart at the seams: the army disintegrated, the old Shah was forced to abdicate, government officials were imprisoned, political prisoners were freed, a Shi'i Islamic revival weakened reforms and advances in female emancipation, renascent tribes seized control of large areas, rural brigandage returned, and a plethora of diverse political groups were formed.

Before the occupation Iran began efforts to balance its foreign relations between British and Soviet interests and to attract American involvement. In 1940 Iran signed a trade agreement with the Soviet Union that reportedly gave the Soviets the use of airfields in Iran and released imprisoned Iranian Communists. An agreement with the British-owned Anglo-Iranian Oil Company ended a dispute over wartime oil production. American claims against Iran for the seizure of missionary school property were settled. The problem facing Iran after the occupation was to reduce the threat to its independence created by its traditional enemies.[3]

Direct appeals for American intervention on the day of the invasion went unrewarded. Iran then took steps to come to terms with the occupiers, placating them with concessions, but it gave up most of those efforts in order to entice America into intervening. Iranians hated the British and feared the Soviets, making it more necessary to employ a third-power *movazaneh* strategy; to create a buffer between Iran and the occupiers. Trust in the United States developed from a history of detached interest and in no small part from the principles announced in the Atlantic Charter. Unable to attract official American government support at first, Iran initiated efforts to attract private American concerns and companies, hoping that the US government could be drawn into intervention when private interests were threatened.

The Iranian government did not attempt to hide its strategy. One prime minister asked for American advisers to reform the army and national police and to run the government's economic administration (the Millspaugh Mission). Another expressed his desire to have additional advisers operate all government industrial and mining enterprises. A third told a personal representative of President Roosevelt that he wanted American business concerns to enter all fields of enterprise in Iran. When the United States notified Iran that it would be operating the British portion of the Trans-Iranian Railway (the supply route to the Soviet Union), Iran urged the United States to take over the entire system, replacing the British and the Soviets. *Ettela'at*, the semiofficial national newspaper, called the United States Iran's only hope for freedom and independence and pleaded for American intervention to end British and Soviet interference in Iran's internal affairs.[4]

One of the Chiefs of Staff of the Iranian army during the war succinctly summarized this policy of courting American interest: "Our policy was to bring as many Americans as possible to Iran to be witnesses of the Soviet political encroachment and by their presence act as a deterrent for the more open violations of our independence and interference in our internal affairs."[5]

Iran kept the United States informed of all Soviet transgressions during the war, helping to convince American officials of the Soviet danger.[6] In 1941 the Iranian ambassador to Vichy France warned President Roosevelt's aide Admiral Leahy that the Soviets would pillage and destroy Iran. The Iranian government made repeated complaints to the American minister in Tehran regarding Soviet interference. The American minister earlier had warned the State Department that Iran was exaggerating its reports of Soviet interference in order to gain American sympathy and support. Consular intelligence reports indicated no signs of covert Soviet activities or serious interference in local affairs, concluding, to the contrary, that Soviet occupation forces were better behaved than the troops of the other three allied nations in Iran – Britain, the United States, and Poland.[7]

The struggle of domestic political forces in Iran for supremacy was linked to these efforts to attract American support. Diverse power centers formed mercurial coalitions to fight in the social, economic, and political conflicts. The Shah and the army he controlled formed one power center, relying on the United States for military advisers and aid. The government and the gendarmerie it controlled also sought American advisers and American intervention but often opposed the Shah. The parliament was a hodgepodge of eight factions: royalists, conservatives, bureaucrats (all three largely pro-American and somewhat pro-British), northern liberals, Tudeh Communist party (both pro-Soviet), southern liberals, southern tribal leaders (both pro-British), and independents (xenophobic).[8] The Tudeh Communist party gained its support from the industrial cities and the Soviet Union. Merchants and clerics in the traditional cities attracted British support. Other political factions organized more than two dozen political parties with various degrees of foreign support and backing by more than one hundred newspapers. Tribal and ethnic minority factions formed autonomous enclaves when the central government lost its power to control rural areas. Many of these enclaves existed within the allied occupation zones.

These disparate elements pursued Great Power sponsorship for the special advantages it could provide in the competition for domestic supremacy. Reaction against the monarchy after the invasion left the Shah with only the army for support, and he turned to the United States to strengthen it. The efforts of three prime ministers to attract American support through economic concessions and advisory programs already have been related. In September 1941 another prime minister called for allied support, warning that the Shah would have to be deposed if basic reforms were to be accomplished. The Shah promised to return previously confiscated properties to certain large southern pro-British landlords in order to gain British support in the power struggle. The Tudeh Communist party served Soviet interests in Iran and flourished in areas under Soviet control. Several government members tried to balance their allegiances. One prime minister, for example, attempted to win an oil concession for American oil firms and was a member of the Iran–America Relations Society. He was also a member of the Irano-Soviet Cultural Relations Society and a large contributor to a relief agency for Soviet war victims. Pro-British and pro-Soviet groups used their connections to the Great Powers to force the recall of a governor-general of Esfahan in 1944 because he had been suppressing their activities. This pattern of factionalism continued until 1944, when crises over labor unrest in Esfahan and over the issuance of an oil concession crystallized the domestic forces into those that supported the Shah and the Western allies and those that supported unrest, northern separatists, and the Soviet Union (though friction continued within the broad coalitions).[9]

Shah Mohammad Reza Pahlavi proved most adept at playing this game for supremacy, establishing ties with America lasting more than three decades. He convinced American diplomats of his progressive views and of his value in solving Iran's problems. His radio broadcast early in the war, for example, identified democracy as Iran's best hope for the future. In December 1942 the Shah used a serious food shortage, blamed on the British, to incite food riots, hoping to force the legal government to resign and open the way for a martial law administration under his control. In 1944 he tried to subvert the parliament in order to establish a martial law administration. Soon after his arrival in Iran in 1942, American military adviser General Clarence Ridley became the object of a governmental disagreement. The Shah wanted Ridley to serve as his aide in reorganizing the army, thereby maintaining court control over the military. The Prime Minister, on the other hand, wanted to make Ridley the Assistant Minister of War, under the authority of the Minister of War, who also happened to be the Prime Minister. The effect would have been to interrupt the chain of command between the Shah and the army. Ridley eventually became inspector-general – a victory for the Shah.[10]

By late 1943 Iran had succeeded in gaining at least a measure of American involvement. American advisers were helping to run the country, the United States had issued the Tehran Declaration, and Roosevelt had stated his desire to make Iran an "example of what we could do by an unselfish American policy." Just two years earlier the United States had refused to intervene in Iran, leaving it to the British.[11]

Actual Soviet aggression and interference in Iranian affairs were limited until October 1944, when Iran announced its decision to postpone all negotiations for an oil concession until after the war. The oil crisis of that month became a catalyst for the Soviet-American confrontation over Iran. The apparent anti-Soviet nature of the postponement encouraged the Soviet Union to see an American attempt to seize Iranian oil for itself.[12]

Iran had tried as early as the 1920s to attract American oil companies to balance the British-owned Anglo-Iranian Oil Company. Standard Oil of New Jersey and Sinclair received invitations for possible concessions but nothing came of them. In the 1930s Iran pursued six American oil companies, succeeding in 1937, over Soviet objection, with Seaboard Oil (a subsidiary of the Texas Company). This Amiranian concession was canceled in 1938 on Seaboard's initiative. In 1940 Standard Oil of New Jersey approached Iran for a concession and Iran responded positively. However, after the Soviet Union informed Iran that any new oil concession granted to a foreign power would be a threat to Soviet security, Iran advised Standard Oil that the concession would be held in abeyance because of the deteriorating world situation. The American minister in Tehran identified this episode as an Iranian attempt to attract American support against a perceived Soviet threat.[13]

In early 1943 the Iranian commercial attaché in Washington approached Standard Vacuum to seek an agreement for an oil concession. The American government and firms jumped on the invitation once it was made, in spite of warnings from the US minister in Tehran and from the head of the American economic advisory mission that oil negotiations in Iran might jeopardize allied unity. In December the Iranian government sent official invitations to Standard Vacuum and Standard Oil of New Jersey. Constant delays in the negotiations over the next year caused the Iranian Prime Minister to encourage American companies to forestall any Soviet or British interference. In February 1944 the Soviets reminded Iran of their "prior rights" to northern oil. Disregarding the warning, the Iranian government in April included the northern provinces in the prospective American concession. British oil interests joined the competition in late 1943, but the Soviets did not join until September 1944. On October 2, 1944 the Soviets made an official offer, followed shortly by the demand for an oil concession. Iran's *movazaneh* strategy had backfired. Instead of attracting the United States as a buffer against Anglo-Soviet participation in oil matters, Iran was left with all three countries simultaneously demanding concessions. The only way out was to deny concessions to all, which Iran did on October 8. After more than a year of visible efforts to win a concession for American oil interests, Iran decided, only six days after the arrival of a Soviet offer, to postpone negotiations until after the war. The employment of two American petroleum geologists as advisers on oil matters made the postponement seem more sinister, raising the specter of American involvement in denying the Soviets a concession. In 1941 the Soviets had attempted to resurrect a defunct oil agreement with Iran, but they were told new negotiations would have to be held. In 1944 the Soviets attempted new negotiations but again were denied.[14]

The Soviet reaction was severe. For the first time in the war, Moscow openly employed the Tudeh Communist party to organize demonstrations against the Iranian government. Traffic heading north into the Soviet zone was halted and food shipments south out of Soviet-occupied Azerbaijan were temporarily stopped. Soviet representatives threatened Iranian officials with dire consequences for the affront. The disruptive acts ended only after the resignation of the Prime Minister and the Cabinet, who were responsible for the postponement, and after announcements of American support for the Iranian decision. This ultimate American backing proved the advisability of the *movazaneh* strategy.[15]

Soviet scholars and American revisionist historians have blamed the United States, specifically the oil companies, for the 1944 crisis, although the evidence indicates they did not create the problem. Iran instigated the affair as another attempt to gain American involvement in Iran. Still, all concerned parties should have anticipated the Soviet response. Throughout the twentieth century Russia continually had indicated its objections to any other foreign powers establishing a presence in northern Iran. In 1921 a Soviet-Iranian treaty canceled a tsarist concession in northern Iran with the understanding that the concession area would never be ceded to a third power. In 1940 the Soviets clearly stated their objection to an American concession anywhere in Iran. In 1941 the Soviets expresssed their continuing desire for an oil concession, and by 1944 they claimed "prior rights" to northern oil. Despite these actions, Iran pursued a concession with American companies. Iran's decision canceling negotiations was aimed clearly at the Soviet Union. The United States, by announcing support for Iran in the crisis, by permitting two American oil experts to advise Iran on oil matters, and by ignoring the warnings of its own officials, came out in strong support of Iran and its anti-Soviet stand. Soviet Ambassador Andrei Gromyko in Washington cited "hidden influences" behind Iran's actions. The lines of confrontation had been drawn, with the United States and Iran opposing the Soviet Union, but the Soviets postponed the battle over Iran until after the war with Germany.[16]

Actions taken by the Iranian government after the oil crisis indicated additional efforts to attract American involvement in Iranian affairs, especially since Iran had goaded its northern neighbor into an aggressive stance. In late 1944 Iran notified the allies that its internal air routes would be closed to all foreign air carriers after the war, but it privately told the United States that the prohibition was aimed at the USSR and not the United States. In early 1945 Iran dropped all pretense and appealed to the United States for direct military intervention to stop Soviet aggression and to support Iran in its efforts to send forces into the northern areas to quell unrest. It also attempted to negotiate an early allied withdrawal, although the treaty of alliance clearly gave the allies the right to remain in Iran until six months after the war with "Germany and her associates." At the same time, the Iranian government was secretly advising the American government that the withdrawal demands applied only to British and Soviet and not American forces.[17]

Beginning in the summer of 1945, local unrest in Soviet-occupied Azerbaijan and Kurdistan, encouraged but not created by the Soviets, led the central authorities in Tehran to initiate military measures to restore order and control. Iran retained the right to maintain internal security, according to Article 3 of the Treaty of Alliance, although that right was subordinate to Iran's

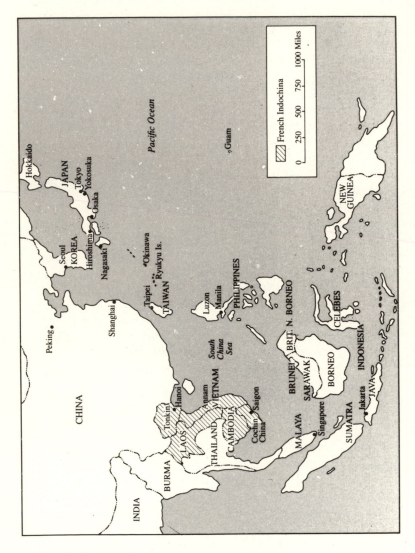

Map 5 The Middle East, 1945–6. Adapted from Wm Roger Louis, *The British Empire in the Middle East, 1945–1951* (Oxford: Clarendon Press,1984), xviii–xix.

responsibility under Article 4 to safeguard the security of Allied forces. Iran exacerbated an already tense situation by moving into direct confrontation with Soviet forces still occupying the northern provinces. The Soviets claimed this threatened the security of their forces in Iran.[18]

On November 19, 1945 Soviet forces at Qazvin, ninety miles northwest of Tehran, halted an Iranian army column ordered into Azerbaijan. The Iranian government assumed a three-sided response to the issue. First, it doubled its efforts to keep the United States constantly informed of all Soviet actions and especially misdeeds. Second, it labored to preserve the crisis atmosphere until the Soviets withdrew from Iran and until the control of the central authorities could be restored in the northern areas. And third, it sent a trusted representative, well known as a friend of America, to Washington, an ambassador capable of working on public opinion and able to pressure government officials.

The greatest immediate problem confronting the United States was the acquisition of accurate intelligence on the incident. With Iran controlling the initial sources of information, reports were forwarded of 6,000 Soviet troops manning the roadblock at Qazvin and of widespread Soviet efforts to encourage revolts against the Iranian government. The American ambassador was careful to warn the State Department that: "Communications difficulties plus the unreliability of even official Iranians as factual reporters make it impossible . . . to vouch for the absolute accuracy of reports forwarded." He described reports of the Soviets arming civilians in the north and reports of 6,000 Soviet troops in civilian clothing pouring over the border as mere "fabrications." After American diplomatic personnel visited the area of the disturbances and observed events firsthand, a different situation was revealed. The American military attaché traveled to Qazvin and Karaj, scenes of the purported obstructions, and called Iranian reports "alarmist." The Soviets had created roadblocks, but at Qazvin the blocking force was composed of two armored cars and a small infantry detachment, not 6,000 armored troops. He found no Soviet troops at Karaj. The ambassador repeated his warning to Washington on the unreliability of information given by Iranian sources. Traveling on into Azerbaijan by car, the military attaché found no evidence of open Soviet intervention, although he felt the Soviets in spirit backed northern insurrectionists. The Soviets had interfered in Iranian domestic affairs but no attempt was made at the time to construct satellite regimes in northern Iran.[19]

The Iranian Army Chief of Staff asked the government for permission to withdraw the column from Qazvin and return to Tehran several days after it was forced to halt. He saw no military reason for encamping there unable to advance. The government denied his request outright and ordered him to keep the troops at Qazvin, because a withdrawal in the face of the enemy would be politically impossible. The case claiming Soviet interference would dissolve unless the evidence was preserved. The American ambassador cited this incident as more evidence of Iran's efforts to exacerbate the crisis and to keep it alive. The troops were not withdrawn from Qazvin until December 18, 1945.[20]

In Washington, Hossein 'Ala, the new Iranian ambassador, arrived in time to further exaggerate the reports. 'Ala was a former court minister, right-hand man of the Shah, and a public figure well known for his pro-American leanings. Stepping off the plane from Iran at New York's La Guardia Airport, he assailed Soviet policy before American newspapermen. In Washington, he insisted on presenting his credentials directly to President Truman, but his petitions were initially rejected. He persevered and on November 29 appeared before Truman. 'Ala told him that the United States alone could save Iran and asked for immediate intervention by American military forces and for an American promise to get a seat on the UN Security Council for Iran. 'Ala's major themes, presented to government officials and to the press, were that the crisis would destroy the United Nations if not met head-on by direct American action and would become the "first shot fired in a third world war." He found a receptive audience among some State Department officials, who seemed willing to ignore the warnings of Iranian exaggerations and manipulations. High-level officials and a majority of the American people, as demonstrated by public opinion polls, remained cautious and perhaps unconvinced of the critical nature of the crisis until early 1946.[21]

The crisis over troop obstructions never was resolved but rather was preempted by a new crisis. On December 12 and 15, 1945 separatist forces in the north established the Autonomous

Republic of Azerbaijan and the Kurdish People's Republic. The declarations of autonomy were the results of domestic issues, though the Soviets certainly had encouraged them, and came only after four years of demands for basic rights by the northern minorities. The central government continually failed to respond to the demands. In 1945 the Tehran government appointed a reactionary as governor-general of Azerbaijan and used the army to suppress leftist forces all over Iran, especially Tudeh offices. Mohammad Mosaddeq accused the government of driving Azerbaijan toward rebellion. Separatist sentiments existed apart from the Soviet occupation and were either supported by or used by the Soviets. The Iranian government used the Soviet presence as an excuse for an age-old internal problem. Under Iranian tutelage, this attempt to dismember the Iranian state intensified the drive toward a direct Soviet-American confrontation. The existence of Soviet troops in the area, the Iranian accusations of Soviet involvement, and the expanding cold war atmosphere in the United States and elsewhere magnified this largely internal concern into what has been commonly declared the first battle of the Cold War.[22]

The crisis developed rapidly. 'Ala, always the *agent provocateur*, identified this crisis as one of Soviet initiative because the northern peoples were true patriots incapable of rebellion. His analysis of events negated the domestic issues and concentrated on what he declared was open and vicious Soviet aggression. He asked for an American military demonstration in Tehran and insisted that the United States confront the Iranian issue at the Moscow Conference of Foreign Ministers. He also pressed for an early hearing of Iran's case at the United Nations. The Shah had tried as early as November 1945 to obtain American support for an appeal to the UN but instead was told to try bilateral negotiations. By January 19, 1946, under the impetus of events both inside and outside Iran, American policy had changed. Iran presented its complaints to the Security Council, thus succeeding in expanding the fledgling Soviet-American confrontation over Iran into an international concern more than a month prior to the March 2, 1946 deadline for the Soviet withdrawal from Iran. Over the following months the initiative behind the crisis shifted from Iran to the United States and the Soviet Union. Soviet troop movements into Iran caused the American consul in Azerbaijan to report a Soviet armored thrust to seize

Iran, Turkey, and the entire Middle East. Stalin reasserted the struggle against capitalism; President Truman became tired of "babying" the Soviets; Secretary of State James Byrnes decided to give the Soviets "both barrels"; Chargé George Kennan from Moscow sent his famous "long telegram"; Winston Churchill identified Soviet "expansive and proselytizing tendencies" and popularized the term "iron curtain"; and the American public turned rapidly against the Soviet Union.[23]

'Ala continued making bellicose speeches to the American public, appealing to America's sense of justice and fair play. He described the Soviets as "contagious bacilli." He disobeyed orders and retained the Iranian complaint before the United Nations at a time when his Prime Minister was attempting to defuse an issue becoming too hot to handle. The Shah dramatically informed the American ambassador in Tehran that the United States should pursue Iran's appeal to the United Nations in case the Soviets captured Iran. The government of Iran continued the pressure on Washington by passing reports of large Soviet troop movements all over northern Iran. The American consul at Tabriz, capital of Azerbaijan, reported similar movements, although some of his reports were based on sightings passed to him by Iranian sources. The *New York Times*'s reporter in Iran wrote that he saw no sign of Soviet troop concentrations or movements at Qazvin, based on a reconnaissance flight over Azerbaijan, but he found fourteen tanks and other vehicles at Karaj. The revelation several years later that the Shah had ordered the Minister of War to announce a Soviet drive on Tehran, in order to inhibit a Prime Minister's efforts to reach a compromise with the Soviet Union, further challenged the accuracy of the accounts. The Soviet advances certainly occurred, but the reports of them probably were exaggerated.[24]

Public exposure at the United Nations, strong statements of American support, and a Soviet-Iranian oil agreement of April 4, 1946 ended the crisis over Moscow's refusal to withdraw from Iran. The oil agreement, the result of purely bilateral negotiations outside the Soviet-American confrontation, gave the Soviets a face-saving excuse to leave Iran and also repaired damaged relations caused by the Iranian decision in 1944 to deny a Soviet request for an oil concession. The Soviet evacuation was completed by May 9, 1946. An agreement in June temporarily reconciled the Iranian government and the northern separatist regimes. The situation was defused for the moment. The *movazaneh* policy had paid off once again. Iran's independence was secured and American support against Iran's foreign enemies had been essential in obtaining it. According to the American ambassador, Iran had invited the United States to interfere in Iranian affairs in order to eject the powerful northern intruder. The American involvement with Iran was firm and growing.[25]

In 1947 in a document handed to the Iranian government, the Soviets listed their grievances concerning the events of the previous seven years. They accused Iran of favoring American oil and aviation companies; of inviting American experts to run the army, police, and economy; and of creating international incidents by dragging the Soviets before the United Nations and then crushing the progressive democratic movements in northern Iran – all without consulting the Soviet government. The dialectics of the Cold War normally mandated blaming the United States for all such actions. The interesting point here is that the Soviets correctly identified the root of the problem: all of these major conflicts between the involved parties occurred from Iranian initiative and not from a preconceived Soviet-American policy of confrontation.[26]

The Iranian Cold War crisis evolved from the interaction of two forces. First, Iranians laid the foundation for the confrontation and worked to enlarge it for Iran's advantage. Second, international representatives entered Iran for their own purposes, reacted to domestic events, became entangled in the maelstrom of Iranian politics, and ultimately assumed the initiative in intensifying the confrontation. They then used Iran as a stage for acting out international disputes arising from additional points of contention outside of Iran. The United States reacted to apparent anarchy in Iran in order to protect Middle Eastern oil and to help Iran by aiding the Iranian government and by intervening in Iranian affairs. American diplomats failed to heed signs of Iranian complicity in creating the perception of a Soviet threat and to recognize the continuity of Iranian politics. Although more than thirty cabinets served between 1941 and 1947, they were formed from a close clique of seventy to eighty politicians.[27] All of the prime ministers during these years were members of the old Qajar (the dynasty ruling Iran from 1794 to 1925) elite, trained in Iranian statecraft, in dealing with the Russians, and in using the *movazaneh* strategy to attract the support of a counterbalancing Great Power. The only newcomer on whom the United States placed its hopes for a stable Iran was the Shah. Over the next three decades, America's ties to the Shah and the Shah's ties to America were solidified, and the interests and perceptions of the United States merged with those of the Shah of Iran.

NOTES

From Stephen L. McFarland, "A Peripheral View of the Origins of the Cold War: The Crises in Iran, 1941–47," *Diplomatic History*, 4 (Fall 1980): 333–51. Copyright © 1980 Scholarly Resources Inc. Reprinted and abridged by permission of the author and the journal.

1 *Washington Post*, November 1, 1945: 11.
2 For a brief essay on the *movazaneh* strategy, see Rouhollah Ramazani, *Iran's Foreign Policy 1941–1973* (Charlottesville, VA: 1975), 70–2. Official Iranian records for the Second World War period either do not exist or are not accessible. This article therefore relies on other sources, including newspapers, foreign diplomatic records, and memoirs, to fill the gaps remaining in the general literature.
3 US Department of State, *Foreign Relations of the United States: Diplomatic Papers, 1940* [hereafter cited as *FRUS*, followed by appropriate year] (Washington, DC, 1958), Vol. 3: 629–30; Nasrollah S. Fatemi, *Oil Diplomacy: Powderkeg in Iran* (New York, 1954), 186; and *FRUS, 1941* (Washington, DC, 1959), Vol. 3: 355–73, 388–99.
4 *FRUS, 1941*, Vol. 3: 418–19; Ramazani, *Iran's Foreign Policy*, 70–2; *FRUS, 1942* (Washington, DC, 1963), Vol. 4: 238–9; *FRUS, 1943* (Washington, DC, 1964), Vol. 4: 417–19; US Department of State, Decimal File, Record Group 59, National Archives, Washington, 891.114/344, November 6, 1941 [hereafter cited by decimal file number]; *FRUS, 1942*, Vol. 4: 316; *Ettela'at*, 17 Azar 1320: 1; 891.9111/436, April 23, 1941; 891.9111/437, May 3, 1941; *Ettela'at*, 30 Mordad 1321: 1; and 891.4081/6, January 23, 1942.
5 Hassan Arfa, *Under Five Shahs* (New York, 1965), 325. See also Fatemi, *Oil Diplomacy*, 219, 234; Hossein Kay 'Ustavan, *Siyasat-e movazaneh-ye manfi dar Majles-e Chahardahom* [The Policy of Negative Equilibrium in the Fourteenth Parliament], 2 vols (Tehran, 1949–50), Vol. 1: 193–4.
6 See, for example, Cordell Hull, *The Memoirs of Cordell Hull*, 2 vols (New York, 1948), Vol. 2: 1253; and *FRUS, 1944* (Washington, DC, 1965), Vol. 5: 442–3, wherein Secretary of State Hull and Secretary of War Stimson clearly expressed their fears of a Soviet campaign to absorb Iran into the USSR after the war.
7 William D. Leahy, *I Was There* (New York, 1950), 49; *FRUS, 1941*,

Vol. 3: 383–477; *FRUS, 1942*, Vol. 4: 318–25; *FRUS, 1943*, Vol. 4: 319–427; *FRUS, 1944*, Vol. 5: 445–86; *FRUS, 1945* (Washington, DC, 1969), Vol. 8: 359–522; 891.00/1827, February 2, 1942; 891.00/1866, May 3, 1942; 891.00/1874, May 15, 1942; 891.00/1875, May 16, 1942; *FRUS, 1941*, Vol. 3: 463–4; 891.43/9–2244, No. 38; 891.00/3012, February 3, 1944; and *FRUS, 1943*, Vol. 4: 338–42.

8 Ervand Abrahamian, "Factionalism in Iran: Political Groups in the 14th Parliament (1944–46)," *Middle Eastern Studies*, 14 (January 1978): 32–5.

9 891.00/1771, September 12, 1941; *FRUS, 1941*, Vol. 3: 461; Office of Strategic Services, Numerical File, 115902, Record Group 226, National Archives, Washington [hereafter cited as OSS, followed by numerical file number], February 13, 1945; 891.43/5, April 6, 1943; and OSS, 84161, July 8, 1944.

10 *FRUS, 1945*, Vol. 8: 384–6; *Ettela'at*, 4 Aban 1320: 1; 891.00/2042–7/8, November 4, 1943; *FRUS, 1942*, Vol. 4: 219–20; 891.00/3005, January 22, 1944; Department of the Army, *United States Army in World War II: The Middle East Theater; The Persian Corridor and Aid to Russia*, ed. T. H. Vail Motter (Washington, DC, 1952; rep. edn, 1969), 172; and *FRUS, 1943*, Vol. 4: 405–6, 408–10.

11 *FRUS, 1942*, Vol. 4: 242; and Hull, *The Memoirs of Cordell Hull*, Vol. 2: 1507.

12 891.00/3012, February 3, 1944; 891.00/7–1944; 891.00/9-2544; 891.00/10–944; A. V. Bashkirov, *Ekspansia Angliiskikh i Amerikanskikh imperialistov v Irane (1941–1953 gg)* [The Expansion of English and American Imperialists in Iran (1941–1953)] (Moscow, 1954), 99–107; and M. V. Popov, *Amerikanskii imperialism v Irane v gody vtoroi voiny* [American Imperialism in Iran in the years of the Second War] (Moscow, 1956), 209–35.

13 *FRUS, 1940*, Vol. 3: 659–63; and 891.6363 STANDARD OIL/430, May 7, 1940.

14 891.6363/12–1144, No. 148; 891.6363/808, October 20, 1943; *FRUS, 1943*, Vol. 4: 625; *FRUS, 1944*, Vol. 5: 343–45; 891.6363/802, June 22, 1943; *FRUS, 1943*, Vol. 4: 627–8; 891.6363/826, February 28, 1944; 891.6363/836, April 3, 1944; *FRUS, 1944*, Vol. 5: 445–6; and 891.6363/12–1144, No. 148.

15 *FRUS, 1944*, Vol. 5: 456–7, 462–3; 891.6363/12–1144, No. 148; OSS, L49460, November 16, 1944; and *FRUS, 1944*, Vol. 5: 457–61.

16 Popov, *Amerikanskii imperialism v Irane v gody vtoroi voiny*, 218–19; Thomas G. Paterson, *Soviet-American Confrontation: Postwar Reconstruction and the Origins of the Cold War* (Baltimore, MD, 1973), 177; Gabriel Kolko, *The Politics of War: The World and United States Foreign Policy, 1943–1945* (New York, 1968), 300–1; Lloyd C. Gardner, *Economic Aspects of New Deal Diplomacy* (Madison, WI, 1964), 229; L. P. Elwell-Sutton, *Persian Oil: A Study in Power Politics* (London, 1955; rep. edn, 1975), 11, 14, 18, 21, 33, 36–42; *FRUS, 1943*, Vol. 4: 626; Fatemi, *Oil Diplomacy*, 244–5; Bashkirov, *Ekspansia Angliiskikh i Amerikanskikh imperialistov v Irane*, 56–7; *FRUS, 1943*, Vol. 4: 625; and 891.6363/12–2844, No. 7288.

On December 2, 1944, under the sponsorship of Mohammad Mosaddeq, the Iranian Parliament passed a law outlawing any discussions with foreigners on the subject of an oil concession.

17 *FRUS, 1944*, Vol. 5: 492–3; and *FRUS, 1945*, Vol. 8: 360–2, 373–4, 383.

18 "Treaty of Alliance Between the United Kingdom and the Soviet Union, and Iran," *Department of State Bulletin*, 6 (March 21, 1942): 249–52; and *FRUS, 1945*, Vol. 8: 470–1.

19 *FRUS, 1945*, Vol. 8: 436–7, 442–3, 433, 440–1, 447–8; 891.00/11–2845, No. 1009; and *FRUS, 1945*, Vol. 8: 470, 472, 477.

20 *FRUS, 1945*, Vol. 8: 491, 501–2.

21 *New York Times*, November 11, 1945: 19; Matthew Connelly (secretary to the President) to Stanley Woodword (acting State Department Chief of Protocol), January 26, 1946, box 569, Official File, Papers of Harry S Truman, Harry S. Truman Presidential Library, Independence, MO; and *FRUS, 1945*, Vol. 8: 461–2, 500–1, 508.

22 Arfa, *Under Five Shahs*, 346; and Mohammad Mosaddeq, speech before Parliament, *Mozakerat-e majles* [Parliamentary Debates], sess. 171, 14th Majles, 23 Azar 1324.

23 Hossein 'Ala, "Iran's Dilemma: Promises of Allies Not Kept," *Vital Speeches of the Day*, 12 (March 1, 1946): 305; *FRUS, 1945*, Vol. 8: 487–8, 500–1, 508; *FRUS, 1946* (Washington, DC, 1969), Vol. 7: 292–4, 309, 340–5.

24 Hossein 'Ala, "Iran's Dilemma," 305; Hossein 'Ala, "Power Politics in the Near East: Crossroads of Russia," *Vital Speeches of the Day*, 12 (August 15, 1946): 662; *FRUS, 1946*, Vol. 7: 350–4, 340, 342–3, 344–5; *New York Times*, March 14, 1946: 1; and Mehdi Davudi, *Qavam al-Saltaneh* (Tehran, 1948), 115–16.

25 *FRUS, 1946*, Vol. 7: 495–6. For a treatment of Iran's case before the United Nations and of American support for Iran, see Richard W. Van Wagenen, *The Iranian Case, 1946* (New York, 1952).

26 *FRUS, 1947* (Washington, DC, 1971), Vol. 5: 906–7.

27 L. P. Elwell-Sutton, "Political Parties in Iran, 1941–1948," *Middle East Journal*, 3 (Winter 1949): 46.

13

REVOLUTIONARY MOVEMENTS IN ASIA AND THE COLD WAR

Michael H. Hunt and Steven I. Levine

China and Vietnam have played critical roles in the Cold War. In these countries revolutionary movements triumphed, consolidated power, and challenged American hegemony. In the Philippines another revolutionary movement, the Huks, sought power and lost. Traditionally, the rise and fall of revolutionary movements have been interpreted in light of Soviet inspiration and US counteraction.

In this important essay Michael H. Hunt and Steven I. Levine emphasize that revolutionary movements must be grasped on their own terms. Their roots were indigenous and their success or failure depended more on their leaders' organizational skills and ideological coherence than on external encouragement or repression. Revolutionary nationalist leaders in Third World countries looked on all foreigners with suspicion. To grasp their aims and aspirations, Hunt and Levine stress that one needs to study the domestic history of Asian nations, their social structure, and their land patterns as well as the sociology and psychology of revolutionary movements and their leaders.

The Americans and Russians were looking for docile allies who would be amenable to their wishes, but in the Third World they often encountered determined and resourceful leaders who rejected a subordinate and dependent status. Readers should discuss the internal social, economic, and political conditions that catalyzed revolutionary movements as well as the international systemic circumstances that nourished or constrained them. They should ponder the roles played by the United States and the Soviet Union. They should examine why it was so difficult for US officials to establish positive relationships with revolutionary nationalist leaders in China and Vietnam whereas they were able to forge a mutually beneficial partnership with a counterrevolutionary elite in the Philippines.

* * *

257

Asia after the Second World War was a region in which "regime collapse" was nearly ubiquitous. From India to Japan political structures and elites, some colonial and others indigenous, were under siege. The rise of elite nationalism, the turmoil associated with Japanese victory and occupation, the surge of American power into the region, and the postwar return of colonial authorities combined to create a fluid political situation. The nature of the ensuing political change varied widely.

In India, Burma, and Indonesia, new regimes emerged with relative ease as former colonial masters began to decamp. In the southern half of Korea and in Japan elements of the old political elites, with the cooperation or acquiescence of American proconsuls, established regimes that were fundamentally conservative in orientation even when, as in the case of Japan, a democratic political system was established.[1] Elsewhere, particularly in China, Vietnam, and the Philippines, revolutionary forces grew apace.

The history of modern Asia and the sociology of revolution suggest some pertinent questions. What manner of men embarked on revolutions? How did they build a base of popular support sufficiently strong to bid for power and challenge the American presence? What conditions favored the emergence of revolutionary nationalism? What was the Soviet relationship to Asian revolutionary movements and regimes? How did this relationship change when revolutionary movements came to power?

Twentieth-century Asian revolutions have passed through two fundamentally different stages. They have begun as *revolutionary movements*, mobilizing resources and people in the process of struggling for power and legitimacy. If and when they succeeded, then as *revolutionary states* they have devoted themselves to realizing the economic and social transformations that had animated them from the beginning.

The revolutions in Pacific Asia were in transition from the first to the second stage in 1953 as Harry Truman yielded the White House to Dwight Eisenhower. The Communist revolution in China had triumphed in 1949, and the new state was in the process of consolidating its political control and pursuing its socioeconomic goals. In French Indochina a second revolution, displaying considerable political strength and military tenacity, was preparing for the battle at Dienbienphu that would soon deal the *coup de grâce* to an over-extended and war-weary colonial power. In the Philippines a third revolutionary movement, the Huks, had gained momentum in 1950, creating panic in the Filipino government and sudden alarm in Washington.

Revolution in these three countries arose out of long-brewing indigenous political crises that can be understood only by taking a broad and long-term perspective.[2] Revolution was initially an elite enterprise that developed through several difficult stages and, where successful, commanded a widening circle of supporters and a growing base of resources. We will gain a better grasp of the revolutionary challenge if we look at the three phases through which a successful revolution had to pass before culminating in victory.

First, the initial impetus to revolution arose from a quiet crisis of confidence that took shape in the minds of politically engaged intellectuals. Concern about the traditional states' diminished capacity to meet foreign and domestic responsibilities goaded these leading players in the drama of revolution into undertaking political activity. In China, the crisis of state and society underlying the collapse of the Qing dynasty in 1911 stimulated a search for alternative political forms that might restore China's strength and glory. By the 1920s some leading intellectuals had begun to find in Marxism-Leninism an attractive idiom for expressing their concerns and a vehicle for political organization.[3] In Vietnam the state crisis was even more profound. There a well-entrenched colonial power loomed over the patriotic intellectuals who wished to restore indigenous political authority. Vietnamese intellectuals followed the pattern established by their Chinese counterparts. By the 1920s patriotic and social concerns – couched often in Marxist concepts and categories – gripped a younger generation of intellectuals and political activists.[4]

Second, the fortunes of revolution depended heavily on the ability of nascent revolutionary elites to construct a shared ideology and forge an effective party organization. They had to translate the esoteric language of an elite ideology into a popular vision of a new order accessible to the masses. Equally important was the creation of a unified, disciplined party capable of challenging both local power-holders and the central government.

By the 1920s activists in both China and Vietnam had discovered in the concept of a Leninist party a powerful tool for achieving revolutionary success and in the Soviet experience a model to emulate. The Communist International (Comintern), established in 1919 by the youthful Soviet regime as an instrument of world revolution, recognized a historic opportunity and stepped in to supply nascent Communist parties with funds, schooling, literature, and advisers. The Chinese Communist Party [CCP] took shape in 1920–1 with a mere fifty members.[5] Its Vietnamese counterpart, the Indochina Communist Party, began in 1925 as a nine-man cell and was formally organized in Hong Kong in 1930, when Ho Chi Minh, already an experienced Comintern operative, brought together rival Communist groups.[6]

Third, ultimate victory turned on the successful application of party ideology and organization to the task of mobilizing the resources – manpower, taxes, labor, and intelligence – that revolutionary organization required. Initially, activity began in the cities with an attempt to forge a proletarian spearhead for the revolutionary movement. When the cities proved inhospitable and dangerous, the urban intellectuals qua early revolutionary leaders took refuge in the countryside where four-fifths of their countrymen lived. The CCP took advantage of the rugged Jinggang mountains in the south and then the primitive Yan'an area in the north, while the Viet Minh established a secure base in the inaccessible mountains of North Vietnam from whence they penetrated the populous Red River delta.

Perhaps the most difficult as well as the most important task required to make revolution self-sustaining was that of mobilizing peasant support. Translating revolutionary abstractions into political practice in rural areas was a fragile and contingent operation that put a premium on an experimental outlook. Success demanded extraordinary sensitivity to the great variety of conditions existing both within and between different regions. The political consciousness of peasants and, in turn, the degree of peasant activism depended on the nature of those conditions. Only by constructing a revolutionary program flexible and ample enough to accommodate the diversity of peasant experience and needs could the revolution make headway.

Revolutionaries struggling to build a base of support within secure zones of operation faced a formidable and changing set of foes. Local power-holders and the central government, sometimes separately and sometimes in combination, exploited the vulnerability of the peasantry to the assertion of state power or, where the revolutionaries had dug themselves in, to the exercise of counterrevolutionary terror. At times the intrusion of foreign powers dramatically redefined the nature of the conflict. The CCP faced first the Nationalists, then the Japanese, and finally the Nationalists again, this time backed, however ineffectively, by the United States. For the Vietnamese Communists the first foe was the French, then briefly the Japanese, and once more the French, now bolstered by increasing levels of American support.

By the late 1930s the CCP had worked out a viable strategy.[7] The Viet Minh for its part solved the riddle of rural mobilization in the course of the early 1940s while organizing resistance to Japan and battling famine.[8] The mark of success in both cases was the establishment of relatively secure rural base areas that gradually evolved into embryonic states containing the seeds of a new social and political order. By 1945, after two decades of struggle against long odds, both the CCP and the Viet Minh had created conditions of "multiple sovereignty" (to use Charles Tilly's phrase),[9] raising hopes for an imminent victory.

The ultimate challenge for revolutionary leaders was to identify the moment for decisive action when sufficient resources had been aggregated to meet and master a vulnerable enemy. In China and Vietnam no less than in the Philippines (to be discussed below) the Second World War set the stage by discrediting the old regime and by weakening its hold on the countryside. During wartime, revolutionary parties firmly seized the chance to extend territorial control and to promote a patriotic united front that appealed to previously uncommitted groups. In 1946 the Chinese Communists drew on the strength accumulated during the anti-Japanese War in meeting the military challenge of their Nationalist foes and then fought their way to victory in a three-year civil war. For the Viet Minh the opportune moment had come in 1945. A policy of revolutionary expansion took advantage of French weakness, the impending defeat of the Japanese, and socially disruptive famine in the north. The Viet Minh offensive culminated in August in the seizure of Hanoi and the creation of the Democratic Republic of Vietnam [DRV]. This gave the Viet Minh at least a tenuous hold on power in the north.

The revolutionary crisis that erupted in the Philippines in the late 1940s and then subsided in the early 1950s departed significantly from the Chinese and Vietnamese patterns. Fundamental to the failure of revolution in the Philippines was the absence of a crisis of the state comparable to that which had proved so troubling to intellectuals in China and Vietnam. Filipinos had known only weak government in Manila. After the ouster of the Spanish in 1898, leading Filipino provincial families ruled in league with American proconsuls. The elite comprised of those families not only lacked a tradition or model of a strong state but was also compromised by a habit of collaboration with foreign masters on a scale unmatched in either China or Vietnam. After briefly resisting the American takeover, the elite had settled into a collaborative relationship with the United States that safeguarded its domestic privileges while promising ultimate political independence. When the Japanese conquered the islands during the Second World War, the elite again accommodated to foreign rule. Finally, when the Americans returned, the Philippines resumed a dependent relationship with the United States, which continued even after the attainment of formal independence in 1946. Rather than forcefully rejecting external domination, the dependent Filipino elite developed at best a kind of submissive nationalism.

The type of collaboration prevailing in the Philippines served as a model for US policymakers with regard to other Asian countries. Local elites that deviated from this norm were at the very least viewed with suspicion by Americans who preferred and expected complaisance from their Asian partners. By explicitly and often passionately rejecting the subordinate and dependent position such a model entailed, revolutionary elites directly challenged American political values and presumptions. This conflict was one of the core elements in the confrontation between the United States and Asian revolutionary movements.

In the case of the Philippines, it appears that the Huk crisis arose not from elite disaffection but rather from peasant discontent, which became pronounced in the interwar period. The deterioration of patron-client ties left peasants without economic security. Landlords with whom peasants had once enjoyed

a mutually supportive relationship increasingly embraced com-
mercialized agriculture and "rationalized" their use of peasant
labor so as to eliminate traditional but costly welfare practices.
The catalyst for peasant resistance was a rural order characterized by increasingly high rates of landlessness and tenant debt.
In the 1920s sporadic, isolated acts of collective peasant protest
threatened the local elites and attracted the attention of the
Socialist Party, which helped organize peasant unions. The
Philippine Communist Party, established in 1930, also embraced
the cause of the peasant, perhaps even before it merged with the
Socialists in 1938.

The Japanese occupation of the Philippines in 1941 set the
stage for the creation of the People's Anti-Japanese Army, popu-
larly known as the Huks.[10] In March 1942 prominent Socialists
and Communists met to organize a united-front, peasant-based
force. They put at its head Luis Taruc, a charismatic Socialist
from a poor, rural background. The Huks resisted the invaders
and punished Filipino collaborators, many of them landlords.
But Huk leaders failed to undertake the ideological and organizational work that was in the long run essential if the movement were to be sustained and made cohesive. In this critical
respect, the practice of the Huks differed from that of the CCP
and the Viet Minh.

As in China and Vietnam, the end of the war brought only a
hiatus in the gathering rural crisis. The Huks disbanded, and
the initiative in the countryside passed to local forces sponsored
by landlords, who were in turn supported by the Roxas government of the newly independent Philippines. As the futility of
peaceful peasant organization and protest became apparent between 1946 and 1948 and as wartime gains evaporated, armed
Huk units sprang back to life, reestablishing themselves in their
stronghold in central Luzon.[11]

In January 1950 the Huk leadership, dominated by the
Communist Party, decided to gamble on an all-out offensive to
seize power.[12] That decision was prompted in part by Manila's
ineffectual response to the Huk challenge and in part by the
Communist leaders' conviction that the United States was on
the defensive in the Cold War and would not be able to save its
Filipino allies. However, the general offensive failed and the
Huk cause suffered a crushing defeat. Under a series of heavy
blows the Huks rapidly declined. At its peak the Huks had

boasted 12,000 to 15,000 combatants and 1.5 to 2 million followers, but by the mid-1950s the Huks had disappeared as an organized force.[13]

The defeat had several sources. Among them was a wrong assessment of how the United States would react to a revolutionary upsurge, and a serious misreading of the mood of the peasantry. Once the gravity of the Huk threat became clear during the first half of 1950, Washington had rushed assistance to Manila. Communist leaders also erred by stressing the threat of American imperialism but failing to link it to the local grievances and personal aspirations of the peasantry.

In Ramon Magsaysay, moreover, the United States had found an effective Filipino partner in turning back the revolutionary challenge. As the Huks scented victory over the Quirino government in September 1950, Magsaysay was made Secretary of Defense at the urging of the Americans. Bolstered by various kinds of American assistance, he transformed the army into an effective instrument of rural pacification, while himself promising land reform. His success at capturing Huk leaders and at sowing dissension within the movement further blunted the revolutionary thrust.[14]

The failure of the Huks may be interpreted in several ways. The United States had found that it could indeed neutralize rural-based revolutionaries by combining the effective application of force with a program of political inducements and promises of reform. From this experience was born the notion of counterinsurgent warfare. An alternative reading of this experience was that in the Philippines the ingredients for a successful social revolution – a disciplined party able to translate elite discontent into a program that could mobilize and sustain peasant support – had not yet appeared. The Huks arose on the basis of strong peasant grievances, but they never acquired an elite leadership armed with the ideological and organizational tools to harness the peasantry to revolutionary goals. The leadership of the Huks, a heterogeneous lot, lacked a common program, and some among them were still psychologically oriented to the cities and not attuned to rural conditions and the military potential of armed Huk units. These leaders were responsible for the ill-advised and disastrous all-out offensive of 1950.[15]

Before considering the transformations undertaken by revolutionary Asian states, let us briefly sum up the implications for the United States of our three cases of Asian revolutionary movements. First, at a time when American power was still very much in the ascendant, the successes of Communist revolutionaries in China and Vietnam already foreshadowed the limits of American influence in postwar Asia. The Chinese revolution in particular forced Washington to abandon the idea that China could be a reliable bulwark against a perceived Soviet threat to the stability of postwar Asia. Second, the United States, which prided itself on being different from and better than the European colonial powers, was reviled by the revolutionaries as merely the latest of the Western imperialist powers to seek domination in Asia. Although American leaders naturally denied the charge, it stung none the less. Third, the coming to power of revolutionary counter-elites who rejected American guidance in no uncertain terms directly challenged the tutelary model of external patron-domestic client relations that Washington favored. This model, first evident in the Philippines' case, was seen by Washington as the way to accelerate political and economic development while blocking Soviet penetration. The successful suppression of the Huk uprising may have strengthened the confidence of policymakers that they could cope with rural-based insurgencies elsewhere.

Revolution in Asia entered a new era as triumphant revolutionary movements in China and Vietnam assumed state power. Revolutionary leaders left behind them the heroic and perilous age of the struggle for survival and confronted a new period filled with formidable policy challenges and fresh perplexities. Among their core tasks was that of creating an efficient state apparatus and tackling the yet unrealized goals of the revolution – social transformation, long-term economic development, and strategic security. Here, as in the earlier phase, the United States discerned danger in the ways that revolutionary leaders pursued these goals.

The transition from revolutionary movement to revolutionary state produced considerable tension in the revolution as some leaders adjusted more easily than others to the new tasks at hand. That tension arose out of a basic dilemma: how to build a strong administrative structure and promote development without losing touch with the revolutionary ethos or abandoning the political style promoted over several decades of intense political and military activity. Those gripped primarily by the statist concerns that had initially driven the elite toward revolution placed priority on building up a strong party and government bureaucracy governed by expertise and regulations. While they wanted to preserve and promote the myths of the revolution, which provided legitimacy and fostered national unity, they deemed the improvisational and voluntaristic practices of the movement days unsuitable to the new age. Those of a more populist persuasion, however, saw in the program of the state-builders a threat to the vision of national unity and popular mobilization that had shaped revolutionary strategy and produced victory.

In China this statist-populist tension is evident in the domestic policy pursued during the first decade of the People's Republic. Most of the leadership, including Zhou Enlai, Liu Shaoqi, and Deng Xiaoping, generally favored a prolonged period of domestic stability conducive to state-building and laying the foundation for the later development of an advanced socialist economy. On the other side, Mao Tse-tung embodied a populist commitment to maintaining revolutionary consciousness and egalitarian values long central to the struggle that he had led. Development would come not through deadening, routinized work but through "storming," directing a burst of energy from the Chinese people against economic obstacles. A period of rest and consolidation would follow, setting the stage for attempting new breakthroughs.[16]

The divergent goals and styles evident in domestic affairs also supply a clue to the tensions at work in the foreign policy realm. Statist concerns made foreign policy an instrument to serve China's concrete development needs once the essential security of the revolution had been attended to. Links to the Soviet Union were important, both in deterring any American-sponsored attack and in guaranteeing economic aid and technological transfers. But links to other states, regardless of their social system, were also valuable for the economic opportunities they might open up and for the diplomatic opportunities and international status such contacts might bestow on China. By contrast, foreign policy initiatives that threatened to embroil China in conflict were unwelcome. China needed to direct its resources into development at home, and it needed a calm and stable international environment to pursue its domestic agenda.

From the populist perspective, most forcefully articulated by Mao, foreign policy was to serve the same essentially revolutionary goals that defined domestic policy. Only an assertive and principled foreign policy could shape a popular revolutionary consciousness, align China with the world's struggling peoples, and isolate ideological backsliders from potential foreign support. Such a foreign policy entailed a vigorous defense against the predictable imperialist attempts to disrupt the revolution and divide the Chinese people against itself. It also meant promoting unity among China's natural allies – the Soviet Union and the weak and oppressed peoples of the world – as a counterpoint to the popular unity Mao sought to promote domestically.

The revolutionary movement in Vietnam did not enjoy a moment of decisive revolutionary triumph such as the Chinese had savored in 1949. Thus the tension between revolutionary and state-building goals was even sharper there.

A crossroads was reached following the August 1945 revolution. On that occasion Ho Chi Minh, convinced that the newly established DRV was too weak to confront the returning French, adopted a policy of moderation that gave priority to building a Vietnamese state. Ho sought to strengthen domestic support by continuing the wartime united-front strategy. The Indochinese Communist Party was (at least on paper) dissolved in November, and the new government promoted domestic policies calculated to appeal to non-Communist patriots. At the same time Ho sought to shield the DRV behind an international united front. He pointedly appealed to the victorious allies for support, expressed goodwill toward his Chinese Nationalist neighbor whose forces occupied the north, and called for French and American support on the basis of a presumed common commitment to the principles of liberty and self-determination. Having set the stage with these domestic and international appeals, Ho tried to convince the French that it was in their own best interests to withdraw gradually from Vietnam.

Ho's "soft" policy, especially his handling of the French, appears to have aroused resistance and criticism from some of his compatriots, if not from party comrades. The French, they suggested, were unlikely to offer acceptable terms, and Ho's

267

effort to avoid a showdown was thus foredoomed and humiliating. Indeed, by the summer of 1946 Ho's negotiations with the French had proven fruitless, as the skeptics had all along predicted. In December the Vietnamese-French conflict began in earnest, pointing the way to the realization of long-term revolutionary goals at the short-term cost of sacrificing Hanoi and the trappings of statehood.[17]

In both China and Vietnam, US intervention disrupted the transition from the movement phase to the state-building phase of the revolution. Beginning in the Truman administration, Washington promoted Taiwan ("Free China") as an anti-Communist alternative to the People's Republic. The Eisenhower administration made a similar attempt to nurture an anti-Communist South Vietnam. These actions in turn justified the arguments of Chinese and Vietnamese Communist leaders who resisted the routinization and bureaucratization of their revolutions. Until American imperialism was defeated, they argued, the unfinished tasks of national unification and the defense of the revolution required popular mobilization and unremitting struggle. Washington for its part interpreted the pursuit of these tasks by Beijing and Hanoi as evidence of Communist bellicosity and aggressiveness that threatened stability and order in Asia. Thus, American actions provoked the behavior that US leaders then condemned and intensified their efforts to oppose.

If the United States abhorred the advent to power of revolutionaries in China and Vietnam, it was no less hostile to their attempts to build socialism once in power. The expropriation of private property, the widespread violence unleashed during land reform, the attacks against religion, "brain-washing" techniques and recurrent campaigns directed against intellectuals, and similar features of revolutionary transformation induced revulsion on the part of most Americans. Moreover, the strident anti-American rhetoric of triumphant Communist revolutionaries and their adherence to the Soviet side in an era of cold war confrontation further strengthened American antipathy and served to justify Washington's efforts to isolate, harass, and destabilize the revolutionary regimes. If pragmatic considerations ultimately suggested the wisdom of dealing with such regimes in the diplomatic arena, this was considered a distasteful and unfortunate necessity. Quite unlike the compliant

Filipino elite, which followed America's lead and gratefully hosted American military bases and corporations, revolutionary elites in Beijing and Hanoi were seen as emulating Soviet socialism at home while joining their countries' fortunes to America's cold war adversary in Moscow.

In Asia, as elsewhere, wherever revolutionary movements threatened the status quo, the United States was inclined to see the hand of the Kremlin. There can be no doubt that in the broadest terms the Soviet Union supported revolutionary change in postwar Asia, but this simple truth masks a complex reality. Indeed, from the very beginning of its involvement in Asia following the October Revolution of 1917, Soviet policy had reflected its own often conflicting revolutionary and statist imperatives. On the one hand, it pursued the traditional statist goal of survival within a hostile international environment. At the same time, as the bearer of the Bolshevik revolutionary tradition, the Soviet state promoted revolutionary change abroad that looked toward the transformation of the international system.

The revolutionary imperative derived initially from Moscow's status as the self-proclaimed center of the "world revolution," the command headquarters of the Comintern. The Comintern assisted in the establishment of revolutionary Marxist-Leninist parties throughout the world and sought to coordinate and direct their strategies for taking power. Moscow recognized in nationalism a revolutionary force with the potential to undermine colonialism and imperialism in Asia. Unfortunately, the leaders of nationalist movements frequently perceived communism as an alien force that fostered class divisiveness instead of national unity and Communist parties as threats to their own power. When Moscow tried to ride the twin tigers of Communism and nationalism simultaneously, as it attempted to in China in the 1920s, the results were disastrous both for the local Communist Party and for Soviet diplomacy. The CCP, which Moscow had forced into a shotgun wedding with the Chinese Nationalists, had been virtually annihilated in 1927, when Chiang Kai-shek turned on his partners in the united front. For good measure, Chiang sent all of his Soviet advisers packing and broke off diplomatic relations with the Soviet Union.

In the late 1920s, concomitant with the onset of the world

depression, the Comintern asserted that the new crisis of capitalism was creating the conditions for another revolutionary upsurge. It was in the grip of this apocalyptic mood that the Communist movement in Indochina was consolidated and the Communist Party of the Philippines established. By the 1930s, as Moscow witnessed the rise of fascism in Europe and Japanese militarism in Asia, it directed Communist parties in the service of Soviet foreign policy objectives to enter broad national coalitions of a popular-front type in which Communist revolutionary goals were subordinated to the quest for national unity. National resistance based on national unity took priority over a peasant-worker revolution with its divisive emphasis on class conflict. The Chinese Communists moved toward a second round of cooperation with their Nationalist foes. The Communists' united-front strategy in Vietnam echoed that of the Popular Front government in France and temporarily ceded the class-based revolutionary ground to unreconstructed revolutionaries such as the Trotskyists. As noted above, the formation of the Huks in 1942 expressed the same strategy in the context of a Japanese-occupied Philippines.

Although a post-Second World War Asia in turmoil was rife with revolutionary opportunities, the Soviet Union acted with considerable circumspection. While Western leaders anxiously scrutinized Soviet behavior in the region for symptoms of rabid Leninism, Stalin accepted the limits that superior American power imposed on the Soviet Union. Thus, even though he got back southern Sakhalin and the Kuriles at Yalta, he had to abandon his demand for a zone of occupation in Japan. In China, Stalin initially expressed skepticism toward the Communist bid for power and counseled caution. Soviet aid was extended to Chinese Communist forces during the Chinese civil war (in northern Manchuria), but it was carefully shielded from prying Western eyes. In Southeast Asia, Moscow scarcely took notice of the Viet Minh and the Huk struggles for power.[18]

If the Bolshevik Revolution still inspired Asian revolutionaries in the 1940s, it was because of what Lenin had written concerning the need for organizational efficiency and ideological coherence and what he had actually accomplished in 1917, not because of what Stalin was doing after the Second World War. Yet foreign Communists persisted in viewing Stalin as the preeminent leader of world revolutionary forces, and Moscow said nothing to disabuse them of this notion. (The Red Army's "liberation" of Eastern Europe was hardly a model for Asian revolutionaries – with the exception of Kim Il Sung in North Korea, who came to power via essentially this same route.)[19]

During the Eisenhower era, American understanding of Soviet policy in postwar Asia lagged considerably behind the evolution of that policy itself. Washington remained fixated with the Kremlin as some sort of corporate headquarters of franchised revolutionaries, actively seeking opportunities to extend its operations. In fact, the Soviet role was actually quite different and far more modest. Soviet policy toward the revolutionary states established in China after 1949 and Vietnam after 1954 clearly demonstrates this point.

In both cases, the post-Stalin leadership escalated the level of Soviet interest in and commitment to the Communist regimes in power. It did so, however, not to nurture Mao's revolutionary romanticism or to encourage the territorial irredentism of Ho's colleagues, but rather to support their statist aspirations for political consolidation and economic development.[20] Moscow regarded the dour party bureaucrats and budding Communist technocrats as its natural partners in the 1950s. The Soviets promoted programs of industrialization via loans and the provision of technical assistance. The growth of these allies' state-run economies would contribute to the overall strengthening of the socialist bloc vis-à-vis the capitalist world while the success of a socialist development model would contribute to the prestige of the Soviet Union, facilitate its entrée into newly independent, nonaligned states, and in general put behind the era of Stalinist isolation in international affairs.

Following Stalin's death in 1953, Nikita Khrushchev brought Moscow's Asian policy full circle, back to its Leninist origins in the early 1920s. This earlier Leninist experience supplied a useful point of reference for Soviet leaders as well as the ideological formulas and the tactical tools to respond creatively to the fluid character of international relations in the 1950s and 1960s. Khrushchev recognized that a historic shift was underway; the accelerating decline of the Western imperium in Asia and Africa was opening the way for some new, yet still undefined, international system. The Soviets believed that what they called the governments of "national democracy" – i.e. the radical nationalist regimes of Fidel Castro in Cuba, Sekou Toure in Guinea, and

Kwame Nkrumah in Ghana – were headed toward socialism and that the most radical of these nationalist regimes were worthy of Soviet encouragement and support. By supporting these regimes rather than by instigating revolution, the socialist world could strengthen its "natural alliance" with Third World nationalism and more effectively undermine American power and influence. Such support, of course, fed American suspicions of radical nationalism and pushed the Third World further into an arena of superpower competition.

NOTES

From Michael H. Hunt and Steven I. Levine, "The Revolutionary Challenge to Early U.S. Cold War Policy in Asia," in Warren I. Cohen and Akira Iriye (eds), *The Great Powers in East Asia, 1953–1960* (New York: Columbia University Press, 1990), 13–34. Copyright © 1990 Columbia University Press. Reprinted and abridged by permission of Columbia University Press.

1 For treatment of some of these "nonrevolutionary" postwar transfers of power, see Bruce Cumings, *The Origins of the Korean War: Liberation and the Emergence of Separate Regimes, 1945–47* (Princeton, NJ: Princeton University Press, 1981); J. W. Dower, *Empire and Aftermath: Yoshida Shigeru and the Japanese Experience, 1878–1954* (Cambridge, MA: Harvard University Press, 1979); and Robert J. McMahon, *Colonialism and the Cold War: The United States and the Struggle for Indonesian Independence, 1945–49* (Ithaca, NY: Cornell University Press, 1981).

2 For an introduction to the Chinese revolution, see Lucien Bianco, *The Origins of the Chinese Revolution, 1915–1949*, tr. Muriel Bell (Stanford, CA: Stanford University Press, 1971); James P. Harrison, *The Long March to Power: A History of the Chinese Communist Party, 1921–72* (New York: Praeger, 1972). Good starting points for Vietnam are William J. Duiker, *The Communist Road to Power in Vietnam* (Boulder, CO: Westview, 1981); James P. Harrison, *The Endless War: Fifty Years of Struggle in Vietnam* (New York: Free Press, 1982); Alexander Woodside, *Community and Revolution in Modern Vietnam* (Boston MA: Houghton Mifflin, 1976); and Huynh Kim Khanh, *Vietnamese Communism, 1925–1945* (Ithaca, NY: Cornell University Press, 1982). For the Philippines, the best brief introduction is by Peter Stanley in James C. Thomson, Jr *et al.*, *Sentimental Imperialists: The American Experience in East Asia* (New York: Harper & Row, 1981), Chaps 8 and 19.

3 For the rise of what might be called "radical statism" in China between the late nineteenth and early twentieth centuries, see Jane L. Price, *Cadres, Commanders, and Commissars: The Training of the*

Chinese Communist Leadership, 1920–1945 (Boulder, CO: Westview, 1976), Chaps 1–2; Maurice Meisner, *Li Ta-chao and the Origins of Chinese Marxism* (Cambridge, MA: Harvard University Press, 1967); Lee Feigon, *Chen Duxiu: Founder of the Chinese Communist Party* (Princeton NJ: Princeton University Press, 1983); Richard C. Kagan, "Ch'en Tu-hsiu's Unfinished Autobiography," *China Quarterly*, no. 50 (April–June 1972): 301–14; and Stuart Schram, "Mao Tse-tung's Thought to 1949," in *Cambridge History of China*, Vol. 13: 789–818.

4 On these developments in Vietnam, see David G. Marr, *Vietnamese Anticolonialism, 1885–1925* (Berkeley, CA: University of California Press, 1971); Marr, *Vietnamese Tradition on Trial, 1920–1945* (Berkeley, CA: University of California Press, 1981); and Khanh, *Vietnamese Communism*.

5 CCP membership did not exceed 1,000 for its first several years. Between 1925 and spring of 1927 it grew to 57,000. Its ranks were thinned by reverses in the late 1920s and early 1930s, but swelled again during the Sino-Japanese War. By 1945 it counted 1.2 million members.

6 The Indochinese Communist Party was submerged in the Viet Minh from 1941 until the fall of 1945, when it was nominally disbanded. It was formally revived and renamed the Vietnamese Workers' Party in 1951 to allow room for the development of separate Cambodian and Laotian Communist parties. As late as 1946 the party could claim no more than 20,000 members (though they were to increase to 700,000 by 1950).

7 For an overview, see Benjamin Schwartz, *Chinese Communism and the Rise of Mao* (Cambridge, MA: Harvard University Press, 1951). For a general discussion of peasant politics in China, see Frederic Wakeman, Jr, "Rebellion and Revolution: The Study of Popular Movements in Chinese History," *Journal of Asian Studies*, 36 (February 1977): 201–37, now somewhat overtaken by new studies; and G. William Skinner, "Chinese Peasants and the Closed Community: An Open and Shut Case," *Comparative Studies in Society and History*, 13 (July 1971): 270–81.

Particularly important local studies are Elizabeth J. Perry, *Rebels and Revolutionaries in North China, 1845–1945* (Stanford, CA: Stanford University Press, 1980); Yung-fa Chen, *Making Revolution: The Communist Movement in Eastern and Central China, 1937–1945* (Berkeley, CA: University of California Press, 1986); Steven I. Levine, *Anvil of Victory: The Communist Revolution in Manchuria* (New York: Columbia University Press, 1987); Donald G. Gillin, "'Peasant Nationalism' in the History of Chinese Communism," *Journal of Asian Studies*, 23 (February 1964): 269–89; and Carl E. Dorris, "Peasant Mobilization in North China and the Origins of Yenan Communism," *China Quarterly*, no. 68 (December 1976): 697–719.

8 For an overview, see John T. McAlister, Jr, *Viet Nam: The Origins of Revolution* (New York: Knopf, 1969). For peasant politics in Vietnam, see James C. Scott, *The Moral Economy of the Peasant: Rebellion and Subsistence in Southeast Asia* (New Haven, CT: Yale University Press,

1976) and Samuel Popkin, *The Rational Peasant: The Political Economy of Rural Society in Vietnam* (Berkeley, CA: University of California Press, 1979); Pham Cao Duong, *Vietnamese Peasants under French Domination, 1861–1945* (Lanham, MD: University Press of America, 1985); Jeffrey Race, *War Comes to Long An: Revolutionary Conflict in a Vietnamese Province* (Berkeley, CA: University of California Press, 1972); and James W. Trullinger, Jr, *Village at War: An Account of Revolution in Vietnam* (New York: Longman, 1980).

9 Charles Tilly, *From Mobilization to Revolution* (Reading, MA: Addison-Wesley, 1978), 190–2.

10 This wartime designation was short for "Hukbalahap," itself an abbreviation for "Hukbo ng Bayan Laban sa Hapon."

11 The postwar Huks operated under the abbreviation HMB, short for "Hukbong Mapagpalaya ng Bayan."

12 The precise role of the party is a matter of some dispute. Compare Benedict J. Kerkvliet's classic *The Huk Rebellion: A Study of Peasant Revolt in the Philippines* (Berkeley, CA: University of California Press, 1977) against the responses to it by William J. Pomeroy in "The Philippine Peasantry and the Huk Revolt," *Journal of Peasant Studies*, 5 (July 1978): 497–517, and by Jim Richardson in "The Huk Rebellion," *Journal of Contemporary Asia*, 8 (2) (1978): 231–7.

13 The unraveling of the Huk leadership is described from the perspective of the influential non-Communist Luis Taruc in *He Who Rides the Tiger: The Story of an Asian Guerilla Leader* (New York: Praeger, 1967).

14 Stephen R. Shalom, *The United States and the Philippines: A Study in Neo-colonialism* (Philadelphia, PA: Institute for the Study of Human Issues, 1981), 68–93; and D. Michael Shafer, *Deadly Paradigms: The Failure of U.S. Counterinsurgency Policy* (Princeton, NJ: Princeton University Press, 1988), Chap. 8. Magsaysay's election to the presidency in 1953 carried the promise of long-term stability in the Philippines. His death in an airplane crash in 1957 cut down those hopes.

15 It remains an open question whether the Huk defeat marks the end of a revolutionary attempt (or even an unsuccessful rebellion, as Kerkvliet describes it), or whether it was merely the first stage in a struggle now being continued by the New People's Army.

16 There is today a consensus among China scholars on the existence of this tension in domestic affairs, though they differ on the precise labels to apply. See Maurice Meisner, *Mao's China and After: A History of The People's Republic* (2nd edn, New York: Free Press, 1986); Lowell Dittmer, *China's Continuous Revolution: The Post-Liberation Epoch, 1949–1981* (Berkeley, CA: University of California Press, 1987); and Carl Riskin, *China's Political Economy: The Quest for Development since 1949* (New York: Oxford University Press, 1987). The origins of this consensus can be found in Stuart Schram's *Mao Tse-tung* (Harmondsworth: Penguin, 1966), Chap. 10, with its stress on Mao's special and debilitating "military romanticism" (p. 293) derived from his pre-1949 experience.

17 Stein Tønnesson, *The Outbreak of War in Indochina, 1946* (Oslo:

International Peace Research Institute, 1984), makes clear Ho's forbearance in the face of a provocative forward policy pursued by French colonial authorities and, as a result, his public vulnerability to nationalist attacks.

18 See Yano Toru, "Who Set the Stage for the Cold War in Southeast Asia?" and Tanigawa Yoshihiko, "The Cominform and Southeast Asia," in Yōnosuke Nagai and Akira Iriye (eds), *The Origins of the Cold War in Asia* (New York: Columbia University Press, 1977), esp. 333–6 and 362–77.

19 See Robert A. Scalapino and Chong Sik Lee, *Communism in Korea* (Berkeley, CA: University of California Press, 1972); Dae-Sook Suh, *Kim Il Song: The North Korean Leader* (New York: Columbia University Press, 1988).

20 On this point, see Steven I. Levine, "Breakthrough to the East: Perspectives on Soviet Asian Policy in the 1950s," in Warren I. Cohen and Akira Iriye (eds), *The Great Powers in East Asia, 1953–1960* (New York: Columbia University Press, 1990).

14

THREAT PERCEPTION AND CHINESE COMMUNIST FOREIGN POLICY

Shuguang Zhang

One of the most exciting aspects of the recent scholarship on the Cold War has been the examination of Chinese Communist foreign policy. As a result of these studies we have a much better appreciation of how the Cold War engulfed Asia as well as Europe. Of immense value in the writing of postwar international history has been the outpouring of Chinese memoir material and the selective dissemination of key documents by Communist authorities in Beijing.

With the use of these primary sources historians have begun to weave a fascinating tale of the complex interrelationships between indigenous conflict and civil war in China, Great Power strife in the international system, suspicion and rivalry within the ranks of the world Communist movement, and capitalist imperatives in the world economy. Any study of the Cold War in Asia must take note of the contest for power between the Chinese Nationalists led by Chiang Kai-shek and the Chinese Communists led by Mao Tse-tung. Nor can one ignore the deep distrust between Stalin and Mao and their complex maneuvering with fellow Communists in Asia like Kim Il Sung in North Korea and Ho Chi Minh in Vietnam. The ideological ties among these Communist leaders often were frayed by their nationalist sensibilities. And in a similar way the cohesion between the United States, Britain, France, and the Netherlands often was undermined by contrasting national strategies for containing revolutionary nationalism in Southeast Asia, coping with Communist rule in China, and coopting Japan into a multilateral economic system.

In this article Shuguang Zhang uses new documents to illuminate the thinking, perceptions, and actions of Chinese Communist leaders. We get a more nuanced picture of the role of ideology, geopolitics, and nationalism in the making of Chinese Communist foreign policy. Zhang

276

adroitly portrays Mao's perception of threat as he sought to consolidate the revolution, seize Taiwan, and crush any domestic resistance that might have been encouraged by either the Chinese Nationalist regime across the straits, the French in Indochina, or the Americans in South Korea. We get a fascinating glimpse of Mao's relations with Stalin and his dealings with Ho Chi Minh and Kim Il Sung. We gain a new understanding of how events in China, Indochina, Korea, and Taiwan were intertwined. We have long known how US officials saw these linkages. Now, we can begin to analyze how they were perceived by the leadership of the People's Republic of China.

Readers should compare the threat perception of government officials in Beijing with the threat perception of leaders in Moscow and Washington. In this context it might be useful to reexamine the essays earlier in this volume by Melvyn Leffler and Michael MccGwire. How did Truman, Stalin, Mao and their respective advisers and colleagues define their vital national security interests? How important were geopolitical, economic, and ideological factors in the making of US, Soviet, and Chinese foreign policy? Did the vastly different cultural backgrounds and ideological predilections of the leaders of the three countries shape their perception of threat and their conception of vital interests? Or did similar strategic and geopolitical concerns transcend the importance of culture and ideology? To what extent does the concept of the security dilemma, referred to at the end of Zhang's article, explain the escalating tensions that culminated in three cold wars: between the United States and the People's Republic, between the United States and the Soviet Union, and between the Soviet Union and the People's Republic?

* * *

The Chinese Communist Party's [CCP] policy toward the United States in 1949–50 played an important role in kicking off a new stage of the Cold War in Asia. Before achieving nationwide victory over the Kuomintang [KMT], CCP leaders openly claimed that the United States was the most dangerous enemy to the new China. Convinced that American military intervention was likely at some future time, they resolved upon preparations for the long-term contingency. A battle-ground to confront perceived American military threat was thus established. To understand the origins of Sino-American confrontation, the security concerns and strategic thinking of CCP leaders deserve a reappraisal.[1]

Why were the CCP leaders so concerned about American military intervention? How did their perception of this threat evolve? One answer had to do with Mao's theoretical concept of the "intermediate zone," which grew out of his understanding of the Cold War. The central argument was that although the United States and the Soviet Union were confronting each other, they were separated by "a vast zone which includes many capitalist, colonial and semi-colonial countries in Europe, Asia and Africa." Mao calculated that "before the U.S. reactionaries have subjugated these countries, an attack on the Soviet Union is out of the question."[2] The Cold War period was thus one in which the United States would fight for the vast intermediate zone, and a general war with the Soviet Union would come only after the United States had consolidated its hold on countries within the zone. Since any anti-American or pro-Soviet forces within the zone would in one way or another weaken American capabilities to fight the Russians, the United States would have to wipe out those forces first.[3] To the CCP leadership Mao's "intermediate zone" argument made sense. Indeed, Chinese Communist officials regarded the Truman Doctrine, the Marshall Plan, the rehabilitation of Germany and Japan, the US occupation of South Korea, and, especially, American military assistance to the KMT and the stationing of US marines along China's coast as strong evidence of a US struggle for this "intermediate zone."[4]

Ideology, too, shaped Mao's perception of Washington's hostile intentions. As a Marxist-Leninist, Mao saw US foreign policy within the context of imperialism. Regarding as irreconcilable capitalist contradictions resulting from the shrinking of domestic and foreign markets, Mao asserted that American imperialism was "sitting on [a] volcano." This situation, he predicted, would drive the American imperialists to "draw up a plan for enslaving the world, to run amuck like wild beasts in Europe, Asia, and other parts of the world."[5] As revolutionary ideologues, Mao and other CCP leaders viewed the US government as counterrevolutionary by nature because of its record of interventions often on behalf of reactionaries.

CCP leaders' distrust of America's China policy also affected their perception of threats. They had not had much experience in dealing with Americans, but from those few occasions when contacts had taken place, they had felt cheated and humiliated. The Marshall mission of 1946, they at first believed, had been intended to mediate China's civil war impartially, but its outcome had not been in line with CCP expectations. Moreover, in the light of continuing American military and economic aid to the KMT, the CCP leadership concluded that to expect America to maintain neutrality was only wishful thinking.[6]

Soviet warnings of possible US military actions in China enhanced the CCP's sense of danger. In April 1948, Mao planned a trip to the Sino-Russian border to meet Joseph Stalin in person. But Stalin abruptly rejected the proposal and replied that since the CCP was facing a "critical turning-point," it would be better for Mao to stay on the spot. Instead, he proposed sending a representative to China if necessary. Stalin explicitly advised Mao that everything – including possible foreign interventions – should be taken into full consideration.[7] Further, when Chinese Communist forces were gathering on the north bank of the Yangtze River, on January 10, 1949, Stalin forwarded a letter from KMT Foreign Minister Wang Shijie asking the Soviet leader to arbitrate the CCP–KMT dispute. Implying his willingness to do so, Stalin expressed concern that the United States might intervene "with its armed forces or navy against the Chinese People's Liberation Army."[8] Anastas Mikoyan, Stalin's personal representative to the CCP, arrived at Xibai Po in Hebei Province, then the CCP headquarters, on January 31, 1949. He told the Chinese leaders to watch for possible changes in the international situation.[9] As a result, CCP leaders were strongly impressed with Stalin's fear that the United States might seize the opportunity in China to act more vigorously against the Soviet Union in the Far East or elsewhere.

Indeed, the activities of US military forces in China worried CCP leaders. "U.S. naval, ground and air forces," Mao asserted in August 1949, "did participate in the war in China." As he noted:

> There were U.S. naval bases in Tsingtao, Shanghai, and Taiwan. U.S. troops were stationed in Peiping, Tientsin, Tangshan, Chinwangtao, Tsingtao, Shanghai and Nanjing. The U.S. air force controlled all of China's air space and took aerial photographs of all China's strategic areas for military maps. At the town of Anping near Peiping, at

Chiutai near Changchun, at Tangshan and in the Eastern Shantung Peninsula, U.S. troops and other military personnel clashed with the People's Liberation Army and on several occasions were captured. Chennault's air fleet took an extensive part in the civil war. Besides transporting troops for Chiang Kai-shek, the U.S. air force bombed and sank the cruiser *Chungking*, which had mutinied against the Kuomintang.

Mao believed that "[a]ll these were acts of direct participation in the war, although they fell short of an open declaration of war and were not large in scale, and although the principal method of U.S. aggression was the large supply of money, munitions and advisers to help Chiang Kai-shek fight the civil war."[10] Especially when CCP intelligence noticed "the sudden increase of [U.S.] marine activities in Qingdao" in the late spring of 1949, he felt the imminent threat of American military action.[11]

Even in late 1949, when immediate US armed intervention seemed to be less likely, Chinese Communist leaders were stressing long-term – if not short-term – American hostility. Mao explained in August that the absence of direct American intervention "was determined by the objective situation in China and the rest of the world, and not by any lack of desire on the part of the Truman–Marshall group, the ruling clique of U.S. imperialism, to launch direct aggression against China." In his view, the United States had made China a top priority in its efforts to control the "intermediate zone," because "China, the center of gravity in Asia, is a large country with a population of 475 million; [thus] by seizing China, the United States would possess all of Asia. With its Asian front consolidated, U.S. imperialism could concentrate its forces on attacking Europe."[12]

The CCP's assessment of the possibility of US military intervention had gone from "no immediate threat" to "imminent threat" and to "long-term hostility." However, CCP leaders consistently regarded the United States as an actual and/or potential challenger to their rule in China during this period. What could the CCP do to inhibit the United States from activating its hostility toward a new China in the long run? Based on his understanding of postwar Soviet-American confrontation, Mao calculated that his new regime would have to identify itself with the Soviet Union. His reasoning was simple: it would never be a mistake to ally with an enemy's enemy.

Yet, to the CCP leaders, such an alliance would not be easy because Moscow's attitude toward Mao's CCP in the past had been one of suspicion, indifference, and passivity. The CCP leadership knew that Stalin was particularly skeptical, worrying that Mao was another Tito.[13] In an attempt to eliminate Stalin's distrust, the Communist leaders decided in May 1949 to dispatch a secret mission of top leaders to Moscow. Liu Shaoqi and Zhou Enlai, assisted by Wang Jiaxiang, were in charge of the preparations. Two months later, Liu led a five-person delegation to the Soviet Union. In Moscow, Liu had four meetings with Stalin and his top aides. At these meetings, Liu reported, Stalin made three important points. First, the Soviet Union had not offered as much help to the Chinese Communists as it should have and had even "hampered your revolution to some extent . . . because we did not know China's situation very well." Stalin therefore expressed his apology. Second, the CCP, after nationwide victory, should immediately establish its government, otherwise "the foreigners would take the chance to intervene or to intervene in collective efforts." Third, the world revolution is now moving eastward and, therefore, the Chinese comrades should be prepared to assume more responsibility [for carrying the revolution]. "This is our wish from the bottom of our hearts."[14]

It seemed that Stalin had unexpectedly changed his attitude toward the CCP. However, the Chinese leaders felt that he remained ambivalent about how to support a Chinese Communist government. They were certain that the Kremlin leaders could not have dissolved their suspicions so quickly and so easily. Moreover, the issue of relationship with the Soviet Union was complicated when a group of pro-CCP "democrats" in China appealed for keeping a distance from the Russians but accommodating the West. These people were small in number but politically important to the CCP's "United Front." Besides, their views would affect both the general public and the Party itself.[15] Under these circumstances, Mao decided to move decisively. On the eve of the party's twenty-eighth anniversary (June 30, 1949) he made his "lean-to-one-side" speech, and released it to the public the next day. For the first time, the CCP proclaimed that it would lean only to the side of the Soviet Union and no one else.[16]

The CCP leadership then speeded up its efforts to reach an alliance with the USSR. The Central Committee decided in early September 1949 that it was high time that Mao should visit Moscow and deal with Stalin face to face. Mao left China for Moscow in early December. Upon his arrival, Stalin and almost all of the top Soviet leaders held a state banquet in Mao's honor. The Soviet leader once again apologized, this time in the presence of East European Communist leaders, for the mistakes that he had made and told Mao, "Now you are a winner, and as a winner, no criticism should be imposed on you." Then Stalin asked what the Soviet Union could do to help the Chinese comrades, enquiring what Mao really wanted from his trip. Interestingly, Mao could have given a direct answer but did not. "For this trip," Mao replied, "we expect to create something that should not only look nice but taste delicious." Mao actually meant to achieve a substantial Sino-Soviet relationship rather than a postured friendship, but his Chinese-style metaphor was so ambiguous that when it was translated into Russian, no one understood what it really meant. Shi Zhe, the main translator present, recalled that Lavrenti Beria even could not help laughing at it. But "Stalin was very serious and kept asking Mao to clarify it." The Chinese leader, however, remained ambivalent.[17]

For the next two weeks Mao remained patient but still ambivalent with regard to his real intentions in Moscow. Stalin acted as if he was sincere to offer whatever Mao wanted. In a short meeting as well as three telephone calls, all made by Stalin himself, he repeatedly urged Mao to express directly what he wanted. But Mao was still evasive, insisting that Zhou Enlai should come to Moscow and that Zhou would present the whole package.[18] Mao also conveyed his ambivalence to the Soviet public when he told the Tass News Agency on January 1, 1950 that "the length of my visit in the Soviet Union will largely depend on the amount of time actually needed to settle the issues concerning the interests of the People's Republic of China." He never mentioned a word about what these interests were or how to settle them.[19]

The Kremlin appeared to have run out of patience. On the day after Mao's comments to Tass, Mikoyan and Vyacheslav Molotov informed him that Stalin had authorized them to talk with Mao about the possible results of the visit. Beginning to see the Russians' sincerity, Mao listed three alternative outcomes:

(1) We may sign a friendship and military alliance treaty as well as new economic cooperation agreements, [so as] to settle the Sino-Soviet relationship on the basis of these new treaties. In this case, Zhou must come to Moscow. (2) We may sign an informal agreement to set some general guidelines for the future Sino-Soviet relationship. (3) We may just sign a communique to confirm the friendly relationship between the two countries. Therefore in both cases of (2) and (3), Zhou need not come.

It impressed Mao when Molotov and Mikoyan said, "We will go along with the first [option]." Mao wasted no time in dispatching a telegram back to Beijing on the same day, in which he reported his meeting with Molotov and Mikoyan and asked Zhou to leave China for Moscow in five days.[20]

When the negotiations started, the Russians did not seem willing to accommodate all the Chinese demands. One great difficulty for Zhou was to obtain an explicit commitment from the Soviet Union to assist China if it was invaded, an objective he regarded as the key to an alliance treaty. It took quite some time for Zhou and his aides to bargain over this with the Russians. The Chinese were happy with the final text, though, which provided that "if one side is attacked by a third party, the other side must devote all its efforts to provide military and other assistance."[21] Zhou did an excellent job as he had to, because Mao had explicitly set the task for him as follows: "the basic spirit of the alliance treaty should be to prevent the possibility of Japan and its ally [the United States] invading China," and "with the treaty, we will be able to use it as a big political asset to deal with imperialist countries in the world."[22]

In addition to the Soviet long-term commitment to China's security, the Chinese leaders expected to incorporate Soviet military forces directly into China's national defense, at least for a short period. In Dalian and Lushun, Soviet armed forces had been stationed at military bases since the end of the Second World War. Although the Chinese would want the Russians to go home eventually, they preferred the Red Army to stay until "things get a little quieter in the Pacific." At the Chinese request, the Soviets arranged that Russian troops would remain there till the end of 1952, the expected schedule for a final peace treaty with Japan.[23] Moreover, during Mao's stay in Moscow, Nie Rongzhen, acting General Chief of Staff of the People's Liberation Army [PLA], telegraphed Mao, asking if the Soviet Union could help defend China's coastal cities against the remnant KMT's air raids. This was immediately arranged between Mao and Stalin. Moscow sent one air force division to Shanghai between February and March 1950 which was immediately deployed to defend that city.[24] Moscow also agreed to send a fairly large group of Soviet military advisers and professionals to assist in the "regularization and modernization" of the PLA. A large group arrived in China in early 1950, and Nie put most of them in high positions of the PLA command.[25]

From late 1949 to early 1950 CCP leaders remained concerned about China's coastal security. They particularly feared that the United States might initiate military conflict either from the Taiwan Straits, French Indochina, or the Korean peninsula. Unfortunately, available materials are insufficient to recount how the leadership had come to such a conclusion. Yet there is no doubt that Beijing was preoccupied with preparations against this perceived threat.[26]

The CCP's immediate concern was the Taiwan Straits where KMT forces occupied Taiwan and most of the offshore islands. In considering the importance of Taiwan, the CCP consistently stressed two main themes: first, the United States, faced with failure in China, would seek to bring the island within its sphere of influence regardless of the outcome of the civil war on the mainland, so as to turn it into a stepping-stone for a future invasion of China; second, the KMT, foreseeing its eventual defeat on the mainland, would by all means try to turn the island into its final stronghold under US military protection in order to gain breathing time for its own return in the future.[27] To inhibit this potential danger, the CCP's strategic plan was to occupy the East China coast as soon as possible and then prepare for a final attack on Taiwan in the future.

When Mao returned from Moscow in the early spring, he did not seem to be enthusiastic about seizing Taiwan. Stalin might have pressured him not to attack Taiwan given his fear that an attack at this point might provoke a vigorous reaction by the United States. The CCP leaders encountered a paradoxical situation: on the one hand, complete control of the Taiwan Straits would lessen the potential US military threat; on the other hand, a premature attack on Taiwan might provoke American armed action. The best they could do was to gain control of the East China coast so as to strengthen coastal defense. There is reason to argue that at no point did the Chinese Communist leadership decide to attack Taiwan in the spring of 1950.

In addition to the Taiwan Straits, the CCP leaders believed that any increase of American influence in Indochina would be devastating to China's security interest. The Sino-Vietnamese border had been historically vulnerable to foreign invasions. The CCP leaders were particularly alert to the fact that French occupation of that entire area, with possible US intervention on behalf of the French, would threaten the Chinese borders in the long run if not immediately. From the beginning of the Vietnamese Communist movement, Chinese leaders were determined to offer political and material support.

That determination was based on the sense that, since they shared the common objective of eliminating imperialist and foreign influence in Asia, and since Communist dominance in Vietnam or Indochina would provide a buffer zone, the Chinese revolutionaries bore the responsibility for supporting their Vietnamese "comrades-in-arms."

The CCP's sense of responsibility heightened after the Communist revolution's victory in China. In late 1949, Ho Chi Minh established the Viet Minh (Vietnamese National Liberation Front) for the purpose of liberating Indochina from French control. In early January of 1950, he sent his foreign minister Huang Minh Chian to Beijing, seeking the People's Republic of China [PRC] diplomatic recognition and the establishment of formal relations. When Mao was informed of the Vietnamese request in Moscow, he immediately instructed Liu Shaoqi on January 17 that "recognition and diplomatic relationship shall be granted to the Viet Minh Government at once."[28]

After successfully obtaining China's recognition, Ho Chi Minh decided to go to Beijing for further assistance in mid-January 1950. During his secret visit, Ho talked a great deal with both Liu Shaoqi and Zhou Enlai, primarily about what the Chinese could do to advance his cause. Liu and Zhou clearly understood what Ho wanted from China, but they hesitated to make any commitment without Mao's endorsement. They then suggested that Ho should go to Moscow and talk directly with Mao and Stalin. Ho immediately contacted the Soviet ambassador to Beijing and requested that arrangements be made for his visit. With Moscow's approval late that month, Ho went to Moscow together with Zhou, who was sent there by Mao to negotiate the details of the Sino-Soviet alliance treaty.[29]

In Moscow, Ho met several times with Mao and Stalin to discuss how the Soviet Union and the PRC could assist the Vietnamese revolution.[30] At one meeting, Stalin explicitly explained to Ho that he was "sincerely concerned about the Vietnamese struggle" but preferred that "the Chinese comrades take over the principal responsibility of supporting and supplying the Vietnamese people." Mao agreed to give some thought to how that could be appropriately accomplished when he returned to Beijing.[31]

While the Vietnamese Communists strove to acquire Beijing's support, the CCP leaders understood Indochina's strategic importance in China's security. The CCP's long-term concern was to enhance the security of the Sino-Vietnamese border. The Beijing authorities were determined to help the Vietnamese to gain control of Indochina so as to deny it to the Western imperialists. Viet Minh domination of that area would diminish the potential threat before it became real. Both Zhou Enlai and Liu Shaoqi had made it clear to Ho Chi Minh in early 1950 that the Vietnamese struggle against the French was part of the Chinese struggle against imperialism in Asia, because if Vietnam was recontrolled by the imperialists, China's southern border would be exposed to direct threat.[32]

But what could the Chinese Communists do to accomplish this objective? Hoang Van Hoan, then Viet Minh ambassador to Beijing, remembered that the top Chinese leaders "expressed their determination without any hesitation that China would provide the Vietnamese people all the necessary material assistance, and would be prepared to send troops to fight together with the Vietnamese people when necessary."[33] Hoang does not mention who said this and when, but if true, it would seem that the Beijing leaders had offered almost a blank check to the Vietnamese.

Available materials, however, suggest that Beijing actively provided the Vietnamese Communists with military assistance but at no point decided to dispatch its own armed forces to

Vietnam. In January 1950 the Chinese began to supply the Vietnamese with larger quantities of artillery ammunitions, trucks, and other military equipment. China's military supplies were large enough to fully equip the Viet Minh's five infantry and one artillery divisions, one anti-aircraft artillery regiment and one guard regiment. In the spring of that year, the Chinese also built several training centers in Guangxi and Yunnan and trained four Vietnamese infantry regiments.[34]

The Chinese sent no PLA combat forces into Vietnam nor were their military advisers involved in direct command. Yet the Chinese military advisers seemed to have satisfied Ho by doing their job well. At and above the division level, the Chinese were closely advising the Vietnamese commanders on military affairs, political mobilization, and rear services. Moreover, the Chinese equipped the Viet Minh's three best divisions (304th, 308th, and 312th) with advisers down to the battalion level. The Chinese advisers were chiefly in charge of combat training and planning.[35]

After the Korean War broke out, Beijing became more cautious and consequently restricted its assistance to the Viet Minh. In September 1950, Mao twice warned Deng Zihui, military commander of Guangxi, that "our troops should not go across the Sino-Vietnamese border by any means or on any occasions; it would be better to keep a distance from the border even in pursuit of KMT remnants." Mao, in particular, wanted Deng to see to it that his order "be strictly observed [because] otherwise we would be in big trouble."[36] By "big trouble," Mao meant the potential danger of increased US military involvement in Indochina if Chinese troops entered Vietnam. Clearly, Indochina remained a major security concern of the CCP leadership.

As much as Indochina, the CCP authorities regarded the Korean peninsula as yet another dangerous spot likely to complicate China's security. In their views, Korea's geopolitical importance was too great to be ignored. Believing that the United States had long "dreamed" of dominating the Far East, Hu Sheng pointed out in late 1949 that the Korean peninsula stood as a "bridgehead" connecting Japan and Northeast China.[37] In addition, Beijing believed that US hostility toward China in that area derived from the fact that the Soviet Union and China were building a common defense against US-dominated Japan in East Asia.[38]

To diminish American influence in the Korean peninsula, Beijing could have offered the same type of assistance to the North Korean Communists as it offered to the Viet Minh. The CCP leaders obviously understood the importance of Communist control in the peninsula, and they had no problem working with Kim Il Sung and his followers, who, along with more than 90,000 soldiers of Korean origin, had fought the Japanese side by side with the CCP in Northeast China throughout the Second World War. Available evidence is insufficient to suggest that Beijing had made the same commitment to the North Koreans as it made to the Vietnamese. The Soviet Union had played a dominant role in assisting the North Koreans. Quite understandably, as long as Moscow kept offering military assistance to North Korea (beginning in late 1948), it would be wise for the Chinese to stay uninvolved.

Scattered Chinese sources do indicate CCP involvement in helping the North Koreans before the outbreak of war. The Beijing authorities signed three agreements with North Korea on January 7, 1950 to establish Sino-North Korean postal services, telegraphic communication, and telephone lines.[39] They also reached an agreement with the North Korean representative that "altogether 14,000 soldiers of Korean origin will be returned to North Korea along with their weapons and equipment."[40] In the spring of 1950, Beijing's military authorities began increasing the ratios of PLA troops stationed in Northeast and North China. Although these troops were to conduct military training and protect economic construction there, their chief mission was to defend China's border rather than to support the oncoming North Korean war efforts.

At the outbreak of the Korean War, Washington's announcement of its intention to intervene in Korea and to send the Seventh Fleet into the Taiwan Straits highly alarmed the Beijing authorities. It seemed that US imperialist policy toward East Asia was just as they had predicted. On June 27 Zhou Enlai proclaimed that the objective of the Truman administration's decision to intervene in the Taiwan Straits was to prevent the PRC from liberating Taiwan and was an act of aggression which the CCP leadership had fully anticipated. He asserted that the United States had instigated Syngman Rhee to initiate the Korean conflict as a prelude to America's grand strategy of invading Korea, Taiwan, Vietnam, and the Philippines.[41] On the evening of June 28, Mao addressed the State Council, emphasizing the duplicity of Truman's statement of January 5, 1950 which had indicated America's intention to stay away from Taiwan. He pointed out that the United States had now made an open declaration of its imperialist policy, thereby removing any disguise of non-interference in Chinese internal affairs. Mao told the State Council that China should by no means be scared of the US military actions.[42] And the Chinese Communists were not intimidated, indeed, when they resolved upon military intervention in Korea to confront the United States four months later.

Taking American hostility for granted, the CCP leadership prepared military counterthreats against a perceived threat before it became real. This deterrence strategy based on a worst-case assumption was hardly difficult for Mao. With a keen understanding of Chinese strategic tradition, he believed and apparently admired such old teachings as "Actions speak louder than words," "One pair of strong fists cannot match two pairs of weak fists," and "The best strategy is to force an enemy into retreat without actually fighting with it." And more importantly, "Preparedness eliminates mishaps" became an unchallengeable principle in the CCP's strategic thoughts.

Unfortunately, such strategic thinking brought counter-productive results. The CCP's active, sometimes hazardous, attempts to build up a national defense line, to some degree, brought about increased suspicion in Washington. During this period, the Truman administration became increasingly worried that the new regime in China was Moscow-directed and, perhaps, spearheading Soviet expansion in the Far East and Asia as a whole. Accordingly, Washington also took precautions against the Chinese Communists, which, in turn, further enhanced the CCP leadership's suspicion and hostility toward the United States. Beijing eventually decided to fight with the USA in Korea, a conflict which seemed inevitable to the Beijing authorities.

It is interesting to note that a security dilemma had largely shaped the evolution of Sino-American confrontation during this period. Establishing a new regime after decades of bloody civil war, the CCP leadership could never be at ease with a sense of insecurity. Perceiving, often imagining, an external threat of American armed intervention, the leaders took preparedness of military counterthreat very seriously, and indeed, they acted drastically and sometimes desperately. The CCP's overreaction in both political and military terms to an exaggerated threat gradually but surely caused the other side to respond in the same way and, perhaps, even more vigorously. This chain of action and reaction laid out a battleground for further confrontation, especially when unexpected crises occurred.

NOTES

From Shuguang Zhang, "'Preparedness Eliminates Mishaps': The CCP's Security Concerns in 1949–1950 and the Origins of Sino-American Confrontation," *The Journal of American-East Asian Relations*, 1 (Spring 1992): 42–72. Copyright © 1992 by Imprint Publications Inc., Chicago. Extracted, with text and footnotes rearranged. Reprinted by permission of the publisher.

1 There have as yet been few works dealing with the CCP's security concerns during this period, let alone those that make use of recently available Chinese materials. Good recent studies include Harry Harding and Yuan Ming (eds), *Sino-American Relations, 1945–1955: A Joint Reassessment of a Critical Decade* (Wilmington, DE, 1989); and Jian Chen, "China's Road to the Korean War: A Critical Study of the Origins of Sino-American Confrontation, 1949–1950" (PhD dissertation, Southern Illinois University, 1990). Chen's work is excellent in reformulating Mao's conception regarding foreign affairs during this period, although his argument that Mao and his contemporaries aimed at expanding China's influence in Asia through an offensive and "revolutionary diplomacy" is debatable.

2 Mao Zedong [Mao Tse-tung], "Talks with the American Correspondent Anna Louise Strong," August 1946, *Selected Works of Mao Tse-tung* (Beijing, 1961), Vol. 4: 99. Also see Lu Dingyi, "Explanations of Several Basic Problems Concerning Post-World War II International Relations" (in Chinese), *Jiefang ribao*, January 4, 1947; Lu was a senior CCP official in charge of political propaganda and the article was drafted by Mao himself.

3 Mao, "Talks with Strong," *Selected Works*, Vol. 4: 99.

4 Lu, "Explanations of Several Problems." Also see Central Committee to Liu Ningyi, March 21, 1948; *Zhou Enlai nianpu, 1898–1949* [Chronicle of Zhou Enlai, 1898–1949] (Beijing, 1989), 767.

5 Mao Zedong, "The Present Situation and Our Tasks," December 25, 1947, *Selected Works*, Vol. 4: 172.

6 Mao Zedong "The Truth About U.S. 'Mediation' and the Future of the Civil War in China," September 29, 1946, *Selected Works*, Vol. 4: 109. See also He Di, "The Development of the CCP's Policy toward the U.S., 1945–1949" (in Chinese), *Lishi yanjiu* (June 1987): 17–18.

7 Shi Zhe, "With Chairman Mao on a Visit to the Soviet Union" (in

Chinese), *Renwu* (May 1988): 6–7.

8 Stalin to the CCP Central Committee, January 10, 1949, cited in Yu Zhan and Zhang Guangyou, "Did Stalin Ever Persuade Us Not to Cross the Yangtze River?" (in Chinese) in Ministry of Foreign Affairs (ed.), *Xinzhongguo waijiao fengyun* (Beijing, 1990), 19. Shi Zhe remembers that the timing of Stalin's letter was "between July and August 1948." See Shi Zhe, "I Accompanied Chairman Mao from Yan'an to Beijing" (in Chinese), *Renwu* (May 1989): 152.

9 Division of CCP Central Archives and Manuscripts (ed.), *Zhou Enlai zuan, 1898–1949* [Biography of Zhou Enlai, 1898–1949] (Beijing, 1989), 742–3; also see Shi, "With Chairman Mao," 6.

10 Mao Zedong, "Farewell, Leighton Stuart," August 18, 1949, *Selected Works*, Vol. 4: 434. As early as 1946, Zhou Enlai had pointed out that "to support Chiang Kai-shek, the U.S. has in fact stationed its troops [in China] and provided ammunitions and financial assistance [to Chiang]." See minutes of Zhou–Stuart talks, August 6, 1946, *Zhou Enlai nianpu*, 685.

11 He, "Development of the CCP's Policy," 21.

12 Mao, "Farewell, Leighton Stuart," *Selected Works*, Vol. 4: 433; Mao Zedong, "Cast Away Illusions. Prepare for Struggle," August 14, 1949, *Selected Works*, Vol. 4: 428.

13 Steven Goldstein, "Communist Chinese Perceptions, 1945–1950," in Dorothy Borg and Waldo Heinrichs (eds), *Uncertain Years: Chinese-American Relations, 1947–1950* (New York, 1980), 253.

14 Shi, "With Chairman Mao," 8–10.

15 See *Youpai yanlunji* [Collection of Rightist Views] (Beijing, 1957), 43–8.

16 Mao Zedong, "On the People's Democratic Dictatorship" (in Chinese), *Renmin ribao*, July 1, 1949.

17 Shi, "With Chairman Mao," 13.

18 ibid., 14.

19 "Chairman Mao in Moscow" (in Chinese), *Renmin ribao*, January 2, 1950.

20 Mao to Central Committee, January 2 and 3, 1950, *Jiangua yilai Mao Zedong wengao* [Mao Zedong's manuscripts since the founding of the People's Republic] (Beijing, 1987–8), Vol. 1: 211.

21 Wu Xiuquan, *Zhai waijiaobu banian* [My Eight Years in the Ministry of Foreign Affairs] (Beijing, 1983), 8–9.

22 Mao to Central Committee, January 2, 1950, *Mao Zedong wengao*, Vol. 1: 213.

23 Wu, *Zhai Waijiaobu banian*, 10; also see *Lun Zhongsu mengyue* [On the Sino-Soviet alliance] (Shanghai, 1950), 55–9.

24 Nie Rongzhen, *Nie Rongzhen huiyilu* [Memoirs of Nie Rongzhen] (Beijing, 1984), Vol. 3: 729.

25 ibid., 730. Nie was in charge of assigning and arranging positions for the Soviet military advisers.

26 Zhou Enlai's address to Korean veterans, February 17 1958, cited in Yao Xu, "A Wise Decision to Resist America and Aid Korea" (in Chinese), *Dangshi yanjiu ziliao* (October 1980): 7.

27 Commentary of Xinhua News Agency, "The Chinese People Must Liberate Taiwan" (in Chinese), March 15, 1949, *Xinhua yuebao* (March 1949): 43; "Carry on Our Fighting to Taiwan and Liberate the Taiwan People" (in Chinese), September 4, 1949, ibid., 44; Wang Mingzhi, "Taiwan is Chinese People's Taiwan" (in Chinese), September 4, 1949, ibid., 45.
28 Mao to Liu Shaoqi, January 17, 1950, *Mao Zedong wengao*, Vol. 1: 238–9.
29 *Mao Zedong wengao*, Vol. 1: 124–5.
30 Wu, *Zhai waijiaobu banian*, 13.
31 Hoang Van Hoan, *Changhai yishu: Huang Wenhuan geming huiyilu* [A Drop in the Ocean: Hoang Van Hoan's Revolutionary Reminiscences] (Beijing, 1987), 259.
32 Huong Zhen, *Hu Zhiming yu Zhonggua.* [Ho Chi Minh and China] (Beijing, 1987), 126.
33 Hoang, *Changhai yishu*, 263.
34 Han Huaizhi *et al.* (eds), *Dangdai Zhongguo jundui de junshi gongzuo* [Military Affairs of the Contemporary Chinese Army] (Beijing, 1989), Vol. 1: 520–1. Also see Li Ke, "The Chinese Military Advisory Group in the Struggle of Assisting Vietnam and Resisting France" (in Chinese), *Junshi lishi*, no. 3 (1989): 29.
35 Li, "Chinese Military Advisory Group," 28.
36 Mao to Deng Zihui, September 16, 1950, *Mao Zedong wengao*, Vol. 1: 519–21.
37 Hu Sheng, "How Did American Imperialists Attempt to Invade China in History?" (in Chinese), *Xinhua yuebao* (December 1949): 275–6.
38 Xinhua News Agency, "U.S. Imperialists Are Making Up Stories" (in Chinese), January 31, 1950, ibid. (February 1950): 1113. See also Zhou Enlai, "Refute Acheson's Speech" (in Chinese), March 18, 1950, ibid. (March 1950): 1360.
39 Huang Daoxia (ed.), *Zhonghua renmin gonghoguo sishinian dashiji, 1949–1989* [Chronicle of Important Events in Forty Years of PRC History] (Beijing, 1989), 6.
40 Nie, *Nie Rongzhen huiyilu*, 748.
41 *Renmin ribao*, June 28, 1950.
42 ibid., June 29, 1950.

THE IMPACT OF THE COLD WAR ON LATIN AMERICA

Leslie Bethell and Ian Roxborough

Historians, political scientists, economists, and sociologists are increasingly interested in studying the interaction between domestic and international trends. As the United States and the Soviet Union became locked into a Cold War relationship, leaders in both nations sought to expand their influence and power. But as we have seen in the cases of many European, Asian, and Middle Eastern countries, the desires and demands of the Great Powers often collided with the aspirations, hopes, and needs of indigenous peoples and local groups. The latter often sought to use the Soviet-American rivalry to enhance their own interests and agendas.

In this suggestive article, Leslie Bethell and Ian Roxborough sketch the confluence of internal and external factors on postwar social, economic, and political developments in Latin America.* The Second World War spurred the economic growth and political mobilization of Latin American societies. However indirectly associated to the allied war effort, large numbers of people especially among the lower and middle classes were affected by the democratic discourse and ideological fervor that inspired the struggle against fascism. Miners, factory workers, and some rural laborers organized, joined unions, supported new democratic parties, and injected strength into Communist movements. Entrenched elites and traditional authorities, including the Church, felt threatened. They looked for outside assistance to thwart the left, preserve stability, and spur economic growth. They used the Cold War to consolidate their power and perpetuate their rule. The United States, Bethell and Roxborough argue, was their accomplice.

* These ideas are elaborated upon in their new book, Leslie Bethell and Ian Roxborough (eds), *Latin America between the Second World War and the Cold War, 1944–1948* (Cambridge: Cambridge University Press, 1992).

This article resonates with many of the themes that have appeared in previous selections. In Latin America, as in Europe and Asia, the war politicized the masses, inspired the disenfranchised, and generated a new democratic discourse. There was great turmoil within nations as groups, classes, and factions struggled for power and sought allies both inside and outside their borders. The United States and the Soviet Union sought to exploit the opportunities presented to them and hoped to capitalize on their own respective ideological appeal. They also forged their own distinctive transnational linkages among labor unions, business associations, and political parties. In the worldwide competition for influence and power, the Kremlin had its ideology and Communist affiliates, but the United States possessed the advantages of its hegemonic position in the world economic system. Local actors were buffeted by these international systemic conditions, but they also tried to manipulate them in their own behalf.

In discussing this article readers should ponder how the Cold War affected indigenous trends. What factors led to the rise of the left in Latin America during the Second World War? Where, why, and how was the left rolled back in 1946, 1947, and 1948? What were the sources and instruments of US and Soviet influence in Latin America?

* * *

The importance of the years of political and social upheaval immediately following the end of the Second World War and coinciding with the beginnings of the Cold War, that is to say, the period from 1944 or 1945 to 1948 or 1949, for the history of Europe (East and West), the Near and Middle East, Asia (Japan, China, South and East Asia), even Africa (certainly South Africa) in the second half of the twentieth century has long been generally recognized. In recent years historians of the United States, which had not, of course, been a theater of war and which alone among the major belligerents emerged from the Second World War stronger and more prosperous, have begun to focus attention on the political, social, and ideological conflict there in the postwar period – and the long-term significance for the United States of the basis on which it was resolved. In contrast, except for Argentina, where Perón's rise to power has always attracted the interest of historians, the immediate postwar years in Latin America, which had been relatively untouched by, and had played a relatively minor role in, the

Second World War, remain to a large extent neglected. It is our view that these years constituted a critical conjuncture in the political and social history of Latin America just as they did for much of the rest of the world.

Each Latin American country has its own history in the immediate postwar years. Nevertheless, there are striking similarities in the experience of the majority of at least the major republics, despite differences of political regime, different levels of economic and social development, differences in the strength and composition of both the dominant groups and popular forces, and different relations with the United States, the region's hegemonic power. Broadly speaking, for most of Latin America the postwar period can be divided into two phases. The first phase, beginning in 1944, 1945, or 1946 (depending on the country concerned), and often tantalizingly brief, was characterized on the political front by democratic openings, political mobilization, and participation, and the relatively successful articulation of popular demands by both movements and parties of the "democratic" or "nationalist-populist" reformist left (many newly formed) and the orthodox Marxist left (hitherto with few exceptions largely ineffective). Even more important perhaps, this phase witnessed unprecedented militancy within organized labor: the end of the Second World War saw strike waves throughout the region (in, for example, Mexico, Brazil, Peru, Colombia, Argentina, and Chile) and a bid for greater union independence in those countries (for example, Mexico and Brazil) where the labor movement was closely controlled by the state. In the second phase, beginning in 1946 or 1947 (in some cases as early as 1945) and completed almost everywhere by 1948, the democratic advance was for the most part contained, and in some cases reversed; the left in general lost ground and the Communist parties in particular almost everywhere suffered proscription and severe repression; most importantly, labor was disciplined and brought under closer control by the state. In other words the popular forces, in particular the organized urban working class but also in some cases the urban middle class, and the left, most decisively the Communist left, suffered a historic defeat in Latin America during the immediate postwar period. As a result an opportunity, however slight, for far-reaching social and political change was lost. This would have involved an expansion of democracy, the incorporation of organized labor into the political system as an autonomous actor, and not simply as a power base for a sector of the elite, and some sort of commitment to greater social justice and a distribution of wealth. The result would have been a decisive shift in the balance of power toward the urban working class (though not yet the rural population) and a concomitant weakening of elite control over politics and society. The failure to follow this path toward an alternative future, which seemed plausible to many actors at the end of the war, had in our view far-reaching consequences for Latin American development in the postwar world.

How is this outcome of the postwar conjucture in Latin America to be explained? It is necessary in the first place to examine the shifting balance of domestic forces at the time. It is also essential to explore the complex interplay between the rapidly changing domestic scene in each Latin American country and the no less rapidly changing international scene as a new political and economic international order was created in the aftermath of the Second World War and as the Cold War began. Here the role played in Latin American affairs, directly and indirectly, by the United States needs to be examined with particular care.

The final year of the war (1944–5) and the first year after the war (1945–6) saw at least a partial extension of democracy in those Latin American countries which already had some claim to call themselves democratic in the sense that their governments were elected (however severely limited the suffrage and however restricted the political participation), political competition of some kind was permitted (however weak the party system) and basic civil liberties were at least formally honored (however precariously at times). This was true in Chile, Costa Rica, Colombia where Jorge Eliécer Gaitán mounted his ultimately unsuccessful campaign against the oligarchy, both Liberal and Conservative, and even Peru where the candidate of the recently formed Frente Democrático Nacional, José Luis Bustamante y Rivero, with Alianza Popular Revolucionaria Americana [APRA] support, won the elections of June 1945 and displaced the traditional oligarchy. Elsewhere there were a number of important transitions from military or military-backed dictatorships of various kinds to democracy broadly defined. In Ecuador in May 1944 a popular rebellion led by the Alianza Democrática Ecuatoriana against Carlos Arroyo del Río led to the military coup which brought José Maria Velasco Ibarra to power. In Cuba the elections of June 1944 witnessed the triumph of the reformist Ramón Grau San Martín over the *continuiste* candidate favored by Fulgencio Batista, who had dominated Cuban politics since 1934 and served as president since 1940. In Guatemala after a dictatorship lasting thirteen years, Jorge Ubico was overthrown in July 1944 and Juan José Arévalo was elected in December of the same year. In Brazil Getúlio Vargas, after fifteen years in power, was overthrown by the military in October 1945, and direct presidential and congressional elections were held in December. In Venezuela a process of political liberalization, begun by the dictator, Isaías Medina Angarita, was accelerated by a military coup backed by Rómulo Betancourt and Acción Democrática [AD] in October 1945 which led to the establishment of an open, democratic system. In Argentina, where the coup of June 1943 had brought to power a nationalist military junta, political liberalization begun in 1945 would lead to free elections in February 1946. The coup by young officers backed by the Movimiento Nacional Revolucionaria [MNR] in December 1943 in Bolivia also eventually produced a political opening as the oligarchy, the MNR, and the Marxist Partido de la Izquierda Revolucionariá [PIR] struggled for the support of the miners and the peasants. In Mexico the election of 1946 was seriously contested, saw considerable citizen mobilization, and produced the first authentically civilian presidency, that of Miguel Alemán, since the revolution. On the other hand massive fraud and the final imposition of the governmental candidate indicated that Mexican democracy was still largely rhetorical.

Thus, almost all the countries of the region moved in the direction of political liberalization and partial democratization. No Latin American country moved in the opposite direction. By 1946 apart possibly from Paraguay and a handful of the smaller republics in Central America and the Caribbean (El Salvador, Honduras, Nicaragua, and the Dominican Republic), all the Latin American states could claim to be in some sense democratic. At least they were not dictatorships.

The principal factor behind the political climate of 1944–6 in Latin America was the victory of the allies (and of democracy over fascism) in the Second World War. Despite the strength of Axis interests and indeed widespread pro-Axis sympathies throughout Latin America during the 1930s, in the aftermath of Pearl Harbor (December 1941) all the Latin American states (except Chile, temporarily, and Argentina) lined up with the United States and severed relations with the Axis powers; eventually most, although until 1945 by no means all, declared war. Formally at least, and in some cases with varying degrees of cynicism and *realpolitik*, they had chosen the side of Freedom and Democracy, although only Brazil sent combat troops to the European theater. The war strengthened existing ties – military, economic, political, ideological – between Latin America (except Argentina and, to some extent, Bolivia) and the United States. As the nature of the postwar international order and the hegemonic position of the USA within it became clear, the dominant groups in Latin America, including the military (and by this time, in some countries, industrialists), recognized the need to make some necessary political adjustments. There was at the same time considerable popular pressure from below, especially from the urban middle class, intellectuals, and students but also from the urban working class, for a more open political future. War and postwar demands for democracy drew upon a strong liberal tradition in Latin American political ideas and culture going back at least as far as the period of independence in the first quarter of the nineteenth century. But they were also the product of wartime propaganda in favor of US democracy and the American way of life directed at Latin America, and orchestrated above all by Nelson Rockefeller's Office of the Coordinator of Inter-American Affairs [OCIAA]. By the end of the war, it should be remembered, the press and radio throughout Latin America had been heavily penetrated by US capital.

Direct US pressure in favor of democratization was not perhaps a decisive factor but it undoubtedly played its part. At the outset of the war the United States had cooperated with *all* anti-Axis regimes in Latin America, both dictatorships and democracies. But as early as April 1943 Roosevelt made it clear to Getúlio Vargas, his closest ally in Latin America, that the Estado Novo would be expected to liberalize itself at the end of the war, especially if Brazil aspired to play a more important role in international affairs in the postwar world. (And throughout 1945 the US ambassador Adolf Berle quietly encouraged the dismantling of the old regime.) There was some US involvement in the downfall of some of the tyrants of the Caribbean and Central America in 1944. In November 1944 Berle, Assistant Secretary of State at the time, in a circular to US embassies in Latin America made it known that the United States felt a greater affinity with and would be more favorably disposed toward "governments established on the periodically and freely expressed consent of the governed."[1] And as the war ended and the opening shots in the Cold War were fired, it became even more imperative that the allies of the United States in Latin America were seen to be democratic. The most sustained US efforts in favor of democracy were directed at the two countries still regarded as "fascist": Bolivia and, more particularly, Argentina. Ambassador Spruille Braden arrived in Buenos Aires in May 1945 with the "fixed idea" according to Sir David Kelly, the British ambassador, of establishing democracy in Argentina. He became virtually the leader of opposition to the military regime and especially to Perón. A timetable for democracy was eventually established and elections were held in February 1946, although faced with the choice of "Braden or Perón" the Argentine people chose Perón.

With limited democratization at the end of the Second World War a number of political parties which sought to extend participation and promote economic and social reform – all of them formed since the 1920s, many of them strongly personalist and populist – came to power or at least to a share of power for the first time. We refer to the Auténticos [PRC-A] in Cuba, Acción Democrática in Venezuela and APRA in Peru among others. In Brazil the popular movement of Queremismo in favour of Vargas and the formation by Vargas of the Partido Trabalhista Brasileiro provided an organizational expression for such reformist aspirations. In Argentina this role was played by the short-lived Partido Laborista, and eventually by Péron's Partido Justicialista. In Mexico the official party of the revolution, renamed the PRI in 1946, remained the principal umbrella under which reformist currents sheltered, though recent changes in the party had done much to shift it to the right. Emerging belatedly (and as a result, abortively) in 1948 as a mass reformist party of the Left was Lombardo Toledano's Partido Popular. Of course, not all of these parties were thoroughly committed to formal democracy, and with the passage of time, even their commitment to social and economic reform was significantly reduced.

Also notable were the gains, albeit more limited, made at this time by the Latin American Communist parties. (Only Chile, and to a lesser extent Argentina, had a significant Socialist party.) After years of weakness, isolation, and for the most part illegality, many Communist parties reached the peak of their power and influence in this period – power and influence never to be repeated except in Cuba after 1959 and (briefly) in Chile in the early 1970s. They were legalized or at least tolerated in virtually every country. Total membership, less than 100,000 in 1939, had reached half a million by 1947.[2] In competition with, at times cooperating with, their traditional rivals, the parties of the non-Communist, nationalist left, they had considerable success in both congressional and local elections all over Latin America but especially in Chile (where in 1946 the Cabinet had three Communist members), Cuba, and Brazil. And as we shall see, they made important advances within the labor unions throughout Latin America.

The explanation for these Communist gains is again to be found in the war. After the German invasion of Russia and the breakup of the short-lived Nazi-Soviet pact wartime imperatives brought a return to the tactics of class collaboration and popular-frontism laid down by the Seventh World Congress of the Comintern (1935). Communists, even where they had no legal status, generally supported national unity and the allied cause; they were part of the anti-fascist, democratic front (in wartime government coalitions in Cuba, Costa Rica, and Chile) and therefore beneficiaries of the democratic advance – together with the temporary but enormous prestige of the Soviet Union – at the end of the war. Meanwhile, the Comintern (which had "discovered" Latin America only in 1928) had effectively ceased to function after 1935 and had finally been dissolved in 1943. During the war and its immediate aftermath the Latin American Communist parties were largely neglected by Moscow and experienced a growing, though relative, independence of action. What became known as Browderism, the belief that Communists should increasingly act as an integral part of nationally oriented, broad popular movements, even to the extent of voluntary dissolution, made headway in several Latin American countries (Cuba, Mexico, Venezuela, for example) during these final years of the war. Nor was there, at least throughout most of 1945, any significant hostility to Communist parties from Washington. On the contrary, in Brazil Berle was unconcerned about Communist support for Vargas, in Argentina Braden accepted Communist support against Perón, and in Bolivia the PIR was encouraged to join the anti-Villarroel campaign.

An independent feature of the postwar years was the emergence of organized labor as a major social and political actor in Latin America. By the late 1930s the export sectors had largely recovered from the world depression and import substitution industrialization had accelerated in the more economically developed countries of the region. The Second World War gave a further impetus to industrial development. Combined with population growth and rural-urban migration the size of the working class had expanded considerably. And its character was being rapidly transformed: besides the already important nuclei of workers in the agricultural and mining export sectors, and workers in transportation and public utilities, white-collar workers, many of them state employees, and industrial workers were increasingly important. In Mexico the number of workers in manufacturing had risen from 568,000 in 1940 to 938,000 in 1945, in Argentina from 633,000 in 1941 to 938,000 in 1946. In Brazil, over the decade between 1940 and 1950, the number of manufacturing workers rose from 995,000 to 1,608,000.[3] While rises of this order of magnitude were not experienced by all countries, the rate of growth of the urban working class, and especially workers in industry, in Latin America as a whole during the war years was impressive. This growth in the size of the working class was accompanied by a widespread expansion of union membership. In Argentina the number of workers enrolled in unions rose from 448,000 in 1941 to 532,000 in 1946 (and then shot up to 2.5 or 3 million by the end of Perón's first term in office). In Brazil, some 351,000 workers were unionized in 1940; by 1947 this had more than doubled to 798,000. Even in Colombia union membership doubled between 1940 and 1947 (from 84,000 to 166,000). By 1946 between 3.5 and 4 million workers were unionized in Latin America as a whole.[4] Even more important perhaps was the trend to more centralized organization, the search for greater autonomy from the state, and militancy over wages. Real standards of living had generally declined toward the end of the war as wages were held down by social pacts and no-strike pledges in the interests of the allied war effort and the battle for production – while inflation rose. The war in any case increased expectations and the new liberal political atmosphere provided the space in which pent-up demands could be released.

The last year of the war (1944–5) and the first year after the war (1945–6) therefore witnessed not only political openings but a marked increase in the number of labor disputes and strikes in, for example, Mexico, Brazil, and Chile. Major concessions were wrung from employers and the state by workers in the export agriculture sector (Argentine meat packers), mining and oil (Chilean coal and copper workers, Mexican and Venezuelan oil workers), transport (Mexican and Argentine rail workers, Brazilian port workers), urban services (Brazilian bank employees and tramway workers), and some sections of industry (Brazilian and Peruvian textile workers, for example). Much of this insurgency in the ranks of labor sprang from the combination of specific grievances, falling real wages, and an increasingly tight labor market (which improved union bargaining power). A number of political parties were able to capitalize on this and expand their influence in the labor movement. In this situation the Communist parties were often in an ambiguous position. On the one hand, their reputation as advocates of broad reforms and their (at least verbal) defence of working-class interests attracted considerable support. On the other hand, their encouragement of the no-strike pledges in support of the allied war effort frequently led to rank-and-file movements by-passing the Communists. To a great extent the eventual outcome depended on the nature of the Communists' rivals in the labor movement. In those countries (such as Chile) where there was a well-established non-Communist left (the Socialist party), it was these forces which often prospered at the expense of the Communists. In other countries relatively new parties like Acción Democrática in Venezuela or personalistic movements of the kind led by Vargas and Perón emerged as serious (and often successful) rivals to the Communist parties. Whatever the outcome, the working class was now being incorporated into democratic politics and was courted by a variety of political leaders, movements, and parties.

Behind all this political effervescence at the end of the Second World War were some profound, if dimly perceived, shifts in the nature of political discourse and ideology. The emergence of "democracy" as a central symbol with almost universal resonance was specific to this period. Of course, the term was used by different actors to mean quite distinct things. For some it meant little more than the façade of formal elections; for others it meant simply a commitment to the allied camp. Nevertheless, for many people in Latin America the meaning of the term underwent a considerable expansion. Democracy was now seen to imply a commitment to wider participation, and had its economic and social dimensions. It came increasingly to be identified with a positive redistribution of wealth and income to benefit the lower income groups, and increasing levels of urban working-class participation in politics.

At the same time, perceptions of the developmental options open to Latin American countries (particularly in those countries which had already experienced significant industrial growth) underwent a fundamental shift. The pursuit of industrialization now became a realistic and widely held policy option. Despite widespread controversy around this issue the body of thought which later came to be known as *cepalismo* or structuralist economics soon emerged as the dominant intellectual paradigm in the region. State intervention in a mixed economy, planning, support for the developing national bourgeoisie, deliberate attention to social and welfare goals, together with the (regulated) entry of foreign capital came to characterize this newly emerging body of thought. The parallels with the development of social democratic welfare ideology in Western Europe, and that region's commitment to an increasingly interventionist state are worth highlighting. Unlike the situation in Western Europe, however, *cepalista* developmental prescriptions came increasingly to be associated with authoritarian statism as the links between economic development, social reform, and democracy became ever more tenuous.

Did these various, mutually reinforcing tendencies in the immediate aftermath of the Second World War add up to an opportunity for significant political and social reform, a potentially decisive step toward a new order in Latin America? Or were they "premature" and destined to fail because of Latin America's continuing economic, social, and political "backwardness" (despite the changes of the 1930s and the war years), the balance of domestic class forces in Latin America at the end of the war, and the impact of the changing international climate marked by the beginning of the Cold War? Certainly a challenge to the established order in Latin America was perceived at the time, and in every country except Guatemala (where the "revolution" survived until the United States-backed invasion of 1954) steps were quickly and successfully taken during the years 1946–8 to neutralize it.

Only in Peru (October 1948) and Venezuela (November 1948) were democratic regimes actually overthrown and replaced by military dictatorships during these years, although reactionary military coups followed in Cuba (1952) as well as ultimately, of course, in Guatemala (1954). Almost everywhere, however, there was a marked shift to the right within democratic or semi-democratic regimes – in Brazil, Chile, Colombia (where the *bogotazo*, the predominantly urban insurrection which was triggered off by the assassination of Gaitán in April 1948, was quickly and effectively quelled), Cuba, Ecuador (where Velasco Ibarra, who had himself suspended the constitution in March 1946, was overthrown in August 1947 in a conservative coup), Mexico, even Costa Rica (despite the apparent victory for democracy in the civil war of 1948) – and within reformist parties which had formerly had democratic pretensions (AD in Venezuela, APRA in Peru, the Auténticos in Cuba). And in country after country popular mobilization was repressed and participation restricted or curtailed. As early as September 1946 in Brazil the constitution which launched the country's twenty-year "experiment with democracy" denied the vote to illiterates (more than half the population) and distributed seats in Congress in such a way as seriously to underrepresent the more densely populated, urban, and developed regions of the country.

In this new political atmosphere – very different from that at the end of the war – Communist parties were no longer legitimate, not least because of their newly discovered "anti-democratic" natures, and were once again excluded from political life. In one country after another – notably in Brazil (May 1947), Chile (September 1948), and Costa Rica (July 1948) – they were declared illegal. (And many Latin American governments took the opportunity to break often recently established diplomatic relations with the Soviet Union.) Party members experienced repression, and in Cuba, for example, from April 1947 physical violence. Communist members were forced out of the Cabinet and Congress in Chile in August 1947 and Congress (as well as state and municipal assemblies) in Brazil in January 1948. Everywhere Communist labor leaders found themselves purged from the major unions, even though they had been elected and in many cases were notable for the relatively moderate positions they had adopted on strikes.[5] The result was a dramatic increase in the strength of some of the Communists' rivals in the labor movement: for example, in Peru APRA, in Colombia the Catholic unions, in Mexico the pro-governmental clique around Fidel Velázquez, and in Brazil the *trabalhistas*.

The purge of Communist labor leaders was, however, part of a more general crackdown on labor aiming at greater institutional and ideological control by the state. In Latin America, as throughout the West (including the United States), national trade union confederations were deliberately split, the state intervened to purge militant leaderships, a tough stand was taken against strikes, and anti-strike legislation was revived and reinforced. Apart from Guatemala under the reformist presidencies of Arévalo and Arbenz, Argentina provided the only exception to this anti-labor trend in Latin America in the late 1940s.

The outcome of the postwar conjuncture in Latin America can, in part, be explained in terms of the relative strength of the dominant classes, rural and urban, civil and military, and their determination to restore political and social control in so far as they perceived it to be threatened by popular political mobilization and especially labor militancy. The commitment of Latin American elites to formal, liberal democracy of the kind espoused by the United States, in so far as it existed in other than a purely rhetorical form, by no means implied an acceptance of wide-ranging social reform and the recognition of organized labor as a major political actor. (The strength of the authoritarian as well as the liberal tradition in Latin American political culture should never be forgotten.) In contrast, Latin American labor unions, despite their impressive growth and the burst of militancy at the end of the war, were still relatively weak and inexperienced (and they still organized only a very small part of the total working population); and the parties of the left for the most part lacked deep roots in society and were often divided and in conflict. Moreover, both parties and labor unions no doubt made strategic mistakes. Here the weakness of the commitment to political democracy and democratic rights on the left, non-Communist as well as, more obviously, Communist, and among some sectors of organized labor should be noted. Similarly, the reluctance of the left, both Communist and non-Communist, to offer "appropriate" political leadership to the working class, and their conciliatory, and at times conservative, policies, have attracted considerable criticism.

At the same time, domestic class conflicts – different in each country – were undoubtedly influenced by the Cold War and the fact that Latin America at the end of the Second World War was even more firmly situated inside the United States' sphere of influence. At one level the Cold War merely reinforced domestic attitudes and tendencies, providing an ideological justification for the counter-offensive against labor and the political left which had already begun. Popular political mobilization and strike activity now became Communist-inspired, Moscow-dictated, "subversive," potentially revolutionary and in the last analysis anti-democratic. Significantly, the Chilean Communist Party was outlawed in September 1948 by a "Law for the Permanent Defence of Democracy." (Here it is important to remember, however, that the Cold War did not introduce anti-Communism into Latin America; it had been an element in the political culture of the Latin American elites since the Russian Revolution and the creation of the Comintern. And the Catholic Church, itself a not unimportant actor in the events of 1945–8, was, of course, a bastion of anti-Communism.) At the same time the Cold War – and United States policy – had an independent role to play. It is easy to exaggerate its significance: Latin America was hardly a central issue in the early years of the Cold War and the United States, as we shall see, did not give Latin America a high priority in the immediate postwar period. But it would equally be a mistake to underestimate its importance.

Historically, US interests in Latin America were strategic – the defence of the western hemisphere against external attack or internal subversion by a foreign enemy of the United States (and therefore, it was assumed, of the Latin American states) – and economic – the promotion of US trade with, and investment in, Latin America. After decades of conflict and increasing animosity the Good Neighbor Policy introduced by Roosevelt in 1933 and, more particularly, the growing dangers of war during the late 1930s, brought the United States and the Latin American states closer together. The Second World War, as we have seen, represented the inter-American system's finest hour. Against the Axis threat, both external and internal, the United States and Latin America (except Argentina) extended their military ties – bases, technical cooperation, lend-lease (although 70 per cent of military aid went to one country, Brazil) – and economic links – the supply of strategic materials from Latin America to the United States, technical and financial assistance by the United States to Latin America, including a limited amount of cooperation in Latin America's industrial development. Although the allied occupation of North Africa in 1942 (and steady American advances in the Pacific) largely eliminated the external Axis threat to the security of the western hemisphere relatively early in the war, the United States continued to plan for the preservation and strengthening of hemispheric solidarity after the war.[6]

At the same time it was clear even before the end of the war that the United States had become for the first time a world power in military, economic, and ideological terms, with different concerns – global in scope – than in the past and able to fashion a new, more open, postwar international order in its own interests. The primacy of US relations with Latin America was no longer unquestioned. This was evident as early as February–March 1945 at the Conference on Problems of War and Peace (the Chapultepec Conference) in Mexico City, where concessions were made to Latin American opinion but where Assistant Secretary of State William Clayton issued the first warning that Latin America should not count on postwar economic aid. That the United States was now to play a world – not just a hemispheric – role was even more apparent at the United Nations Conference in San Francisco in April 1945 where growing signs of US distrust of the Soviet Union, the United States' only rival at the end of the war, emerged. (Many historians would date the beginnings of the Cold War here, if not earlier.) Anti-Communism would soon replace anti-fascism as the dominant feature of American foreign policy. It is important, however, to stress the degree to which US foreign policy at the end of the war was marked by hesitancy, confusion, and division. It took some time for a unified and coherent approach to develop.

Nelson Rockefeller, Assistant Secretary of State for the

American Republics since December 1944, took the view at San Francisco that "we couldn't do what we wanted on the world front" unless western hemispheric solidarity were guaranteed. (Not insignificant was the fact that at the outset Latin America represented two-fifths of the votes at the United Nations.) This view of the fundamental importance of Latin America to the United States was never seriously questioned. But it is interesting to note that almost without exception the key policymakers in Washington in the immediate postwar years showed little interest in, were largely ignorant of, and indeed had a certain contempt for, Latin America. Compare Truman, James F. Byrnes, George C. Marshall, Dean Acheson, and George F. Kennan with Cordell Hull, Sumner Welles, Berle, Rockefeller (who was in fact fired in August 1945), and for that matter Roosevelt himself. ("Give them [the Latin Americans] a share," Roosevelt had told a meeting of business editors in January 1940 in a famous remark. "They think they are just as good as we are and many of them are.")

A conference of American states in Rio de Janeiro to formulate a regional collective security pact against external attack under article 51 of the UN Charter was planned for October 1945. But this was never given top priority and in any case continuing problems between the United States and Perón's Argentina were permitted to delay it. The Inter-American Treaty of Reciprocal Assistance (the Rio treaty) was not signed until August 1947. In the meantime, no significant military assistance was offered to Latin America. An Inter-American Military Cooperation bill was drafted in May 1946 but failed to make progress in Congress and was finally abandoned in June 1948. There was in fact no Soviet threat to Latin America. The Russians had no atomic bomb, no long-range strategic air force, and an ineffective navy. From the US point of view Latin America was safe, whereas the Eurasian land mass – western Europe and the Near East – was in great danger: the Truman Doctrine (March 1947) – the doctrine of containment – was a result of the perceived Soviet threat in Turkey and Greece. In any case there were limits even to American resources. Latin America therefore was given low strategic priority and remained firmly at the periphery of United States strategic concerns. The Mutual Defence Assistance Act (1949) allowed for the expenditure of $1.3 billion; not a cent went to Latin America.[7]

Latin America was secure from external aggression and to some extent it was safe for the United States to neglect it in global terms. This is not to say, however, that the United States was unconcerned at the possibilities for *internal* subversion (from Communists rather than fascists now, of course). The Soviet Union had neither the military means (except perhaps in Europe and the Near East) nor the economic means seriously to challenge the United States. But it did retain enormous political and ideological influence throughout the world. In the domestic conflicts of Latin America immediately after the war, just as in the final years of the war itself, the United States played a role – official and unofficial, direct and indirect – in determining their outcome that, while not perhaps decisive, was certainly important.

Communist activities in Latin America in the immediate post-war period were carefully monitored by legal attachés (almost always FBI agents), military and naval attachés, and labor attachés in the United States embassies, and by CIA agents. The intelligence apparatus set up during the war for dealing with Nazi subversion was given a new lease of life in the struggle against Communism. Behind-the-scenes pressure was a factor in moves against Communist parties, certainly in Chile, possibly in Brazil, Cuba, Bolivia, and elsewhere. Although a CIA review of Soviet aims in Latin America in November 1947 contended there was no possibility of a Communist takeover anywhere in the region, United States anti-Communism in Latin America was made explicit in State Department Policy Planning Staff document PPS 26 (March 22) and National Security Council document NSC 7 (March 30), on the eve of the ninth International Conference of American States meeting in Bogotá (March–April 1948), a conference which had been called for the express purpose of establishing a new institutional framework for the inter-American system in the postwar world. Resolution XXXII of the Final Act concerned the Preservation and Defence of Democracy in America and asserted that the continuing legality of Communist parties in Latin America was a direct threat to the security of the western hemisphere.[8]

The United States approved of, where it was not actively involved in, the more general shift to the right which we have already noted in postwar Latin American politics – in Brazil as early as 1945, Bolivia, Chile, and Ecuador in 1946–7, Cuba in

1947–8, Venezuela and Peru in 1948 (where the military coups which established the dictatorships of Pérez Jiménez and Odría were a strong signal to reactionaries throughout the region). The United States certainly preferred and favored *constitutional* democracy, but this did not mean a commitment to wider participation and broad-ranging social reforms and certainly not to an enhanced role for labor and the left (particularly the Communists): all this, it was feared, could only prove antagonistic to the United States' strategic and economic interests. What might have been acceptable in 1944 or 1945 or even 1946, when ambiguous and occasionally contradictory signals were emanating from Washington, was no longer so in 1947 or 1948. As George F. Kennan stated during a visit to Rio de Janeiro in 1950: "it is better to have a strong regime in power than a liberal government if it is indulgent and relaxed and penetrated by Communists."[9]

The United States was especially concerned about Communist penetration of the Latin American labor unions. As in Western Europe (especially France and Italy), and for that matter in the United States itself, organized labor was the major battleground of the Cold War. The struggle to defeat or contain labor insurgency was a global one, and concerted efforts were made to reverse the gains which had been made by the left during and immediately after the Second World War. In the United States the passage of the Taft-Hartley legislation in June 1947 imposed considerable restrictions on strike activity and collective bargaining and made it illegal for Communists to hold union office. Outside the United States the international trade union movement now became the site for bitter ideological rivalry. A campaign was undertaken by conservative forces, operating largely through the American Federation of Labor [AFL] to drive the Communists in particular out of the ranks of international labor. With State Department "informal assistance," roving labor "ambassadors" like Irving Brown in Europe and Serafino Romualdi in Latin America were sent out to organize support for pro-American unionism. The upshot was a series of splits in the international trade union movement.

In Latin America a major offensive was launched against the Confederación de Trabajadores de América Latina [CTAL]. The CTAL had been established by Vicente Lombardo Toledano in 1938; by 1944 it claimed to represent some 3.3 million members in sixteen countries. It controlled several unions in strategic industries (many of the dock workers' unions in the Caribbean region were affiliated with the CTAL, for example) and was well known for its nationalist, leftist, and pro-Communist positions. At the end of the war it affiliated with the World Federation of Trade Unions [WFTU]. By 1947 or 1948 the conservatives or moderates had won the internal struggles in Latin American unionism, and the major national union confederations disaffiliated from the CTAL, often after bitter internal conflicts and splits. In January 1948 the Confederación Interamericana de Trabajadores [CIT, later to become ORIT] was established in Lima. And in December 1949 the non-Communist unions also left the WFTU and formed the International Confederation of Free Trade Unions [ICFTU].

The drive behind this shake-up of the international trade union movement was, of course, largely ideological. As the Cold War hardened, Communism became increasingly unacceptable and had to be defeated on its own preferred terrain: within the labor movement. There was also, however, strategic thinking behind this attack. The end of the Second World War and the emergence of the Cold War produced considerable uncertainty about the future of the world. In the late 1940s it was far from clear to all participants that a long period of mutual stand-off and relatively peaceful coexistence was on the horizon. Certain policymakers, at least, expressed fears of an impending third world war. (That this was not entirely unrealistic may be seen from the dangers of escalation inherent in the Korean War.) Were a third world war to break out, independent, militant unions, whether Communist-controlled or not, might pose a threat to the United States, especially in strategically important industries like petroleum in Mexico, Venezuela, and Peru (almost all US petroleum imports at the end of the war came from Latin America), copper in Chile and Peru, even sugar in Cuba, and also in transport and in industry generally. Moreover, as in the United States itself, militant unions were a potentially destabilizing force hostile to postwar capitalist development – exerting direct economic and political pressure through strikes and demonstrations and forming a base for both the parties of the democratic left and the Communist parties.

This leads us to a wider aspect of the interaction of domestic and international trends in the resolution of the postwar conjuncture in Latin America: the perception the ruling groups had of the new international economic order, and its consequences, short- and long-term, for Latin American economic development. At the end of the war the more economically advanced Latin American nations looked to promote further development through industrialization. Economic policymakers did, however, face some dilemmas and uncertainties. The end of the First World War had seen an international recession, and there was every reason to expect something similar at the end of the Second World War. There were considerable doubts about the likely performance of Latin America's exports: it was unclear what sort of demand there would be in the devastated postwar world, and the prices for Latin America's principal commodities were unpredictable. On the other hand, as a result of the accumulation of substantial gold and foreign reserves during the war, most Latin American economies were in a relatively favorable position. Even this advantage, however, was less than it appeared on the surface: reserves held in sterling continued to be blocked, and the world inflation of the dollar was steadily eroding the real value of reserves held in that currency. Clearly, if industrialization was to proceed, considerable transfers of capital and technology would be required. It was by no means clear that these would be forthcoming, or on what terms they could be attracted.

During the war the United States had provided financial and technical assistance to Latin America, mainly for the increased production of strategic raw materials but also in some cases (in Brazil and Mexico in particular) for the promotion of industry. At the end of the war many Latin American governments had expectations – or hopes – that the United States would continue and indeed expand this role, providing them with long-term development capital. The United States, however, repeatedly headed off an inter-American conference on the economic problems of Latin America and at this stage refused to support the creation of an Inter-American Development Bank. The United States focused its attention instead on the security and economic rehabilitation of Western Europe (and the link between the two was clearly recognized). The result was the Economic Recovery Program (the Marshall Plan) of June 1947. One consequence was that in 1950 Latin America was the only area of the world without a

US aid program, apart from the meagerly funded Point Four technical assistance program established in 1949. Compared with $19 billion in US foreign aid to Western Europe in the period 1945–50 only $400 million (less than 2 percent of total US aid) went to Latin America. Belgium and Luxembourg alone received more than the whole of Latin America.[10]

Although there was some modest increase in lending by the Export-Import Bank, Latin America, it was made clear, should look to *private* capital, domestic and foreign. In fact, there was very little new US investment in Latin America in the immediate postwar period; and most of it went into Venezuelan oil. If more US capital were to be attracted the right climate had to be created: political stability (not necessarily by means of democratic institutions), a commitment to liberal, capitalist development and to an "ideology of production," nationalism curbed (no more "Mexican stunts" – Bernard Baruch's reference to the Mexican nationalization of oil in 1938), the left marginalized, the working class firmly under control, unions not necessarily weaker but bureaucratized.

Here was a clear point of coincidence of different imperatives. Domestically, militant unions and an increasingly mobilized working class threatened dominant classes and elites with moves in the direction of social reform and an expanded democracy which they found unacceptable. At the same time, in terms of the links between the domestic economies of Latin America and the US-dominated world economy, economic policymakers in Latin America had cogent reasons for taming labor and the left. If foreign capital was to be attracted to Latin America, various guarantees and assurances, both symbolic and real, had to be given. And all this is quite apart from cold war pressures and the revival of the barely latent anti-Communism of large sections of the elites and indeed the middle classes. The attack on labor and the left, especially the Communist left, was, in this sense, clearly overdetermined.

Whether the *defeat* of labor and the left was equally overdetermined must remain largely a matter of speculation. The odds were clearly weighted in favor of a conservative victory. In this article we have indicated the variety of factors, both domestic and international, many of them very powerful, which worked to bring about the defeat of the reformist aspirations of the immediate postwar period. Nevertheless, it does seem that, however limited the prospects of the left, if there was a favorable moment for consolidating democracy and moving ahead on a broad reforming front, this was it. The survival, however tenuous, of the reformist regimes, however timid, of Arévalo and Arbenz in Guatemala seems to indicate that defeat was by no means absolutely certain in the late 1940s. Moreover, Argentina under Perón (the candidate who had won against the explicit opposition of the US ambassador in 1946) with its pro-working class, albeit authoritarian, regime may perhaps suggest that some move toward a more egalitarian developmental path was not entirely a matter of wishful thinking. Both Guatemala and Argentina serve to illustrate the limits and constraints of the processes we have identified; equally, they indicate the possible historical alternatives which were open to Latin America at the end of the Second World War.

In the end, of course, at least in the West, the forces of conservatism, both domestic and international, won out. By 1948 or 1949 (and in some countries even earlier) the postwar crisis or, more correctly, the set of overlapping and interacting crises which had their origins in the depression years of the 1930s and their more immediate origins in the Second World War, had been resolved. In Western Europe the resolution of the crisis led to the implantation of an enduring social democracy constructed around the key institutions of a mixed economy, planning, a welfare state and a major consultative role for organized labor. The resolution of the crisis in the United States took a different form. There, the last years of the 1940s led to the complete abandonment of any reformist project: the New Deal and progressive coalitions were now a thing of the past, the age of mass consumption had arrived, the "end of ideology" was proclaimed, and a conservative, and at times reactionary, consensus came to dominate domestic politics until it began to be eroded by a variety of challenges in the 1960s. As Michael Harrington has said, "1948 was the last year of the 1930s."

In Latin America, where the hegemony of the United States had been expanded and consolidated in the course of the war and during the postwar years, the resolution of the immediate postwar crisis also took the form, as we have argued, of a conservative victory. And this victory was a necessary precondition for the region's successful participation in the unprecedented expansion of the international economy, in which the

United States played the dominant role, during the thirty years following the Second World War. With the decisive defeat of labor and the left a "favorable climate for investment" had been created. Foreign capital and technology had always been important in Latin America but had previously been largely confined to export enclaves and public utilities. Now, by means of transnational corporations, it would invade all sectors of the economy, not least manufacturing industry which was to become the principal engine of growth in the major Latin American countries. The postwar economic "model" would be one which put growth ahead of employment, distribution, and welfare. And the developmental strategy adopted would have political as well as social consequences. While in many countries a competitive electoral system was maintained, Latin American democracies would be increasingly restricted and authoritarian. Marxism, in the form of the Communist parties, had been almost eliminated as a viable political force in Latin America, but the democratic left had also suffered a decisive setback, and the democratic middle class parties of the centre were also to a large extent on the defensive. Even more important, democracy was widely seen as dispensable if it stood in the way of sustained economic growth. A democratic government in Latin America would more often than not live in the shadow of a vigilant and increasingly ideologically motivated military, and if it moved too far toward labor or the left it could be overthrown.

NOTES

From Leslie Bethell and Ian Roxborough, "Latin America between the Second World War and the Cold War: Some Reflections on the 1945–8 Conjuncture," *Journal of Latin American Studies*, 20 (May 1988): 167–89. Reprinted and abridged with the permission of the authors and of Cambridge University Press.

1 Quoted in D. M. Dozer, *Are We Good Neighbors? Three Decades of Inter-American Relations, 1930–60* (Gainesville, FL, 1959), 213.
2 Fernando Claudin, *The Communist Movement. From Comintern to Cominform* (London 1975), 309. Compared to the absolute size of the French and Italian parties, of course, even the largest of the Latin American parties (the Brazilian, the Cuban, and the Chilean) were still quite small.
3 J. Fuchs, *Argentina, su desarrollo capitalista* (Buenos Aires, 1966), 260, 268; B. Torres Ramírez, *México en la Segunda Guerra Mundial* (Mexico,

D. F., 1979), 299; T. Merrick and D. Graham, *Population and Economic Development in Brazil* (Baltimore, MD, 1979), 158.

4 L. Doyon, "Conflictos Obreros Durante el Régimen Peronista (1946–55)," *Desarrollo Económico* (1977): 440; L. Martins, "Sindicalismo e classe operária," in B. Fausto (ed.), *História Geral da Civilizaçào Brasileira*, Vol. 10 (São Paulo, 1981), 535; M. Urrutia Montoya, *The Development of the Colombian Labor Movement* (New Haven, CT, 1969), 183; S. Baily, *Labor, Nationalism and Politics in Argentina* (New Brunswick, NJ, 1967), 101; V. Alba, *Politics and the Labor Movement in Latin America* (Stanford, CA, 1968), 211, 258.

5 Edward J. Rowell, labor attaché at the United States embassy in Rio de Janeiro from 1944 to 1948, commented ironically in February 1947 on how confusing this could be for the independent observer of the labor scene in Brazil: there was to be sure on the one hand "the unquestioned participation and influence of Communist leaders" but on the other "a trade union program which is sympathetic to trade union status and activities as recognized by Western democracies." Rowell, Monthly Labor Report no. 25 (February 1947), April 8, 1947, RG59 State Department, 850.4, National Archives, Washington, DC.

6 See David Green, *The Containment of Latin America. A History of the Myths and Realities of the Good Neighbor Policy* (Chicago, 1971), 343; Chester J. Pach, Jr, "The Containment of United States Military Aid to Latin America, 1944–1949," *Diplomatic History*, 6 (1982): 226.

7 Pach, "Containment," 242. See also Stephen G. Rabe, "Inter-American Military Cooperation 1944–51," *World Affairs*, 137 (1974): 132–49.

8 See Robert A. Pollard, *Economic Security and the Origins of the Cold War, 1945–1950* (New York, 1985), 201; Roger R. Trask, "The Impact of the Cold War on United States–Latin American Relations, 1945–1949," *Diplomatic History*, 1 (1977): 279–80.

9 Quoted in Pollard, *Economic Security*, 212.

10 Pollard, *Economic Security*, 213; see also Stephen G. Rabe, "The Elusive Conference. US Economic Relations with Latin America, 1945–52," *Diplomatic History*, 2 (1978): 293.

EPILOGUE
The End of the Cold War
David S. Painter and Melvyn P. Leffler

By focusing on the international system and on events in all parts of the globe, this volume has sought to offer a fuller understanding of the origins of the Cold War. Rather than chronicle the subsequent evolution of events from the 1950s through the 1980s, this epilogue seeks to outline some of the key changes in geopolitics, technology, ideology, and political economy that help explain the end of the Cold War. In brief, the Cold War ended when the structure of the international system and the dynamics of the world political economy no longer supported it.

Although the Cold War involved much more than Soviet-American relations, that rivalry – strategic, political, ideological, and economic – lay at its core. This competition ended because Soviet strength eroded and the Soviet empire disintegrated. Although it is now almost impossible to identify independent variables, the Soviet Union's inability to compete economically with the United States was probably the decisive factor in its demise. The Kremlin gained rough military equivalency, but this success came at tremendous cost. Compared to the United States the Soviet Union was forced to devote a much larger share of its much smaller gross national product to defense. Diverting investment from more productive sectors and from consumer goods ultimately undermined the regime's capacity to satisfy its own people and to act as a Great Power.

If one defines power not in terms of troops, tanks, ships, airplanes, bombs, and missiles, but in terms of industrial infrastructure, raw materials, skilled manpower, and technological prowess, the postwar era was bipolar only in a narrow military sense. By any broad definition of power, the United States was always far ahead of the Soviet Union. This imbalance was even more stark when one measures the strength of the Western alliance against that of the Soviet bloc. Even in narrow military terms the Soviet position had as many elements of weakness as strength. The Soviet Union and its Warsaw Pact allies possessed numerical superiority in ground forces along the central front in the heart of Europe. Around 1970, the Soviet Union also achieved rough parity with the United States in strategic nuclear weapons. The Soviets, however, were never able to count on the loyalty of their Warsaw Pact allies, and after the Sino-Soviet split they had to deploy a quarter of their ground forces along their long border with the People's Republic of China [PRC]. In terms of nuclear weapons, the Soviets also had to take into account the arsenals of the other nuclear powers – the United Kingdom, France, and the PRC – as well as that of the United States.

The Soviet strategic situation worsened over time. Although the destruction of German and Japanese power initially seemed to benefit the Kremlin, these advantages were transitory. The defeat of the Axis and the decline of Britain and France left undisputed leadership of the non-Communist world to the United States. Subsequently, the successful reconstruction of Western Germany and Japan, the economic recovery of Western Europe and the United Kingdom, and the incorporation of all these countries into a US-led alliance meant that four of the world's five centers of industrial might stayed outside Soviet control. While the United States adroitly practiced double containment, coopting German and Japanese power while limiting Soviet expansion, the Soviet Union split with the People's Republic of China in the late 1950s. The growing hostility between the two Communist giants put enormous strains on the power position of the Soviet Union.

The arms race was one of the most dynamic aspects of the Cold War. At various times, technological advances threatened to give one superpower or the other a dangerous edge over its rival, thereby triggering vigorous countermeasures. But gradually, leaders in the United States and the Soviet Union started to come to terms with the implications of the nuclear revolution. Nuclear wars, they concluded, might be fought but could not be won. While possession of nuclear weapons might help expand influence abroad and deter encroachments on their truly vital interests, marginal increments in nuclear weaponry did not provide commensurate additional leverage in the struggle for influence and often decreased rather than increased security.

The key breakthrough came in the 1980s when Soviet leaders and defense planners recognized that military expenditures were crippling the Soviet economy and concluded that a limited number of nuclear weapons provided sufficient security. At the same time, US President Ronald Reagan and his advisers abandoned their emphasis on winning the arms race, tried to regain control over the US budget, and decided to make serious overtures to the Kremlin. Faced with upheaval in Eastern Europe and turmoil at home, Soviet leader Mikhail Gorbachev and his reformist colleagues in the Kremlin agreed to limit, and eventually reduce, the Soviet arsenal. More astonishingly, they acquiesced to the erosion of their influence in Eastern Europe and to German unification. They probably believed that their nuclear capabilities, however they might be limited, would still suffice to deter any prospective attack from either the United States or a united Germany, the Kremlin's traditional enemy. Germany's peaceful behavior for almost two generations and its integration into a web of military (NATO) and economic institutions (the European Community) that circumscribed its autonomy also probably prompted Gorbachev and his colleagues to take risks that their predecessors never would have contemplated.

The collapse of Communism as an ideology preceded the collapse of Soviet military power. At the end of the Second World War, the future of capitalism as an organizing principle for society was anything but secure. The Soviet Union enjoyed enormous prestige as a result of its leading role in defeating Nazi Germany. At the same time Socialist parties came to power in Great Britain and Scandinavia and Communist parties were strong in France and Italy. There was a widespread belief in many European countries that economic planning was necessary to ensure economic growth as well as equity. And for many people in the Third World the Soviet model of development seemed to provide a compass for a rapid transition from a backward agrarian society to a powerful industrial nation.

But over the years the prestige of the Soviet Union and the appeal of Communism and the Soviet model of development faded. Continued repression at home and oppression abroad (especially the purge trials of the late 1940s and the invasions of Hungary in 1956, Czechoslovakia in 1968, and Afghanistan in 1979) tarnished Communism's image. Attempts by European Communist parties to reform themselves and to divorce Communism from the harsh reality of Soviet practice had no lasting impact. Growing publicity about human rights abuses inside the Soviet Union discredited its appeal as did its faltering economy. Economic growth in the Soviet bloc, which had soared in the late 1940s and the 1950s, began to drop sharply in the early 1960s and never reversed itself. The failure of Communism to deliver the goods contrasted sharply with the appeal of Western consumer culture. Younger people in the Soviet bloc and the Third World measured their economic well-being not against the experiences of their parents but against those of their contemporaries in the West. The nuclear disaster at Chernobyl and the failed attempt to cover it up delivered the final blow to Communist rule, demoralizing the few who still believed the system could be transformed from within. By the end of the 1980s, Communism inspired and attracted almost no one, least of all those who knew it best.

The reconstruction, reform, and relative resiliency of the world capitalist system contrasted sharply with the failure of Communism. The United States and its allies experienced unprecedented economic growth in the 1950s and 1960s. Playing the role of economic hegemon, the United States buttressed the reconstruction of Western Europe and Japan, promoted economic integration, supported a stable financial order, and encouraged international trade and investment through the lowering of tariffs and the removal of other impediments to the free flow of goods and capital. Moreover, US economic assistance helped its allies finance reconstruction and expand exports without imposing socially explosive austerity programs at home. Although the Third World did not share equally in the resulting prosperity, the United States, Western Europe, and Japan flourished. Prosperity associated with the long boom stretching from the early 1950s to the early 1970s undercut the appeal of leftist and Communist parties, perpetuated the ascendancy of moderate elites who associated their own well-being with that of the United States, and sustained the cohesion of the Western alliance. Although the oil crises of the 1970s caused immense economic difficulties and financial disorder in the

West, the dislocation did not redound to the advantage of the Soviet Union. The vitality of the West German and Japanese economies and the emergence of Western-oriented "newly industrializing countries" ensured the West's economic dominance over the East even as the US share of world production declined. In short, the ability of the world capitalist system to avoid another great depression and the inability of the Soviet Union to compete with the West economically were key factors in the end of the Cold War.

Revolutionary nationalism in the Third World was at the heart of one of the most significant transformations of the postwar years. The era of decolonization, roughly 1945–75, provided a window of opportunity for the Soviet Union and a window of vulnerability for the United States and its allies. During the course of three decades, scores of former colonies attained their political independence. Many national liberation movements wanted to expropriate foreign-owned properties, overthrow traditional power structures, and challenge the West's cultural hegemony. For a time, there seemed to be at least a symbiotic relationship between social transformation in the Third World and the interests of the Soviet state. But appearances were deceptive. National liberation movements were authentic expressions of the popular will for autonomy and freedom and proved to be beyond the control of any foreign power.

The United States was acutely aware of the importance of the Third World from the outset of the Cold War. American officials deployed their superior resources to ensure that the markets and raw materials of the periphery remained accessible to the industrial core of Western Europe and Japan as well as to the United States. The Soviet Union, preoccupied with problems closer to home, was actually slow to seize the opportunities offered by the "revolt against the West" in the Third World. Only after Stalin's death in 1953 did the Soviets try to harness national liberation movements for their global advantage. Communist parties came to power in several Third World nations, but the gains were usually marginal or ephemeral. In fact, Soviet intrusions in the Third World often galvanized Western counteractions. And experiments with Soviet-style development often failed miserably, leaving less developed countries with little choice but to look to the United States and its allies for capital, technology, and markets. Paradoxically, the

Cold War began with expectations that the Soviet Union would exploit the breakup of Western colonial regimes, but it closed with the Soviet empire itself collapsing and with the Kremlin's subject nationalities asserting their own autonomy.

By the time the Cold War ended, it had become increasingly irrelevant to many of the problems plaguing humankind: chronic poverty; environmental degradation; religious, racial, and ethnic conflict; and nuclear proliferation. Whether the peoples of the world have the imagination, the determination, and the resources to forge a more peaceful, more prosperous, and more just world order remains to be seen.